READINGS OF ŚĀNTIDEVA'S *GUIDE TO BODHISATTVA PRACTICE* (*BODHICARYĀVATĀRA*)

COLUMBIA READINGS OF BUDDHIST LITERATURE

COLUMBIA READINGS OF BUDDHIST LITERATURE

SERIES EDITOR: STEPHEN F. TEISER

This series is published with the sponsorship of the Dharma Drum Foundation for Humanities and Social Science Research.

Readings of the Lotus Sūtra, Stephen F. Teiser and Jacqueline I. Stone, editors

Readings of the Platform Sūtra, Morten Schlütter and Stephen F. Teiser, editors

Readings of the Vessantara Jātaka, Steven Collins, editor

READINGS OF ŚĀNTIDEVA'S *GUIDE TO BODHISATTVA PRACTICE* (*BODHICARYĀVATĀRA*)

Edited by Jonathan C. Gold and Douglas S. Duckworth

COLUMBIA UNIVERSITY PRESS NEW YORK

Columbia University Press
Publishers Since 1893
New York Chichester, West Sussex
cup.columbia.edu

Library of Congress Cataloging-in-Publication Data
Names: Gold, Jonathan C., 1969– editor. | Duckworth, Douglas S., 1971– editor.
Title: Readings of Śāntideva's Guide to bodhisattva practice / edited by
Jonathan C. Gold and Douglas S. Duckworth.
Description: New York : Columbia University Press, 2019. | Series: Columbia readings
of Buddhist literature | Includes bibliographical references and index.
Identifiers: LCCN 2018055393 (print) | LCCN 2018056563 (ebook) | ISBN 9780231549905
(electronic) | ISBN 9780231192668 (cloth) | ISBN 9780231192675 (pbk.)
Subjects: LCSH: Śāntideva, active 7th century. Bodhicaryāvatāra. |
Mahayana Buddhism—Doctrines.
Classification: LCC BQ3147 (ebook) | LCC BQ3147 .R43 2019 (print) | DDC 294.3/85—dc23
LC record available at https://lccn.loc.gov/2018055393

Cover image: Bronze and silver image of the bodhisattva Manjushri, Bengal, Pala Dynasty,
11th century / Pictures from History / Bridgeman Images

In memory of
Luis O. Gómez (1943–2017)

CONTENTS

A Note to the Reader ix
Acknowledgments xi

Introduction. Participatory Authorship and Communal Interpretation: The *Bodhicaryāvatāra* as a "World Classic" 1
Jonathan C. Gold

1. Śāntideva: The Author and His Project 27
Paul Harrison

2. Reason and Knowledge on the Path: A Protreptic Reading of the *Guide* 45
Amber Carpenter

3. On Learning to Overhear the "Vanishing Poet" 60
Sonam Kachru

4. An Intoxication of Mouse Venom: Reading the *Guide*, Chapter 9 84
Matthew T. Kapstein

5. Seeing from All Sides 99
Janet Gyatso

6. Bodies and Embodiment in the *Bodhicaryāvatāra* 114
Reiko Ohnuma

7. Ritual Structure and Material Culture in the *Guide to Bodhisattva Practice* 132
Eric Huntington

8. *Bodhicaryāvatāra* and Tibetan Mind Training (*Lojong*) 146
Thupten Jinpa

9. Taming Śāntideva: Tsongkhapa's Use of the *Bodhicaryāvatāra* 162
Roger Jackson

10. The Middle Way of the Bodhisattva 180
Douglas S. Duckworth

11. Seeing Sentient Beings: Śāntideva's Moral Phenomenology 192
Jay L. Garfield

12. Śāntideva's Ethics of Impartial Compassion 209
Charles Goodman

13. Śāntideva and the Moral Psychology of Fear 221
Bronwyn Finnigan

14. Innate Human Connectivity and Śāntideva's Cultivation of Compassion 235
John D. Dunne

Appendix 1: A Guide to Guide *Translations: Advice for Students and Instructors* 253
Appendix 2: Index of Guide *Verses Cited* 257
Bibliography 271
Contributors 285
Index 291

A NOTE TO THE READER

THERE IS no standard English translation of the *Guide to Bodhisattva Practice* (*Bodhicaryāvatāra*). Each author in this volume makes plain which translation is being cited in her or his chapter. Unless otherwise noted, chapter and verse citations (e.g., 4.5) refer to traditional numbering (and not to Dunhuang versions). For advice and discussion of some widely used English translations, see "Appendix I: A Guide to *Guide* Translations: Advice for Students and Instructors."

Different authors also use different translations of certain technical terms, such as "thought of enlightenment" or "Mind of Awakening" for the term *bodhicitta*. Each of these translations appears in the index, and each refers the reader to the index entry for the original Sanskrit, which in turn lists all of the translations and their various locations in the book.

ACKNOWLEDGMENTS

The contributors to this volume met to share their work and plan the volume at a conference at Princeton University in February 2017 that was generously sponsored by the Numata Foundation (BDK), as well as the Princeton University Center for the Study of Religion and the Department of Religion. The Center for the Study of Religion has also provided financial support for this book's production. A sabbatical leave from Temple University enabled Douglas Duckworth to lay the groundwork for his work on this project.

As always, thanks go to our families, with love and appreciation for cultivations of generosity and patience.

READINGS OF ŚĀNTIDEVA'S *GUIDE TO BODHISATTVA PRACTICE* (*BODHICARYĀVATĀRA*)

INTRODUCTION

PARTICIPATORY AUTHORSHIP AND COMMUNAL INTERPRETATION: THE *BODHICARYĀVATĀRA* AS A "WORLD CLASSIC"

Jonathan C. Gold

THE BOOK you are reading contains fifteen scholars' assessments of what you might want to know as you read and study a much beloved work of late Indian Buddhism, the *Guide to Bodhisattva Practice* (*Bodhicaryāvatāra*, hereafter *Guide*) by Śāntideva (eighth century). This chapter is an introduction to this introduction. In the first section, I provide my own first pass at what I think Śāntideva is up to, by explicating the overarching themes of karmic merit, *bodhicitta*, and the unusual composition of a work that intertwines prayer, meditation, and philosophy. This is the reading of the *Guide* that I have to offer. In the second section, I turn to the reception history of the *Guide*, focusing especially on the relatively recent phenomena that have brought the *Guide* to prominence as a "world classic." I argue that readers should not feel that they are doing anything new or unexpected when they appreciate the work for qualities only indirectly intended by its author(s). I wish to defend, therefore, the diverse employments of the *Guide* by historical as well as modern readers, while remaining respectful of traditional readings. In the final section, I summarize the chapters that follow, and wish you well.

BODHICITTA AND THE *GUIDE*'S INVITATION TO PARTICIPATORY AUTHORSHIP

The *Guide* is distinctive within Indian Buddhist literature for its practical, psychologically vivid articulation of the Mahāyāna path. Although it is clearly composed for an audience well versed in Buddhist thought and experienced in philosophical and doctrinal analysis, it serves on its own as a complete guide to the practice. In the opening verses, Śāntideva says, with traditional modesty, that his work contains nothing that is new and is only intended "for my own mind's cultivation" (*svamano bhāvayituṃ*, 1.2).[1] Yet this first-person perspective, through which Buddhist doctrines and meditative strategies appear in an order and in language suited to cultivate the author's own mind, *was* something new.[2] There is an invitation to others "with just my same constitution" (*matsamadhātur eva*, 1.3), who may benefit as well, but the implied reader is the author himself, and one gets the feeling of reading over the shoulder of a medieval Buddhist practitioner at prayer, study, and intensive personal psychological work.

Prayer composed in the first person was widespread and well known among Buddhists during Śāntideva's time. Also, there were countless scriptures and several comprehensive summaries of the doctrine in circulation that recommended various practices, assembled the stages of the bodhisattva path—the cultivations that can transform an ordinary person into an enlightened buddha—and surveyed the final attainments. The *Guide* weaves this literature together into a study of the Mahāyāna Buddhist path in the form of an extended aspirational prayer. It also includes within it, all tightly integrated: one of the most influential digests of "Middle Way" (Madhyamaka) philosophy; a great deal of ingenious theorization on the moral and practical implications of karma; and several innovative approaches to meditation.

The thread that reworks and binds these elsewhere distinct topics and genres is "*bodhicitta*." Literally the "mind of awakening," *bodhicitta* is the distinctive mindset of a bodhisattva, an aspiring and inevitable future buddha. This is what distinguishes a practitioner of the so-called "Great Vehicle" (Mahāyāna) from other Buddhists, who pursue liberation but do not presume to seek buddhahood.[3] This special kind of "mind" or mental attitude is the *Guide*'s central theme and central object of praise. After all, it is the distinctive, transformative mental state that allows a bodhisattva to advance on the path and eventually become a buddha. This special mindset allows the bodhisattva to be of unlimited benefit to himself and others.[4] For this reason, *bodhicitta* is likened to a rare, magical gem or an alchemical elixir that turns base metals into gold (*Guide* 1.10–11).

What exactly is this mental state, and why is it so beneficial? It starts with compassion—expanded, deepened, and universalized: compassion that sees and knows the suffering of all living beings, everywhere, and wants nothing more than to alleviate it. Upon this ground, *bodhicitta* grows with the awareness, shared by all Mahāyāna Buddhists, that the only way to be truly free from suffering is to be established in buddhahood—and that therefore the best and most effective (the only truly effective) way to help beings attain freedom from suffering is to become, oneself, a fully enlightened buddha who can guide other beings to liberation. *Bodhicitta,* then, is the mental state that seeks to attain buddhahood in order to save all beings from suffering.[5]

Realistically, of course, the fact that only Buddhist practice is truly effective in helping others may be known directly by advanced bodhisattvas, but remains a matter of faith for ordinary beings. The full and proper activation of this "mind of awakening"—the mental state that drives one toward awakening—depends, therefore, upon a direct understanding, a vision, of the truth of the Buddhist path. It is not a beginner's attainment; it is rather the fruit of a mind already significantly awakened.[6] Yet the *Guide to Bodhisattva Practice* provides a smooth ramp, an entryway for the cultivation of this crucial mental state. It allows that in addition to the inconceivable *bodhicitta* that motivates the unending work of advanced bodhisattvas, there is *aspirational bodhicitta* that can be cultivated by anyone, here and now:

> The Awakening Mind should be understood to be of two kinds; in brief: the Mind resolved on Awakening and the Mind proceeding towards Awakening. (1.15)
>
> The distinction between these two should be understood by the wise in the same way as the distinction is recognized between a person who desires to go and one who is going, in that order. (1.16)
>
> Even in cyclic existence great fruit comes from the Mind resolved on Awakening, but nothing like the uninterrupted merit that comes from that resolve when put into action. (1.17)[7]

Once one has adopted the true Awakening Mind and can act on it, one receives a flow of karmic benefits that surpasses all previous good deeds. But great fruit still comes from the resolution to attain this state. Perhaps a bit of context will help. Good works and generosity toward other beings are venerable Buddhist acts, and they yield karmic benefits to their practitioners in the form of merit—what we conventionally call "good karma." Good deeds yield good results in birth and fortune. The ideal for this practice of virtue is exemplified in the stories called *Jatakas*, tales of the Buddha's lives *before* he became the Buddha—that is, when he was a bodhisattva.[8] As a bodhisattva, the (pre-)Buddha cycled from death to rebirth just like everyone else does, but no matter what kind of creature he became—a fish, a monkey, a prince, a merchant—he always displayed exemplary virtue. His virtuous deeds contributed to a vast store of merit, which eventually (after a *very* long time) allowed him to be born with the special, auspicious circumstances and body suitable for him to become a fully enlightened buddha. How did he act so virtuously across countless lifetimes? This process is what Śāntideva and his readers are seeking to replicate by adopting the special mindset of *bodhicitta*.

To return to the point of the verse above, Śāntideva feels the need to mention how much more merit accrues from *bodhicitta* put into action by advanced bodhisattvas than by ordinary beings only aspiring to true *bodhicitta*. But one of the key contributions of the *Guide* is its ingenious manipulation of Buddhist karmic logic and Buddhist psychology to justify and bring to life an effective *aspirational bodhicitta*:

> From the moment that he takes on that Mind to release the limitless realm of beings, with a resolve that cannot be turned back, (1.18)
>
> From that moment on, though he may doze off or be distracted many times, uninterrupted streams of merit like the bursting sky continuously pour forth. (1.19)

A practitioner who dedicates himself, sincerely, to the cultivation of *bodhicitta* will gain uninterrupted merit "though he may doze off or be distracted many times"—which suggests that *even a beginner* can take advantage of *bodhicitta*; even aspirational *bodhicitta* is an effective mechanism for the production of merit.

The karmic logic here deserves some exposition, since it is crucial to the understanding of *bodhicitta* that holds the work together. It is, we will agree, better to *heal* a person of her headache by providing her some aspirin (say) than it is to just *wish* to heal her headache, or to rejoice in someone else doing it. But Buddhist karma theory recognizes that mental actions—such as rejoicing in or aspiring to meritorious deeds—are genuinely consequential. It is therefore sometimes deemed better to aspire to or rejoice in great deeds than to *perform* lesser ones.

Now, Buddhists generally accept that karma works as an unseen causal relation between morally significant actions and experientially significant results; if I kill someone, or even if I fervently pray for someone's painful death, I might end up reborn in hell. But much of the causal mechanism operates in the minds of ordinary living beings—without having to posit anything unseen—and the moral logic of praiseworthy mental actions may work even in ordinary life. If I give a dollar to a hungry person, that is surely better for that person today than if I only praise someone else's gift. But if I sincerely rejoice in the gift of a great donor today, it makes me just a bit more predisposed to make a large donation myself, sometime in the future. Add to this that praise is inexpensive, and relatively easy to do (depending on how much sincerity I muster). And if I can develop a *habit* of praising certain kinds of acts, that should (in time) substantially increase the chances that I will end up being the kind of person who is capable of performing those acts. In a purely utilitarian calculus, then, I can be confident in the value of my praise and aspiration to give, as long as the gift to which I aspire is sufficiently large. If I give away one dollar every day for eighty years, it will total $29,219 (or $29,220, if the centennial is a leap year). But if I aspire to a great gift and my accumulated aspirations someday lead me to make even one $30,000 gift, it will be a larger gift in the end. What's more, once I have given $30,000, I am likely to do it again.

Śāntideva capitalizes on this karmic logic, which places a significant value on mental self-transformation. He praises the "Awakening Mind" even in its intention, given its maximal character. He asks, if it is meritorious to wish to cure a few beings' headaches (which of course it is), how much better is it to wish for *eternal* buddhahood for *all* beings? (*Guide* 1.22) Even gaining the capacity to *wish*, sincerely, for such a meritorious occurrence is a massively powerful moral act with extreme karmic benefits. It is therefore worth a significant effort just to practice at this *aspiration*.

For this reason, after praising *bodhicitta* (conflating, somewhat, the benefits of aspiring to it with its real enactment), the work moves through a ritual intended to aid in the development and adoption of this very special mental state. This takes up the first three chapters. The full ritual structure is discussed in Huntington's and Harrison's chapters below. In brief, the *Guide*'s first chapter praises the Awakening Mind, the second chapter is a confession of sins and a refuge prayer, and the third chapter is the official adoption of the bodhisattva vow. Then, in the fourth chapter, once he has recognized its value, made an effort to cultivate it, and expressed the sincere intent to continue to cultivate it, Śāntideva pretends to realize, as if for the first time, that to abandon it now would be to abandon all beings—the very opposite of *bodhicitta* in karmic effect. A misstep here threatens to plunge one into hell. With this concern always present for the remainder of the work, forward motion on the path becomes essential, and the opening of each subsequent chapter—from chapters 5 to 9—includes a verse in the optative mood, expressing a new kind of cultivation that *must be done*.

Since one can only keep the vow one has made to all beings if the mind is held firm, he says, "therefore I must guard and control my mind well" (*tasmāt svadhiṣṭhitaṃ cittaṃ mayā kāryaṃ surakṣitam*, 5.18). This introduces and motivates the chapter on how to cultivate mindfulness. The next chapter opens with the point that, since any and all karmic benefits can be wiped away by anger, "therefore patience must be cultivated with diligence" (*tasmāt kṣāntiṃ prayatnena bhāvayed*, 6.2). The patience chapter, to which we will return below, leads one through some of the most original and psychologically sophisticated meditations in the work—not just on combatting anger but on the implications of the universality of compassion implicit in the *bodhisattva* vow. Yet it is the fear of karmic decline, which might come from a moment of anger, that provides the motivation and the energy that propels the chapter. Once patience is valued, though, one's merit is understood as yet again subject to decline if one does not continue forward on the path and cultivate vigor—the topic of chapter 7—lest sloth set in (*evaṃ kṣamo bhajed vīryaṃ*, 7.1), and then meditative quiescence (*samādhī*)—the topic of chapter 8—to stabilize one's ability to prevent slippage into the negative emotions, the *kelśas* (*samādhau sthāpayen manaḥ*, 8.1). Finally, at the opening of the ninth chapter, Śāntideva argues that, since it is all for naught unless one gains a clear and accurate vision of emptiness, "therefore one must develop wisdom" (*tasmād utpādayet prajñāṃ*, 9.1). This introduces Śāntideva's famous treatment of Madhyamaka philosophy. The final, tenth chapter uses dramatic language to dedicate the merit gained from these previous cultivations to the benefit of all beings. Even the karmic benefits of good practices for the sake of living beings are not kept for oneself; they too are shared with living beings.

This integrated textual structure, by which the whole Buddhist path of practice, including its philosophical defense, is woven on the thread of *bodhicitta* and motivated repeatedly by reference to karma, was recognized by some of the earliest commentators. The thirty-verse *Summary Meaning* (*Piṇḍārtha*), a digest of the work by Suvarṇadvīpa, contains all of those optative constructions—what *must be* done—that link the chapters together, and not much else.[9] At the same time, there is reason to believe that, in spite of Śāntideva's strategic motivational integration, some readers selected from the work and used separately its sections on ritual, meditation, and philosophy. For instance, Tibetan practitioners recite sections from the opening chapters as a way of ritually adopting the bodhisattva vow. In this context, it is interesting to note that the Chinese translation of the *Guide* (which received no commentaries) is actually missing the chapters that enact the vow.[10] It is as though someone had borrowed but not returned the ritual chapters before the book was included in the canon, and henceforth ignored. Where there are commentaries, some sections attract far more attention than others. There are commentaries available that focus most, sometimes all, of their attention on the ninth chapter, which covers Madhyamaka philosophy.[11] There is also an entire genre of Tibetan practice texts, called "Mind Training" (*lojong*) literature, that is based in the *Guide* but primarily illuminates methods of meditative cultivation that are found only in the eighth chapter.[12]

In addition to the commentarial traditions, we can use manuscript history as a lens into an otherwise dark corner of the Indian scholastic world. Recently studied manuscripts of the *Guide* from Dunhuang give evidence of a substantially shorter version of the work than the one that appears in the Tibetan canons and the previously known Sanskrit edition.[13] The earlier, Dunhuang manuscripts present a problem in speaking of Śāntideva as the author of the *Guide*, when we are used to thinking of the work as a text of 900 verses, 200 of which are not found within the oldest extant version. The difference disrupts our sense of authorial intention behind the longer work. There must be some cause for the addition of the extra verses, but what was it?

The scholar Paul Harrison has suggested that the change represents Śāntideva's own continuous reworking of the text. He proposes that, since many of the verses added in the later version are also cited in Śāntideva's scriptural source book, the *Training Anthology*, perhaps Śāntideva included these additions as he found them, ostensibly because they aided in the project of self-cultivation that was the work's declared purpose.[14] Another possibility is that the text was used—taught and perhaps studied for personal practice—by others at Nālandā monastery, where Śāntideva taught, and that additions crept in through added marginal notes or other editors' markings. A teacher or student might have annotated the text with additional verses for his (probably not her) personal use, and a copyist might have included those additions in the body of the text when recopying that manuscript.

On the other hand, I wonder whether it is a mistake to suggest that any alterations must be either the author's own or erroneously attributed to the author. Perhaps the people behind the alterations did not understand the changes as a violation of the norms of authorship. Recall Śāntideva's opening verse, which allows a reader "with just my same constitution" to benefit by adopting the author's own first-person voice in search of mental cultivation. Recall as well that Śāntideva claimed that his work contained *nothing new*. He wanted it to represent the Buddha's teachings, not his own understanding as a unique interpreter. This dovetails with the ideal of aspirational *bodhicitta*; we have the impression of an author who wanted to see himself not as an authority, but as an aspirant to *bodhicitta*. Here the speaker's self-effacement allows the reader not only to adopt the same perspective and *read* along with the author but also to take his position as an aspiring bodhisattva engaging in a specific textual practice that involves study, meditative cultivation, and (why not?) writing—in other words, to *adopt fully the subject position of the work's author*. The *Guide*'s logic of aspirational *bodhicitta* suggests to me a strong possibility that devotees within the work's immediate authorial context might read the *Guide* as an invitation to a kind of extended, participatory authorship. Perhaps, then, a copyist was expected to *include* the additions of a learned teacher or practitioner when recopying—not out of error, but out of an intention to aid the next reader and more fully express the goals of the text.

If this is an accurate representation of the text's self-presentation, then we must be careful to check our modern tendency to read the vivid first-person expressions in the text as personal or individual. They are expressions of an aspirational ideal—from a certain perspective, of course, but one that even the author is training himself to adopt.

If the difference between the editions mentioned above is the result of a kind of participatory authorship, then we have reason to take the fact that the alterations are centered in the chapters on meditative quiescence and Madhyamaka philosophy as evidence that these parts drew special attention from the scholastic community that kept the work alive, even before there were any commentaries. In its origin, then, it was a philosophically engaging text tied to an original and influential meditative practice. To be sure, not all readers were equally engaged by the meditational and philosophical teachings; but the work itself presents them both as indispensable culminations of the path. A second problematic, then, for modern readers is the potential oddness of a philosophical treatise that is also a meditation guide. Once again, we should be careful about imposing a modern understanding—in this case, a modern approach to philosophy.

As Matthew Kapstein has argued, the *Guide* gives us one of the most direct examples of a meditation text that makes explicit, and repeated, use of philosophy as a method for personal growth and mental development.[15] It is evidence that at least some Buddhists understood their doctrinal analysis to be "spiritual exercises," or "philosophy as a way of life," to apply the phrase that Pierre Hadot famously used to describe classical Greek and

Roman philosophy. We have already seen that Śāntideva places his philosophical discussion within the frame of mental cultivation and the acquisition of aspirational *bodhicitta*. If the ninth chapter on Madhyamaka's philosophy of emptiness is considered as operating within this pragmatic context, we could read philosophy itself as serving the purpose of training the aspirant to think in specific ways that are beneficial and lead to positive development. It is certainly a sensible reading of the central verse from chapter 9, often considered the culmination of the Madhyamaka argument, to say that it is expressing how philosophy's greatest success, once it has disproven all false views, is that it issues in a state beyond all thought: "When neither entity nor non-entity remains before the mind, since there is no other mode of operation, grasping no objects, it becomes tranquil. (9.34)."

Other chapters also include philosophical analysis that can be read in this kind of pragmatic way, such as where an argument disproving the nature of self is used to dissolve anger toward a potential adversary. (Are you angry at his hands or his feet?) Here it is difficult to know whether the argument is intended to be fully convincing or just a useful chastisement.

We can find philosophy described in a similarly supplementary role in other locales across the Indian Buddhist tradition. From Śāntideva's own monastery in his own century, the great Haribhadra refers to philosophical analysis (specifically epistemology, *pramāṇa*) in his explanation of the meaning of "Perfection" in the "Perfection of Wisdom" (*prajñāpāramitā*), which is the term for an advanced bodhisattva's understanding of ultimate reality.[16] The "perfection" here, he says, refers simply to the three scholastic methods of hearing, investigation, and meditative cultivation. And in glossing the nature of investigation, he makes it quite clearly *philosophical investigation*, the analytical work of removing the thorn of doubt. Once doubts are removed, and only then, can one proceed to the meditative cultivation that is the stated intent of the *Guide*. The *Guide* thus includes the philosophical analysis *within* its extended meditative cultivation because the recitation of the arguments is what allows their proper understanding to bring about wisdom.

In this way, philosophy's purpose is to facilitate personal transformation. But the wisdom chapter is introduced with the claim that it itself is made possible by the attainments that precede it, especially meditative quiescence. This notion—which is, again, quite different from modern philosophy's ordinary expectation of philosophy as abstract rational analysis—reflects an approach to knowledge and reason deeply embedded in the Buddhist tradition. One of the texts most commonly cited by modern Buddhists to defend the view that Buddhism is a rational and empirical philosophy, rather than a religion, is the *Kālāma Sutta*, in which the Buddha tells the Kālāma people not to take his word, or anyone's, on faith alone but to investigate it for themselves.[17] The Buddha does indeed say this, but just after he says this, he gives precision to the investigative method he is recommending: most people are so distracted by greed, hatred, and delusion that they cannot be trusted; they lie. The Buddha's own followers, however, have cultivated meditative quiescence based upon the four immeasurables (compassion, loving-kindness, sympathetic joy, and equanimity). Go and look for yourselves, he says, and you will see that his followers, unlike ordinary people, can be trusted. Their rationality is not hampered by ordinary mental afflictions, by moral and cognitive defects—so, anyone who sees them can have confidence in the Buddha's teachings. I see a parallel here, where Śāntideva cultivates meditative quiescence as a prelude to philosophical reasoning.

Philosophy, for Buddhist traditions, is thus part of the virtuous circle (with meditation and moral behavior) that allows the practitioner to advance toward wisdom. Yet, as verse 9.34 says, the final goal is ultimately beyond any particular argument or view. This pragmatic approach to rationality on the path is not an indication that the philosophical arguments themselves should not be taken seriously. On the contrary, understanding the doctrines correctly and acting with proper intentions are matters of the utmost significance: life and death, heaven and hell, advancement and regression. Mistaken interpretations *just are* what prevent good practice. But that does mean that Buddhist philosophical arguments, even their best interpretations, should be understood as aspects of a path where right understanding is in service of a greater goal (i.e., *nirvāṇa*), with respect to which all conceptual understandings are insufficient.

Buddhist philosophy had initially grown out of the interpretation of the Buddha's teachings in a variety of traditions called "Abhidharma" schools, which sought to resolve conundrums and confusions about everything from the Buddha's understanding of perception and cosmology to the meaning of his doctrines of no-self and impermanence. In the early first millennium CE, the rise of the Mahāyāna stimulated a new philosophical movement that emphasized the conventional or "empty" nature of all of the Buddha's teaching components (*dharmas*), even those that Abhidharma schools had taken to be the final word. Two modes of arguing for this notion of universal emptiness, the Madhyamaka and the Yogācāra, diverged and in turn ramified into a range of distinct positions. By the middle of the first millennium, Buddhists had turned outward in debates with non-Buddhist opponents and developed a versatile and influential epistemological tradition. By Śāntideva's time, Buddhist philosophers were engaging with newly emergent tantric traditions as well. Śāntideva's work inherits many arguments—he claims to say nothing new—but he was probably also innovative in arguing against Yogācāra (and perhaps tantric) opponents of his time. Here is not the place to fill in the details in this sketch. Suffice it to say that Śāntideva's placement of his Madhyamaka arguments at the pinnacle of a path text represents a return to the pragmatic origins of Buddhist philosophy, but renewed (as always) with the most current understandings.

Philosophy as a practice is not distinct, in this way, from the more obviously embedded practices of ritual and meditation; but since the ideas themselves *can* be isolated and abstracted, they may end up serving a rather more diverse array of functions. Śāntideva's work contains a set of practices and concerns that are very far from those of most modern readers, whether or not they consider themselves to be on a Buddhist path. As I discuss in the next section, this does not prevent the widespread acceptance of the *Guide* as relevant to contemporary concerns.

THE MAKING OF A "WORLD CLASSIC"

In his introduction to the Oxford World Classics translation of the *Bodhicaryāvatāra*, the scholar Paul Williams cites a verse from the *Guide*'s final chapter, the dedication of merit, which is also, he notes, frequently cited by His Holiness the Dalai Lama: "As long as space abides and as long as the world abides, so long may I abide, destroying the sufferings of the world" (10.55).

Let us acknowledge that this is an astonishing aspiration, a truly vast, imaginative expansion of the human potential for compassion. It is, at the same time, a logical, if poetically expressed, extension of aspirational *bodhicitta*. The purpose of the work, from start to finish, is fulfilled if it helps one generate the greatest amount of good karma (merit) possible, which is achieved by making as sincere a play as possible at the mental state of a bodhisattva. The dedication chapter collects the merit assembled throughout the previous cultivations and dedicates it (i.e., aspires to give it), again, toward the goal of the attainment of buddhahood for the sake of the liberation of all beings. If the logic of aspirational *bodhicitta* works, then whatever merit one has acquired thus far will be multiplied exponentially by this culminating aspiration. If it doesn't work, one has literally nothing to lose.

For this reason, even though I find the verse moving, I also find it surprising that Williams comments upon it with the declaration that, "There can perhaps be no higher human sentiment."[18] Yes, but that's the point. The higher you aim, the better the result, even if the intended goal is not achieved. Through the logic of aspiration, the text projects a kind of self-transformation and self-transcendence.[19] After all, to aspire to aspirational *bodhicitta just is* to enact aspirational *bodhicitta*, which is to develop *bodhicitta*.

If karma works, then all the merit generated throughout the text's many prayers and aspirations will affect the mind, and at some point (perhaps through the lofty language of the dedication chapter) the instrumental account gives way (might give way?) to a kind of enactment of the attainment. I may have good instrumental reasons to try to say the words with feeling, but as in method acting, eventually the feeling kicks in. The *Guide* seems unaware of Buddhist tantra, which was coming into efflorescence during the time of its composition; but here the use of aspiration to enact *bodhicitta* in a way that transforms an imagined, resultant goal into the path of practice seems a quintessentially tantric move.[20] If it works, then the text rises above its karmic context and becomes, as Williams intimates, a genuine expression of a maximal, universal morality.

But *does* it work? Perhaps the proof is in the pudding. Williams is hardly the only modern, extratraditional reader to find inspiration in this work; there is, after all, a reason it is included among the Oxford World Classics.[21] My reading here, which provides the verse above with a studied contextualization within Buddhist karmic theory, may seem forced and cynical in the face of the widespread, present admiration for the *Guide*. And surely, modern readers who are not Buddhists are more likely to admire the work for its expressions of universal compassion than for its effectiveness as a merit-generating engine. In fact, although I think it is a mistake to attribute the work's modern political implications (see below) to the time period of the author, I would not want to deny the resonant meanings present in its more recent receptions. *Bodhicitta* may be a more powerful sentiment than ever, since it has emerged into modernity. I would argue, then, that the *Guide*'s communal expression, that is, the combination of its multiple readings through the history of its interpreters, has *made it* mean what it is now taken to mean. Part of what makes the text, deservedly, a classic is what the text has *come to mean*.

As the great twentieth-century German philosopher Hans-Georg Gadamer has taught us, a "classic" is an ancient work that is not just an interesting historical or cultural artifact but one that speaks to the present as though it belongs to our world.[22] Gadamer's point is not that the classic has some eternal essence that transcends time and culture; rather, it is that *our prejudices* provide the window or horizon of meaning that conditions our interest in a given work, from our time or another's. He uses the notion of a classic to show that a historian might pretend to be following objective, scientific methods but is always in fact a *critic* of cultures, and should acknowledge and accept that role. The point is that the *Guide* has entered our time as a work that modern readers can *use* as a moral model. We have developed a community of interpretation that finds meaning in this text, but we should not be fooled into imagining that it was always read in the ways that we like to read it.

Along with our contextualizations and close readings that seek the author's intention, then, our preparations for reading the text should include some treatment of the historical circumstances that have brought about some of the felicitous misreadings that make the work appear meaningful to many modern readers. The full story is beyond telling in my remaining space here.[23] What I wish to emphasize is one crucial set of shifts, beginning in the nineteenth century, whereby a realistic political reading of the text emerged among a small but growing lineage of Tibetan teachers. This group of Tibetan interpreters has provided the text with a bridge to modernity.

Before turning to this transition, though, note that the *Guide* had a wide, diverse readership well before its emergence into modernity. Ten Indian commentaries (extant in the Tibetan canon) display continual interest in the work among the monastic colleges of northern India from the eighth to the thirteenth centuries. The best known of these is a complete commentary by Prajñākaramati, still extant in Sanskrit.[24] Premodern translations from the Sanskrit into Tibetan, Chinese, and Newari, and from Tibetan into Mongolian, attest to the work's broad geographic reach. The *Guide* was first translated from Sanskrit into Tibetan shortly after it was composed, in the ninth or perhaps the late eighth century, and retranslated and revised several times. The work has received an unknown number of Tibetan commentaries—there is much uncharted territory here—but it was the subject of major commentaries by scholars from all of the major Tibetan Buddhist orders. As important as the work might have been throughout Tibetan history, a major change seems to have taken place in the nineteenth century, and this is the story I now wish to tell.

I begin with the great yogi Shabkar Tsogdruk Rangdrol (1781–1851), who aimed his ascetic's critique of hypocrisy not just at individual monks, as previous yogis did, but at the growing "mass monastic" institutions of his day.[25] Shabkar was a teacher of the "Mind Training" practices mentioned above that Tibetans, following Atiśa, used to cultivate aspirational *bodhicitta* according to the eighth chapter of the *Guide*. One thing that was unusual about Shabkar was his vegetarianism, which was almost unheard of in Eastern Tibet of his day.[26] Even more important, in his work, *Nectar of Immortality*, he argues that if you are a meat eater, you have yet to successfully cultivate your aspirational *bodhicitta*.[27] This moral stance allowed him to draw critical attention to monasteries, which at festival times received large donations of meat: "The result is that when one goes on pilgrimage to a monastery, intending to make offerings and pay one's respects, one is confronted by the spectacle of stacks of carcasses, before one has even seen the images of the enlightened beings."[28]

This and similar examples make of meat eating a sign of the corruption of monastic institutions; vegetarianism, by contrast, is cast as a precondition, if not an outright sign, of developed *bodhicitta*.

In the next generation, Patrul Rinpoche (1808–1887) was a beloved teacher famous for teaching the *Guide* constantly, to everyone. He also continued Shabkar's program of advocating for vegetarianism and the end of hunting. Patrul's teachings had the effect of reviving the study of the *Guide* in Tibet. At least two major traditions of interpretation were rejuvenated. Most famously, the philosophical study of the ninth chapter became a major topic of disputation after Patrul's disciple Mipam composed a controversial commentary on it. In addition, under Mipam's instruction, the practice of the full series of meditations became widespread, for perhaps the first time.[29] Both movements were instrumental in providing the ground for the so-called "Nonsectarian" revival of the non-Geluk schools of Tibetan Buddhism.[30] The lives of Shabkar and Patrul provided implicit and explicit critiques of institutional corruption and hegemony, and of the short-sighted disputations that had kept the various schools in mutual competition.

By the time the Fourteenth Dalai Lama studied the *Guide* with his teacher Khunu Lama (1894–1977), a disciple of a disciple of Patrul, the work represented not just a private, karmic method of cultivating aspirational *bodhicitta* but also a *political* ecumenism that was linked to a potential method for transforming oneself into a living model of universal compassion. The work provided, and continues to provide, a kind of public litmus test for the legitimacy of a Buddhist teacher and his or her institution—and a challenge to the legitimacy of those who fail to live up to its maximally compassionate standard. After the Dalai Lama went into exile, the *Guide*'s political ecumenism and the implicit critique of corrupt institutions it had acquired over the past century could be read anew to express the self-declared compassionate approach to the Chinese Communists occupying Tibet. For many Tibetan teachers in exile who teach this work, the *Guide*'s project of cultivating compassion is commensurate with humanity, in contrast to the cruelty and injustice of the Chinese occupation.

In making this claim, to which I will return below, I do not mean to slip into a cynical critique of Tibetan teachers; on the contrary, I am arguing that the practical methods and the psychological realism of the *Guide* do provide a (now) clear method for generating and displaying a genuine aspiration to embody Buddhist ideals. This possibility, I think, was not exactly the initial intention of the author, but it is now an indelible part of the work's explicitly practical application of the Buddhist path. In fact, I would argue that the political purposes that the work serves have helped to "supercharge" the personal cultivation potential within its tradition and to underline its very significant real-world ethical implications. This helps us account for the work's modern following not just among Tibetan religious followers but among many modern non-Buddhist admirers as well.

The political import of the work, then, is significant for us today even if it has a comparatively recent history. Still, this dynamic requires us to place a caveat on the *Guide*, given that its version of universalism is premodern and will inevitably fail to express norms identical to contemporary liberal expectations. This does not prevent it from being instructive in many ways, but ought to alert us to potential hazards in adopting it without a critical eye. As an example of the utility of the work's psychological, practical approach that nonetheless strays from a modern ideal, we could look at the sixth chapter on the cultivation of patience, *kṣānti*. Here the bodhisattva is instructed to work as hard as possible to avoid a mental state afflicted with hatred, since even a *moment* of hatred might wipe out eons of merit ("good karma") collected across countless lifetimes of virtuous behavior. This seems extreme, and if taken too literally is in fact contradicted by other advice that comes later. We should probably read it to mean that hatred *can* wipe out one's previous merit. After all, hatred is a powerful emotion that can override your better judgment, and if you end up *acting on* your hatred and, say, killing someone, you could indeed launch yourself into hell and effectively counteract the benefits of any merit you might have stored up.[31]

In any case, hatred is extremely dangerous. So how can one avoid it? Śāntideva provides numerous strategies, but they begin with the cultivation of a kind of courageous and unflinching sympathetic joy. Hatred is said to find its moment when one is feeling dejected (he calls dejection hatred's "food," 6.7), and one girds oneself against dejection with its antidote, the feeling of gladness about the many ways that living beings experience happiness. This is psychologically subtle: out of fear of *future* suffering in hell, one motivates oneself to endure *present* suffering and discomfort without feeling dejected, by imaginatively trying to feel glad about other beings' happiness. This might seem arbitrary or oddly specific from an abstract, logical perspective, but from a practical perspective the question is just whether it works.

We could attempt to answer this question from the perspective of Buddhist philosophy, interrogating Buddhist texts for their views of degrees of fear and gladness as psychological motivations, and karmic rewards and punishments. Another, more modern and less historically minded method, however, would be to turn for an assessment of its practical success to the self-declared experience of the most beloved Buddhist practitioner in the world, the Dalai Lama. The *Guide* verse most often cited by the Dalai Lama to explain his own celebrated optimism (an emotion perhaps related to sympathetic joy) in the face of continued Chinese aggression and intransigence employs exactly this pragmatic, emotional logic:

> If there is a solution, then what is the point of dejection?
> What is the point of dejection if there is no solution? (6.10)

In several of his works—speeches and writings—the Dalai Lama takes the discussion from this chapter and applies it directly to the circumstances of his own life. He takes the notion of compassion for one's "enemy" literally and declares often that he wishes nothing but peace and liberation for the Chinese as well as the Tibetans. The Dalai Lama himself is only one of many, many Tibetan teachers to have declared the *Guide* as the key that unlocked the compassion for which they became famous. Under his influence and that of the Tibetan exile community, the *Guide* has become emblematic of the Tibetans' claim to civility, ecumenism, and humanity in their confrontation with the Chinese occupation.

So far everything appears beneficial and instructive to a modern sensibility. Still, although I have no doubt that the text has provided a means for the Dalai Lama's spiritual development as he claims, Śāntideva's verses themselves are less perfectly ecumenical than the Dalai Lama would like them to appear. The dozen or so verses that follow the hypothetical question above suggest ways that the aspiring bodhisattva should cultivate himself to endure suffering. And among them, encouraging himself, he writes: "In Karṇāṭa the devotees of Durgā willingly endure to no purpose the pain of burns, cuts and worse. Why then am I a coward when my goal is liberation?" (6.13).

Here, it would appear, xenophobia is being put to use in the cultivation of sympathetic joy. Needless to say, the worshipers of the goddess Durgā do not consider their ritual pains to be for "no purpose." But within the text's assumed Buddhist monastic context (evident here, and at many other points) the bodhisattva can rightly be seen as chastising those who are unwilling to accept what even non-Buddhist sectarians are able to endure for their gods. The Dalai Lama says often that he believes people should keep to their own religions, and that all of the major spiritual traditions serve important needs for their adherents.[32] This would appear to contradict the point of Śāntideva's verse.

Going on, Śāntideva says that pain is worse when you are sensitive and cowardly, whereas practice with small pains eventually allows you to bear major discomforts. The goal, then, is to learn to adopt a heroic attitude toward pain of every kind: "Those who conquer the enemy taking the blows of their adversary on the chest, they are the triumphant heroes, while the rest kill what is already dead" (6.20).

The point that we should learn to endure pain, like a hero receiving blows, seems to be in line with the previous discussion. But the idea of ordinary heroes only killing "what is already dead" may seem callous, and I think it is intentionally so. What is meant by this elusive expression? Here we must avail ourselves of not just the cultural context, as in the Durgā example, but the textual context—what is sometimes referred to as the work's intertextuality. This line seems like a reference to, and a jab at, a famous passage from the Hindu scripture, the *Bhagavad Gīta*:

> It is just these *bodies* of the indestructible, immeasurable, and eternal embodied self that are characterized as coming to an end—therefore fight, Bharata! (2.18)
>
> Anyone who believes this a killer, and anyone who thinks this killed, they do not understand: it does not kill, it is not killed. (2.19)
>
> . . . .
>
> Death is inevitable for those who are born; for those who are dead birth is just as certain. Therefore you must not grieve for what is ineluctable. (2.27)[33]

This is Krishna's opening argument to Arjuna, explaining why he should not be worried—dejected—about taking on his heroic responsibilities and killing his teachers and cousins on the opposing side of the battlefield. Death is inevitable and unreal, so killing is only an illusion. For Krishna, the emotion that Arjuna must "learn to endure" (2.14) is the fleeting feeling of grief that he naturally, but unjustifiably, experiences due to the impending loss of his family members.

Śāntideva's reference tips the reader off to the fact that he has playfully reconfigured the *Gīta*'s argument. Ironically, he agrees with Krishna that Arjuna, as an ordinary hero, is ineffective as such because he is engaged, like the worshipers of Durgā, in a pointless activity that avails nothing. The Buddhist even shares the *Gīta*'s view that death follows inevitably from birth. But Śāntideva's Buddhist reader rejects the notion that mass killing could be salutary, let alone salvific: the purpose of the comparison is to notice, with pride, the superiority of the virtuous, karmic logic of *bodhicitta*, which preserves heroism without its traditional violence.

Given this analysis, the relation between the *Gīta* and the *Guide*—two prominent Indian religious "world classics"—deserves closer scrutiny. Śāntideva lived in and wrote for the Buddhist community of Nālandā, a vibrant, multicultural center of learning. Was the *Gīta* a "classic" for him and his colleagues?[34] To what degree might we read this reference as an implicit expression of indebtedness in a text that could make no explicit mention of such? Or is it simply disrespectful mocking? Surely an attitude of reverence toward the *Gīta* is lacking, but that may be an unfairly anachronistic understanding.

Yet I bring up the comparison not to initiate a close intertextual reading but to note that the historically original reading is not the only Buddhist one. The Dalai Lama's reading, which is a modern reading, suggests a perspective from which the text *ought to be* more respectful than the historically accurate reading suggests it is. In fact, there is a good deal that many modern readers may wish to leave behind in this text, from its monasticism to its sexism to its views about hells and magical powers. At the same time, Gadamer, in agreement with all Buddhists, is poised to remind us that our readings are only made possible by succumbing to our own biased projections. It may be a Buddhist way of viewing things to accept that it is futile to expect a resolution of the multiplicity of perspectives this side of nirvana, given that all things change. Even the received manuscript tradition suggests a participatory authorship that violates the individuality of the work. If we dive in ourselves and imaginatively take on its aspirational mode, we might find ourselves able to participate in the *Guide*'s living community of interpretation, seeking together to help one another advance toward freedom.

FINALLY: ADVICE FOR READERS OF *READINGS OF THE* GUIDE

The fact that a classic is variously interpretable guarantees a diversity of interpretations not just across time but within any given time as well. Different readers will approach the text in search of different types of connection—and not every reader approaches a classic text like the *Guide* with the expectation of discovering *any* connection to the present. The contributions to this volume run the gamut from readings that bracket the contributor's interpretive perspective in an effort to disclose the intention of the author (or authors) with as much clarity and textual precision as possible, to those seeking resonances in contemporary thought while knowing full well that they present arguments the *Guide*'s author would not recognize. We hope that this diversity of methods helps to disclose the multivocality of the *Guide*'s reception history as well as the diversity of materials within the work itself.

The chapters that follow, then, provide fifteen (fourteen more) brief readings of the *Guide to Bodhisattva Practice*, each of which illuminates the contemporary significance of the *Guide* from a distinctive scholarly perspective. The authors are all specialists in Buddhist studies, drawn to the work from a range of specialties and areas of interest. The resultant multiplicity of envisionings constitutes a complex cross-section of current understandings of the work, a feast of new insights from leading lights as well as new voices in the field, and a promising collection of incitements to future research. It is intended to provide multiple points of entry for those newly interested in the *Guide*, as well as rich contemplation for experienced readers.

As noted above, the *Guide* has been in constant use as a ritual, contemplative, and philosophical manual since its eighth-century composition by the monk Śāntideva, most likely at Nālandā monastery in northern India. Śāntideva was honorifically designated "Akṣayamati" to link him to the scriptural bodhisattva of that name who also provided brilliant instructions on the cultivation of the six perfections.[35] The opening chapters of our volume—including this one—orient the reader through analysis of the author's textual and intertextual identity, and the characteristic traits of the *Guide*'s structure and genre. Paul Harrison's chapter attempts to establish the wider project of the author by comparing the *Guide* with Śāntideva's other extant work, the *Training Anthology*—a scriptural collection that Harrison concludes stands in the background and is "suggested reading" for those hoping for an in-depth understanding of the *Guide*.

Amber Carpenter's chapter provides a strong defense of reading the *Guide* as a kind of "protreptic," a genre of (Greek) literature that attempts not merely to *convince* the reader but to "turn [her] toward" the truth. Sonam Kachru analyzes the work as a literary accomplishment, emphasizing not just its linguistic play but also its distinctive authorial mode of "self-overhearing"—an enrichment of the idea of participatory authorship from the present chapter.

The next chapters focus on complex moments and recurring themes. Matthew Kapstein's chapter uses a close reading of the "mouse venom" analogy from chapter 9 to study Śāntideva's Madhyamaka approach to illusion and subjectivity. Janet Gyatso's chapter resonates with the literary characterization from Kachru's essay and dives deeply into a theory of the unique ethical cultivation enacted in the moment from chapter 8 on "exchanging self and other." This study of the benefits of "alternative body" envisioning is followed by Reiko Ohnuma's careful classification of the many kinds, and uses, of *bodies* in the *Guide*. Ohnuma shows that while many will naturally think of Buddhist practice as above all a kind of mental cultivation, the body is present throughout the process, whether as vehicle or as an image for contemplation and analysis. Next, Eric Huntington continues the theme of acknowledging the physical world with a study of rituals and references to material culture in the *Guide*. These chapters partake of the crucial shift in Buddhist studies in recent years that has illuminated many hidden corners of Buddhist worlds through understanding texts not only as abstract conduits of ideas but also as historically located enactments of culture and human motivation.

For a millennium, Tibetans have studied, taught, and interpreted the *Guide*, so that it has arrived into modernity as a living text. The next three chapters elucidate and partake of the rich Tibetan *Guide* traditions. Thupten Jinpa explains the widespread Tibetan method for cultivating *bodhicitta* called *lojong*, "mind training," which is based in and inspired by the *Guide* but evinces the creative expansion and insight of many generations of Tibetan interpretation. Roger Jackson shows how the great forefather of the Geluk tradition, Tsongkhapa, relies upon and draws from the *Guide* but also reworks and reshapes it, in constructing his own masterful treatise outlining the path. Here we see how a classic is adapted and molded as the *Guide* is subsumed under Tsonghkhapa's systematic project. Douglas Duckworth's chapter uses the sophisticated lens of the nineteenth-century Tibetan philosopher Künzang Sönam to elucidate why and how Tibetans read the *Guide* as an exemplification of the Prāsaṅgika-Madhyamaka view.

Recent years have seen an efflorescence of scholarly interest in the *Guide* as a quintessential source for Buddhist ethics. The final section of the volume is dedicated to a range of approaches to the work in the mode of philosophical ethics. Jay Garfield reads Śāntideva as a moral phenomenologist and elucidates how this reading makes sense of moral cultivation in the *Guide*. Charles Goodman, in contrast, defends his view that the *Guide* is "act-utilitarian," explaining that this way of reading Śāntideva finds consistency across his works and allows him to meet common objections to utilitarianism, but lands Śāntideva in a position more suitable to the monastery than to broadly shared, public discourse. Bronwyn Finnigan's chapter formulates a distinctive Buddhist moral psychology of fear based on a study of passages from the *Guide* in which Śāntideva uses fear as a motivator to move the practitioner to fearlessness. Finally, John Dunne argues that Śāntideva's approach to moral cultivation assumes and deploys a fundamental human capacity for connectedness—an assumption that is confirmed by current psychological research on the evolution of cooperative cognition.

Although the volume is intended to exist as a physical book and must therefore have a linear order, the categories of the chapters as just noted should not be taken as exclusive. Carpenter and Kapstein, for instance, are important aspects of the volume's contribution to Buddhist ethics. Kapstein's chapter may also be paired with Duckworth's for a fruitful conversation on the *Guide*'s approach to the doctrines of emptiness and two truths. And the literary qualities of the *Guide* are mentioned across many chapters, though they are the central focus only in Kachru's. A variety of other themes exemplified in many chapters could be mentioned, such as a pragmatic approach to knowledge, an interest in contextualization and intertextuality, or the changing, though continuing relevance of a classic text. Readers interested to find verses, sections, or chapters addressed across the essays may find it useful to consult the "Index of *Guide* Verses Cited." To find terms used (sometimes in different translations) across chapters, see the index.

The *Guide* is a tremendously rich source for students of Buddhism, and we hope these essays provide an entry point and a wealth of contributions to this exciting, active area of Buddhist studies. At the same time, we cannot claim to have thoroughly plumbed the text's depths in these essays. In particular, Saitō's scholarship (1993) comparing the early Dunhuang manuscripts of the *Guide* with the later version that ended up incorporated in the Tibetan canon (and studied here) has opened many questions about the history of the work that we have not had the opportunity to address. What can be gleaned about the history and character of Buddhist monastic and intellectual life from the *Guide* in its different versions? Why, for instance, are almost all the chapters expanded in the later version, but two *reduced*?[36] Furthermore, as is inevitable with such a complex text, many topics in the *Guide* are untouched by our essays. We have hardly mentioned, for instance, how the countless Indian and Tibetan commentaries illuminated each of the perfections, or the nature of *bodhicitta*. We have hardly acknowledged the massive, almost daily, contributions of contemporary Tibetan teachers or the dozens of translations into modern languages. The editors are humbled by the recognition of how many questions are left not only unanswered but even unasked. We hope that readers will be stimulated to pursue these questions further, while of course discovering their own.

NOTES

1. Sanskrit citations in the *Bodhicaryāvatāra* are given with associated chapter and verse numbers and are based upon the edition of Minayeff, "Çāntideva: 'Bodhicaryâvatāra.'"
2. A clear precedent is the *Seventy Verse Aspiration* (*Praṇidhānasaptati*) attributed to Aśvaghoṣa/Mātṛceta. See Lindtner, "Mātṛceta's *Praṇidhānasaptati*."
3. For an introduction to the traditions of Great Vehicle Buddhism, see Williams, *Mahāyāna Buddhism*.
4. The work is sexist and assumes that the reader/aspiring bodhisattva is male (and heterosexual)—and should aspire to remain so until liberation (10.30).
5. One question the editors of this book considered was whether we should regularize the different chapter authors' translations of terms such as *bodhicitta*. Since there is no single standard translation of the *Guide* and the various translations in use adopt different translation terms, we have opted to allow our authors to persist with their favorites. These include "mind of awakening," "Awakening Mind," "thought of enlightenment," and others. Readers will find all of the different translations brought together under the index entry for the Sanskrit term.
6. The full activation of *bodhicitta* and the consequent definition of the practitioner as a true bodhisattva is the achievement of the so-called Path of Seeing, at which point one's vision of the path makes future buddhahood inevitable (as if one has possession of a map to a desired destination), but the practitioner is not there yet. See Gethin, *Buddhist Path to Awakening*, 201–207.
7. For complete verses, I am using Crosby and Skilton's Oxford World Classics translation, i.e., Śāntideva, *The Bodhicaryāvatāra*.
8. See Shaw, *The Jatakas*.
9. Eimer, "Suvarṇadvīpa's 'Commentaries' on the *Bodhicaryāvatāra*."
10. Liland, *Transmission of the* Bodhicaryāvatāra, 37ff.
11. Prajñākaramati's Sanskrit commentary focuses most of its attention on chapter 9. In nineteenth-century Tibet, Mipam's commentary on the ninth chapter stimulated a whole literature of polemics on this topic.

12. Sweet, "Mental Purification (*Blo sbyong*)," and Shönu Gyalchok and Könchok Gyaltsen, eds., *Mind Training.*
13. Saitō, *Study of Akṣayamati's (=Śāntideva)'s* Bodhisattvacaryāvatāra, and van Schaik, "The Original *Bodhicaryāvatāra.*"
14. Harrison, "The Case of the Vanishing Poet."
15. Kapstein, "Stoics and Bodhisattvas."
16. Here I am relying on Gareth Sparham's translation (Vimuktisena and Haribhadra, *Abhisamayālaṃkāra with Vṛtti and Āloka*), 198–199.
17. Harvey, "Extract from the *Kālāma Sutta.*"
18. Paul Williams, "General Introduction," in Śāntideva, *The Bodhicaryāvatāra*, trans. Crosby and Skilton, ix.
19. I am grateful to Eric Huntington for helping me develop the ideas in this paragraph. See his chapter in this volume for an adjacent reading.
20. Douglas Duckworth (personal communication) has suggested that another move that resembles tantra can be seen in the eighth chapter's section, discussed in this volume by Janet Gyatso, where the reader identifies with the enemy in order to overcome resentment. This imagined perspectival shift does not go so far as the envisioning of oneself as a divine other, but it is the perspective of an other nonetheless. In his chapter in this volume, Thupten Jinpa notes that this section is in contrast to the Tibetan *lojong* practices, where one maintains one's own identity and does not literally adopt the gaze of the other.
21. The work has been paid great respect by numerous scholars and other extratraditional readers, including those contributing to this volume.
22. Gadamer, *Truth and Method*, 296–302.
23. Also, this is an ongoing research project for me, and I do not yet have the full narrative in hand.
24. For details and sources, see Liland, *Transmission of the* Bodhicaryāvatāra, 17–19.
25. On the Tibetan system of "mass monasticism" as opposed to the "virtuoso monasticism" of other Buddhist areas, see Dreyfus, *Sound of Two Hands*, 32–53.
26. Barstow, *Food of Sinful Demons.*
27. Shabkar, *Food of Bodhisattvas*, 23–30; 97–99.
28. Shabkar, *Food of Bodhisattvas*, 113.
29. Smith, "Mi pham and the Philosophical Controversies of the Nineteenth Century," and Viehbeck, "An Indian Classic in 19th-Century Tibet and Beyond."
30. Perhaps more precise would be to refer to the *Gemang* movement, which overcame divisions even between the Geluk and the other schools. See Duckworth's introduction to Künzang Sönam, *Profound Reality of Interdependence.*
31. Although this reading makes sense of Śāntideva's position, it somewhat oversimplifies traditional accounts of Buddhist karma. It should be allowed that there is disagreement among Abhidharma philosophers about whether karma is cumulative. Some believe that one's next rebirth is conditioned, in each instance, by the overall character of one's mind at the moment of death. This allows one to compensate and, in effect, repent for negative acts with positive acts. Others argue that, on the contrary, morally significant acts *each* result in karmic recompense. This would mean that no matter how terrible one acts today, one will eventually reap the positive rewards of previous good deeds. Under such a view, it would be difficult to imagine how a single act of hatred could have any effect on previously accumulated merit—unless it is just meant to apply to one's next rebirth.

32. For example, Dalai Lama, *Mind in Comfort and Ease*, 8: "I believe the different religions and philosophies of the world—Christianity, Judaism, Islam, or any of the many branches of Hinduism—are all extremely beneficial and truly help many people. And so I admire and respect them all."
33. *Gīta* quotations are from Johnson, *The Bhagavad Gīta*. Another possible allusion here is the *Discourse on the Fruits of the Contemplative Life*, wherein non-Buddhist ascetics are criticized for their mistaken views, such as one Pakudha Kaccayana, who says that "When one cuts off [another person's] head, there is no one taking anyone's life. It is simply between the seven substances that the sword passes." Using the Pāli canon for convenience, this translation is from Thanissaro Bhikkhu, trans., "*Samaññaphala Sutta*." We don't necessarily have to choose between these passages as the proper target of Śāntideva's critique; he could be alluding to both, and thereby likening the *Gīta*'s view to that of the Buddha's early opponent.
34. It was at least well known. Śaṅkara, who lived more or less at the same time as Śāntideva, wrote a commentary on it.
35. Based on a clever conjunction of the Derge catalog story with Bu-ston's narrative, Saitō, "*Study of Akṣayamati (=Śāntideva)'s* Bodhisattvacaryāvatāra," 20–22, concludes that the name Akṣayamati was an epithet that Śāntideva acquired after his famed public reading of the *Guide*.
36. Saitō, *A Study of Akṣayamati (=Śāntideva)'s* Bodhisattvacaryāvatāra, 20.

REFERENCES

Barstow, Geoffrey. *Food of Sinful Demons: Meat, Vegetarianism, and the Limits of Buddhism in Tibet*. New York: Columbia University Press, 2017.

Dalai Lama. *Mind in Comfort and Ease: The Vision of Enlightenment in the Great Perfection*. Boston: Wisdom, 2007.

Dreyfus, George B. J. *The Sound of Two Hands Clapping: The Education of a Tibetan Buddhist Monk*. Berkeley: University of California Press, 2003.

Eimer, Helmut. "Suvarṇadvīpa's 'Commentaries' on the *Bodhicaryāvatāra*." In *Studien zum Jainismus und Buddhismus: Gedenkschrift für Ludwig Alsdorf*, ed. Klaus Bruhn and Ambrecht Wezler, 73–78. Wiesbaden: Franz Steiner Verlag, 1981.

Gadamer, Hans-Georg. *Truth and Method*. 1974; reprint, London and New York: Bloomsbury Academic, 2013.

Gethin, R.M.L. *The Buddhist Path to Awakening*. Classics in Religious Studies. Oxford: Oneworld, 2001.

Harrison, Paul. "The Case of the Vanishing Poet: New Light on Śāntideva and the Śikṣā-Samuccaya." In *Festschrift für Michael Hahn, zum 65. Geburtstag von Freunden und Schülern Überreicht*, ed. Konrad Klaus, and Jens-Uwe Hartmann. Vienna: Arbeitskreis für Tibetische und Buddhistische Studien, 2007.

Harvey, Peter, trans. "Extract from the *Kālāma Sutta*." In *Buddhist Philosophy: Essential Readings*, ed. William Edelglass and Jay L. Garfield, 177–178. New York: Oxford University Press, 2009.

Johnson, W. J., trans. *The Bhagavad Gīta*. Oxford World Classics. Oxford: Oxford University Press, 1994.

Kapstein, Matthew T. "Stoics and Bodhisattvas: Spiritual Exercise and Faith in Two Philosophical Traditions." In *Philosophy as a Way of Life: Ancients and Moderns—Essays in Honor of Pierre Hadot*, ed. Michael Chase, Stephen R. L. Clark, and Michael McGhee, 99–115. Hoboken, NJ: Wiley-Blackwell, 2013.

Künzang Sönam. *The Profound Reality of Interdependence: An Overview of the Wisdom Chapter of the Way of the Bodhisattva*. Trans. Douglas Duckworth. New York: Oxford University Press, 2019.

Liland, Fredrik. "The Transmission of the *Bodhicaryāvatāra*: The History, Diffusion and Influence of a Mahāyāna Buddhist Text." M.A. thesis, University of Oslo, 2009.

Lindtner, Christian. "Mātṛceta's *Praṇidhānasaptati*." *Asiatische Studien/Études asiatiques* 38 (1984): 100–128.

Minayeff, Ivan Pavlovich, ed. "Çāntideva: 'Bodhicaryāvatāra.'" In *Zapiski Vostochnago Otdeleniya Imperatorskago Russkago Arkheologicheskago Obshchestva* (Transactions of the Oriental Section of the Royal Russian Archeological Society) 4 (1889): 153–228. Retrieved from "Bibliotheca Polyglotta," February 2017, http://www2.hf.uio.no/common/apps/permlink/permlink.php?app=polyglotta&context=volume&uid=433c2dda-4412-11df-870c-00215aecadea.

Saitō, Akira. *A Study of Akṣayamati (=Śāntideva)'s* Bodhisattvacaryāvatāra *as Found in the Tibetan Manuscripts from Tun-huang*. Unpublished project report. Tsu, Japan: Miye University, 1993.

Śāntideva. *The Bodhicaryāvatāra*. Trans. Kate Crosby and Andrew Skilton. Oxford World Classics. New York: Oxford University Press, 1995.

van Schaik, Sam. "The Original *Bodhicaryāvatāra*." 2014. Retrieved from "early Tibet," February 2017, https://earlytibet.com/2014/02/04/the-original-bodhicaryavatara/.

Shabkar [Tsokdruk Rangdrol]. *Food of Bodhisattvas: Buddhist Teachings on Abstaining from Meat*. Trans. the Padmakara Translation Group. Boston: Shambhala, 2004.

Shönu Gyalchok and Könchok Gyaltsen, eds. *Mind Training: The Great Collection*. Trans. Thupten Jinpa. Library of Tibetan Classics. Boston: Wisdom, 2006.

Smith, Gene E. "Mi pham and the Philosophical Controversies of the Nineteenth Century." In *Among Tibetan Texts: History and Literature of the Himalayan Plateau*, 227–234. Boston: Wisdom, 2001.

Shaw, Sarah. *The Jatakas: Birth Stories of the Bodhisatta*. New York: Penguin, 2006.

Sweet, Michael J. "Mental Purification (*Blo sbyong*): A Native Tibetan Genre of Religious Literature." In *Tibetan Literature: Studies in Genre*, ed. José I. Cabezón and Roger R. Jackson, 244–260. Ithaca, NY: Snow Lion, 1996.

Thanissaro Bhikkhu, trans. "*Samaññaphala Sutta: The Fruits of the Contemplative Life* (DN 2)." *Access to Insight (BCBS Edition)*, published November 30, 2013. Retrieved October 18, 2018, http://www.accesstoinsight.org/tipitaka/dn/dn.02.0.than.html.

Viehbeck, Markus. "An Indian Classic in 19th-Century Tibet and Beyond: Rdza Dpal sprul and the Dissemination of the *Bodhi(sattva)caryāvatāra*." *Revue d'Etudes Tibétaines* 36 (2016): 5–44.

Vimuktisena and Haribhadra. *Abhisamayālaṃkāra with Vṛtti and Āloka. Volume One: First Abhisamaya*. Vṛtti by Ārya Vimuktisena. Āloka by Haribhadra. English translation by Gareth Sparham. Fremont, CA: Jain Publishing Company, 2006.

Williams, Paul. "General Introduction." In Śāntideva, *The Bodhicaryāvatāra*, trans. Kate Crosby and Andrew Skilton, vii–xxii. Oxford World Classics. New York: Oxford University Press, 1995.

——. *Mahāyāna Buddhism: The Doctrinal Foundations*. 2nd ed. New York: Routledge, 2008.

[1]

ŚĀNTIDEVA

THE AUTHOR AND HIS PROJECT

Paul Harrison

ON THE TRAIL OF THE DISAPPEARING AUTHOR: INTRODUCTORY REMARKS

The other chapters of this book address themselves primarily to the *Bodhicaryāvatāra* (the *Guide*) of Śāntideva, with only occasional reference to his second major work, the *Śikṣāsamuccaya* or *Training Anthology* (the *Anthology*).[1] The two works are quite different in various ways. The *Guide* is a unified and extended verse composition, which is, as far as we can tell, entirely the creation of its author, and as poetry it is crafted with a fair degree of skill and art.[2] The *Anthology*, by contrast, is a much longer composite work, in which Śāntideva's own words, in both prose and verse, are combined with extensive citations from a wide variety of scriptural texts, over 110 in number. Written in an equally wide variety of registers, the passages cited also consist sometimes of prose, sometimes of verse, which is to be expected given the standard prosimetric style of the Mahāyāna sūtras to which Śāntideva gives pride of place; he quotes Mainstream Buddhist or Śrāvakayāna texts much less frequently, and even then not at great length.

The general style of the *Anthology* is consequently quite uneven, more prosaic and expository than artistic and evocative, although occasionally the verses that Śāntideva inserts, whether his own or taken from his canonical sources, rise to the heights of expressiveness achieved in the *Guide*. The *Guide* and the *Anthology* are thus very different in form and style, but what about their purpose? In this chapter we will make an attempt to understand who Śāntideva was and what he was about, asking whether each of these two works has its own agenda or somehow contributes to one coherent and comprehensive project clearly initiated by a single person.[3] We will see in the end that the *Guide* and the *Anthology* do serve a common agenda, and that neither work can be fully understood independently of the other.

We arrive at this conclusion on the basis of internal evidence. That evidence is not always easy to interpret, but we have no alternative but to rely on it. The traditional biographies, such as they are, hardly help us to get a grip on Śāntideva's purposes, and with them we face a problem endemic to the study of the authors of Buddhist treatises and commentarial works, of having to deal with a tissue of legends of uncertain and unverifiable historical validity. In the case of Śāntideva, who also seems to have gone by the name Akṣayamati ("Inexhaustible intelligence"), the core of the story is quite simple: a monk at the great monastic university of Nālandā,[4] he appeared not to be applying himself to his studies and acquired a reputation for being lazy and unmotivated, so much so that his fellow monks grew used to treating him with contempt, bestowing on him the highly derogatory nickname Bhusuku, a composite of three verbal roots that we might translate as Mr. Eat-sleep-shit. One day the monks hatched a plan to compound the embarrassment and shame of this good-for-nothing slacker and invited him to preach the Dharma to them. To begin with, they made the preacher's throne extremely high, but somehow he managed to seat himself upon it, after which he asked the assembled company whether they wanted to hear something old or something new. Choosing what they thought would be the more challenging option, they asked for something new, and to their great astonishment Śāntideva began to recite the *Guide*. Furthermore, as if the polished elegance and deep erudition of the work were not impressive enough, when Śāntideva got to verse 34 in chapter 9, he rose into the sky and vanished from sight, although his voice could still be heard reciting the rest of the poem. He never returned to Nālandā, and when his shamefaced tormenters searched his cell later for clues as to what had happened to him and why they had got him so terribly wrong, they found the manuscript of the *Anthology*.

Of course we cannot help but pay some attention to such legends, even if it is but a sideways glance, and in the case of Śāntideva in particular there is an almost irresistible temptation to try to salvage something from his hagiography on which to peg our understanding of his authorial impulses. After all, do we not know such characters in the world of academia, the colleague who seems to be doing nothing, who is looked at askance for letting the side down and not justifying his or her tenure, but eventually turns out to have been all along incubating a masterpiece, that one big prize-winning book, indeed the only one produced by the faculty of the department to be hailed as a field changer? Or in Śāntideva's case, two books—the double whammy, an even better payoff! This is a tale of undeniable appeal, of the dunce who turns out to have been a genius in disguise putting the learned to shame, the plodder who is at last revealed as a superstar, leaving everyone dumbstruck with amazement. As emotionally satisfying as the story is, however, we can hardly rely on it as a record of what actually happened and must turn to the works themselves. To know the author and discern his project, we have no alternative but to read his words and try to interpret them as best we can.

STATING THE INTENT, SETTING THE AGENDA

Letting the works speak for themselves turns out to be easier said than done, even if we begin by looking at explicit statements of intent and instructions to the reader, for there we discover several things that complicate the picture. The *Guide*, to start with that work, opens with such a statement of intent, and elsewhere in the text it makes reference to the *Anthology* by name. Let me take these passages in order. The statement of intent in chapter 1.1–3 runs as follows:

> Bowing down in devotion to the Exalted Ones
> With their sons and with their bodies of Dharma, and to all those worthy of worship,
> I shall provide an introduction to the vow of the sons of the Exalted Ones,
> In accordance with scripture and in a concise fashion. (1.1)
>
> I do not have anything new to say here,
> Nor do I possess any skill in composition.
> For that reason I am not thinking about benefiting others:
> I have done this to perfume my own mind. (1.2)
>
> By this the impulse of my faith to cultivate
> What is wholesome grows a little.
> If anybody else with the same disposition as I
> Should see this, he may derive benefit from it too. (1.3)[5]

This seems fairly straightforward: Śāntideva promises the reader a succinct "introduction to the vow of the sons of the Exalted Ones," that is to say, to the vow or vocation (*saṃvara*) of bodhisattvas, who are, metaphorically speaking, the offspring of the Exalted Buddhas. The Sanskrit term *saṃvara*, literally "restraint," is not so simple, and is variously translated as "observance" or "vow"—Crosby and Skilton double-translate it as "the undertaking of the observance"—and it implies moral restraint or discipline. Perhaps we could also understand it as a regime.[6] The rest—nothing new to say, no skill in composition, primarily for his own edification but others may find it useful—is more or less a conventional expression of modesty, adding little or nothing to our knowledge.

Interestingly, this same sequence is not found in the *Bodhisattvacaryāvatāra*, the putative earlier version of the *Guide*, extant only in Tibetan translation, knowledge of which we owe to the research of the Japanese Buddhologist Akira Saitō.[7] However, it also appears at the beginning of the *Anthology*, with some differences in the wording, especially in the last line of the first verse (in italics):[8]

> Bowing down in devotion to the Exalted Ones
> With their sons and with their bodies of Dharma, and to all those worthy of worship,
> I shall provide an introduction to the vow of the sons of the Exalted Ones,
> *Using an anthology of meaningful passages.*

If we hold that the order in which the two (or three) texts were composed runs *Guide*$_1$—*Anthology*—*Guide*$_2$ (see below), then it follows that some of the opening verses of the *Anthology* were subsequently repurposed for the revised version of the poem. Their use in both contexts can be seen as the first indication that both works serve the same agenda of introducing the reader or hearer to the disciplined way of life of a bodhisattva—and indeed that they were composed by the same person.

When we look into how other works are referred to in the text, we see that there is some change from *Guide*$_1$ to *Guide*$_2$.[9] First, *Guide*$_1$ 4.90–91 runs as follows:

> The rules of training are to be seen in the sūtras.
> Therefore one should recite the sūtras,
> And one should look first of all
> At the *Ākāśagarbha-sūtra*. (4.90)

And since the *Sutra Anthology* (*Sūtra-samuccaya*)
By the Noble Nāgārjuna
Ought to be looked at carefully,
You should look at it after that. (4.91)

These two verses are expanded into three in *Guide*$_2$ 5.104–106:

The rules of training are to be found in the sūtras.
Therefore one should recite the sūtras,
And one should consider the cardinal transgressions
In the *Ākāśagarbha-sūtra*. (5.104)

The *Training Anthology* (*Śikṣā-samuccaya*) should by all means
Be looked at again and again
Since good conduct[10] is propounded
At length in it. (5.105)

Alternatively, [for the same thing] in brief,
You should just look carefully
At the *Sutra Anthology* (*Sūtra-samuccaya*),
The companion work [of this type], composed by the Noble Nāgārjuna. (5.106)

These verses have been the subject of a fair amount of scholarly discussion, with different interpretations advanced depending in part on whether Śāntideva himself is credited with a second anthology entitled *Sūtra-samuccaya*.[11] I believe, however, that the correct interpretation of the text of *Guide*$_2$ at this point turns on the contrast between "at length" and "in brief," which replaces the advice concerning the sequence or order of study in the verses of *Guide*$_1$ ("first," "after that"). Once the *Training Anthology* was composed, the student of the bodhisattva path had two commentaries of the *samuccaya* or anthology type to inform and guide his or her study of the sūtras, and thus two possible pathways (making a simple "first"/"after that" order less appropriate). The *Training Anthology* covers the material at length, whereas the *Sutra Anthology* attributed to Nāgārjuna[12] does the same thing in briefer or more condensed form, being roughly a third of the size. If this interpretation is accepted, then these verses do suggest that the text of the *Guide* in the form we now have it (i.e., *Guide*$_2$) was finalized after the *Training Anthology*, but when Śāntideva produced the first version of his poem (i.e., *Guide*$_1$), he had not yet finished the larger commentary, and may not even have started it. After the composition of the *Training Anthology*, however, perhaps in his mature years, he turned back to *Guide*$_1$ to rework it into the *Guide* as we now know it (i.e., *Guide*$_2$). In fact, the revision and enlargement of the *Guide* may have been an ongoing project, a work continually "in progress," with multiple drafts being released into the communication networks of the Indian Buddhist community. Such a scenario is suggested by traditions reporting different verse counts for the poem.

The verses dealt with so far thus tell us something about the purpose of the two works under review here and also throw light on the order in which they were composed and the relationship between them. The other connection between the two works is seen in the verses interspersed throughout the *Anthology*, some of which have counterparts in *Guide*$_2$ (and *Guide*$_1$).[13] This is a more enigmatic connection, since it is not always clear what function these verses have in the text of the longer treatise or how and why they were inserted in it. We could of course conclude that they are there by happenstance, and that folios of the manuscripts containing the two different works were simply jumbled up in a way that, once again, calls to mind the traditional biography, which states that the longer work was discovered in Śāntideva's cell after his disappearance from Nālandā. But however we explain them, these verses, along with the ones in the *Guide*, do not tell us everything we need to know. To understand the structure of the two works in more detail and get a firmer grip on the agenda they serve, we need to look elsewhere.

SUMMARY VERSES AND CHAPTER TITLES: NOTES ON THE STRUCTURE OF THE *GUIDE* AND THE *ANTHOLOGY*

Starting with the *Anthology*, that there is an explicit program to the work is apparent from the twenty-seven verses around which it is structured.[14] I call them the "Root Verses" for the sake of convenience. They even appear as a separate work, the *Verses of the Training Anthology* (*Śikṣā-samuccaya-kārikā*), in editions of the Tibetan Tengyur.[15] The key stanzas are 3 and 4:

> Because the vow of the bodhisattva
> Is hard to know, since it is set forth at such length,
> So that one can be free of transgression,
> One should understand what its key points are: (3)

The giving for the sake of all living beings
Of one's person, one's possessions,
And one's merit accrued in the past, present and future,
And the preserving, purifying and enhancing of these things. (4)

In these two verses Śāntideva lays out his agenda for the whole work, to convey the key points of the vow of the bodhisattva (*saṃvara* again, perhaps here better construed as vocation, discipline, or regime than vow, which seems too restricted in meaning) so that any transgression or wrongdoing may be avoided. Interestingly, he justifies the need to do this with a reference to the prolixity of Mahāyāna sūtras, the sheer length and number of which make it difficult to grasp what the path of a bodhisattva is all about. There's just too much material to assimilate; how can it be reduced to the essentials? The key points can be laid out in a simple three-by-four matrix, as in table 1.1. Some of the Sanskrit terms used are not altogether straightforward, but we will not discuss them in detail here.[16]

TABLE 1.1

	A. person (*ātmabhāva*)	B. possessions (*bhoga*)	C. merit (*śubha, puṇya*)
1. giving (*utsarga*)	1A	1B	1C
2. preserving (*rakṣā*)	2A	2B	2C
3. purifying (*śuddhi*)	3A	3B	3C
4. enhancing (*vardhana*)	4A	4B	4C

So Root Verses 3 and 4. The remaining Root Verses working out the details of this scheme are scattered throughout the text, often dismembered and in an uneven fashion, as Śāntideva attends to the various topics they raise. The result is that the three-by-four matrix, neat as it is, cannot be laid evenly over the whole work. Although all the points are presumably vital, Śāntideva devotes more attention to some than to others.[17]

An alternative way of thinking about the sequence of topics in the *Anthology* is in terms of the Six Perfections (*pāramitās*): giving or generosity (*dāna*); morality (*śīla*); patient acceptance (*kṣānti*); fortitude, valor, or heroism (*vīrya*); meditation (*dhyāna*); and insight or wisdom (*prajñā*). However, if we look at how these are arranged in terms of the chapter divisions of the work, we see that the plan laid down in the Root Verses cannot be mapped onto the Six Perfections evenly or symmetrically.

TABLE 1.2

Chapter No.	Chapter Title	3 x 4 Matrix	Perfection
1	Perfection of Generosity	1A, 1B, 1C: giving one's person, possessions, and merit	giving
2	The Embrace of the True Dharma in the Perfection of Morality	2A, 2B, 2C: preserving one's person, possessions, and merit	morality
3	Preserving the Preacher of the Dharma, etc.	2A: preserving one's person	morality
4	*No title [see next]*	2A: preserving one's person	morality
5	Avoiding the Unprofitable in the Perfection of Morality	2A: preserving one's person	morality
6	Preserving One's Person	2A: preserving one's person	morality
7	Preserving One's Possessions and Merit	2B, 2C: preserving possessions and merit	morality and giving
8	Purifying Evil	3A: purifying one's person	morality
9	Perfection of Patient Acceptance	3A: purifying one's person	patient acceptance
10	Perfection of Fortitude	3A: purifying one's person	fortitude
11	In Praise of the Wild	3A: purifying one's person	various perfections, chiefly morality, meditation, and insight
12	Mental Preparation	3A: purifying one's person	meditation (and insight?)
13	Foundations of Mindfulness	3A: purifying one's person	meditation (and insight?)
14	Purification of One's Own Person	3A: purifying one's person	insight
15	Purification of Possessions and Merit	3B, 3C: purifying possessions and merit	giving, morality, and insight
16	The Rule of Virtuous Conduct	4A, 4B, 4C: enhancing one's person, possessions, and merit	[resolve, vow, etc.]
17	Advantages of Paying Homage (and so on)	4C: enhancing merit	giving
18	Calling to Mind the Triple Gem	4C: enhancing merit	[faith, etc.]
19	Enhancement of Merit	4C: enhancing merit	various perfections, chiefly giving and insight

Further, certain other qualities are highlighted in some chapters, one of which is also regarded as a perfection when the list is extended to ten: vow (*praṇidhāna*). Table 1.2 presents a preliminary analysis, which can no doubt be refined considerably as we continue to deepen our understanding of this complex work.

Several things become evident here, the most salient being the amount of attention devoted to morality and the tendency to weave giving and to a certain extent insight throughout the work. This tendency is hardly surprising, since all the perfections are underpinned by the perfection of insight, while at one point Śāntideva remarks, apparently quoting the *Ratnamegha*, that giving or generosity *is* awakening for a bodhisattva.[18]

As is clear from some of the chapter titles, the Six Perfections also provide part of the basic armature on which the *Guide* is strung, even though there is no explicit program to address them. That is to say, no verse in the *Guide* sets out a plan to deal with the perfections one by one—or indeed any plan at all—but in practice we see chapters 5–9 addressing perfections 1–6 in the standard order, and a case can be made that giving and morality are also addressed in chapters 1, 3, and 10 and chapters 2 and 4 respectively. However, there is a second organizing principle, combined with the Six Perfections and to a certain extent interwoven with them: the Supreme Worship (*anuttarapūjā*).[19] This important liturgical schema, attested already in some of our earliest datable Mahāyāna sūtras (second century CE), blends older Buddhist ritual practices like the Triple Refuge with Mahāyāna innovations to produce a ritual sequence that can be performed publicly or privately as needed, one that remained influential in Vajrayāna Buddhism as well. It takes various forms, but a common sevenfold arrangement includes the following components, not always in the same order: (1) salutation; (2) offering; (3) confession of one's own transgressions (or sin, if one prefers); (4) rejoicing at or giving thanks for the good deeds of others; (5) exhortation to teach; (6) supplication, or entreating the buddhas to remain for the benefit of the world; and (7) dedication of merit. Sometimes making the aspiration to awakening or taking refuge is substituted for one or another of these. The sequence is far from stable, although whatever combination of moves is chosen, the ritual logic remains much the same.[20] If, then, we were to use the Supreme Worship and the Six Perfections to chart the sequence of chapters in the *Guide* in the same way as we have just done for the *Anthology*, the result would be something like table 1.3:

TABLE 1.3

Chapter No.	Chapter Title	Supreme Worship	Perfection
1	In Praise of the Aspiration to Awakening	salutation	{giving}
2	Confession of Sin or Evil	offering, refuge, confession	{morality}
3	Embracing the Aspiration to Awakening	rejoicing, exhortation, supplication, dedication, aspiration	{giving}
4	Not Being Careless with the Aspiration to Awakening	aspiration	{morality}
5	Guarding Full Awareness	—	giving, morality
6	Perfection of Patient Acceptance	—	patient acceptance
7	Perfection of Fortitude	—	fortitude
8	Perfection of Meditation	—	meditation
9	Perfection of Insight	—	insight
10	Dedication (of Merit)	dedication	{giving}

Here the perfections assigned to chapters 1–4 and 10 are given within curly brackets to indicate that they are not the primary focus of these chapters but play a secondary role in relation to the elements of the Supreme Worship being addressed.[21] Nor are they the only perfections implicated in these chapters, which are thematically quite rich and diverse. However, even with this complexity, a clear overall picture of the *Guide* emerges, which shows it wrapping the Supreme Worship around a treatment of the perfections, in doing so generating a text that can itself be used, partly or wholly, to perform the Supreme Worship. This is especially true of chapter 10, which is often recited in liturgical contexts by itself.[22] There are, no doubt, other ways of thinking about the intersection of these two structures. It is not so much that when the Supreme Worship is primary, the Six Perfections become secondary, but that the Supreme Worship encapsulates and enacts the entire training, providing a framework within which one moves from the ritual voicing of the aspiration to awakening to the cultivation of the key qualities, morality and so on, that move the bodhisattva along the path toward that goal, generating in the process the merit required for the ritual dedication. Seen in this light, the structure of the *Guide* is quite ingenious. (See Gold's contribution to this book for a similar analysis of this sequence.)

READING IN STEREO: CONCLUDING REMARKS ON THE AUTHOR AND HIS AGENDA

The evidence reviewed to this point is useful, but it takes us only so far. We need to think about less explicit indications of the author's purposes as well, and the connections they imply between the two works. When one reads the *Anthology* carefully, for example, it becomes evident that neither of the two schemata (three-by-four matrix, sequence of the Six Perfections) addressed in the last section seems to provide a completely satisfactory way of grasping Śāntideva's project and its basic shape. In fact, the way the work bulges out of its frame and the uneven and lumpy fit between schemata and exposition merit closer attention. We have already seen definite indications as to where the author's emphases will lie, in the statement of purpose, in the Root Verses, and in the brief characterization of the *Anthology* in *Guide* 5.105 as a work in which good conduct—or the conduct of good people—is propounded at length. This seems to be picked up by the concluding words of the work, probably added by a later hand, which run, "Here ends the Training Anthology, a code of conduct (Sanskrit: *vinaya*) for bodhisattvas made of extracts from numerous scriptures."[23] In other words, the *Anthology* as a whole is characterized as a kind of *vinaya*, the name given to the corpus of disciplinary regulations governing the lives of members of the saṅgha, which seems consistent with the repeated use of the term "vow" or "vocation" (*saṃvara*), as noted. Accordingly we would expect the emphasis in this work to be on guidelines for conduct, rules by which a bodhisattva may live his or her life so as to be without transgression and morally irreproachable. Whereas the *Guide* appears to focus on aspiration and motivation and can be read as, among other things, an inspirational piece (hence the use of the first-person voice), the *Anthology* provides the practical instructions for the religious life of those so inspired and motivated. However, this rather bland way of formulating the difference hardly conveys Śāntideva's almost obsessive concern in the *Anthology* with urging bodhisattvas to stay on the right side of the law of karma—if we can put it in such crude terms—not only to avoid damnation themselves but also to make themselves acceptable to others and arouse their faith.[24] As Susanne Mrozik has observed, this has a bodily dimension, i.e., it involves looking good as well as behaving virtuously. It is a theme that Śāntideva develops at great length and with some surprising flourishes.

The next point to observe—and we have already seen a number of hints of this—is that what is implicit in the *Guide* becomes explicit in the *Anthology*: that Śāntideva is writing primarily for members of the saṅgha, i.e., for monks and nuns who have taken on themselves, in addition to the usual rules of life for ordained followers of the Buddha, the vocation of the bodhisattva. Although the *Guide* can be and has been read as a call to altruism addressed to all, renunciant and lay alike, when read in tandem with the *Anthology* it clearly addresses primarily Śāntideva's fellow renunciants, his brothers and sisters in robes. The *Anthology* presupposes the observance of the monastic code of conduct (*vinaya*) on the part of bodhisattvas, and in fact makes detailed reference at various points to rules of training and even etiquette whose observance would make little sense for laypeople (so does the *Guide*, for that matter). What is more, it also presupposes an engagement in the study of the Buddha's Dharma that would, if its injunctions were followed to the letter, constitute a serious time commitment for anyone, a commitment perhaps unfeasible for someone not fully devoted to the religious life.[25] Even the minimal reading recommendations in *Guide* 5.104–106, touched on above—*Ākāśagarbha-sūtra* plus *Sutra Anthology* or *Training Anthology*—could only with difficulty be followed by someone without access to a monastic library, to say nothing of the way the prescriptions of the first of these three texts speak directly to the experience of monastics. At many points in the *Training Anthology* we meet the same situation: Śāntideva rounds off his citations by suggesting that further consultation of this or that work is possible, with such words as "and so on" or, more commonly, "and so on at length."[26] Alternatively, he directs his readers to investigate the topic at greater length in sources that he names without quoting from them, doing this sometimes implicitly,[27] sometimes in more explicit terms.[28]

In terms of extra reading, then, he asks for a certain amount, but often in a way that implies that it is optional. Generally, however, he supplies the relevant material in the *Anthology* itself. Here we might consider a characterization of the relationship between the *Guide* and the *Anthology* suggested by Jay Garfield, that the former is like a course textbook and the latter like a course pack of supplemental readings.[29] One could perhaps tweak this a little and think of the *Guide* as the text of the professor's lectures—which in the Indian context would effectively have been the textbook—and the *Anthology* as the required readings for the students, but however we frame it, the analogy is a useful one. A careful reading of the *Guide* adds further force and nuance to it. Although Śāntideva's poem contains a fair number of allusions to scripture,[30] it is generally quite self-contained, making very few explicit references to other texts by name in a way that invites the reader to consult sources external to itself. The injunctions at 5.104–106 are one such case, but what is interesting in that regard is that the *Anthology* provides extensive quotations precisely from those sections of the *Ākāśagarbha-sūtra* that deal with the "root downfalls" or cardinal transgressions mentioned in 5.104.[31] This is a pattern repeated elsewhere whenever the *Guide* invokes sūtras by name. Verse 1.14 makes mention of Maitreya's commendation of the aspiration to awakening to Sudhana, which is a reference to a sequence of verses in chapter 54 (Maitreyavimokṣa) of the *Gaṇḍavyūha*.[32] The relevant verses are given in full in the *Anthology*.[33] At 5.103 in the *Guide* the reference to the Śrīsaṃbhava-vimokṣa is again to a chapter of the *Gaṇḍavyūha* (chapter 53), and, sure enough, we find the relevant passage from it in chapter 2 of the *Anthology*.[34] Verse 7.46 calls for specific practice in accordance with the *Vajradhvaja*,[35] and this too is matched by prodigiously long quotations from that sūtra in the *Anthology*.[36] The only exception to this rule is the reference to the *Subāhu-paripṛcchā* at 1.20 (1.20 also in *Guide*$_1$), which does not appear to be taken up in the *Anthology*.[37] In all cases but one, then, when Śāntideva refers to other sources in the *Guide*, he provides the relevant passages in the *Anthology*, once again confirming the organic connection between the two works.

In the Buddhist monastic context that Śāntideva's work presupposes, reading inevitably shades into ritual. Especially interesting from the point of view of practice are injunctions in the *Anthology* to perform particular rituals, as for example in chapter 8, which addresses the topic of purification, i.e., removal, of evil or sin. Organizing his material using the rubrics of the *Sutra on the Four Qualities* (*Caturdharmaka-sūtra*—in Goodman's translation these four qualities are rendered as remorse, remedy, resolve, and reliance), Śāntideva not only discusses the results of misdeeds in the past in terms of their categories, philosophical implications, and so on but also gives detailed and lengthy practical instructions for the ritual recitation of certain texts to eliminate what we have all grown used to calling "bad karma." The *Suvarṇaprabhāsa* is one such text, the *Upālipariprcchā* another, but toward the end of the chapter many different scriptures are recommended, which call for the repetition of mantras, circumambulation, worship of images of the Buddha, making offerings, taking refuge, making the aspiration to awakening, and so on. Here of course we find ourselves back in the land of the Supreme Worship, and this is no accident. One supposes that bodhisattvas need not do all the things enjoined of them, but to do even some would require a great deal of time and, evidently, access to the appropriate ritual spaces and to a good monastic library.

This is consistent with at least one element in the story of Śāntideva's life, that he lived and worked in Nālandā, which we nowadays assume to have had a library the equal of any in India, and possibly vast enough to rival the Great Library of Alexandria. Whether those who perused the *Guide* would have followed up all Śāntideva's references, or even some of them, we do not know, but there is no doubting his own wide reading and prodigious erudition, which he poured into an anthology so comprehensive as to spare his readers a trip to the stacks. It is only natural that he was devoted to the bodhisattva Mañjuśrī, often regarded as the incarnation of wisdom and learning. His dedication to this figure is seen clearly in chapter 10 of the *Guide*, with its multiple invocations of the great bodhisattva. It is also attested at the end of the *Anthology*, after a long series of verses, some of which also appear in the *Guide*.[38] Whatever we make of the life story of Śāntideva, it is somehow not surprising that his chosen deity or *iṣṭadevatā* appears to have been Mañjuśrī, who, at least in his later Chinese manifestations, was himself given to appearing in unexpected disguises and vanishing into thin air afterward.

Śāntideva did not in fact vanish without trace: he remains in his works. It is true that the *Guide* speaks to us eloquently across the intervening centuries and directly addresses certain aspects of the human condition in words that resonate with us even today. At the same time it is a work of its time, born in a particular historical, social, and institutional context. While much of it is relatively plain sailing, there are sections that can only be fully understood when one knows the background of its author and has some idea what his training might have been, what his daily life as a renunciant entailed, what practices he engaged in, and what he was reading. This is most evident in chapter 9, where Śāntideva is dealing at length and in detail with rival philosophical positions (Yogācāra, Sāṃkhya, etc.) that, absent detailed commentarial support, are likely to remain opaque to the uninitiated. The ninth is a difficult chapter, to be sure, but it is simply the most extreme expression of the embeddedness of the whole work in the doctrinal, ritual, and institutional context of late first-millennium Indian Buddhism. The payoff of reading the *Anthology* is that it makes the contextual embeddedness of the *Guide* much clearer, and we get an even stronger sense of its author's concerns, his hopes, and his fears.

Through both works we can hear Śāntideva's voice, in stereo, as it were, still speaking some twelve centuries or more after his death. We *can* hear it, and we *should*. To return to the analogy of the course textbook (or lectures) and reading pack suggested by Jay Garfield, and to repeat what we ourselves tell our own students every year when we meet them for the first time: you always have the option of just reading the textbook or listening to the lectures, but if you want to get the most of the course, you had better do the recommended reading as well.

NOTES

1. The Sanskrit text of the *Anthology* as we know it has survived in a single manuscript now in the Cambridge University Library, which was first edited by Cecil Bendall, *Çikshāsamuccaya: A Compendium of Buddhistic Teaching*. It has been translated twice into English, almost a century ago by Bendall himself in collaboration with W. H. D. Rouse, *Śikshā-samuccaya*, and recently by Charles Goodman, *The Training Anthology of Śāntideva*. Goodman's translation is superior to that of Bendall & Rouse, and we recommend its use. References to the *Anthology* will be in the form B52:G55, where B stands for Bendall's edition of the Sanskrit text, G for Goodman's English translation.
2. This makes it challenging to translate. We will refer in this chapter to the English rendition by Kate Crosby and Andrew Skilton, Śāntideva, *The Bodhicaryāvatāra*, which is enhanced by useful chapter introductions and notes. Also well worth looking at is the almost complete translation made by Luis Gómez, "How to Be a Bodhisattva."
3. Modern scholarship generally follows the Tibetan tradition in accepting the attribution of the two works to Śāntideva, and I see no good reason to call this into question. For a useful survey (in French) of material relating to questions of ascription and to Śāntideva's life, see Pezzali, *Śāntideva: mystique bouddhiste des VIIe et VIIIe siècles*. See also Saitō, "Facts or Fictions: Reconsidering Śāntideva's Names, Life, and Works," for a concise summary of the issues.
4. The extensive ruins of this vast monastic complex can still be seen in the North Indian state of Bihar, near the city of Patna. One of the greatest centers of learning in the ancient world, Nālandā attracted students from every part of Asia, and many celebrated Buddhist scholars and teachers received their training within its walls. Even today the XIVth Dalai Lama likes to refer to himself as an heir to the Nālandā tradition, and a modern international university established in the area capitalizes on its image.
5. The translation presented here is a slightly modified form of that given in Harrison, "Verses by Śāntideva in the *Śikṣāsamuccaya*," 90; cf. Śāntideva, *The Bodhicaryāvatāra*, trans. Crosby and Skilton, 5.
6. This prompts reflection on the pervasiveness in Indian religious discourse generally, and certainly in Buddhism, of the metaphor of restraint (negatively, bondage) and its opposite, release. *Saṃvara* is something one takes upon oneself or binds oneself with, which closes off certain possibilities, which one freely chooses (another sense of *saṃvara* is choice); it is a kind of commitment.

7. For the sake of this discussion, we will call this earlier version *Guide*$_1$ and use the name *Guide*$_2$ for the later version of the work when comparing the two. In the rest of this book *Guide*$_2$ is simply called the *Guide*. *Guide*$_1$, attested by four manuscripts from Dunhuang, has not yet been published in its entirety. It consists of 701.5 verses as opposed to the 913 of *Guide*$_2$, and is divided into nine chapters (its chapter 2 becomes chapters 2 and 3 in *Guide*$_2$, with consequential renumbering of the later chapters). There are also differences in the order of verses and in their content.
8. For the Sanskrit and an alternative English translation see B1:G1–2.
9. Here I reproduce the translations presented in Harrison, "The Case of the Vanishing Poet," 224–226, with some modifications. These render the Tibetan text of *Guide*$_1$ IV.90–91 as given in Saitō, "Notes on the Interpretation of *Bodhi(sattva) caryāvatāra* V.104–106," 135–147, and the Sanskrit of *Guide*$_2$ V.104–106 as found in de La Vallée Poussin's edition of Prajñākaramati's commentary on the text, *Bodhicaryāvatārapañjikā*, 159–164.
10. Or "conduct for good people," if one follows Prajñākaramati's interpretation of the Sanskrit compound *sadācāra*.
11. See Harrison, "The Case of the Vanishing Poet," 226, n. 49 for a discussion of the problems of interpretation raised by these verses. See also Saitō, "Notes on the Interpretation of *Bodhi(sattva)caryāvatāra*."
12. But certainly not the work of the great Nāgārjuna who wrote the *Mūlamadhyamaka-kārikās* (*Fundamental Verses on the Middle Way*).
13. For a full discussion see Harrison, "The Case of the Vanishing Poet"; for an English translation see Harrison, "Verses by Śāntideva."
14. On the structure of the *Anthology* see also Goodman, *Training Anthology*, xxvii–xxviii and Clayton, *Moral Theory in Śāntideva's* Śikṣāsamuccaya, 39–40. Their analyses proceed along similar lines to mine.
15. For example, they appear twice in the Derge Tengyur, once in the dBu ma or Madhyamaka section (Tōhoku 3939) and once in the Jo bo'i chos chung section (Tōhoku 4549). See Bendall, *Çikshāsamuccaya: A Compendium of Buddhistic Teaching*, xxxix–xlvii for Sanskrit and Tibetan texts with English translation; cf. Goodman, *Training Anthology*, lxxiii–lxxvi.
16. For example, *vardhana* ("enhancing") means literally "growing" or "increasing," which would work for possessions and merit, but not for one's person (*ātmabhāva*), which in many contexts simply means "body." However, we are not talking about bodybuilding here. Similarly, *śuddhi* ("purifying") can denote clearing away as well as cleaning up, so that "purification" will not work in all contexts. Cf. Goodman, *Training Anthology*, xxvii.
17. The framework that Śāntideva uses here is presumably intended as a complete and exhaustive analysis of the bodhisattva's training from one point of view, and is reminiscent of another well-known scheme of Buddhist practice, the four right efforts (*samyak-vyāyāma, samyak-pradhāna*), which resolves spiritual cultivation into the efforts one puts into making sure one does not acquire the bad qualities that one does not yet have, eliminating the bad qualities one already has, acquiring the good qualities one does not yet have, and increasing the good qualities one already has. The two schemes are not reducible to each other, but both illustrate a propensity for thinking in terms of grids that cover all the relevant possibilities.
18. B34:G37. Śāntideva makes the same point using his own words in the *Guide*, at 3.11.

19. Both Crosby and Skilton, in their introduction to Śāntideva, *The Bodhicaryāvatāra* xxxiv and 9–13, and Goodman, *Training Anthology*, xxviii–xxx, draw attention to the role of the Supreme Worship in the structure of the *Guide*.
20. Crosby and Skilton, in their introduction to Śāntideva, *The Bodhicaryāvatāra*, 9–13, provide a useful discussion of the issues.
21. This is only to be expected, given that confession is obviously linked with considerations of morality, dedication is clearly a form of giving, and so on.
22. The foregoing comments apply equally well to *Guide*$_1$, even though chapters 2 and 3 are combined into one.
23. See Bendall, *Çikshāsamuccaya: A Compendium of Buddhistic Teaching*, 366. Cf. *Śikshā-samuccaya: A Compendium of Buddhist* Doctrine, trans. Bendall and Rouse, 320: "Here endeth the Śikṣāsamuccaya set forth in a number of chapters for the discipline of Bodhisattvas." Goodman, *Training Anthology*, does not provide a translation.
24. For an explicit statement see Root Verses 10–12. This important theme is explored at length in Mrozik, *Virtuous Bodies*.
25. In this light it is significant that the chapter devoted to the perfection of fortitude or heroism, chapter 10, reads this perfection entirely as energetic application to the study of scripture.
26. See, e.g., B69:G73; B104:G106; B166:G164; B203:G200; B209:G206; B243:G234; B256:G244; etc.
27. Examples include the reference to the following texts: *Bodhisattvaprātimokṣa* at B55:G59; *Adhyāśayasaṃcodana* at B95:G97; *Ratnacūḍa* at B117:G115; *Sāgaramati* at B145:G140; *Upāyakauśalya* at B168:G166; *Gaganagañja* at B271:G259; *Akṣayamati* at B290:G274.
28. E.g., the reference to the *Bhaiṣajyaguru* at B14:G15 (what follows is not a citation, contra Goodman); *Ugraparipṛcchā* at B193:G190; *Candrapradīpa*, *Bhadracarī*, and *Vajradhvajapariṇāmanā* at B291:G274–275; *Gocarapariśuddhi* at B350:G325.
29. Quoted in Goodman, *Training Anthology*, xii.
30. Sometimes these are signaled with words such as "the Exalted One said" (*Guide* 4:20), "so said the Omniscient One" (5.16), "has therefore been said by the Sage" (6.112), "it has been said by the Lord of the World" (9.17), and so on. Sometimes, however, even though no such markers are used, it is clear that Śāntideva is alluding to specific texts, as, e.g., to some version of the *vinaya* at 5.88–95. In some cases particular stories or episodes involving named figures are referred to, such as that of Supuṣpacandra at 8.106 (see also 8.118, 10.28).
31. See B59–66:G63–70.
32. This verse also appears in *Guide*$_1$.
33. B101–104:G103–106; cf. also B9:G11.
34. B35–36:G38–39. This verse is also found in *Guide*$_1$. The citation in the *Anthology* is not in fact continuous: Śāntideva cherry-picks freely from the text without inserting a single ellipsis marker.
35. This verse does not appear in *Guide*$_1$.
36. B279–283:G265–268; see also B26–36:G29–36; B213–216:G209–212.
37. It is possible that this text from the Ratnakūṭa collection is cited in the *Anthology* under another name, but so far no passages from it have been identified. It is not quoted in the *Sūtra-samuccaya* either.
38. See Harrison, "The Case of the Vanishing Poet" and "Verses by Śāntideva."

ABBREVIATIONS

B Bendall, ed.
G Goodman, trans.

REFERENCES

Bendall, Cecil, ed. *Çikshāsamuccaya: A Compendium of Buddhistic Teaching* (*Bibliotheca Buddhica I*), St. Petersburg: Imperial Academy, 1897–1902. Reprint, Delhi: Motilal Banarsidass, 1971.

Bendall, Cecil, and W. H. D. Rouse, trans. *Śikshā-samuccaya: A Compendium of Buddhist Doctrine*. London: John Murray, 1922. Reprint, Delhi: Motilal Banarsidass, 1971.

Clayton, Barbra. *Moral Theory in Śāntideva's* Śikṣāsamuccaya*: Cultivating the Fruits of Virtue*. New York: Routledge, 2007.

Gómez, Luis. "How To Be a Bodhisattva: Introduction to the Practice of the Bodhisattva Path (*The Bodhicaryavatara*)." In *The Norton Anthology of World Religions: Buddhism*, ed. Donald S. Lopez, Jr., 395–441. New York: Norton, 2015.

Goodman, Charles. *The Training Anthology of Śāntideva: A Translation of the* Śikṣāsamuccaya. New York: Oxford University Press, 2016.

Harrison, Paul. "The Case of the Vanishing Poet: New Light on Śāntideva and the *Śikṣā-samuccaya*." In *Indica et Tibetica: Festschrift für Michael Hahn, Zum 65. Geburtstag von Freunden und Schülern überreicht*, ed. Konrad Klaus and Jens-Uwe Hartmann, 215–248. Vienna: Arbeitskreis für tibetische und buddhistische Studien Universität Wien, 2007.

——. "Verses by Śāntideva in the *Śikṣāsamuccaya*: A New English Translation." In *Evo ṣuyadi: Essays in Honor of Richard Salomon's 65th Birthday*, ed. Carol Altman Bromberg, Timothy J. Lenz, and Jason Neelis, 87–103. Bulletin of the Asia Institute, New Series, 23 (2009) [actual year of publication 2013].

de La Vallée Poussin, Louis, ed. *Bodhicaryāvatārapañjikā: Prajñākaramati's Commentary to the Bodhicaryāvatāra of Śāntideva*. Calcutta: Asiatic Society, 1901–1914.

Mrozik, Susanne. *Virtuous Bodies: The Physical Dimensions of Morality in Buddhist Ethics*. New York: Oxford University Press, 2007.

Pezzali, Amalia. *Śāntideva: mystique bouddhiste des VIIe et VIIIe siècles*. Firenze: Vallechi Editore, 1968.

Saitō Akira. "Notes on the Interpretation of *Bodhi(sattva)caryāvatāra* V.104–106." In *Gedenkschrift J. W. de Jong*, ed. H. W. Bodewitz and Minoru Hara, 135–147. Studia Philologica Buddhica, Monograph Series, XVII. Tokyo: The International Institute for Buddhist Studies, 2004.

——. "Facts or Fictions: Reconsidering Śāntideva's Names, Life, and Works." *Journal of the International College for Postgraduate Buddhist Studies* 22 (2018): 1–20.

[2]

REASON AND KNOWLEDGE ON THE PATH

A PROTRETPTIC READING OF THE *GUIDE*

Amber Carpenter

> The Guide enjoins giving only vegetables and the like at first. Later, by degrees, one acts in such a way that one is even able to give up one's own flesh!
>
> When the understanding arises that one's own flesh is no more than a vegetable, what difficulty is there in giving away one's flesh and bones? (7.25–26)[1]

MECHANISMS OF PROTREPTIC

The Greco-Roman philosophical tradition had a genre of literature called "protreptic." *Protrepsis* means "turning toward," and while the genre might broadly be taken as a call to turn toward a different form of life,[2] the metaphor embedded in this term for it comes from Plato's *Republic*, where at issue is specifically a turning of the soul toward reality:

> The power to learn is present in everyone's soul, and the instrument with which each learns is like an eye that cannot be turned around from darkness to light without turning the whole body. This instrument cannot be turned around from that which is coming into being without turning the whole soul until it is able to study that which is and the brightest thing that is . . . education is the craft concerned with doing this very thing, this turning around, and with how the soul can most easily and effectively be made to do it. It isn't the craft of putting sight into the soul. Education takes for granted that sight is there but that it isn't turned the right way or

> looking where it ought to look, and it tries to redirect it appropriately . . . the virtue of reason . . . never loses its power but is either useful and beneficial or useless and harmful, depending on the way it is turned.
>
> (*REPUBLIC* VII.518C–519A)[3]

Insofar as talk of "turning souls" refers to souls, such a phrase may seem singularly inappropriate to a Buddhist context. But there are deeper affinities in the metaphor. The very notion of protreptic as a genre contains a sense of literature that does not just say something but *does* something. It does something to the audience; and what it does is transform their outlook wholesale. More specifically, protreptic aims, as Plato puts it, to turn us toward reality, or reorient us toward a comprehension of reality.

There is a further, related affinity in the presumption that such reorientation—grasping reality aright, in a way one ordinarily does not—is a moral matter. Such transformation is no mere accumulation of facts; turning toward reality transforms one's engagement with the world. Thus, for Śāntideva,[4] all virtues are essentially and primarily mental. For instance, "The perfection of generosity is said to result from the mental attitude of relinquishing all that one has to all people, together with the fruit of that act. *Therefore the perfection is the mental attitude itself*" (5.10, *emphasis mine*).

And similarly with *śīla* (discipline, or restraint):[5] "Where can fish and other creatures be taken where I might not kill them? Yet when the mental attitude to cease from worldly acts is achieved, that is agreed to be the perfection of *śīla*" (5.11).

And so with anger and the rest.[6]

Such reorientation implies a revised conception of what is possible, necessary, and appropriate, which in turn issues in feelings and actions. Actions and individual choices carry moral weight, of course—in the Buddhist idiom, they have karmic consequences. But they carry these because of the intentionality and ways of seeing that they contain, express, and perpetuate. It is our ways of seeing reality that inform our conceiving of intentions to act; and so it is through seeing reality that we transform ourselves, and the quality and nature of our actions.[7] This process of coming to see reality does not, for Śāntideva at least, arise suddenly and all at once.[8] It arises rather through several more minor or local revisionings, which it is the work of the *Guide* and other such texts and related exercises to effect.[9] The transformation of outlook, the perspective thus attained, are the core and substance of the moral life—as epitomized in the perfection of wisdom or insight (*prajñā*) standing at the culmination of the path.

While a great deal of modern moral theory attends to action, decision, and the principles underlying correct choice, by the time we reach the point of choosing an action we are already fairly well down the road of ethical formation and ethical thought. All the truly decisive elements occur upstream, as it were, where the world is characterized in a certain way and categorized, where meanings take shape and options emerge. At the point of choice among a few well-articulated options, we might say with Sartre, *les jeux sont faits.*[10]

Buddhist ethical thought, reflective and hortatory, respects this fact implicitly, and Śāntideva's *Guide to Bodhisattva Practice* (*Bodhicaryāvatāra*, hereafter *Guide*) exemplarily so. Rather than argue for this or that ultimate ground of normativity, the *Guide* aims to change the categories in which we experience the world, the perspective we take on our own experiences, and to modify quite comprehensively what is "on our minds." This emphasis on transforming experience is what makes so apt Garfield's preferred characterization of Śāntideva's ethics as "phenomenological."[11] This transformation should alter what we see as possible, necessary, and reasonable regarding action and feeling, and leave choice a theoretically quite uninteresting part of the chain of explanation.

Such protreptic texts appeal to reason and offer arguments—because after all, it is a feature of human creatures that they do also recognize and respond to these in distinctive ways. But it belongs to the very nature of the genre that such rational appeals do not swing free in some rarefied logical space (as claims like $2 + 2 = 4$ seem to do). For protreptic attempts to alter what one recognizes as a reason; the "turning of the soul" consists in the recognition that what you took before to be a good reason is no reason at all, while something you had never properly seen is now appreciated as the salient rational consideration. Exactly this shifting appreciation of what counts as a reason makes the genre of protreptic an apt point of reference for a Mādhyamika like Śāntideva.[12] For it allows categories and conceptualizations to be evaluated as progressively more apt, without implying commitment to any one set of categories as capturing the final and ultimate truth of the matter.

The difficulty for any Mādhyamika is how to eschew any reference (or commitment) to ultimate reality and yet retain teleological notions of progress and path. Any Buddhist thinks our ordinary ways of looking at the world are terribly flawed and the cause of persistent suffering, but without recourse to some sort of "seeing things as they actually are" (in the metaphysical sense that a Mādhyamika eschews), it is difficult to evaluate any ordinary conceptions as better and worse. They cannot be rejected on account of their being wrong or false, nor can changes in ordinary views be validated on the basis of being correct or closer to correct. A protreptic understanding of how Śāntideva is working here addresses the difficulty inasmuch as protreptic arguments do not aim to—and do not need to—prove that alternative positions are just plain false (in the way that $2 + 2 = 5$ is just plain false), nor need they demonstrate that the preferred outlook is the *only* intelligible one. The everyday outlook is superseded and replaced, not proved wrong; the opening of the mind to new things as reasons counts as an improvement primarily on moral grounds (such ways of looking make us better persons and are better at ending suffering), but also on peri-epistemological grounds such as the ability of the new ways of seeing to shed more light on more of our moral lives, or to accommodate and explain the old ways of seeing and their inferiority.

To illustrate what it means to say that the *Guide*, like any protreptic text, deliberately alters what we recognize and respond to as a reason or argument, we will look closely at two such transformations: the first, working on the audience of the text through the course of chapters 2 to 4, transforms how we conceive of ourselves and our situation; the second examines the way a transformation of outlook is effected through the depiction of the mind as menagerie in chapter 5, and how this prepares the audience for understanding an argument in chapter 6 in the right way. While these two instances are significant, they are primarily offered as illustrative: tracing their workings should give us tools for approaching the *Guide* as protreptic and articulating much of the rational work done implicitly through choice of categories and metaphor, which determine where and how to focus the audience's attention.

A SAMPLE TRANSFORMATION: HUMAN LIFE AS A FANTASTIC CHANCE TO DO GOOD DEEDS

We begin by tracing out a movement through chapters 2 to 4 by which the text uses reason and argument to bring us along the path.[13] In chapter 2, after a general and fairly anodyne "confession of faults," the text begins leveraging the anxiety we can all be presumed to have about death, and about what we conceive of as "our own" future suffering. Death is tacitly presented as something fearful *in virtue of the prospect of future suffering it implies*. (The audience is clearly not thought to be of the ancient Epicurean sort, where death is by definition the end of all sentience, painful or pleasant.) To the ordinary way of thinking, there is no need to ask whether avoiding my own intense future suffering is a good reason to act, think, or feel. Of course it is.

The text works by taking this natural presumption and, first, intensifying it:

> How can I escape it? I am continually in a state of alarm, O leaders. Let death not come too soon to me, before my mass of evil is destroyed. (2.32)
>
> How can I escape it? Rescue me quickly, lest death come swiftly, before my evil is destroyed. (2.33)

There may be—in the abstract—many reasons to fear death: fear of the unknown, loss of relationships, and projects unfinished. But we are not "in the abstract." Here it is not just death that is fearful, but an early or sudden death—specifically, death before the "mass of evil is destroyed." To an audience that takes death to be the end, there is nothing particularly terrifying in this. Only with the background conviction that evil is suffered after death, proportionate to evil done before, does fear arise, for then such a death entails unspeakable suffering for the deceased. The text does not make this latter claim explicitly here but rather relies on it as a suppressed premise, so obvious and commonly shared that there is no need to state it in order for it to be present in the hearer's mind at the mere suggestion of dying with evil deeds unexpiated. The presentation of death as terrifying *because of the evil that will persist* through that transformation should already effect an initial reorientation, should bring us to see the world in a completely different way: "Even someone taken away today to have a limb cut off withers, throat parched, gaze wretched. He sees the world in a completely different way. But that is nothing to the feverish horror which grips me . . . as Death's terrifying messengers stand over me" (2.44–45).

The line of reasoning invokes a kind of parallelism: someone facing the prospect of lesser suffering (merely a limb cut off) sees the world differently; therefore, the prospect of much greater suffering ought certainly to cause one to see the world differently.

In what way differently? Enlivening our sense of the implications of death without atonement, life no longer appears as a field of potential self-fulfillment through projects and relationships, which would be sadly cut short when death comes. Instead it appears suddenly a minefield, an omnipresent danger—life itself is a chance at every turn to create more suffering by "clinging to this transient life" (2.43), with all the negative actions that entails, and to incur more future suffering for oneself rather than less.

This is an appeal to pure pragmatic thinking, within categories that we could assume to be available to everyone, presenting specific considerations—intelligible from that perspective—that cast our situation in a specific light. It leads with the stick rather than the carrot. It causes me to see my situation differently, but by using all the same categories and presumed values.

But the next major move, in chapter 3, presents something entirely new. There is no balancing list of all the charms and advantages of timely expiation of evils, so that we may weigh the available alternatives and make a rational choice from among the options as we already understand them. Instead we get something quite different—something that does not figure in the calculative, self-interested reasoning motivating the great fear, and the reconception of everyday life as fraught with danger. Chapter 3 invites us to envisage morally perfect beings (accomplished bodhisattvas, buddhas), and at first simply to "rejoice" (3.1–3) in how marvelous they are.

This taking joy in a perfectly *and effectively* benevolent being is inspiring. Once the option is presented as a possibility, one wants to be *like that*. By 3.6, the "I" of the text is not content to rejoice at the someone who is an ocean "bearing happiness to every being" (3.3); "I" want to be like that too: "may I allay all the suffering of every living being" (3.6)—a series of ardent wishes to alleviate the suffering of others follows (3.7–23). All talk of fear for self has vanished, drawing our attention to another dimension of the picture to which we had been hitherto oblivious. Notice what the text does *not* do: the buddhas and bodhisattvas are not presented as themselves perfectly happy and fearless—though they surely are—and so they are not being presented as a straightforward solution to the predicament as made vivid in chapter 3 on its own terms ("Want to relieve your suffering? Try caring for others!"). The will to emulate does not spring out as a solution to my fear of my own suffering. It is rather a reasonable form of recognition of a sort of goodness hitherto unacknowledged—the world does not have to be a system of traps, fraught with danger, in which my best hope is to escape with less suffering than happiness. The world can be a glorious opportunity to alleviate all suffering; and I can participate in that.

Merely adducing the possibility may add a new dimension to our understanding of reality and the possibilities for action within the human condition; it may even be inspiring. But glimpsing the world as the buddhas and bodhisattvas see it does not suffice for us to inhabit that outlook. The mere introduction of new categories, associations, and possibilities does not yet stably transform our orientation toward reality, or ensure the sustained effort required to live it consistently over time. Still, the sharp contrast between the two does give us a basis for confidence to undertake the painstaking, piecemeal labor of undoing our default ways of thinking that are incompatible with that perspective. Chapter 4 acknowledges the tension, or rather the vacillation, between these two perspectives—"Swinging back and forth like this in cyclic existence, now under the sway of errors, now under the sway of Awakening Mind" (4.11)—and attempts to use the resources of our default perspective to reason us into inhabiting the bodhisattva perspective.

To work us from one perspective into the other, calculating reasons are offered for persisting in our inspired undertaking. "How much worse will it be for me, having proclaimed aloud the unsurpassed happiness with great enthusiasm," if I renege on my promise? "After breaking my word to the entire world, what would be my future birth?" (4.6). But over the course of the chapter, we see that the recollection of hell is deployed for a different purpose. Instead of terrorizing us, the recollection of hell aims to reveal our current human circumstances to us in a certain light. Now this could amount to the familiar thought—familiar in the European tradition—that earthly life, and humans in particular, are in-between beings, no saints perhaps, but not as badly off as some are. Think, for instance, of Odysseus's conversation with Achilles in the underworld: "I'd rather slave on earth for another man—/ Some dirt-poor tenant farmer who scrapes to keep alive—than rule down here over all the breathless dead" (*Odyssey* 11.467–564). The main thrust of such a reflection on inferior rebirths is that we should stop grumbling—however bad it is here, it's not as bad as it could be.

This is decidedly not the view taken in *Guide* chapter 4. Achilles misses passion in the underworld, human contact and society, zest for life; dwellers in Śāntideva's hell, by contrast, miss chances to behave morally (4.18, 4.22)—*this* is what we should notice about them, this is the lack that constitutes their real misery. What makes the human condition stand out from all others is the rare chance to be virtuous: "There is no greater waste of time than this, nor is there greater folly: that after attaining such a fleeting opportunity I do not practice good deeds" (4.23; cf. 4.15).

Human life is precious *because it allows one to do good deeds.* Consider for a moment how odd that thought is, stripped naked of any context. When extolling life, some people speak of each human life being precious, or life being a gift; some speak of the dignity of human beings; some of gratitude for life or for being alive. None of them is alluding to the marvelous chance to practice virtue. Even the Greeks, for whom morality was uniquely human, did not therefore think of human life as an exciting opportunity for practicing virtue that we must urgently take up with all our energy.

But because chapter 3 already introduced the radical possibility of participating in ending all suffering for all beings, we are primed to see *just this aspect* of hell-dwelling as particularly hellish: namely, that this marvelous alternative is unavailable. This contrast allows us to appreciate keenly *just this difference* between the human condition and *all others*—hellish or divine: namely, that a mode of being beyond all calculation of selfish pleasures, the complete dedication to the removal of all suffering, is possible.[14] In the light of this possibility, the consideration of our own fears and pains becomes something paltry—inconsequential, when one keeps well in view the great, inspiring goal.

> Without cause, they display the wounds from the enemy on their limbs as if they were decorations. Why then, when I am striving to fulfil the Great Cause, do I let my sufferings oppress me? (4.39)
>
> Their minds set only on their own livelihoods, fishermen . . . and the like withstand such distress and extreme cold. Why have I no endurance though it is for the advantage and well-being of the universe? (4.40)

The argument buried in here is simple and—thus abstracted—unconvincing. Other people are proud of their wounds incurred for lesser causes; therefore, I should not be bothered by my own suffering for a greater cause. Thus abstracted, the argument tendentiously neglects the fact that my sufferings may be much greater, that the fishermen have no choice, that we are all naturally more motivated by our own immediate welfare. Taken independently of any context or commitments, this is so far from being compelling argumentation that it might be accused of begging the question against the egoist.

But the whole point is that neither the argument nor we who must consider and evaluate it are abstracted from context—and if we were, we would not be any better able to make sense of considerations offered as a reason. Contrasting the greater goal, and the conception of my own activity and possibilities, with the goals of fisherman and soldiers gives me good reason to seek endurance and fortitude in my own endeavors *because* I have already seen what the world could look like from the bodhisattva's perspective—where ending all suffering *is* a goal, where the world appears as the joyful opportunity of generating joy, rather than as an arduous, unending task of accounting pleasures and pains, defending the bottom line so it comes out more favorable than otherwise.

We must not mistake the character of the *Guide* as offering irrational appeals masquerading as bad arguments. Śāntideva is reasoning in the mode of invitation, offering new aspects to be considered as relevant and salient—which is a perfectly legitimate mode of reasoning; and the arguments work, just as any arguments do, by taking their meaning and connotations from a surrounding network of categories, possibilities, and values. Protreptic joins these by using our current commitments and categories to introduce the salience and value of new possibilities that come to replace the initial outlook.

A SECOND TRANSFORMATION: THE MENAGERIE MIND

A second strand of reorientation may be traced from chapter 5, which opens by likening the undisciplined mind to a rutting elephant. It is a fun and familiar image. It is also a mechanism for engendering a distinctive and pragmatically efficacious model of mind. In 5.2–4, our inner life is likened to so many wayward forces, to "tigers, lions, elephants, bears, serpents" (5.4). The simile draws us to regard mental life in a certain way: as a menagerie of arbitrary, willful creatures in need of discipline. I introspect and discover aliens.

Contrast this with a Freudian-type way of regarding the emotions and the mind. On the Freudian picture, emotions and compulsions are eruptions to the surface of the buried truth of our real desires, our real fears, our *real selves*. We are encouraged to "own" our darkest impulses, to make sense of our seemingly irrational whims, by connecting them to deep sources within ourselves. Perhaps we will eliminate some unwanted impulses, but only by explaining them, tracing them back to something more true in us, more lasting, stable, real. On this familiar picture (and it *is* a picture), I introspect, and—like so many followers of the Vedas—I find my true self.

Śāntideva's menagerie mind cuts against this notion that if I just dig deeper, I will strike the real truth about myself. Śāntideva's use of wild animals to figure our mental lives has us externalize the mind *tout court*, setting in place an attitude toward it that makes disidentification obvious and natural. It picks up on work already under way in chapter 4, where the various vices are depicted as The Enemy Within, which we are roused to eliminate. In 4.28–34 and 4.43, the defilements are us and are also *in us*—fifth columnists so firmly entrenched that we must be ready to battle them every day, on every front. The menagerie mind of chapter 5 builds on this externalization of mental factors, but it goes further. Its more specific characterization of mind carries with it more helpful expectations about appropriate attitudes and actions to take toward our mental states, and promises surprising results from introspection. It also thereby lays the groundwork for a correct apprehension of no-self. No-self as it arises for the first time in the middle of the chapter is not so much the conclusion of a mereological argument as it is the implication of an outlook dominated by the metaphor of the menagerie, rather than the metaphor of archaeology.

Instead of the real truth about who we really are, deep down, what goes on in the mind is an "it," an "other"—and not some tame, docile Other, but some thing to be restrained and disciplined. Lions, tigers, and bears are not my true essence,[15] and I do not come to know myself better by coming to know *them* better, identifying with or affirming them. Nor does one seek deep explanations for why the tiger roars or the elephant ruts—that is just what tigers and elephants do. Characterizing our mental life as menagerie is an invitation to attend to the waywardness, the wildness, the vehemence of the mental events arising. This menagerie mind is, moreover, what *everyone* sees upon introspection (that is, every unawakened ordinary person)—there is nothing special about *me* here. The simile, while encouraging disidentification with introspected reality, encourages at the same time the implicit recognition of commonality with others.

This simile suggests a different response to the mental life, and the further verses of chapter 5 follow this up—for a wild animal is not tamed through behavior equally wild, nor through deep understanding of its childhood traumas. It is tamed through restraint. What, in this case, however, is the appropriate restraint? Should we think of nooses and cages and other violent forms of restraint, as the battle language of chapter 4 suggests? On the contrary, in this discourse on Guarding Awareness (and mindfulness, 5.23), it is mindfulness itself that should be the restraining tether of these wild beasts (5.3).

Mindfulness may seem a paltry device for such labor. How indeed does mere mindfulness operate as a *restraint* at all? The chapter does not offer an explicit account. But we may discover a clue by considering *what it is* that we should be mindful *of*. In verse 29, we are admonished to "remember the torment of hell"—but this is in order to generate the motivation to reinstate mindfulness, if it has slipped. One should also "recollect the Buddhas in this way," namely "meditating thus . . . possessed of shame, respect, and fear" (5.32). But what we recollect about the Buddhas is that they "have unobstructed vision in all directions" (5.31)—so this is again using a recollected object to inspire the motivation to *remain mindful*; it is not that *of which* we are mindful.[16] We are not told to bear in mind the perfection of the Buddha, or his many examples of perfect living in his previous lives as a bodhisattva; nor are we instructed to be mindful of the precepts—or of Rules to be Obeyed. Indeed, we are not told so much as we are *shown* what we are to be mindful of—and that is *our own minds*, all the random stuff arising, and in particular (to start with) the unreasoning, groundless impetuosity and harmfulness of our menagerie minds. Being constantly mindful that our desires, impulses, fears, ambitions, and frustrations are just so many willful forces arising to no purpose—they are not a need of the soul, or my true self, or demanded by reason—prevents them setting in motion manifold further unwholesome mental events and actions. It enables us to guard awareness (5.27) of right and wrong, and thus avoid inadvertent offenses (5.26).

This is why "mindfulness remain[ing] at the door of the mind in order to act as guard" suggests the much-reiterated advice to be "like a block of wood" (5.34, 48, 49, 50, 51, 52, 53)—unyieldingly firm and still. This is terrible moral advice *in the end*, as the final statement on how we should be in the world. Its implicit unresponsiveness is even inconsistent with the bodhisattva vow. But if ordinary mental life is a confusion of wild, ungrounded pushes and pulls, then "be like a block of wood" is terrific advice for what to do with the unruly mind "at first" (5.33), in order to get oneself into a condition to be able to act morally at all. I can only have the responsiveness of the bodhisattva when the wild cacophony of strident voices composing my mental life is no longer clamoring for attention (this is why "the thief, lack of awareness . . . *comes after* the theft of mindfulness," 5.27); and the clamoring only stops when I refuse to go along with their demands, or as the metaphor from 5.33 suggests, when I turn them away at the door.

Although the mind-as-menagerie image discourages seeking deep and meaningful sources of mental events, which would enable us to "own them" (as the current jargon has it), Śāntideva *can* of course adopt the Freudian—or (less anachronistically) let us call it the Yogācāra *ālayavijñāna* (store consciousness)—approach to the mind, tracing current experiences to earlier causes. He must do so, in fact, for precisely such tracing will be necessary to undermine anger. But this tracing of effect back to cause will be importantly impersonal or detached, and it will be so precisely in virtue of the work done by the menagerie mind metaphor.

Consider for a moment a concern we might have with chapter 6, if we read it in isolation. In order to diffuse anger and cultivate patience, the "I" of the *Guide* draws upon his unspecified misdeeds in a previous life to undermine any sense of righteous indignation he might feel at his own "unjust" suffering. How, we might wonder, is Śāntideva entitled to do this? Surely such tracking of karma and fruit, and attributions of belonging and identity, reinforces the "I"-thinking we are supposed to abandon. *In the abstract*, this is a common and not unwarranted anxiety about the compatibility of karmic thinking with the pragmatics of no-self.[17] But we need not be worried, because chapter 6 is not context free (indeed nothing is!). The advice in chapter 6 is, in particular, directed to someone who has been through chapter 5's exercises in disidentification and disavowal of seeking meaning in the activity of tracing out the genesis of emotions. The use of the menagerie mind image has inoculated us against engaging in the activity of tracing cause and consequence in the wrong sort of way, as an act of appropriation.

More precisely, the reorientation of chapter 5 means that by the time we come to chapter 6, we are already approaching what we call "our own lives" as impersonal, even alien events, and using I-attributions in the purely locative and pragmatic sense. Practiced in regarding our minds as dangerous and also vulnerable (5.20), alien and willful ("when the mind" does this or that, 5.49–54), to be watched over and guarded, we are no longer in any danger of making the genetic fallacy—of mistaking the (conventionally discriminated) cause of effects for the identification of any real essence or truth. To accomplish this, Śāntideva does not need to point out that the mind is "not me"—indeed, explicitly declaring *some* things "not I" can implicitly strongly suggest that some *other* unnamed thing is the real me, failing completely to perform any of the vital work of reorientation. Śāntideva's whole procedure and whole way of speaking, by contrast—the metaphors (mind as menagerie, but also mind as wound, 5.19), the distancing locutions ("the mind" does this or that), the block of wood—reorient our outlook so that "What is *really* the Real Me?" is simply not a question on the table. When no-self is finally explicitly introduced (5.60–64, regarding the body; not generalized until 6.25–32), it simply falls into the place prepared for it, working rather as a *reminder* of what was already implicit.

CONCLUSION

Other such transformations could be traced through the progress of the *Guide*. Śāntideva's implausible claim that suffering makes one compassionate (6.21), for instance, is to be understood not as an assertion but as an invitation to make it so—and indeed, an invitation efficacious in the production of the invited effect. My suffering may shock me into compassion for those in cyclic existence, *when* I have a framework for experiencing suffering as a portion of an interconnected network without any loci of overall command. And this is the framework Śāntideva goes on to give in the verses that follow (6.24–26, 31), picking up on the impersonal orientation to reality set up in chapter 5, and showing how this leads to an opening toward others' suffering (6.34). Chapter 8 then takes this further, showing how our habit of creating unity where there is none can be turned to good effect: we know what it is to think of our hands and feet as parts of a single whole (8.91, 99); although *believing* this would be unhelpful, we are by now far enough from such an outlook that we can draw on our previous experience to isolate the activity of whole-making itself. This activity succeeds not by tracking truth, but by composing wholes in such a way that suffering is diminished (8.115). Many other instances could be identified, once we revise our understanding of the genre of the *Guide* and our expectations of how reason works.

To approach the *Guide* as protreptic is to ask, in each case, how are we being reoriented *here*? What are the particular elements of the mode of presentation that enable a thought to be compelling *here*? When we identify these, we will have seen how it is that our souls have been turned, as Plato would put it; we will make explicit what changes in attention, in categories and classifications, in possibilities and relevances, enable the meaningfulness of the reasons offered to come into view.

If image and metaphor are among the tools deployed to effect this change, this does not make the text irrationalist, or the means of persuasion underhanded. On the contrary, we should ask why we ever expected in the first place that reason should be an appeal to some thin, pure, wholly indeterminate "rational being." This conception of reason, and what counts as a reason, is itself a moral matter; the shared unquestioned assumption that this is the gold standard of a good reason has a history, and it is political.[18] To understand the use of reason and argument in the *Guide*, we must lose the frankly bizarre expectation that this will look like an abstract appeal to pure rational beings, and be more honest—as Śāntideva was—about what reason is actually like. Rational appeals and arguments are only compelling because of the way they draw their meaning from a wide range of tacitly accepted presumptions, categories, and perspectives. The whole is what must be targeted and adjusted, piecemeal, if we are to be reasoned into a different point of view.

NOTES

1. Translations taken from Śāntideva, *The Bodhicaryāvatāra*, trans. Crosby and Skilton, with occasional minor emendations.
2. Stowers, "Letters of Exhortation and Advice," 92.
3. Grube's translation, rev. Reeve as in Cooper, ed., *Plato: Complete Works.*
4. For the purposes of this essay, I use the name "Śāntideva" as indicating the author or authors combined with any unknown editors responsible for the text currently received under the name *Bodhicaryāvatāra.*
5. Often translated, as in Śāntideva, *The Bodhicaryāvatāra*, trans. Crosby and Skilton, as "morality."
6. Patience in 5.12; the famous verse at 5.13 ("where would there be leather enough to cover the entire world?") targets *vīrya* (zeal, resoluteness, diligence); 5.14 highlights controlling the mind in the manner of mental cultivation; and 5.15 describes the perfection of wisdom with its "no fruit comes from a dull mind that bears comparison with a sharp mind on its own."
7. This reverses the consequentialist interpretation of Goodman in *Consequences of Compassion*, which takes action to be the means of character transformation; on the view taken here, if there is to be talk of means and ends, it will be transformations of seeing or understanding that are the means of transforming action. However, the character transformation (consisting, as it does, in increasing insight into reality) is the only part of this that could claim to be good in itself; the improved actions that follow are themselves instrumentally useful so long as one is but imperfectly enlightened, and dry up altogether (in some sense) when one has attained full understanding of reality.
8. The question was apparently the great point of dispute at the legendary "Council of Lhasa" debate (supposed to have taken place at Samye Monastery in Tibet, in the late eighth century CE), as a consequence of which (so the legend goes) the Chan view of sudden enlightenment was banished from Tibet in favor of the position of the Indian faction (represented by Kamalaśīla) that enlightenment is gradual.
9. See for instance Buddhaghosa's *Path of Purification*, which details exercises for effecting revisions of reality in specific ways, suited to specific characters. Buddhaghosa often recounts or refers to Buddhist tales to illustrate his points—that is, to get the audience to see things as he is recommending we see them. Such tales are a vast store of literature used to shape outlook and categories for experiencing the world differently.
10. Not for nothing do latter-day Buddhists such as Stephen Batchelor see a common cause between existentialist and Buddhist ethics.
11. See Garfield, "What It Is Like to Be a Bodhisattva," and Garfield, *Engaging Buddhism*, ch. 9; also, this volume.

12. Śāntideva is working within the Mahāyāna tradition inaugurated by Nāgārjuna, called Madhyamaka. One hallmark of Nāgārjuna's approach is a thoroughgoing anti-essentialism and anti-foundationalism, which nevertheless makes use of ordinary claims and conceptions for advancing along the path toward enlightenment.
13. There are many ways to parse these chapters, and the *Guide* as a whole; for instance, the way that Śāntideva is here picking up on and reworking the Mahāyāna "Supreme Worship" liturgy is surely revealing of text and context. To read it protreptically need not exclude multiple other approaches revealing different vital insights into the text.
14. To say straight out "think of human life this way" would be no more effective than simply telling someone, "think of yourself as a unique child of a unique and loving God." You have to *show* the person the world in which that is the case.
15. Contrast Plato's use of the man-lion-beast image in *Republic* IX, where he aims to show precisely that this *is* our real nature.
16. This description of the buddhas follows the observation that mindfulness "comes easily to those . . . [who] live with their teacher" (5.30). We are to make our teachers and their all-seeing powers present to us ("before them I stand" 5.31) through recollection, in order to make mindfulness easy to maintain.
17. This moral "no-self/karma" difficulty is more difficult to address than the more familiar, metaphysical "no-self/karma" compatibility concern (as I argue in *Indian Buddhist Philosophy*, 105–107).
18. For concrete details of one historical manifestation, see McCumber, *The Politics of Reason in the Early Cold War*; short read at https://aeon.co/essays/how-cold-war-philosophy-permeates-us-society-to-this-day.

REFERENCES

Carpenter, Amber. *Indian Buddhist Philosophy*. New York: Routledge, 2014.

Cooper, John, ed. *Plato: Complete Works*. Indianapolis: Hackett, 1997.

Garfield, Jay. *Engaging Buddhism*. New York: Oxford University Press, 2014.

——. "What It Is Like to Be a Bodhisattva." *Journal of the International Association of Buddhist Studies* 33, no. 1–2 (2010–11): 333–335.

Goodman, Charles. *Consequences of Compassion*. New York: Oxford University Press, 2009.

McCumber, John. *The Politics of Reason in the Early Cold War*. Chicago: University of Chicago Press, 2016.

Śāntideva. *The Bodhicaryāvatāra*. Trans. Kate Crosby and Andrew Skilton. Oxford World Classics. New York: Oxford University Press, 1995.

Stowers, Stanley. "Letters of Exhortation and Advice." In *Letter Writing in Greco-Roman Antiquity*. Philadelphia: Westminster Press, 1986.

[3]

ON LEARNING TO OVERHEAR THE "VANISHING POET"

Sonam Kachru

You and one companion are an adequate theater for each other; or you for yourself.

—SENECA

TRULY, ŚĀNTIDEVA is "the vanishing poet." Paul Harrison once memorably characterized him thus when speaking of Śāntideva's *Training Anthology* (*Śikṣāsamuccaya*). He had in mind the curious fact that editors and readers often found themselves lost in the woods of what was presented as continuous prose in our editions, failing to see that more than a few trees among the thickets were lyrical verses. When verses were identified as such, many were identified as being citations rather than Śāntideva's own compositions.[1] To speak of "the vanishing poet," then, can mean that we have not always been in a position even to begin to hear Śāntideva aright, much less to interpret him.

In a sense, the poet Śāntideva vanishes even when we read the *Guide*. It is easy enough to speak of the beauty of individual verses, but Louis Gómez is right: "Alas, for all our expressed admiration for the poetical beauty of [the *Guide*], we do not have to date any detailed explorations of the literary characteristics and merits of the work."[2] Nor, to the best of my knowledge, have even individual verses received the kind of literary attention they so richly deserve. Consider what follows, then, to be a very tentative introduction to the vanishing poet, and merely one cautiously suggested orientation to an altogether remarkable work.

MEETING THE VANISHING POET

Let's consider three moments from the *Guide* to get an initial feel for Śāntideva's skills in poetic craft and a first taste of the kind of sensibilities we might need as auditors to keep the poet in view. The examples range from instances of care in language that are (or at least can be made) evident in translation to those not so easily preserved.[3]

First, let us attend to the meditating voice of the text in chapter 8. We join the poet after his long (and often claustrophobic) description of our frailties and failings (8.70–8.84), infelicities that the poet would have us see as being particularly evident when we persist in orienting ourselves to success and the satisfactions of our desires with the help of a calculus of means and ends. Śāntideva's conclusion is abrupt (8.85–86):

Thus recoil
from desires—one should
bring into being ravishing delight
in solitude:
in the undisturbed,
the tranquil
woods, empty of
all wearing effort
and strife. (8.85)
The lucky ones walk about
on delightful surfaces of rock stretching wide across
wide as palaces the surfaces of rock cooled by the sandal-
balm rays of moonlight as the air's being stirred about
them by wind through the forest, gentle, soft, soundless,
and they're thinking all the while of the well-being of others. (8.86)

I have tried here to capture the phonetic texture of these verses, even resorting to the prose-poetic mannerisms of Jack Kerouac at the close, in order to highlight a change of pace and voice. It is not the content alone that changes at the end, but even the texture of the voice in verse. There is, for one thing, the remarkable twinning of phonemes (which in English literature are called assonance and alliteration, and literary critics in Sanskrit knew as *yamaka*). Thus, the word for rocks (*śītaleṣu* [8.86a]) reverberates in an anagrammatic rearrangement of syllables in the compound description of their cool surfaces (*śilā-taleṣu* [8.86b]), and the word for the delightful affordances of the scene (*ramya*) in 8.86 resounds with the verb to move (*caṅkram-*) in that verse, as if to make real the suggestion of embodied felicities through phonetic movements.

Such effects of texture are here in service of a cooling delight, and entirely unlike the beginning frame of this long sequence (in 8.70) where phonetic twinning is in service of revulsion at what a different sensibility finds delightful:

> When in the charnel ground, seeing
> not a few corpses, you're
> apparently put off in disgust, delighting
> in this charnel ground: a village
> choked with walking corpses. (8.70)

You don't need to know much Sanskrit to hear the juxtaposed possibilities of delight and revulsion enacted at the level of phonemes in the last two feet of that line, with the soft nasalization in the word for delight (*ram-*) echoing the word for village (*grāma*), only to be drowned out with the clanking consonants of the animated skeletons (*kaṅkāla*).

However directed, such heightening of lyrical concentration through phonetic texture is rarely idle. With the shift to the moonlight-cooled wildness of delightful rock we hear a control of genre, a shift to an "aesthetic of the wild,"[4] the use of which involves conjuring the virtues of place and potential qualities of mind.

Such use has a long history. Though not restricted to Buddhism, in Buddhist verse this is a genre of attention long associated with exhortations to contemplative exercises and cognitive and affective achievement.[5] Moreover, Śāntideva's literary evocation of this genre is here enjoined on us as a conclusion—"*Thus* recoil from desires." The description of our lives that has preceded this moment is intended to incline us to a variety of revulsion from which we are now enjoined to pivot. The lyricism of the description of solitude that follows, briefly considered above, enacts the quality of mind that is about to be invoked and engaged in contemplative exercise. For "solitude" (*viveka*), a word that echoes in the verses that conclude the chapter from here on out, is a complex word: it can mean the withdrawal of a person from a crowded, domestic setting to the solitude of wildness; the withdrawal of attention from distracting thoughts and emotions; and even the capacity for and quality of calm and controlled analytic discernment.[6] The lyrical use of language enacts a mood meant to attune one to receive the arguments and contemplative exercises (such as "the exchange of self and other") that are to follow (see chapters by Gyatso and Jinpa).

But shifts in genre can happen more quickly than this, and with less programmatic effects. Take another example from a little before the passage cited above. Śāntideva says:

> For the desiring ones
> there's all too much
> of such want of luck
> and misery; the relish
> of enjoyments small:
>
> snatchings
>
> at
>
> cuts of grass,
>
> as the beast shoulders the cart along. (8.80)

I have spaced the single simile to allow one to hear in it a found poem, as it were, hidden so as almost to challenge us to juxtapose the pleasure in acknowledging it with the relish of small enjoyments the poet has just censured. Whether or not you hear in this an allusion to the first image of the *Dharmapada*[7]—suffering follows him who acts with an unskillful mind as a wheel follows the foot of the ox—the poem will now move along a different track, switching from what premodern intellectuals in South Asia would have recognized as a discourse of power and profit (*artha*, for which see particularly 8.73–77) to a discourse of virtues (*dharma*). Our attunement to a possible change of tone and diction in the space of a single image, and the consequent possibility of a new register with which to bring our life under a description, functions as a kind of crossing, a threshold of heightened care and attention, but one not easily settled or determinable in meaning or mood.

To see how the attention of the speaking voice, and correspondingly that of the auditor, can be modulated by Śāntideva the poet requires a sensitivity to even finer grain at smaller scales of literary craft. Let us consider now a third example, a moment from Śāntideva's concluding dedication of merit (chapter 10) in the translation by Kate Crosby and Andrew Skilton:

> May they experience the sword-leaved forest as the splendor of the divine grove, and may the thickets of torturing thorns grow into magical trees that fulfill every wish. (10.6)
>
> May the regions of hell become glades of delight, with lakes scented by a profusion of lotuses, splendid and delightful with the chorus of song from grey geese, ducks, *cakravākas*, swans and other water-birds. (10.7)

The lyricism is apparent even in translation, as is the texture of ornamented speech. But let us consider what is not, despite the care the translators have taken with alliteration.

The "magical trees," *kalpapādaḥ* (10.6d), close the verse, phonetically echoing with the abrasive "*ka*" sounds distributed in the compound that serves to name what the poet prays will be replaced: the "thickets of torturing thorns (*kūṭa-śālmalī-vṛkṣāḥ*, 10.6c)." Note that the open vowels and absence of harsh consonants in "*kalpapādaḥ*" ease the constriction and torture of the thorny thickets of those dental and conjunct consonants.

This transformation sets up the dramatic effect to follow. The next verse enacts in its texture what it wishes to be the case: that the horrors of hell vanish. And so, poetically, it is: hell has for its place only the last word in the last foot of the verse (10.7d), with the atmosphere of suffering reoccupied by a graceful zoology and a pleasing environment: "Splendid and delightful with the chorus of song from grey geese, ducks, *cakravākas*, swans and other water-birds" (10.7ab).

You might hear in this an echo of the idyllic space of the heavenly gardens shared in the common aesthetic imaginaire of urban sophisticates and the makers and users of Buddhist monastic environs. The ideal beautiful monastery, after all, is often described as "made lovely (*śobhite*)" in stenciled descriptions, not only by the presence of flowering trees and fruit but also by resounding birdsong. Many of the same birds feature in such lists of places that join wild nature with cultural products and values, though I would hazard that Śāntideva's reverberating chorus, because he carefully restricts in his choice of names to those that begin with "*ka*" or "*ca*," more artfully seeks to enact the birdsong it evokes.[8]

To understand that point you need to hear Śāntideva in Sanskrit. Listen now to the verse-inaugurating "ecological" description in Sanskrit, "*kādamba-kāraṇḍava-cakravāka-haṃsādi-kolāhala-ramya-śobhaiḥ*" (10.7a–b). And you might also hear something else. The long, unfolding description is a map of the full complement of sounds available to Sanskrit: every class of articulable sound the grammarians recognized in the language is present, and correspondingly, your tongue must move over the entire mouth to produce it: there is the guttural (called *kaṇṭhya*, such as "*ka*," for example); the palatal (*tālavya*, such as "*ca*"); the cerebral (*mūrdhanya*, such as "*ḍa*"); the dental (*dantya*, such as "*da*"); the labial (*oṣṭhya*, such as "*ma*"), and all semivowels (*antaḥstha*, the in-between, such as "*ya*," "*ra*," "*la*," and "*va*"); not excluding a generous helping of the class of sibilants (*ūṣman*, such as "*ha*," "*śa*," and "*sa*"). This does not appear to be mere statistical chance. The modulation of the world that some Buddhist texts tell us is possible due to the extraordinary power of awakened beings—a transformation, we are told, we ought to imagine as taking place even on the scale of the very elements of material reality[9]—is here performed within language. For a moment, it is as if the work of literature consists in the transfiguration of what there is, making real for us new experiences of possibility through the manipulation of the least units of linguistic texture in such "extreme phonetic figures."[10]

At the very least, the above examples evince impressive control of and care for the affordances of language, going far beyond a concern with merely propositional content. Śāntideva's workmanlike verse is often unadorned by the kind of phonetic and semantic ornamentation some critics in Sanskrit considered criteria for the use of language to count as poetic literature (*kāvya*).[11] But his use of language is never idle. There is, for one thing, the care taken with the suggestion of moods, and the impressive range of "the varying moods evoked from chapter to chapter, and within each chapter."[12] And in any case, we should not forget that a later generation of literary critics in Sanskrit (beginning in the ninth century CE) would have us seek the true criterion of poetic literature in such suggestion afforded by overarching literary contexts rather than in any explicit, individual, and localizable instances of figurations of semantic content or phonetic texturing and ornamentation.[13]

But even recognizing in the *Guide* an astonishing theater of changing moods will not get us to what is truly distinctive about the poetic work of the *Guide*. I will introduce below a feature I take to be related to the evocation of moods, but one not overtly discussed by critics in Sanskrit, despite being exemplified in the poetry available to them (including the kind of literature they used to particular effect in order to exemplify the suggestion of moods as a new criterion for the work of poetry).[14] What I have in mind is an affordance of lyric whose context is dramatic, and which, along with the evocation of a heightened self-consciousness through attunement to the experience of moods, brings into view the prospect of a lyrical subject overhearing themselves, and so becoming capable of change.

SPEAKING TO YOUR OWN MIND

"Overhearing," John Stuart Mill believed, is what is distinctive about lyric. Many have since sought to refine Mill's criterion to include more than his solipsistic theater, in which all we get to overhear in lyric is a voice not principally addressing itself to us but peculiarly unconscious of its audience.[15] Yet the various demands lyric voices can make on their auditors are not insulated from the dramatic contexts of their performance and reception,[16] and we might well be constrained to confront in lyric a far more dramatic range of possible stances and lyric personae than Mill ever entertained as possible.[17]

In some cases, lyric subjects, like dramatic characters, change by overhearing themselves,[18] which is an extension of Mill's sense of "overhearing." This notion is especially helpful, I believe, when trying to put one's finger on Śāntideva's literary achievement. At least that's what I'll try to show below: how Śāntideva's "I" is a lyric persona capable of *self*-overhearing in a work composed in a way that allows us to enter into the drama of a mutable mind, one that thinks and feels as it speaks, changing even as it speaks, thinking through and feeling what it says.

Let's unpack this slowly, beginning with what I mean by "entering into" the work. The stage of Śāntideva's drama of awakening, though first-personal, is anonymous. Its psychological textures and the contoured background it acquires over the course of the work are not biographically afforded—the first-person "I" does not necessarily represent a specific individual but a generic psychological type.[19] The literary conceit would have it that if the poet is skilled enough, nothing insulates us from moving ourselves into the position of the speaker and finding in Śāntideva's meanings our experiential possibilities.[20]

The work might fairly well be described as not so much finding its ideal reader but making one up. The anonymity of the first-person voice ensures that potential auditors are not insulated from the variety of "self-composition" we are told the *Guide* involves (as when the speaker tells us that "I didn't compose this work thinking of others: I did it to perfume my own mind"[21]). Indeed, the capacity at issue in the fact that others can enter into the *Guide*, taking up its first-person perspective and voices as their own, increasingly becomes an explicit and thematic focus.

The reader who sets off with Śāntideva, making the meditator's voice his or her own, will at last be called on to formally test the presumptive insulation of self from other and the value of any such insulation. I have in mind the formal exercise and regimen of imaginative experimentation called the exchange of self and other that serves as the dramatic climax of the *Guide* 8.90–184, where the ability to bring oneself under a third-person description, offered by another (perhaps only offered "as if" by another), and the ability to realize and feel ourselves into the truth of first-person descriptions uttered by another (perhaps only "as if" uttered by another), is made real for us:

> Generating a sense of self
> with respect to one's inferiors,
> among others, and a sense of otherness
> with respect to oneself, make real
> and bring into being envy and pride
> with an uncalculated mind: (8.140)
>
> He is honored, not I. I don't receive the alms he does.
> He is praised. I am blamed. I suffer. He's the happy one. (8.141)
> I do chores while he takes it easy. He, apparently,
> is the best in the world. Apparently, I'm not worth a damn:
> There is nothing good about me. (8.142)

Such an exercise of the imagination would have us experiment with feeling oneself *as an object* of another's subjective attitudes while allowing oneself, as it were, to move into subjective stances that were either simply not entertained before or treated as being, in some brutal sense, either metaphysically unavailable or entirely different in kind from one's own case. Such an exercise has at least two effects. Guided by the imaginative use of social affects (like envy and pride, rooted in the social concepts of praise and blame), one can use such an experiment to experience, and so potentially to reconsider, the massive asymmetry that otherwise habitually characterizes the experience and valuation of one's own subjective location as opposed to those of others. Less proximately, such an imaginative reframing of the links between one's (subjective and social) location, orienting affects, and habits of first-person identification might also serve to call into question default vectors of attention, even as it reorients us in a constitutive way such that it shifts the axis of our cognitive and affective moral concern.

The point of the imaginative exercise is to have us experience, and not just entertain propositions about, the possible scope for our first-person attitudes and the reach of our concerns (8.81–100; 8.158). My contention is that this variety of experientially consequential imaginative exercises taken by Śāntideva to be constitutive of the development of our affect-constrained varieties of attention and moral concern serves also as the tacit dramatic conceit of the work. The philosophical work of the *Guide* might just depend on what reading—or, more properly, enacting—the *Guide* might show us of what we are like (and what we could be). Part of the philosophical success of the *Guide*, I am arguing, requires that Śāntideva be able to make sufficient imaginative room in his work, as it were, to move us into the position of enacting his drama within ourselves, and so convincingly allow us to experience that drama as our own.

What is dramatized thereby are not only the possibilities for the anonymity of the first person but also no more and no less than the power of thought—when imaginatively exercised and minutely experienced—to change us. This can change not only how the work is read but also what it can do. I have suggested that the work is composed in a way that we might find ourselves to be among its subjects. One literary way this is indexed has to do with one of the distinctive textural features of this work, namely apostrophe, or the turning away to address something or someone else: "So, heart, free yourself from fear."[22]

Now read that out aloud as if it were a script for you to speak to yourself, and you'll have at least one condition for how the work seeks to convince us by dramatizing the ability of reasons to address, reach, and possibly change us. You will also create the conditions for the variety of dramatic *self*-overhearing I have in mind to recommend as being distinctive of the *Guide*.

While apostrophe is not uncommon to lyric in Prakrit, Pāli, Sanskrit, or, even later, Apabhraṃśa, the sustained and directed use of such address in Śāntideva is, to the best of my knowledge, unprecedented. It is, moreover, qualitatively distinct from many of its precedents. Unlike the erotic first-person female subject of the lyric collection *Sattasaī*,[23] or even (in the Southern recension) the aging and increasingly disenchanted voice in Bhartṛhari's *Śatakatraya*,[24] this is a voice not limited to mere exhortation or admonishment. Śāntideva's lyrical voice can demand reasons of itself, following out entailments in arguments to which it holds itself accountable, as in chapter 5:[25]

> Why, mind, do you protect
> this carcass, identifying
> with it? If it's really separate
> from you, what loss
> is its decay to you? (5.60)

> Fool! You do not
> identify with a doll made
> of wood, even if pristine:
> why, then, guard this
> festering contraption of filth? (5.61)

Śāntideva's "heart" and "mind" are not mere grammatical props in a rhetoric of address; nor yet are these used as mere indices for a rhetoric of affective excess, the kind of insistence sometimes found in lyric in South Asia to the effect that our embodied life forever exceeds the reach of the normative expectation of reasons.[26]

If Śāntideva's mind is brought within a space of reasons, it is no mere passive witness of the inner life: it plans, projects ideals, transvalues the meaning of individual emotions and the value of the passions in general;[27] it recollects what it has done and thought, weighs and considers normative commitments enjoined by both theoretical and practical reasons:[28] it is a person, subject to all the confusions that change and self-reflection can involve.[29] All this, again, anonymously, if first-personally presented.

With respect to the literary space afforded by the *Guide* we are far removed from the literary texture Bernard McGinn discerned in early modern mystical writing of Europe, exercised as those authors were with the issue of privacy of feeling and the ineffability of experience.[30] If anything, the *Guide* is a literary context whose distinctive texture is in part characterized by nothing in it being long hidden or beyond the reach of articulation. Everything can be brought into view, through a variety of dialogical attentiveness the poet sometimes considers "anatomical"—for here what is initially concealed (and so indistinct) is soon analyzed by being pulled into view with "the knife of discernment" (as in *Guide* 5.62) and at last articulated. The mind is not immune to the reach of such analysis. The first person's many voices are articulate, the dispositions and moods recognizable: nothing is *ultimately* obscure to its meditating subject (however occasionally bewildered or under their spell he might be, as in *Guide* 4.27); nor, consequently, is anything of this drama not made available to us to enter into, as reading the work we stage a performance of the meditation in ourselves.

But to get the full character of this literary space and the central conceit that we may dramatize the ability of thought to change us, we have to experience that anonymously first-person voice *changing* based on what it is saying. And we have yet to see that peculiar sensitivity unfold.

OVERHEARING

What is it like to experience overhearing? To hear it, let's join with the meditation beginning at *Guide* 8.50. This meditation involves the contemplation of the body in a particular way, with the goal of inducing a visceral disgust at the loathsomeness brought into view by the exercise. In what follows, the "cover" is one's own skin:

They don't make love
to their silk
pillows, soft
to the touch,
stuffed with
cotton: "It doesn't
smell foul,
ejaculate"—that's
sensualists thinking for you,
or lovers, infatuated
with feces. (8.50) This
passion, even when it
was covered over—why
once uncovered is it not
held dear? If the cover's beside
the point, why touch
or rub against it? (8.51)

Remember, the speaking voice and the quoted contents need not involve an other. "The sensualist" need not be an extrinsic type of person, but a sensibility in all of us—not so much an untutored or unconscious proclivity as a practiced internalization of a culture of sensibility and value, a possible style of being a person available even to us. It acquires a certain valence as the meditation develops:

If you have no passion
for what's not clean,
why later embrace
the sinew-bound bone-
cage, smeared over
with the muck of flesh? (8.52)
You have excrement enough

of your own—go satisfy yourself
with just that! Glutton
for crap! Forget her, that
other skin-bottle for shit! (8.53)

You can almost hear the spit that enters the voice at "Glutton" and is let out in that last imperative. In Sanskrit, the last word is "forget! (*vismara*)." That strikes me as being far more psychologically revealing and effective than ending with a loud expletive could be.

As memorable as it is, however, this moment is only an exclamation mark on a movement of feeling that develops over time, climaxing at last in the strained syntax leading up to the release of expletives. You can spot the movement, almost, even in the English above. The pace of thought accelerates as we shift from the general ("the sensualist [in general]") to the specific ("you," that is, the lover, or the sensualist in us). So quickly does the thought move that its central analogy goes by in a blur: the body, paradigmatically the truth of which is concealed or covered over, is grammatically and metaphorically hard to pin down in that first argument, tagged only by an indeterminate pronoun—"This passion, even when it was covered over—why... is it not held dear? If the cover's besides the point, why touch... it?" The varying syntactic textures of Śāntideva's verses and the occasional compression of his thought, of which many translators have spoken, seems here to enact a psychological unease. The suggestion is this: even as the voice of reason brings our attention to bear on the body, our syntax betrays our psychological evasion of what such attention would have us acknowledge about ourselves.

Contrast the evasive reference to the body above with the increasingly forceful tone to which the speaker resorts, and the simultaneous expostulation of anatomical precision evident in the care with which the speaker's attention now environs itself within the body:

the sinew-bound bone-
cage, smeared over
with the muck of flesh...

The long compounds in 8.52c–d (*māṃsa-kardama-saṃliptaṃ snāyu-baddhāsthi-pañjaram*) recapitulate the kind of anatomical attention long valued in contemplative exercises directed at inducing revulsion as an antidote to being indiscriminately enamored of the body. The sudden apposition of these relatively long and weighty compounds skillfully slows us down.[31] It creates an environment of particularly charged and disquieted attention, in which you might orient yourself by taking your attention from the outside of the body inward, or the other way around. Here it contributes to an environment within whose horizons the voice quickens unto frank and explosive invective, and after which there is the slow invocation of reason again.

If in 8.54–55 we begin to hear a new thought, this is a tentative exploration of self-cognizance in the wake of the above psychological release:

I'm infatuated
with flesh—that's what
you think, wanting to
see it, to
touch it.
Flesh intrinsically is
without animating mind;
How can you want it? (8.54)

What you want,
that mind, you can't
see it, touch it;
and what can
does not
realize it—why
embrace it so

to no viable end? (8.55)

The repetition is a thing to feel in the original, as is the accumulating weight of the searching questions and the wondering pause after:

It's no wonder
you don't know
the body of another
to be excrement—
What's astonishing
is that you don't get
that your own body is crap. (8.56)

The argument has resulted in a moment of astonishment, surprise—dismay, even. The repetition in verses 8.55 and 8.56 of words from the verbal root *vid*, meaning "to know" or "to realize," suggests a persisting concern in this argument: the nature, limits, and consequences of self-knowledge in philosophical therapy. Arguments aimed at therapy don't float free in an abstract space of reasons; if they are to work at all, they must gain traction in a mind replete with dispositions, defenses, and extraordinary capacities for avoiding acknowledgment.

What is that like? The work of Śāntideva's poetry, I have been suggesting, allows us to enter into such an experience. In our example the voice of persuasion is arrayed against the "sensualist" in us. The arguments do not simply make explicit the propositional commitments such a culture entails but seek to counterpoint one style of seeing and feeling with another. Each has reasons that are, or can be, associated with it. And the dialogue between these two styles of reasoning, carried out in a single mind, involves what is worth calling a phenomenology of thought.[32]

To link Śāntideva's art to a phenomenology of thought is to task it with the capacity to present and make real a phenomenology of cognitive experience, a range of felt textures associated with what it is like to understand or fail to understand, what it is like to see or purposefully overlook. To be able to experience Śāntideva overhear himself is for us to begin to experience what thinking involves, the variable and contingent power of thinking to change us. To speak of Śāntideva's having given us in the *Guide* an example of dramatic self-overhearing entails his having provided us with a phenomenology of thought. This can be abstractly or more poetically put, as when Galen Strawson speaks of the experience of reading the argumentative prose of Mark Johnston: "Philosophy for Johnston is a profoundly concrete, sensual activity; he's someone for whom ideas seem tangible, with specific savours, emotional tones, curves, surfaces, insides, hidden places, dark passages, shining corners."[33] I think this is even truer of the experience of reading Śāntideva, or at least can be, if you're persuaded now of the way Śāntideva's subject—and potential auditor—thinks, feels what it thinks, and changes as it thinks and feels.

There's wonder in such an achievement. Consider how the argument quoted above ends. It is telling that the moment of self-cognizance ends in a moment of wonder that involves not so much an acknowledgment of a proposition but a consideration *of what self-cognizance* involves. Wonder here seems to involve not a step back so much as a step within; to step inside, however, involves turning ourselves inside out—to re-describe ourselves, and, momentarily, to make it all strange, as in the following verse that memorably concludes the argument:

Except for
the tender,
young mud-
born lotus, shining
open with the rays
of the sun
in a cloudless
sky, what delight
in a cage
of feces, for
a mind
addicted to getting high
on filth? (8.57)

Even as the voice lifts with the image of the mud-born yet transcending lotus, the thought unfolds by dragging you back down into the starting horizon of its inquiry and its searching, restless art of reasoning: the cage-bound, the filth-environed.

CONCLUDING THOUGHTS

One last time, take up the verse above with its mixed metaphoric resonance: the mind by turns imagined to be a sun-responsive lotus in bloom and then the ghost of a bird, caged in palpable, repulsive opacity. This mixing of metaphorical vehicles resonates rather well with Śāntideva's anonymously first-person "heteronomous self" and even the *Guide* as a whole, constituted of an incredible range of genres and affording the persona of its lyrical subject many moods and voices:

These enemies—
craving, aversion, and more—
have neither hands nor feet.
They're neither heroic, nor wise.
How, then, have they made me
their slave? (4.28) Dwelling within
my own mind, they're well poised
to strike me down!

Matthew Kapstein has adduced the above verse as illustrative of "the heteronomous self" of the *Guide*.[34] And indeed, there are at least two relevant senses of heteronomy one might wish to keep in mind when considering the achievement of the work as a whole.

There is, first, the sense in moral philosophy of "being subject to the rule of another being or power."[35] Over the long course of the *Guide* Śāntideva's subject ritually internalizes an exemplary ideal and increasingly comes to a sense of his distance from it and the recalcitrance of his embodied life to the ideals he has committed to, and for which he tasks himself to provide reasons. What is on offer, then, may fairly well be described as an exploration and anatomy of the many forms resistance to reasons in defense of an ethical ideal can take, along with what you might call a drama of power, as is suggested in the verse above, with its prospect of a slave struggling to master impersonal masters within.

A second sense of heteronomy, the simple sense of "the presence of a different law or principle,"[36] is relevant as well. Śāntideva's meditating subject is a creature in pursuit of psychical health, but not necessarily the ostensible psychological wholeness conferred by a stable identity. The work can read as an experiment in voices, an exploration of the many dispositions that make us up, a contoured map of the many people we are. (Compare this with Amber Carpenter's recognition of the "menagerie mind" of the *Guide* in her contribution to this volume.) Such an exploration can take the form of inner dialogues with the anonymous *styles* of life in us, as with the sensualist we overheard Śāntideva's subject speak with above; it can also comprise more formal and more carefully controlled experiments using first-person and third-person ascription, as in the exchange of self and other, after which the difference between the "others in us" and the first-person subjectivity of others begins to blur (as discussed in Janet Gyatso's contribution to this volume). You could do worse than to construe the *Guide* as a whole, and its achievement of an echo chamber of voices in an anonymously first-personal space that a reader might enter "from within," so to speak, as such a controlled experiment in the nature and the sometimes opaque, sometimes transparent boundaries of first-personal presence.

To appreciate the relevance of literature to all this, we ought to take what Śāntideva says in the *Guide* and the *Training Anthology* (*Śikṣāsamuccaya*) seriously: "I didn't compose this work thinking of others: I did it to perfume my own mind."[37] What is here involved in *bringing into being* a mind, a certain way of being a person, even—these being ways to get at the exercise in habituation implicit in talk of "perfuming"—has something to do with a textual practice, a kind of writing of one's life.

We might usefully say that Śāntideva's poetic craft is in service of "meditation," but only if we take "meditation" to mean what it once used to mean, an exercise intimately bound up with textual practices. As Hugh of St. Victor put it in the twelfth century, widening the sense of this art beyond the retention of scripture, "meditation takes its start from reading, but is bound by none of reading's rules or precepts; for it delights to range along open ground."[38] Thus oriented, it would indeed be helpful to think of Śāntideva's poetry of self-cultivation as a poetics of meditation: ranging along open ground, effectively involving the creation of a new genre and a new exercise of self-composition.

This might be illustrated by distinguishing between Śāntideva's two achievements in genre, the *Anthology* and the *Guide*. If the *Anthology* is a work gathering occasions for a practice of "responsive listening" to the words of others, words that if attended to in a principled way can change us,[39] we might do well to think of the meditation in the *Guide* as the enactment of such an exercise of responsive listening "from the inside": when one is given to experience what it is like to listen, to exhort, to challenge, and to respond, but to oneself, or at least to others within one.

An image from Śāntideva can help here. I am effectively suggesting that we orient ourselves to take it that the poetic work of the *Guide* lies in giving us to witness, and to possibly enter into, the drama suggested by some of the later verses of the *Anthology*:

With conduct guarded by strength
may the teacher, myself,
always instruct myself,
as one would a good student,

and without one's having to ask oneself.

Who indeed would be pained
by my pain, frightened
by my fear, or know
my faults, my dispositions

as well as my own master, myself?

And where would one find a student
to rival oneself, in being
far from indifferent, unlikely
to run away, and within
the scope of care, even,

always close to hand?[40]

Whether you render the first-person pronoun "*ātman*" colloquially, as above, or seek a clumsier formulation with the rhetorical invitation of potential paradox ("May the teacher, the self, always instruct the self... without the self's having to ask the self"), I think you can agree that the intimate responsiveness to oneself here recommended, on which one is both teacher and student, is evocative of what we hear in the *Guide*. "Overhear," I should say, for this art must involve an art of overhearing not unlike that thought to be involved in lyric poetry more generally.

To conclude my tentative orientation to the *Guide* as literature, such "overhearing" is here pressed into service as a special variety of a long-valorized practice of self-knowledge, mastery, and care. Lyric, we might then say, affords new possibilities for the way the traditional work of philosophical therapy is carried out and how it can be made available to us.

Hold on to this thread when exploring the labyrinth of what is involved in the creation of an anonymously first-person drama where oneself is the stage and all the players in a theater of instruction and hard-won change, a drama that, the *Guide* shows us, reverberates with many moods, with wonder at what we are like (and can be) not the least among them.

NOTES

1. Harrison, "The Case of the Vanishing Poet," 215–248; see also Harrison, "Verses by Śāntideva in the 'Śikṣāsamuccaya.'"
2. Gómez, "The Way of the Translators," 267. See also the remarks of Kate Crosby and Andrew Skilton about being cautious when assessing Śāntideva's literary merits, particularly in light of the norms and values of literature (*kāvya*) in Sanskrit, in Śāntideva, *The Bodhicaryāvatāra*, trans. Crosby and Skilton, xxxviii–xxxix.
3. Unless otherwise explicitly marked, all translations are my own. I have used the edition of the Sanskrit text found in Prajñākaramati's commentary on the *Guide*, the critical edition of which was prepared by Louis de la Vallée Poussin, published between 1904 and 1914, and for details of which see Śāntideva, *The Bodhicaryāvatāra*, trans. Crosby and Skilton, xl–xlii.

4. Since writing this (and drawing inspiration from Usabha's talk of a monk's "forest-sentiment" in verse 110 of Norman, *The Elders' Verses I*, I now find that Patrick Olivelle has already had occasion to use the same phrase. See Olivelle, "Review of Trautmann." Olivelle writes, "Importantly, the aesthetic of the wild is intertwined with the tradition of asceticism that located hermitages in the forests and with the aesthetic valorization of forests, woods, and parks, all of which are termed *vana* in Sanskrit. We find the aesthetic of the wild in the Indian literature from at least the last centuries BCE." Such an aesthetic conjoins civilizational with natural values.
5. For complementary descriptions as old as the *Theragāthā*, see verses 22, 49, 110, 113, (and especially) 1064–1071, among others, in Norman, *Elders' Verses I*, 3, 7, 14, 15, 98; it is worth using this allusion in connection with the point made by Luis Gómez that the *Guide* "combines elements of several genres in a manner that must be characterized as unique in Sanskrit literature." Gómez, "The Way of the Translators," 266.
6. On this complex word and the tenor of this part of the *Guide*, see the excellent discussion in Gómez, "The Way of the Translators," 285–288.
7. In every edition known to me, Sanskrit, Gāndhāri, and Pāli. For a translation from the Pāli, see Norman, *The Word of the Doctrine (Dhammapada)*, 1. See also Brough, *The Gāndhārī Dharmapada*; Shukla, *The Buddhist Hybrid Sanskrit Dharmapada*. To calibrate our sense of what such a possible allusion might intimate, it is useful to recall that "*dharmapada*" is not only the name of a text but also a word meaning something like "Buddhist doctrine." See Norman, *The Word of the Doctrine*, xxv.
8. This can be seen most easily by comparing Śāntideva's compound with the description in the *Cīvaravastu* (GMs iii.2, 107.15), quoted in Gregory Schopen, "The Buddhist 'Monastery' and the Indian Garden: Aesthetics, Assimilations, and the Siting of Monastic Establishments," in *Buddhist Nuns, Monks, and Other Worldly Matters*, 224–251, 230. Such descriptions are also continuous with the standard formulas used when enumerating the constituents of such utopias as the so-called "pure lands," such as Sukhāvatī, the Land of Bliss, for which see Gómez, *The Land of Bliss*, 87, 147.
9. Even power, in Buddhist theory, has what might best be described as an associated poetics to chart its conditions of intelligibility. It would be a useful exercise to compare Śāntideva's dedication, particularly verse 8, with the section on power as transformation in the *Bodhisattvabhūmi*, for example; see Engle, *The Bodhisattva Path to Unsurpassed Enlightenment*, especially 109.
10. This paragraph is indebted to an observation made by Calvert Watkins with respect to the last foot of 10.125 of the *Ṛg Veda*: *śrudhi śruta śradhivaṃ te vadāmi*; of this "extreme phonetic figure" Watkins observed that it serves as an exhaustive classification of the speech sounds of the Vedic language. Watkins, *How to Kill a Dragon*, 111. One might contextualize the value of such phonetic figures with the use made of literary realizations of utopic experiential possibilities in contemplative exercises, on which the text is something to be "done" rather than merely "read." See Harrison, "Mediums and Messages,"120–122.
11. Cf. the judicious, if brief, discussion in Śāntideva, *The Bodhicaryāvatāra*, trans. Crosby and Skilton, xxxviii–xxxix.
12. Śāntideva, *The Bodhicaryāvatāra*, trans. Crosby and Skilton, xxxix.

13. For a history of which paradigm, and the shift it entailed from prior theoretical approaches to literature, see McCrea, *The Teleology of Poetics in Medieval Kashmir*.
14. Such as the Prakrit *Sattasaī*, lyrics from which are used by Ānandavardhana in his *Light on Suggestion* (*Dhvanyāloka*). Despite the right-headedness and truth in the arguments Lawrence McCrea brings to bear against thinking, with Edwin Gerow, for example, that it is a new literary practice or the availability of a new and peculiar lyric genre (such as devotional lyric) that drives the new aesthetics of Ānandavardhana, there is at least an intrinsic affinity between some long-available literary genres (such as the dramatic lyrics of the *Sattasaī*) and the new theory, such that it is easier to illustrate and motivate the new critical vocabulary and paradigmatic orientation to literature with them. McCrea, *The Teleology of Poetics*, 12–17.
15. Developments since John Stuart Mill's "Thoughts on Poetry and Its Varieties" are usefully discussed in Tucker, "Dramatic Monologue and the Overhearing of Lyric," 226–243.
16. See Smith, "Apostrophe, or the Lyric Art of Turning Away."
17. See Pollard, *Speaking to You*, 8–9.
18. See, for example, Bloom, *Shakespeare*, xix, 455. The history of meditation as a literary genre will not allow us, I think, to credit this variety of self-consciousness to Elizabethan drama alone. See Rorty, "Experiments in Philosophic Genre"; C. Mercer, "The Methodology of the Meditations," , 23–47.
19. As is telegraphed in verse 1.3: "Moreover, should another, of the very same humours as me,/also look at this, then he too/may benefit from it." See Śāntideva, *The Bodhicaryāvatāra*, trans. Crosby and Skilton, 5.
20. To get a feel for the distinctive weight of a first-person staging of such a work, consider the difference between self-overhearing and the *dialogue* of self and mind in the metrical part of the perhaps contemporary *Upadeśasahasrī* of Śaṅkara, for which see Mayeda, *A Thousand Teachings*, 203–207. For the philosophical salience of the anonymous first-person voice (or anonymous autobiography) and the distinction between meditation and dialogue, I am indebted to Frankfurt, *Demons, Dreamers, and Madmen*, 3–5; see also Bernard Williams, "Introductory Essay on Descartes' *Meditations*," in Williams, *The Sense of the Past*, 246. Of course, such anonymity (often exemplified in a voice thought to be unmarked by gender, social location, and the contingencies of history and culture) has typically been claimed as the unique affordance of males in dominant social positions. Whether either Descartes or Śāntideva *achieves* true anonymity and whether readers—from their own time or ours—can really "enter into" the work is an empirical question worth taking up.
21. From verse 2 of the *Guide*, for which, see Śāntideva, *The Bodhicaryāvatāra*, trans. Crosby and Skilton, 5. See also my conclusion below for more on this.
22. Verse 4.47, in the translation of Śāntideva, *The Bodhicaryāvatāra*, trans. Crosby and Skilton, 29.
23. See, among others, verses 99, 101, 105, in Khoroche and Tieken, *Poems on Life and Love in Ancient India*, 43–44. The emphatic affective texture associated with the richly felt (and thus perhaps only ostensible) censure of affect, the link between such censure and self-consciousness, and the association of these with the gendered voice of the female erotic subject in these verses ought to contextualize the

force and valence of the apostrophic address in later lyrical personae of even male Buddhist ascetics, such as Saraha, as in verses 23 and 25 in Jackson, *Tantric Treasures*, 65, 66. More work needs to be done on the issue of the gendered and socially situated voices of lyrical personae more generally, and the meditating persona in the *Guide* is no exception; for a helpful start and a way of framing the salience of such a concern for Śāntideva, who ultimately requires that the meditating "I" become aware of, then recontextualize its social location (and possibly even gender), see *Guide* 8.153 and 8.166, and the remarks on these in Śāntideva, *The Bodhicaryāvatāra*, trans. Crosby and Skilton, 81.

24. See verses 4–7 of Bhartṛhari's *Vairāgyaśatakam* in Joglekar, *Bhartrihari*, 73–74.
25. Cf. the translation in Śāntideva, *The Bodhicaryāvatāra*, trans. Crosby and Skilton, 39.
26. As in the examples of apostrophe in the *Sattasaī* and even the *dohas* of Saraha. In ancient Buddhist lyric there is at least one astonishing early precedent on which the mind is more than a rhetorical prop: see the remarkable meditation ascribed to Tāḷapuṭa, and the dialogue with his mind, in verses 1091–1145 in Norman, *The Elders' Verses I*, 101–105. A complete account must naturally also take into account the therapeutic use made of the literary conceit of an internal dialogue, as in Buddhaghosa's prescription of a miniature dialogue involving self-admonishment in IX.22 of *The Path of Purification* (*Visuddhimagga*); this example, a contemplative exercise targeted at the continued availability and appeal of anger, is indicative of the availability of small-scaled precedents, as it were, for the exercises in the *Guide*. See Ñāṇamoli, trans., *The Path of Purification*, 295–296.
27. For the transvaluation of passion, see *Guide* 7.62, Śāntideva, *The Bodhicaryāvatāra*, trans. Crosby and Skilton, 73; see also their discussion of this on 65. For the revaluation of pain, see *Guide* 6.123; Śāntideva, *The Bodhicaryāvatāra*, 61.
28. See for example *Guide* 4.2–4.4a–b and 5.27 in Śāntideva, *The Bodhicaryāvatāra*, trans. Crosby and Skilton, 25, 71.
29. See *Guide* 4.11. Note that the rich psychological texture of the persona the *Guide* sustains is continuous with what is afforded to us by the use of Sanskrit lyric in Buddhist devotional verse, as is the value accorded to such texture. Compare, for example, 2.45–66 of the *Guide* with verses 13–16 in Carpaṭi's *In Praise of Avalokiteśvara* (in Hahn, "Carpaṭi's *Avalokiteśvarastotra*," 11–22). Often, however, the *Guide* reads like an *internalization* of the kind of psychological drama and the psychological room made for self-doubt, psychological ambiguity, and varieties of ambivalence evoked and sustained by the best of Buddhist devotional lyric. Thus the external addressee of the devotional lyric becomes in the *Guide* an instance of the second person within. Compare verses 3.26–27 of the *Guide* (Śāntideva, *The Bodhicaryāvatāra*, trans. Crosby and Skilton, 27) with Carpaṭi's verses 9–10 and 22–23 in Hahn, "Carpaṭi's *Avalokiteśvarastotra*."
30. McGinn, "The Language of Inner Experience in Christian Mysticism."
31. The use of long compounds of harsh (or, at the very least, disquieting) internal assonance to configure and modulate attention to the body is by no means new. See verse 473c–d of the *Therīgāthā*, where Sumedha uses a similar compound to the same effect, in Hallisey, *Therigatha*, 221; see also verse 469, page 219, in the same volume.
32. See Strawson, "Cognitive Phenomenology." To my mind this is continuous with Jay Garfield's sense that Śāntideva is offering what is best described as a "moral phenomenology," insofar as I take it that Śāntideva's ability to present a

cognitive phenomenology makes available to us the distinctive variety of moral phenomenology Garfield discerns in the *Guide*. See Garfield, *Engaging Buddhism*, 279, 294–310, as well as Garfield's contribution to this volume.

33. Strawson, "Religion is a Sin," 26–28.
34. *Guide* 4.28–29a–b, adapted from a translation by of 4.28–29 in Kapstein, "Stoics and Bodhisattvas," 107.
35. This is the second definition for "heteronomy" in the *Oxford English Dictionary* Online, June 2017, Oxford University Press.
36. The first definition for "heteronomy" in the *Oxford English Dictionary*.
37. From verse 2 of *Guide* (for which, see Śāntideva, *The Bodhicaryāvatāra*, trans. Crosby and Skilton, 5) and verse 6 of the *Śikṣāsamuccaya*, for which see Harrison, "Verses by Śāntideva," 90.
38. *Didascalicon* 3.10; quoted and discussed in Robertson, *Lectio Divina*, xvii.
39. As is intimated in verses 1 and 2 of the *Śikṣāsamuccaya*, and the introduction more generally; see Harrison, "Verses by Śāntideva," 90. On "responsive" listening and the ethical charge of this dimension of Buddhist philosophy of language, see Nance, "The Voice of Another."
40. Cf. the translation of verses 145–147 (or verses 55–57 of chapter XIX) in Harrison, "Verses by Śāntideva," 99–100. My translation is indebted to his.

REFERENCES

Bloom, Harold. *Shakespeare: The Invention of the Human*. New York: Riverhead, 1998.

Brough, John. *The Gāndhārī Dharmapada: Edited with an Introduction and Commentary*. London: Oxford University Press, 1962.

Engle, Artemus B. *The Bodhisattva Path to Unsurpassed Enlightenment: A Complete Translation of the* Bodhisattvabhūmi. Boulder, CO: Snow Lion, 2016.

Frankfurt, Harry G. *Demons, Dreamers, and Madmen: The Defense of Reason in Descartes's* Meditations. Princeton, NJ and Oxford: Princeton University Press, 2008.

Garfield, J. *Engaging Buddhism: Why It Matters to Philosophy*. New York: Oxford University Press, 2015.

Gómez, Luis. *The Land of Bliss: The Paradise of the Buddha of Measureless Light: Sanskrit and Chinese Versions of the Sukhāvatīvyūha Sutras*. Honolulu: University of Hawai'i Press, 1996.

——. "The Way of the Translators: Three Recent Translations of Śāntideva's *Bodhicaryāvatāra*." *Buddhist Literature* 1 (1999): 262–354.

Hahn, Michael. "Carpaṭi's *Avalokiteśvarastotra*: Critical Edition of the Sanskrit Text and Its English Translation." In *Buddhist Texts From Kashgar and Nepal*, ed. I. P. Minayeff and S. Oldenburg, 11–22. New Delhi: International Academy of Indian Culture, 1983.

Hallisey, Charles. *Therigatha: Poems of the First Buddhist Women*. Murty Classical Library of India. Cambridge, MA: Harvard University Press, 2015.

Harrison, Paul. "Mediums and Messages: Reflections on the Production of Mahāyāna Sūtras." *The Eastern Buddhist* 35, no. 1/2 (2003): 115–151.

——. "The Case of the Vanishing Poet: New Light on Śāntideva and the *Śikṣāsamuccaya*." In *Indica et Tibetica: Festschrift für Michael Hahn, Zum 65. Geburtstag von Freunden und Schülern überreicht*, ed. K. Klaus and J-U. Hartmann,

215–248. Vienna: Arbeitskreis für Tibetische und Buddhistische Studien, Universität Wien, 2007.

——. "Verses by Śāntideva in the '*Śikṣāsamuccaya*': A New English Translation." *Bulletin of the Asia Institute*, New Series, 23 (2009): 87–103.

Jackson, Roger R. *Tantric Treasures: Three Collections of Mystical Verse from Buddhist India*. Oxford: Oxford University Press, 2004.

Joglekar, K. M. *Bhartrihari: Niti and Vairagya Shatakas*. Bombay: Oriental Publishing Company, 1911.

Kapstein, Matthew T. "Stoics and Bodhisattvas: Spiritual Exercise and Faith in Two Philosophical Traditions." In *Philosophy as a Way of Life: Ancients and Moderns*, ed. Michael Chase, Stephen R. L. Clark, and Michael McGhee. Oxford: Wiley, 2013.

Khoroche, Peter, and Herman Tieken. *Poems on Life and Love in Ancient India: Hāla's Sattasaī*. Albany: State University of New York Press, 2009.

Mayeda, Sengaku. *A Thousand Teachings: The* Upadeśasahasrī *of Śaṅkara*. Albany: State University of New York Press, 1992.

McCrea, Lawrence J. *The Teleology of Poetics in Medieval Kashmir*. Cambridge, MA: Harvard University Press, 2008.

McGinn, Bernard. "The Language of Inner Experience in Christian Mysticism." *Spiritus: A Journal of Christian Spirituality* 1, no. 2 (2001): 156–171.

Mercer, C. "The Methodology of the Meditations: Tradition and Innovation." In *Cambridge Companion to Descartes'* Meditations, ed. D. Cunning, 23–47. Cambridge: Cambridge University Press, 2014.

Ñāṇamoli, Bhikkhu, trans. *The Path of Purification: Visuddhimagga by Bhadantācariya Buddhaghosa*. 4th ed. Kandy: Buddhist Publication Society, 2010.

Nance, Richard. "The Voice of Another: Speech, Responsiveness, and Buddhist Philosophy of Language." In *A Companion to Buddhist Philosophy*, ed. S. Emmanuel. West Sussex: Wiley-Blackwell, 2013.

Norman, K. R. *The Elders' Verses I: Theragāthā*. London: Pali Text Society, 1969.

——. *The Word of the Doctrine (Dhammapada)*. Pali Text Society Translation Series No. 46. Oxford: Pali Text Society, 2000.

Olivelle, Patrick. "Review of Trautmann, Thomas R., *Elephants and Kings: An Environmental History*." *H-Asia, H-Net Reviews* (August 2016).

Pollard, Natalie. *Speaking to You: Contemporary Poetry and Public Address*. Oxford. Oxford University Press, 2012.

Robertson, Duncan. *Lectio Divina: The Medieval Experience of Reading*. Cistercian Studies Series 238. Collegeville, MN: Liturgical Press, 2011.

Rorty, A. O. "Experiments in Philosophic Genre: Descartes' *Meditations*." *Critical Inquiry*, 9, no. 3 (1983): 545–564.

Śāntideva. *The Bodhicaryāvatāra*. Trans. Kate Crosby and Andrew Skilton. Oxford: Oxford University Press, 2008.

Schopen, Gregory. *Buddhist Nuns, Monks, and Other Worldly Matters: Recent Papers on Monastic Buddhism in India*. Honolulu: University of Hawai'i Press, 2014.

Shukla, N. S. *The Buddhist Hybrid Sanskrit Dharmapada*. Tibetan Sanskrit Works Series no. xix. Patna: K. P. Jayaswal Research Institute, 1979.

Smith, J. Mark. "Apostrophe, or the Lyric Art of Turning Away." *Texas Studies in Literature and Language* 49, no. 4 (Winter 2007): 411–437.

Strawson, Galen. "Cognitive Phenomenology: Real Life." In *Cognitive Phenomenology*, ed. Tim Bayne and Michelle Montague, 285–325. Oxford. Oxford University Press, 2011.

——. "Religion is a Sin: Review of Mark Johnston." *London Review of Books* 33, no. 11·2 (June 2011).

Tucker, Herbert F. "Dramatic Monologue and the Overhearing of Lyric." In *Lyric Poetry: Beyond New Criticism*, ed. Chaviva Hošek and Patricia Parker, 226–243. Ithaca, NY and London: Cornell University Press, 1985.

Watkins, Calvert. *How to Kill a Dragon: Aspects of Indo-European Poetics*. Oxford: Oxford University Press, 1995.

Williams, Bernard. *The Sense of the Past: Essays in the History of Philosophy*. Princeton, NJ and Oxford: Princeton University Press, 2006.

[4]

AN INTOXICATION OF MOUSE VENOM

READING THE *GUIDE*, CHAPTER 9

Matthew T. Kapstein

ŚĀNTIDEVA'S "WISDOM CHAPTER"

The *Guide to Bodhisattva Practice* (*Bodhicaryāvatāra*, hereafter, *Guide*) of Śāntideva is, before all else, a *practical* guide for those who aspire to the life of a bodhisattva, an individual whose determining principle is the attainment of *bodhi*, or spiritual awakening. Not just his or her personal awakening, but rather the awakening of all, for *bodhi*, in the Mahāyāna Buddhism that Śāntideva espouses, is a universal principle. To become an individual determined by an orientation to awakening in this tradition, one must abandon the personal, self-centered viewpoint that is our habitual condition, in favor of a growing embrace of an all-encompassing vision.[1]

To accomplish this requires a severe ethical and spiritual discipline. Egoistical tendencies to possessiveness, impulsiveness, indolence, and the like must be overturned by a rigorous commitment to generosity, dignified behavior, forbearance, and effort, while the mind itself must be collected and calm. The goal, however, is not merely to become a well-mannered person adept in tranquility meditation, however praiseworthy that may be. For manners and meditative calm alone remain compatible with the narrow perspective of the self-regarding individual. Indeed, they may well become sources of personal pride, wherein lies an inevitable danger. For Buddhism, as for the other wisdom traditions of India, the sole means to avert such pitfalls on the path to spiritual perfection is to be found in the acquisition of wisdom, insight into the real nature of things. But just how this is to be understood is by no means immediately evident.

Within classical Indian thought, just what constitutes wisdom came to be sharply contested, not only between differing schools but also within them. Debate and philosophical inquiry thus became indissociable from the pursuit of wisdom, and in the ninth chapter of Śāntideva's book his preeminently practical concerns seem sometimes to give way to wrangling over philosophical fine points. However, philosophy in this case is placed in the service of the cultivation of contemplative insight. Śāntideva's practical and theoretical concerns are found, in the end, to be one.[2]

The subject of the ninth chapter of the *Guide* is *prajñā*, often translated "wisdom," "higher knowledge," or "discrimination." As such, it is the "Perfection of Wisdom" (*prajñāpāramitā*), the pinnacle of the six perfections of the bodhisattva's path and identified as the goal of insight (*vipaśyanā*), the contemplative "seeing through" that, conjoined with tranquility (*śamatha*), forms the heart of Buddhist meditation. *Prajñā*, as Śāntideva expounds it, corresponds to the teaching of the Madhyamaka tradition of Buddhist philosophy, spearheaded by Nāgārjuna during the second century CE. Nāgārjuna is widely known for his emphasis on the universal "emptiness" (*śūnyatā*) of phenomena, but the meaning of this concept has been subject to much debate.[3] Just how Śāntideva understands it will be among the chief concerns throughout this chapter.

In accord with the conventions of much of classical Indian philosophical literature, the arguments developed in the ninth chapter are presented tersely and are frequently impenetrable without the aid of substantial commentary. Sometimes, a single eight-syllable line of verse may embody a complex line of reasoning that requires whole paragraphs to unpack—the example explored below is a case in point. Today, the commentaries on the *Guide* that have become well known to readers of Buddhist philosophy are by Tibetan authors, who studied the *Guide* in its Tibetan version, not the original Sanskrit, though this by no means diminishes the excellence of their discussions of the text.[4] The best evidence we now have of the *Guide*'s reception in India itself is to be found in the detailed commentary by Prajñākaramati, a noted scholar from the monastery of Vikramaśīla in northeastern India, who was active close to the year 1000. It is his work, the only Sanskrit commentary on the *Guide* now available in the original almost in its entirety, that we shall follow here.[5]

Although Prajñākaramati's text very much influenced the later Tibetan commentarial tradition on the *Guide*, with respect to the ninth chapter there is an important difference between his approach and that of his Tibetan successors. For the Tibetans (as may be seen in Douglas Duckworth's chapter in this volume) were very much preoccupied by the question of just how Śāntideva was to be categorized among Indian Mādhyamika authors. Did he represent primarily the Prāsaṅgika subschool, which favored only arguments by indirect proof, that is, *reductio ad absurdum*? And, if so, could he be taken as fully consistent with the thought of the leading representative of that tradition, Candrakīrti? For Prajñākaramati, however, none of the Tibetan haggling about this would have made much sense, given that Tibetan efforts to classify in minute detail various subschools of Madhyamaka were unknown in India. The word *prāsaṅgika*, for instance, when used by Prajñākaramati, refers not to a school of thought but instead to a method of argument, which might be employed by the adherents of any school. And though he sometimes cites Candrakīrti in his exposition, he does not hesitate to quote other philosophers, notably Śāntarakṣita, whom the Tibetans would classify as representing the Svātantrika subschool rivaling Candrakīrti and as holding that, besides the indirect proof achieved through *reductio* arguments, the Mādhyamika philosopher might seek to demonstrate the thesis of universal emptiness by positive proofs affirming the emptiness of things as their conclusion.[6] Prajñākaramati, however, helps us to address Śāntideva's text without venturing into the debates that later erupted in the Tibetan monastic schools.

The "Wisdom Chapter" of the *Guide* is 168 verses in length, and it often compresses complex arguments into a single verse.[7] The difficulties that Indian and Tibetan Buddhists may have had in understanding it are compounded by our temporal and cultural distance from the text's frame of reference. To comprehend this chapter, more than any other part of the *Guide*, thus requires reference to its commentaries.[8] It will not be possible to do more here than to illustrate some of the challenges the work presents to contemporary readers and the ways these may be addressed. To do this, we shall focus upon one of the oddest arguments in the "Wisdom Chapter," concerning the aftereffects of contact with a venomous mouse.[9] But we must first understand the context in which this argument is introduced.

ENTERING EMPTINESS

Śāntideva's point of departure in introducing Mādhyamika thought is the classical Buddhist conception of "two truths" (*satyadvaya*), the "relative" or "superficial" truth (*saṃvṛtisatya*) of how things conventionally appear to us and the "ultimate" or "absolute" truth (*paramārthasatya*), which is how things really are.[10] In early Buddhism, this distinction had applied primarily to the assessment of the Buddha's discourses: some, for example those that used the pronoun "I" and spoke of "persons" as enduring entities ("this person in a past life had been . . ."), were regarded as conforming with ordinary, superficial speech conventions; others, affirming there to be no real and enduring self (*anātman*) but rather that the world of experience was to be analyzed in terms of more fundamental phenomena (*dharma*), were held to represent the Buddha's definitive, ultimate meaning. With a change of nuance, however, the two truths came to be regarded by subsequent thinkers as primarily designating two levels of reality, or perhaps two ways of experiencing reality, rather than just two ways of speaking about reality. With this understanding, Śāntideva introduces the two truths as follows:

> Convention and ultimate significance—this is thought to be the pair of truths.
> Reality belongs not to the field of intellect; for intellect is said to be conventional usage. (9.2)
> In this case the world is twofold: there are adepts and commoners,
> And the common world is defeated by the adept's world. (9.3)
> Defeated, too, according to the distinctions of their thought, are adepts in ascending succession. (9.4ab)[11]

Here the commoner who knows only convention is distinguished from the adept (*yogin*) who realizes the truth of ultimate significance, with a hierarchically ordered realm of lesser adepts intervening between them. The latter, though free from the constraints of the commoner, have not yet realized the highest reality. Thus, the apparent bivalence of the two truths notwithstanding, the scheme as deployed here in fact embraces a whole spectrum of philosophical views.

Prajñākaramati amplifies the essential concept of the two truths in his commentary, beginning with his explanation of the term *saṃvṛti*, so far translated as "conventional usage." He writes: "*Saṃvṛti* is so called because by it the comprehension of what is as it is is concealed, or occluded, due to the occlusion of essential being. . . . Ignorance, stupefaction, and error are synonyms [for *saṃvṛti*]. For ignorance, being the imputation of the forms of nonexisting things [to that which exists], and hence of the nature of occlusion of the vision of inherent being, is *saṃvṛti*."[12]

Thus, for Prajñākaramati "concealment" takes precedence over "convention" as the primary sense of *saṃvṛti*.[13]

Prajñākaramati's discussion of ultimate significance (*paramārtha*) reveals a subtle intermingling of two themes that had been associated with this term from antiquity. On the one hand, following a tradition established in the analytical aspects of Abhidharma thought (i.e., early Buddhist scholasticism), it is that which is ultimately real, that which is not destroyed through a reductive analytical procedure. For the fifth-century philosopher Vasubandhu this meant that it was paradigmatically two sorts of things: physical atoms and phenomenal atoms or *dharmas*. For Prajñākaramati as a Mādhyamika thinker, however, analysis can find no such points of termination; it must be pursued until it reveals the radical contingency of all conditioned phenomena, their ultimate emptiness. The ultimate, highest significance is "the uncontrived form of things owing to the comprehension of which there is the abandonment of affliction. . . . It is the absence of the inherent being of all *dharmas*, [their] emptiness, just-so-ness, genuine limit, the sphere of the highest principle—these are among its synonyms."[14]

Analytical ultimacy here is closely associated with a second theme, soteriological ultimacy—at the limit of analysis there is an "abandonment of affliction." For *paramārtha* can mean not just "ultimate significance" in a analytic sense but also *paramapuruṣārtha*, that is, the "highest end of man," *mokṣa*, liberation.[15] In the tradition represented by Prajñākaramati, there is a perfect convergence between these notions.

The doctrine of two truths, having assumed an all-embracing character, begins to look increasingly like a general doctrine of reality. This entails that *saṃvṛtisatya*, the conventional or superficial truth, though ultimately false, is nevertheless part and parcel of the truth of our world:

> It may be [objected], how is it that *saṃvṛti*, being of the nature of what is revealed in ignorance, and which is devastated by hundreds of investigations because its nature is the imputation of what is not, is truth? But it too *is* truth. It is spoken of as the "truth of concealment" in that it is a determination of the common world. For it is the world that is here the truth of concealment. In conformity with it, the Lord too has just so spoken [in terms of] that truth of concealment, without reference to those seeking [ultimate] reality. Hence, the qualification "and the truth of the world's conventional usage" has been asserted by the venerable teacher [Nāgārjuna]. But, in reality, ultimate significance is the only truth.[16]

Conventional truth, in short, is pragmatically justified and so valued. Hence, so long as the ultimate has not been realized, the dialectic of the two truths must be posited. In the final analysis, however, for the sage who has realized the ultimate, the truth can only be one. The theory of the two truths, therefore, belongs to the very domain of the conventional that ultimately it undermines.

MAGIC, MINDS, AND MOUSE VENOM

For Śāntideva, this undermining begins when we take stock of the significance of *māyā*, variously translated as "illusion," "apparition," or "magical appearance." The occurrence of such phenomena, including also mirages, dreams, hallucinations, and the like, suggested to Buddhist thinkers like Śāntideva that we are entitled to be skeptical of the everyday assumption that what we experience is a firm and durable reality.[17] As in Buddhism, in Western philosophy this is a well-known strategy; for example, Descartes' use of the thought that we might be dreaming or subject to deception by an evil demon.[18] Might all that we experience be nothing but a fabulous hoax? Descartes famously found a response to such doubts in his assurance that he was thinking and was therefore a thinking being, *res cogitans*. But Śāntideva may be said to have turned the tables on Descartes. For when his interlocutor asks just who it is who perceives the illusion once ignorance is dispelled (*Guide* 9.15cd), Śāntideva replies that the perceiver, the mind, *is* the illusion, and that therefore, once that is dispelled, who is left to perceive at all (*Guide* 9.17ab)? So, with apologies to Descartes, "thinking being" turns out to be just a further dream.

Immanuel Kant thought of Descartes' argument as "skeptical idealism,"[19] by which he meant that Descartes, by casting doubt on the real existence of the objects of experience, had in effect left the thinker, the mind, as the last man standing. Interestingly, Śāntideva's commentator, Prajñākaramati, saw things similarly and considered the interlocutor, who wants to know who perceives the illusion, to be a representative of the Yogācāra school of Buddhism, which is often considered to have espoused a form of idealism, the doctrine that minds and ideas are what are truly real, what are left standing after all the rest has been reduced to illusion.[20]

This reading of Śāntideva's text poses some difficulties, for it is not quite clear that the major Yogācāra philosophers would have affirmed the position that is here attributed to them, namely that in the absence of real objects the subject's consciousness remains the touchstone of reality. For earlier Buddhist philosophy had generally affirmed that objects and subjects cannot be defined apart from one another, so that, in the absence of an object, one is not entitled to speak of a conscious subject at all. One is conscious only if one is conscious *of* something.[21] Could it have been that Yogācāra ignored this basic principle?

Certainly one of the greatest Yogācāra thinkers, Vasubandhu, mentioned above, is explicitly clear about this issue. What he affirms is not an objectless subject, but rather a consciousness to which the subject-object dichotomy no longer applies.[22] This is, as Vasubandhu himself acknowledged, a difficult concept, but perhaps for present purposes we can say that he was positing a sort of basal awareness, logically prior to the manifestation of consciousness as subject and object. In this case, it would seem that Śāntideva and Prajñākaramati may be treating the Yogācāra philosopher as a straw man, misrepresenting what he actually holds.

It is possible, of course, that they had in mind not Vasubandhu but some of his later followers, who may have been not so clear about these points. But I think it more likely that they wished to argue that Vasubandhu's "nondual consciousness" cannot be posited in good faith: if it is consciousness, then by definition, it is implicated in the subject-object dichotomy, and if it is not so implicated, then there is no reason to think that Vasubandhu is talking about consciousness at all.[23]

Śāntideva's imagined interlocutor, however, responds with an appeal to the notion of consciousness as "self-illuminating," meaning that consciousness functions reflexively, without requiring a distinction of subject and object.[24] Śāntideva rejects this, first by eliminating some obviously problematic interpretations: the idea that consciousness might literally act on itself (where the example is the absurdity of a sword cutting itself) or that it illuminates itself in the manner of a light (where the objection is that, because the light was never in the dark, it makes no sense to hold that it illuminates itself) (*Guide* 9.17–23).

The concept of reflexive awareness, however, was important for Yogācāra thought and was particularly developed among Vasubandhu's successors in the epistemological school of Buddhism. For them, the simplistic understandings that Śāntideva has just dismissed would have been regarded as missing the central point, that reflexive awareness, self-consciousness, must be affirmed as a fundamental feature of our mental lives. As philosopher Franz Brentano emphasized, whenever I am aware of something, I am also aware that I am aware.[25] This awareness of our awareness, taken as a gestalt that cannot be analyzed in terms of the structures of subject and object, is only roughly indicated by the idea of self-illumination and is not to be reduced to the image of the light shedding light on itself that Śāntideva ridicules. It is here, therefore, that Śāntideva's opponent introduces his key argument: without self-consciousness, we would not be able to form memories (*Guide* 9.24ab).[26] In response to this, we are given a dose of mouse venom: "If something was experienced on another occasion, and there is a connection to that, there is a memory; as in the case of mouse-venom."[27] This tersely formulated rebuttal of the opponent's argument is clearly in need of some unpacking.

It is likely that the example of the mouse venom, which is intended to problematize our ideas of how memories are made, merely repeats a now-forgotten old wives' tale from ancient India.[28] It seems that one who had been poisoned by a mouse or rat would have not been quite aware of it when it occurred and so would have forgotten it altogether, until the beginning of the monsoon thunderstorms, at which time the venom remaining in the body would be reactivated and with it a recognition of the contact with the poisonous mouse. But just how is this intended to overturn the notion that self-consciousness is a necessary precedent to memory?

One common assumption, affirmed in everyday life as well as by many philosophers in both Western and Indian traditions, holds that I cannot actually remember something of which I was not, in some appropriate sense, the subject. I cannot remember, from a participant's perspective, an event at which I was not present (e.g., my grandfather's birth). I cannot remember information I never encountered. I cannot remember a face I never saw. I may come to have knowledge of these things, but if so, it is not memory knowledge. And I may even think that I remember them, but in that case we would say that these are instances of false or apparent memories, mental events that seem when they occur to be memories, but on examination prove to be not memories at all. One of the considerations that can lead to their being discounted as memories is my discovery that I was not there, that I could not have been involved in the formation of the supposed memory in question. This conception of the distinction between apparent and real memories seems to imply that the self, the I, in some sense endures.[29]

In our present context, this has two important entailments: the proponent of Yogācāra to whom Śāntideva addresses his critique is charged with tacitly affirming the existence of an enduring self and thus contradicting a fundamental Buddhist tenet; and, as a corollary of this critique, the Mādhyamika philosopher must demonstrate that we may truly speak of memory without the assumption, "M is *my* memory because, when the state of affairs giving rise to M occurred, *I* was there as the subject."

To achieve this, Śāntideva, via the mouse-venom example, seeks to show the viability of an alternative causal chain, one leading to memory formation without requiring an enduring self, or an act of self-consciousness that serves as a stand-in for such an entity, as the subject of memory.[30] If he is to succeed, he must do so without recourse to an assumption that has figured prominently in some interpretations of the argument, which hold that, when the previously unnoticed bite grows painful, the victim *infers* that he was bitten by a mouse.[31] But, in my view, this cannot be correct, for inference is not memory, and to infer that something must have occurred is not at all what we mean when we say that we remember that it did.

Śāntideva, therefore, must have had something else in mind. To see what it might have been, we need to bring together two ideas. One is a causal theory of memory that does not make reference to an actually persisting "I" as the subject of memory. Such a theory had been developed in earlier Abhidharma philosophy; in essence, it held that if, within a causal continuum of the type that we conventionally designate as a person, there occurs an act of consciousness that is causally linked to a later act of consciousness that resembles the earlier act, and the occurrence of the subsequent act is accompanied by an awareness of the resemblance to and the link with the former act (as expressed in the thought, "I was there"), then the subsequent act counts as a memory.[32]

Now, with some such view in mind, the break between Śāntideva and his Yogācāra interlocutor may be said to concern the nature of the initial act of consciousness in its relation to what follows. For the latter, the traditional Abhidharma formulation was too weak and so had to be supplemented by reference to the phenomenon of self-consciousness, or apperception. This was thought, in effect, to create the idea of an enduring self without there actually being such a thing. For Śāntideva, however, the Yogācāra insistence on self-consciousness is too strong; even a peripheral act of consciousness—the overlooked moment of contact with a poisonous mouse—will suffice so long as it operates causally in the right way. The Yogācāra posit of necessary self-consciousness serves only to reintroduce into Buddhist discourse, by the back door, as it were, the discredited idea of an enduring self.

This reconstruction of Śāntideva's argument, however, will be credible only if we can reasonably hold that we do have some memories that are formed on the basis of perceptual events of which we were not quite conscious when they occurred. Śāntideva used the mouse-venom example just because it was current in his place and time—the classical Indian rules of debate required that philosophical examples be "well known," i.e., acceptable to all parties taking part in the debate—but we will need to find an example that works for us as well.[33]

It occurs to me that some nights ago I was at the theater. There were many faces in the crowd but, recognizing no one there, I regarded them indifferently. Sometime later, on returning home, I turned on the television and recognized M. D., a local television anchor person, as someone I had seen earlier that evening. In the theater, therefore, I formed no idea of seeing M. D., but later on I was able to say truly that, "I recall seeing M. D. at the theater."[34] A memory event, by this account, is just one of the many acts of consciousness churned up in the causal stream that is the person; in this, it is no different from an apparent memory or a false memory. Our use of the term "memory" is warranted just by the surrounding relevant conditions, as in our example:

(1) I (= a phase of the continuum M. K.) was indeed at the theater;
(2) I (= that phase of the M. K. continuum) saw a person there;
(3) that person happened to be a phase in the continuum of M. D. (whether or not M. K. knew this at the time);
(4) and, at some later time, in response to the picture on the television, I (= a later phase of the continuum M. K.) had the thought, "I saw that person, M. D., at the theater."

A variety of characteristic connections thus justifies our use of "memory," but not a connection to an enduring self or to a special class of mental acts called "self-consciousness." And our use of the concept of memory is warranted only conventionally; ultimately, none of this finds real ground.[35]

COURSING IN EMPTINESS

If the above illustrates the difficulties we sometimes confront in fleshing out the arguments of the "Wisdom Chapter," we may nevertheless now return to the broader context and consider where it fits in Śāntideva's overall trajectory. It is clear that Śāntideva wishes to eliminate all points that might permit "grasping-at-self" to find even the smallest foothold, as exemplified by his concern to uproot the Yogācāra conception of self-consciousness. One may begin to wonder whether he is even a nihilist, taking the Mādhyamika idea of emptiness to be literally nothing at all, a perfect vacuum. To this he responds, however, that what is seen, heard, and cognized, as it appears, may be left in place (*Guide* 9.26ab). Where we go wrong is in our disposition to try to push beyond appearance and attribute some sort of deeper reality to what merely appears; it is here that our suffering and discontent are rooted (*Guide* 9.26). Though the words were no doubt written with a very different intent, one cannot help but be reminded of Oscar Wilde's famous lines, "It is only shallow people who do not judge by appearances. The true mystery of the world is the visible, not the invisible."

The concept of the illusory nature of appearance, *māyā*, is not advanced by Śāntideva in order to posit, as is suggested by some understandings of Vedānta thought, that "illusion" exists as an independent force in the world, operating to ensnare us in a web of deception. Rather, the idea of *māyā* is intended as an antidote to our self-defeating disposition to grasp reality where it is not, whether in objects or in self. When the antidote has done its work, it becomes clear that no particular reality can be attributed to it; *māyā* is no being, but rather a way of coming to terms with that which appears to be. We are subject to a pervasive fallacy of reification, and this is Śāntideva's target, until we realize, as he famously says, that

> When neither being nor nonbeing stand before the mind,
> Then, with no further recourse, without objectification, one finds peace. (9.34)

NOTES

1. I have examined Śāntideva's approach to the Mahāyāna path in relation to what French philosopher Pierre Hadot, in the context of Hellenistic philosophy, has termed "spiritual exercise," forging a passage between an inauthentic, troubled existence and authentic peace and freedom. See Kapstein, "Stoics and Bodhisattvas."
2. On the relationship between the theoretical concerns of Buddhist philosophy and Buddhism's practical ends, see Kapstein, "Introduction," in *Reason's Traces* and Kapstein, "'Spiritual Exercise' and Buddhist Epistemologists in India and Tibet."
3. A nuanced philosophical introduction, with reference to much of the earlier scholarship, can be found in Westerhoff, *Nāgārjuna's Madhyamaka*.
4. Useful translations of pertinent Tibetan commentaries on the "Wisdom Chapter" may be found in Brunnhölzl, *The Center of the Sunlit Sky*, and Padmakara Translation Group, *The Wisdom Chapter*.
5. The Sanskrit text was first edited by La Vallée Poussin in 1901. In the present chapter, I follow the edition given in Vaidya, *Bodhicaryāvatāra*. Although I characterize Prajñākaramati's commentary as the only one in Sanskrit now available, the extant manuscripts are missing some pages. The editions we have are therefore not quite complete, though the contents of the missing sections are known on the basis of the extant Tibetan translation. Prajñākaramati's commentary on the ninth "Wisdom Chapter" of the *Guide*, however, is completely preserved in the original Sanskrit. Some small fragments of another Sanskrit commentary, by the early

thirteenth-century teacher Vibhūticandra, are also known. Besides this, several additional Sanskrit commentaries are now preserved exclusively in their Tibetan translations.

6. However, for the Tibetans, the Prāsaṅgika and Svātantrika subschools of Madhyamaka were to be distinguished by many philosophical issues besides just the method of argument. The question of reflexive awareness, examined below, is a case in point. Moreover, in his citations of Candrakīrti and Śāntarakṣita, Prajñākaramati uses them for rather different purposes and on some occasions views Śāntarakṣita's arguments unfavorably, so that it cannot be said that his reference to both suggests that he considered them indifferently. See, for instance, chapter 3 of Williams, *The Reflexive Nature of Awareness*, on an important passage from Śāntarakṣita cited in the present context.
7. In fact, the ninth chapter as we now know it was the result of an expansion of the entire *Guide* dating to some centuries after the work's original eighth-century composition. The ninth chapter, in particular, was almost doubled in size to include substantial new material, particularly in its arguments criticizing non-Buddhist schools. I believe that this augmentation of the work was carried out at the monastery of Vikramaśīla toward the end of the tenth century, and possibly under the direction of Prajñākaramati, though my reasons cannot be detailed here. What is important to note is that the mouse-venom argument was introduced into the text as part of this expansion and was not to be found in Śāntideva's original work. For the textual evidence demonstrating that there were at least two versions of the *Guide*—a shorter early version and an augmented later edition—refer to Saitō, "A Study of Akṣayamati (= Śāntideva)'s *Bodhisattvacaryāvatāra*" and "A Study of the Dūn-huáng Recension of the *Bodhisattvacaryāvatāra*." Interestingly, Tibetan hagiographical accounts of Śāntideva also speak of the existence of differing versions of the *Guide*. This issue is also discussed by Gold and Harrison in this volume.
8. Besides the Tibetan commentaries mentioned in n. 4 above, the reader will find a useful outline of the chapter in Śāntideva, *The Bodhicaryāvatāra*, trans. Crosby and Skilton, *The Bodhicaryāvatāra*, 111–112.
9. Skt. *akhu* typically refers to a mouse or rat. Crosby and Skilton take it in this case to be a "shrew," no doubt alluding to the fact that some species of shrew figure among the rare venomous mammals. However, it is not clear that the species current in India, the Asian house shrew (*Suncus murinus*) is venomous or that, if it is, this was known in premodern times.
10. The discussion of the two truths in the paragraphs that follow is based upon Kapstein, *Reason's Traces*, chapter 8, to which readers are referred for a more thorough discussion of the topic.
11. Vaidya, *Bodhicaryāvatāra*, 170–178. Here and in the discussion that follows, I refer to the text of the *Guide* using the verse numbers established in Vaidya's edition. For Prajñākaramati's commentary, I provide a reference to the same edition. Translations are my own.
12. Vaidya, *Bodhicaryāvatāra*, 170.
13. For further discussion of *saṃvṛti*, refer especially to chapter 2 of Nagao, *Mādhyamika and Yogācāra*.
14. Vaidya, *Bodhicaryāvatāra*, 171.
15. For reflections on the idea of "freedom" in the Indian philosophical context, see Kapstein, *Reason's Traces*, chapter 2, and Kapstein, "Interpreting Indian Philosophy: Three Parables."

16. Vaidya, *Bodhicaryāvatāra*, 175.
17. For an insightful and entertaining account of the philosophical use of these metaphors, see Westerhoff, *Twelve Examples of Illusion*.
18. Descartes, *Meditations on First Philosophy*, First Meditation, 12–15.
19. Immanuel Kant, *Critique of Pure Reason*, trans. Norman Kemp Smith (New York: St. Martin's Press, 1965), 244–47, 344–52.
20. See also Kapstein, "Buddhist Idealists and Their Jain Critics on Our Knowledge of External Objects."
21. Vasubandhu, *Abhidharmakośa* 1.34ab, for instance, explicitly identifies the mental with having an object (*sālambanam*).
22. For instance, in the autocommentary on *Viṃśikā* 10 (Silk, *Materials Towards the Study of Vasubandhu's Viṃśikā*, 78–79), where the subject-object distinction is qualified as "imaginary" (*parikalpita*).
23. Candrakīrti, *Madhyamakāvatāra*, 6.51ab, puts it this way: "Just as your external object does not arise in dreams, neither does the mind." Because Candrakīrti clearly restates, at 6.45, the Yogācāra formula denying both subject and object, his objection as expressed here strongly suggests that he does not take it at face value. Refer La Vallée Poussin, ed., *Madhyamakāvatāra* for the Tibetan and Li, "*Madhyamakāvatāra-kārikā* Chapter 6" for Sanskrit.
24. The question of reflexive consciousness in Buddhist philosophy is considered broadly in Yao, *The Buddhist Theory of Self-Cognition*, and with particular reference to the *Guide*, in Williams, *The Reflexive Nature of Awareness*.
25. Brentano treats this issue in considerable detail in *Psychology from an Empirical Standpoint*. In sum (143): "Every mental act . . . is accompanied by a twofold inner consciousness, by a presentation which refers to it and a judgement which refers to it, the so-called inner perception, which is an immediate, evident cognition of the act."
26. For the background of this assumption, see Yao, *The Buddhist Theory of Self-Cognition*, 75–78; 114–118, esp. 115, on the argument of Vasubandhu's disciple, and the founder of the Buddhist epistemological school, Dignāga (fifth century).
27. *Guide* 9.24cd. The verse is so compact that it has been necessary to fill out the translation. Literally, it reads: "If other-experienced, owing to connection, [there is] memory; like mouse-venom."
28. The inclusion of the mouse or rat among poisonous animals is discussed in Schmithausen, *Maitrī and Magic*, 38n78. I am indebted to Seishi Karashima for this reference.
29. Memory has been frequently invoked in connection with personal identity, but not always in quite the same way. The philosopher John Locke, for instance, famously argued that personal identity is itself constituted on the basis of memory—if I lose all my memories, so too in a crucial sense I lose my identity. His "memory theory of personal identity" has played an important role in subsequent Western reflection.
30. On the treatment of memory in relation to causality in Buddhism, refer to Kapstein, *Reason's Traces*, 120–129.
31. Williams, *The Reflexive Nature of Awareness*, 152–154.
32. Kapstein, *Reason's Traces*, 42–44; 122–124.
33. See above, n. 28. As Prof. Karashima also kindly conveyed to me, the evidence for the mouse-venom example's having been well known, as required for use in debate, is demonstrated by its wide occurrence in Abhidharma literature, as well as one

reference in the *Laṅkāvatārasūtra*. I extend thanks too to Dan Lusthaus for a fruitful correspondence on the use of this example in the context of the *Guide*.

34. I do not construe the act of recognition and the ensuing memory in this example as inferences. An inference would occur if, for instance, I were to see that the news anchor was wearing the same distinctive outfit as someone I saw at the theater and then to conclude from this that the anchor and the theatergoer were the same person. But in that case the inference would be perfectly compatible with an absence of recognition or memory: "I suppose from the suit she's wearing that a person I saw must have been her, but I honestly don't recall seeing anyone who looked like M. D." is an intelligible, noncontradictory statement.
35. Tibetan thinkers were much preoccupied by the question of whether Śāntideva's argument excluded the idea of self-consciousness in both relative and absolute terms or in absolute terms alone. The question is taken up in detail in Williams, *The Reflexive Nature of Awareness*.

REFERENCES

Brentano, Franz. *Psychology from an Empirical Standpoint*, trans. Antos C. Rancurello, D. B. Terrell, and Linda L. McAlister. International Library of Philosophy and Scientific Method. London: Routledge & Kegan Paul, 1973.

Brunnhölzl, Karl. *The Center of the Sunlit Sky: Madhyamaka in the Kagyü Tradition*. Ithaca: Snow Lion, 2004.

Descartes, René. *Meditations on First Philosophy*, First Meditation. In *The Philosophical Writings of Descartes*, vol. II, trans. John Cottingham, Robert Stoothoff, and Dugald Murdoch. Cambridge: Cambridge University Press, 1984.

Kapstein, Matthew T. *Reason's Traces: Identity and Interpretation in Indian and Tibetan Buddhist Thought*. Boston: Wisdom, 2001.

——. "Stoics and Bodhisattvas: Spiritual Exercise and Faith in Two Philosophical Traditions." In *Philosophy as a Way of Life*, ed. Stephen Clark, Michael McGhee, and Michael Chase, 99–115. Oxford: Blackwell, 2013.

——. "'Spiritual Exercise' and Buddhist Epistemologists in India and Tibet." In *The Blackwell Companion to Buddhist Philosophy*, ed. Steven Emmanuel, 270–289. Oxford: Blackwell, 2013.

——. "Buddhist Idealists and Their Jain Critics on Our Knowledge of External Objects." In *Philosophical Traditions*, ed. Anthony O'Hear, 123–148. Royal Institute of Philosophy Supplements 74. Cambridge: Cambridge University Press, 2014.

——. "Interpreting Indian Philosophy: Three Parables." In *The Oxford Handbook of Indian Philosophy*, ed. Jonardon Ganeri, 15–31. New York: Oxford University Press, 2016.

de La Vallée Poussin, Louis, ed. *Prajñākaramati's Commentary to the Bodhicaryāvatāra of Çāntideva*. Calcutta: Asiatic Society, 1901.

——, ed. *Madhyamakāvatāra par Candrakīrti*. St. Pétersbourg: Impr. de l'Académie impériale des sciences, 1912.

Li Xuezhu. "*Madhyamakāvatāra-kārikā* Chapter 6." *Journal of Indian Philosophy* 43 (2015): 1–30.

Nagao, Gadjin M. *Mādhyamika and Yogācāra*. Trans. Leslie S. Kawamura. Albany: State University of New York Press, 1991.

Padmakara Translation Group. *The Wisdom Chapter: Jamgön Mipham's Commentary on the Ninth Chapter of* The Way of the Bodhisattva. Boulder, CO: Shambhala, 2017.

Saitō, Akira. "A Study of Akṣayamati (= Śāntideva)'s *Bodhisattvacaryāvatāra* as Found in the Tibetan Manuscripts from Tun-Huang." Unpublished project report. Tsu, Japan: Mie University, 1993.

——. "A Study of the Dūn-huáng Recension of the *Bodhisattvacaryāvatāra.*" Unpublished Project Report. Tsu, Japan: Mie University, 2000.

Schmithausen, Lambert. *Maitrī and Magic: Aspects of the Buddhist Attitude Toward the Dangerous in Nature.* Vienna: Verlag der Osterreichischen Akademie der Wissenschaften, 1997.

Silk, Jonathan A. *Materials Towards the Study of Vasubandhu's Viṃśikā* (*I*). Harvard Oriental Series 81. Cambridge, MA: Department of South Asian Studies, Harvard University, 2016.

Vaidya, P. L., ed. *Bodhicaryāvatāra of Śāntideva with the Commentary Pañjikā of Prajñākaramati.* Buddhist Sanskrit Texts 12. Darbhanga: Mithila Institute, 1960.

Westerhoff, Jan. *Nāgārjuna's Madhyamaka: A Philosophical Introduction.* New York: Oxford University Press, 2009.

——. *Twelve Examples of Illusion.* New York: Oxford University Press, 2010.

Williams, Paul. *The Reflexive Nature of Awareness: A Tibetan Madhyamaka Defence.* Surrey: Curzon Press, 1998.

Yao Zhihua. *The Buddhist Theory of Self-Cognition.* London: Routledge, 2005.

[5]

SEEING FROM ALL SIDES

Janet Gyatso

It is an extraordinary sensation to catch a glimpse, somewhere on one's subjective landscape, of oneself from the outside. Often vague or indistinct, it nonetheless adumbrates a picture of "me" as I might be perceived by others. A mirror image does something like that too, although it is as lucid as could be, in fact, often a lot clearer than one might like. But in the case of the psychic image of ourselves that sometimes comes upon us—in a dream, in reverie, or sometimes even randomly in the course of a day—it may be that the very act of shifting perspective itself, of allowing a novel and indeed surprising angle or perspective to dawn, is what carries the most moral potential, even more than the specific content of the image itself. Unlike when we see a mirror image that is offered automatically (or a selfie provided by our phone's obliging lens reversal), the psychic shift required to see oneself from a foreign angle—however vaguely—needs cultivation and ingenuity. Such an image of oneself may arrive in visual, audial, or some other sensual modality; it may be accompanied by an idea, verbal judgment, or some combination thereof. In whatever form, it often requires fortitude to take in, since it can be surprising, if not shattering to our ego. But perhaps the more we are able to cultivate and incorporate external vantages into our way of seeing ourselves, the more we render ourselves available to an expanded and more ethical way of being in the world.

Śāntideva definitely thought so. His *Guide* highly recommends a practice it calls "exchanging self and other" (*parātmaparivartana*).[1] His presentation of this practice comes at the climax of a long discourse on the importance of relinquishing attachment to oneself and caring instead for the welfare of others. It is achieved by empathically taking on the view that others have of one. It requires giving up attachment to one's own view of things. Śāntideva calls the achievement of this exchange of subject positions a "supreme mystery" (*parama guhya*; 8.120). I suspect he means by this the challenge and difficulty of setting aside one's own perspective and making it possible for another to dawn inside oneself instead.

It has long been understood in Buddhist philosophy that we have no direct access to the minds of others.[2] One of the most detailed studies of empathy in Western philosophy, written by Edith Stein (1891–1942), student of Edmund Husserl, agrees. Stein analyzes, rather, the indirect means we have to access the viewpoints of others.[3] But a positivist knowledge of exactly what another person is thinking in the privacy of their own mind does not seem to be what Śāntideva is after in any case. Nor is his exercise of exchanging self and other about targeting the viewpoint of any particular individual. And so the question of whether our perception of another's view of us accurately represents what that person is actually thinking is not appropriate to the practice that the *Guide* describes.

However, there is an issue around connecting with a kind of reality, a reality about ourselves, that may be accessed and assessed through this practice. The other voices and visions that appear in the text, although not tied to particular individuals, do seem to resemble plausible and typical reactions of people in Śāntideva's actual milieu. In other words, the practice assumes that by relinquishing our own idiosyncratic desires and perspectives we can cultivate a special *capacity*. This would be the ability to access a social reality, however indistinct and multiform, that is true to our actual environment and gives us novel and important vantages upon ourselves. And in this, as I have already suggested, what may be most crucial are the effects merely of *trying* to see oneself from the perspective of that larger world, rather than the exact content of what is thereby seen as such.

The following reading is based in my own interest in why—and especially how—we might come to see ourselves through others' eyes. Philosophers and theologians like Rowan Williams have pointed out that such an act may not be intrinsically ethical or guarantee benevolence; the cruel can well be aware of their effect upon others and how their victims are feeling.[4] And yet the stance from which we try to detect the feelings of the other remains fundamental to achieving the ethical orientation of empathy, not to mention understanding of any kind between people. For Śāntideva, exchanging self and other demands that one has already begun to cultivate a benevolent commitment to the welfare of others; without that, the practice he has in mind will not work.

For my part, convinced of its ethical potential, I am interested in the contours of the phenomenon on its own terms. What are we in fact seeing when we see our self-image from the perspective of another? And what does that help us see about ourselves? What do we learn from it about how best to live and act in the world? What kind of gaze, or gesture, or stance do we need to cultivate in order best to detect it? And how is such a stance-shifting gesture to be represented, or otherwise taught, to others?

This chapter will explore Śāntideva's presentation of the practice of substituting one's own perspective on oneself with that of another. It will focus especially upon his literary strategies to create in his readers the capacity to perform this practice. A lot of the chapter will center upon the logic and the metaphors within the text itself. It will also consider some provocative statements on the different, but perhaps relevant way a master actor sees herself from the viewpoint of her audience. In this I will draw upon the writings of the renowned Japanese dramatist and theorist of Nōh Zeami Motokiyo (c. 1363–c. 1443). I want to explore the phenomenon of seeing oneself from the vantage of others both in terms of Śāntideva's goal of compassion and in terms of its larger potentials in the phenomenology and ethics of being in the world, as intimated in Zeami's artistic vision.

I

The *Guide*'s overt goal is entirely ethical. It is to develop *bodhicitta* (enlightened mind). This is the compassionate mindset, or attitude, of the bodhisattva, the mainstay of Mahāyāna Buddhist ethics. As Śāntideva puts it, enlightened attitude is the desire to "dispel the headaches of beings" (1.21). It is the wish to alleviate all suffering and to create "deep-welling happiness" (1.7) in others. This aspiration issues into activity, "persistent effort for the complete happiness of every being" (1.27).

The narrator showers enlightened mind with devotion and praise in the opening passages of the text. Enlightened mind is a precious gem, a protector, a guide, a consumer of evil, and the cause of great serenity. This is so for both the recipients of its ministrations and the individual who harbors it. It is also the object of amazement. How could such a thing as caring for others even be? We never even have a completely compassionate impulse toward ourselves, let alone others (1.24). How does someone with such superlative concern for others ever get born (1.25)? Moreover, enlightened mind dawns suddenly, like a flash of lightning (1.5). It is both elusive and powerful. It is "quicksilver elixir" that transmutes into the "priceless Buddha gem" (1.10). And yet reflection and meditation can help to bring that rare "opportune moment" (1.4) into being, the opportunity to practice and achieve *bodhicitta.*

The *Guide* is ostensibly written for the narrator's own edification, so that, as he says, it would "perfume my own mind." While the narrator grants in the next stanza that it might be possible for others of similar proclivities to benefit from his words as well, he introduces the text with appropriate humility. He is saying nothing new (1.2–3). But the work proceeds into a powerful reflection on the overrated value of the self. Its compelling logic and hortative exclamations seem clearly intended for readers to take in. Perhaps the powerful self-abnegation that the text frequently recommends is best delivered in the first person, as it often is in the work. But the narrator also addresses himself as "you," which may often be read as direct address to the audience/readership as well. He also often makes normative, propositional statements in the third person. The creative liberties he takes with verb forms and personal pronouns are in fact a key tool of his persuasive agenda. Throughout the text, the boundary between the narrator as protagonist-practitioner and the reader as protagonist-practitioner is unstable. And germane to the focus of the present chapter, a similarly fluid boundary enables the radical deconstruction of any absolute distinction between the practitioner and the beings for whom one is cultivating compassion.

The path of reflection that the *Guide* unfolds is harsh in the extreme against self-cherishing and everything the conventional person holds dear. The narrator quickly establishes that he himself has no merit. He only has his own self to offer to the compassionate buddhas, their teachings, and their followers. He would therefore become their slave, trained only upon worshiping them and submitting himself to their virtue (2.7–9). This subjection of the self to the buddhas' program of compassion sets up the conditions for the narrator/protagonist to relinquish all attachment to his own perspective altogether.

Much of the discussion in the *Guide* argues logically and instrumentally. Given Buddhist notions of karma and rebirth, the only thing that will be of use when we die is our accumulated store of merit. And as the narrator tells himself and his audience, he will die at any time, so there is nothing more urgent than making merit (2.42). That means to follow his own advice in this text and to cultivate *bodhicitta*. Otherwise his chances of reproducing his present state of fortune in his next life are, like an old

Buddhist trope says, as rare as those of a tortoise, when it occasionally comes up for air, to manage to poke its neck through the hole of a yoke that is floating somewhere out on the ocean (4.20). On the other hand, a single instant of evil can eventuate in an aeon in hell (4.21), entirely a product of the "untrained mind in the flame of self-reproach" (4.25). While the hell denizen does not comprehend this, it is actually one's own greed and hatred that enslaves one, condemning one to the hell of one's own mind, the "cage of greed" (4.25; 28).

But logic only goes so far in this rambling diatribe. Often it is clear that the powers—and even the activities—of imagination and determination are more compelling than logic. In one unsettling passage the narrator wishes that beings would play with his body and be derisive of it (3.12 seq.). This is difficult even just to imagine. But then the narrator adds the hope that the anger others feel at him in the course of abusing him will be the very cause of their achieving every goal. In fact, he goes on to wish that those who harm or degrade him will share in enlightenment. The latter would be indeed at the expense of all logic—or even faith in the doctrines of Buddhism. It is not possible for anger or abuse to be the cause of gaining Buddhist enlightenment. Such a passage tells us that the practice is about the narrator's own attitude and transformation; it is not something that he can actually think would ever happen in the way he describes it. Indeed, he knows quite well that those who harm him will go to hell (even if he takes responsibility for that, in the sense of inciting their hatred) (6.47). And so here we see that in producing such extreme imagined scenes, the narrator is even giving up attachment to consistency and to the teachings of the Dharma—all in order to cultivate the best attitude, which is an ultimate wish for the happiness of other beings.

Giving up all attachment had long been basic to the Buddhist path, but the extent to which Śāntideva takes it is exceptional. At one point, he advises becoming like a block of wood, "as if lacking senses" (5.34). "When one notices that one's own mind is attracted or repelled, one should neither act nor speak, but remain like a block of wood" (5.48).

Part of the point of this seems to be to think of the body as insensate, and therefore not worthy of our identification with it. The body is like a wooden doll; it is useless and not worth guarding or protecting, except as food for vultures and jackals, or somehow to help humankind (5.61–66). This rejection of the body is a salient theme of these chapters, but I will point at the end of this chapter to how the body also turns out to be of crucial value to the *Guide's* path after all.

II

Śāntideva's practice of "exchanging self and other" only comes up after a long meditative reflection. He circles around and around the uselessness of attachment to his body and himself, the importance of self-discipline, and the need to endure his own suffering as minor, to strive to benefit others, to take sympathetic joy in the successes of others, to control his carnal desire, to convince himself of the foulness of his own body, to realize the uselessness of his anger at other beings, to eschew honor and pride, to seek serenity, discipline, and energy, and to achieve the highest happiness and good in buddhahood. Then, in the middle of the *Guide*'s meditation chapter, the narrator announces the commencement of the actual development of enlightened mind (8.89).

> The first step is realizing "the equality of self and other:"
> All equally experience suffering and happiness. I should look after them as I do myself. (8.90)

Indeed, why privilege one's own suffering over that of others, since the suffering of the other people in the world vastly outweighs in quantity that of one's single self (8.105)? In the course of considering this point, Śāntideva admits that one can't experience another's suffering directly. But rather than inferring what that experience is from their outer expressions, as phenomenologist Edith Stein would have it, Śāntideva assumes a fundamental similarity between myself and another.[5] I should care about the suffering of others because it is similar to my own (*ātmaduḥkhavat*) (8.93–94):

> Even though suffering in me does not cause distress in the bodies of others, I should nevertheless find their suffering intolerable because of the affection I have for myself. In the same way that, though I cannot experience another's suffering in myself, his suffering is hard for him to bear because of his affection for himself (8.92–93). . . . When happiness is liked by me and others equally, what is so special about me that I strive after happiness only for myself? (8.95)

The last question is especially germane. As time passes, I will be a different self anyway, so why not care for the welfare of other selves as much as I care for the welfare of the other self that I will become in the future (8.97 seq.)? What's more, the narrator goes on, I have only imposed my idea of my self on my body, even though it does not actually have a self. So why can't I project an idea of my self on the body of another (8.115)?

The last point opposes self and body, and turns on the classical Buddhist logic of "no-self," the idea that the self in the end is just a projection and an illusion. This point is systematically and rationally developed in detail in the ninth chapter of the work, the philosophical one, on the "perfection of understanding." But here in the eighth chapter on meditation, the tenor is different, focusing instead on the expansion of imagination, perception, and experience. As the narrator now broaches "the supreme mystery" (8.120), the actual "exchange of self and other" practice, the approach shifts to a new register. The narrator instructs us—and/or himself—to create a sense of self located in others: "Creating a sense of self in respect of our inferiors, and a sense of otherness of oneself. Then imagine the envy and pride on the part of our new self with respect to our old self" (8.140).

Strikingly, the following verses obey this order immediately and directly: "He is honored not I. I do not receive such alms as he. He is praised. I am criticized. I suffer. He is happy" (8.141).

The process has just moved from imagination to spontaneous ventriloquy. We realize that we are now reading direct quotations that are spoken, or thought, by the new self *qua* the other. I'm calling these the "special verses" (8.141 seq.). They are the voice of the other. The narrator is now being perceived, or better, is perceiving himself, from the outside. This is the climactic scene of the book, but it appears without much warning. There are no quotation marks or other overt sign that these verses are not in the voice of the narrator. We realize the shift only through analysis of the grammar. In fact, in what follows, it frequently is not clear who is speaking, and to whom. Be that as it may, it seems that suddenly, as a result of all the careful preparation that the text has proffered, the practitioner is able to hear messages of other subjectivities.

The new voices express envy and resentment toward the protagonist. This in itself was already set up in the course of developing empathy, where it was pointed out how others have the same desires for advancement as oneself (8.127). And that they have. What they say is very stark: "I do chores while he remains at ease. He, it seems is great in the world. I, it seems, am inferior, without virtue" (8.142).

In other words, it appears that in doing this practice, what the practitioner has exchanged with others are his own resentments and disgruntlements. He is sharing his bad side, the very side that he wishes to rid himself of, as when previously he castigated himself for "burning inside" when seeing someone else honored, or when they take on tasks, like supporting his family, that he himself should be doing, or even when they simply gain merit or accept donations (6.81 seq.).

There is much in these comments that may actually be autobiographical for Śāntideva, or at least representative of his guilty conscience. But not only do they seem to mirror his own resentments in life, they also may reflect what others actually thought of him, he who doubtless was well regarded for his talents. These comments by the others all concern issues that would have obtained in a scholastic/monastic setting: receiving alms; doing chores; getting prestige, honor, and status; desire for learning; desire for people to listen to one. This suggests that the specificities of the practice that the *Guide* describes refer to actual life in Nālandā Monastery during Śāntideva's period. It is a life that seems to have been, at least in his eyes, competitive, even around things like making merit (8.86) and gaining praise and renown (6.93).

"He has no compassion for people who stand in the vicious jaw of an evil rebirth" (8.146). The exercise helps the narrator/author/protagonist to see things about himself that heretofore he didn't realize. He realizes his privilege and good fortune, as compared to others. He realizes how much esteem he is held in, how he has failed to be appreciative of that, and how he has rather been embroiled in competitive scrambling and *schadenfreude*. He starts to see his moral failings. But he sees these in a different light than a strictly confessional one, as previously in the text. Rather, he now hears others complaining about his faults, which previously he was only presuming that he had. And by virtue of identifying with those others, he feels their pain even as he simultaneously feels the chagrin of being the one who has caused it.

III

Giving up attachment to the self is one thing, seeing the self from the outside may be quite another. What else comes into view? According to the phenomenological analysis of Edith Stein, seeing ourselves as an object is similar to how we see others as objects. She points out that we use a lexicon of values and bodily expressions to assess others, and eventually to assess ourselves from that same perspective. Like Śāntideva, Stein finds empathy ultimately to be valuable for our own moral development. It is a powerful way for our own self-conception to be mediated by cultural norms.[6]

The *Guide*'s narrator's gaze at the self-*qua*-object on the part of the self-*qua*-other also participates in such a lexicon of values. Realizing the perspective of the other helps him to bring to bear a sharp self-critique of the distasteful selfishness that he displays. However, the others' normative judgements upon him shift as the practice proceeds. The voices begin to move from relatively quotidian envy and condemnation to severe invidiousness and then to downright cruelty and aggression: "Delighted we shall watch while at last he is crushed, the object of everyone's ridicule, criticized from all sides" (8.150).

Or again, "Even if he is given alms we must snatch them from him by force, giving him only enough to live by if he does some work for us" (8.153).

At this point the scene being witnessed has quite exceeded any salvific self-correction driven by Buddhist ethics. It is far too harsh to be normative or even edifying for the practitioner. Rather, perhaps it represents a guilt-ridden, if not paranoid dimension of the narrator's own psyche. He owns up to such guilt: "In brief, whatever malicious act you performed upon others in order to benefit yourself, cause that same predicament to befall yourself for the benefit of living beings" (8.165).

In fact we already saw him wishing that people would play with his body and hurt him. But did the narrator really crush others with ridicule or snatch their alms? And is he actually discerning the feelings of other people in the world toward himself, or is he simply projecting his own fears and self-hatred? Or is it some combination thereof, accessed precisely as a result of allowing his imagination to run free?

Such questions are impossible to answer with certainty. But we can say at least that the latitude the narrator grants the specter of the other subject seems to be given value in itself, and is indicative of how such specters dawn. The vision of self-as-other is shown to ramble, cycling through a veritable stream of consciousness from everyday jealousy to extreme aggression, self-congratulation, self-critique, and conspiracy (e.g., 8.149–153). This roller coasterlike stream of thought even hits upon an occasional realistic self-assessment, such as when the subject counsels himself: "Each person has his own virtues. There are those among whom I am the worst. There are those among whom I am the best" (8.143).

It may be that the manner in which voices and insights dawn during exchanging-self-and-other practice has a significance of its own, quite apart from the particular content of any given insight. Perhaps the license to see things from every possible angle is a prerequisite to getting a new, fuller sense of oneself, a sense that breaks out of strict subject-object bifurcation. That same license may also have something to do with the openness needed to allow the image of ourselves in the eyes of others to dawn to us in the first place. Indeed, the very way that Śāntideva portrays the onset of the voice of the other may be morally instructive. Śāntideva makes clear at the very beginning of the treatise that enlightened mind dawns suddenly, like a flash of lightning (1.5). So, apparently, do the voices of the other. As already noted, the first set of special verses beginning at 8.141 just start speaking without warning, and without quotation marks. What does herald the shift, however, appears to be a studied fluidity in the use of pronouns, a fluidity that mirrors what we have just observed in perspective, voice, and content.

Strikingly, the first line of the special verses suddenly uses the first-person pronoun to refer not to the narrator but rather to the other subject (or better, the narrator *qua* his new self). And it uses the third person to refer to the old narrator: "He is honored, not I." The ending of the rant of the new "I" also comes without warning at 8.155, recognizable only by the way that the voice switches out of the first-person plural and we find our old narrator talking to himself in the second person singular: "Immeasurable aeons have passed while you sought to realize your own well-being."

Or is the second person singular the reader/audience? At 8.156 the verse seems to show the narrator talking to his reader (or is it his better self, talking to his demeaned self?) about the virtues of exchanging-self-and-other practice: "At my entreaty proceed in this way right now without delay. Later you will see the virtues of this, for the word of the Sage is true."

Then a few verses later the voice of the other is back, albeit this time marked off by quotation marks (Skt. *iti*), and overtly provided by the narrator, who is telling the other what to say about himself: " 'He is well situated, another badly off . . . He is exalted. The other works. He does not.' In this way engender jealousy toward yourself" (8.160).

Soon the unmarked voice of the other is back again: "Tarnish his reputation with reports of the superior repute of others. . . . He should not be praised. . . . Act so that no one might know of his virtue (8.163–64).

At 8.168 it is the narrator speaking again, who has become critical of the other, addressed in the second person and now identified as his own mind: "If despite being instructed in this way you do not do it, you it is, Mind, that I shall punish." But is it the same addressee in the next verse? "Where are you off to?. . . I shall knock all the insolence out of you. Things were different before, when I was ruined by you" (8.169).

The reader may be getting disoriented. By 8.171 the second person appears to be addressed to the narrator's body: "If I do not give you away joyful to living beings, you will hand me over to the guards of hell" (8.171).

And then at 8.174 we find the narrator making normative propositions again: "The more this body is protected, the more fragile it becomes, the more it degenerates" (8.174).

The literary effect may well be intentional, to baffle readers and force them to take a few minutes, and perhaps reread several times, before they realize what is going on.

The uncertainty that the reader starts to feel about to whom the personal pronouns refer, and who is talking to whom, would seem to fit well with the exercise of exchanging self and other, wherein destabilization of one's own subject position is the very aim. But far from constructing a panopticon, the exchange-of-self-and-other practice entails a fluidity of particular subjectivities. Neither the narrator nor the practitioner purports to know what everyone, from every vantage point, is thinking and feeling. Rather, the idea seems to be to exercise the ability to drop one's particular attachment to one's own dearly held particular perspective in order to perceive those of particular (if only hypothetical) others. It turns out that in many ways the latter have similar feelings and desires as oneself, albeit from different angles.

IV

There may be something else important about the way the voice of the other dawns on us (that is, we, the would-be practitioners of exchanging self and other), sometimes seemingly of its own accord. Those cases where the verb person and pronouns shift abruptly from narrator to the other might serve to train the reader/practitioner to maintain a certain kind of unfocused attention. By this I mean an alertness that is open to a wide horizon of possibility, rather than fixed upon a narrow intentional object or desire. It may be that cultivating this wider scope of possibility makes us more available to seeing/hearing the perspective of another with regard to ourselves.

I take this idea from a specialized kind of training coming out of a very different corner of the Buddhist world than that of Śāntideva, that of medieval Japanese artistic culture. Zeami Motokiyo wrote several treatises on the art of dramatic performance, some aspects of which I find to resonate with Śāntideva's exchanging-self-and-other practice. What Zeami says about the actor's relationship to the audience watching him is particularly suggestive. In his essay *Mirror Held to the Flower,* Zeami writes of the importance of creating an entire atmosphere rather than focusing on mere techniques and particular forms: "Such a performance resembles a bird that opens its wings and trusts itself to the movement of the winds."[7]

It would appear that the practitioner of self-and-other-exchange needs such trust as well when she exposes herself to the gaze, not to mention the invidious comments, of others.

It is also the broadness of that atmosphere, in fact its entire 360 degrees, that is essential to the effective actor, and is in some ways akin to the necessarily open scope of the *Guide*'s self-other exchange. In another essay, Zeami explores the need for the actor to adjust his voice and style to the weather, the season, the time of day, and the general mood of the atmosphere.[8] The actor also needs to be closely in sync with the mood and feeling of the audience. This begins as he first steps onto the stage, when he must take cognizance of the audience. The actor's feeling needs to be aligned exactly with that of the audience. This allows an entrance onto the stage at the exactly right moment.[9]

Most relevant of all to the *Guide*, the actor needs to see himself as he appears from the outside, in the way that the audience does. He must align his internalized self-image with that of his audience, in order to perform most effectively. This means to create an "internalized outer image." The latter requires "assiduous training."[10] Again, the vision entails a 360-degree perspective. The actor must keep within his purview the views from the space to the left and to the right of him, as well as to his front and his rear. Interestingly, among these four directions, Zeami stresses the ability on the part of an actor to see his image from behind: "If an actor can achieve this, his peerless appearance will be as elegant as that of a flower or a jewel and will serve as a living proof of his understanding."[11]

The image of oneself that one sees from the perspective of others, for both Śāntideva and Zeami, does not consist in a simple subject-object reversal. For Śāntideva it is fluid and shifting, and for Zeami it is multidirectional. For both there is a dimension of the other that is broad and generalized. For Śāntideva, the other is sometimes specified as a we, when he seems to be talking about all sentient beings (although it may also just refer to his colleagues and family): "Because of him we have all suffered the afflictions of cyclic existence hundreds of times" (8.154).

For Zeami, the image is not from the perspective of a single person either, but from that of the audience as a whole. This means in turn that the actor should not gaze directly on the spectators.[12]

Likewise, the image of the self that is gained from the perspective of others must be vague and perhaps indistinct, but essential information is gained from it nonetheless. This becomes clear in Zeami's preference for the actor's image of himself from the back: "If the actor cannot somehow come to a sense of how he looks from behind, he will not be able to become conscious of any possible vulgarities in his performance."[13]

Why would Zeami make such a specification? Surely the audience is seeing him primarily from the front. So in fact the actor is not accessing anything remotely like the precise image that anyone in the audience sees. Somehow the vaguer image seen by "the eyes of the spirit looking behind" is what gets the actor in touch with his inauthenticities, which, like Śāntideva's faults, need seeing and correcting. Perhaps the focused details seen from the front get in the way of perceiving this larger gestalt.

V

It is not too far of a stretch to say that Śāntideva's bodhisattva in training is indeed preparing for a career in acting, that is, acting on behalf of others. As in the prayers of the *Guide*'s final section, the dawning images of bodhisattvas such as Vajrapāni and Mañjughoṣa cause vileness to vanish and fearlessness and joy to be generated in those who look at them (10.11–16). Indeed, an essential dimension of the bodhisattva's activity is to be, or act as, whatever sentient beings need them to be or to look like.[14] There is even one particularly relevant verse in the *Guide* that comes right before the exchange-of-self-and-other verses, where the name of Avalokiteśvara is said to drive away the shyness people feel in front of an audience (8.118). One would imagine Śāntideva means by this that within the arena of bodhisattva activity, the "self-consciousness" that often plagues us is gone. We can say that it has been replaced by another kind of self-consciousness, which the entire text endeavors to inculcate in the reader.

The bodhisattva schooled in the path of the *Guide* maintains a 360-degree awareness of her own image from the outside. We have seen how attaining this involves a willingness to allow the voices of others to impinge on one's attention from unexpected angles. It also involves a willingness for those voices to be critical, prepared earlier in the text by long passages of fierce self-critique regarding one's selfishness, greed, and neglect of others. This self-critique also prepares one for similar selfishnesses in those others whose perspectives one now incorporates. Indeed, much of the leveling of the playing field that exchanging-self-and-other practice entails has to do with the sameness of the samsaric predicament.

Once again, this shared predicament means that the exchanging of self and other in the *Guide* is ultimately not about a single, particular other but rather about a general "we" of all sentient beings. Even if the other's rant against the *Guide*'s narrator begins as the complaint of a familiar colleague within the competitive setting of Nālandā, it evens out later to encompass the larger world of others toward whom the *Guide*'s bodhisattva must be oriented. Zeami's account of the actor's incorporation of his audience's perspective helps us to get a glimpse of the phenomenology of such an experience. It is both indistinct and powerfully self-transformative.

Both paths of practice require exceptional discipline, Zeami's intricate account of which I do not have the space to explore. The self-discipline of the *Guide* that enables a loosening of attachment to oneself includes not only self-castigation but also sometimes a radical separation of mind and body, with the body rendered completely senseless, or at least passive before the will of the mind. And yet the power to render it senseless entails close attentive vigilance, both upon and within it. One needs to maintain constant awareness of one's eyes, one's precise bodily position, how one walks, and even idle motions like handling clods of earth or grass (5.35; 39; 46).

Long a mainstay of both monastic discipline and bodily mindfulness meditation practice in Buddhism, such intense consciousness of the body is not so far from what a dancer must cultivate. In the case of the *Guide*, the self-curtailment entailed in remaining like a "block of wood" ends up becoming the basis for becoming "full of serene confidence, steady . . . , eager to help others" (5.55). Going as deep into the recesses of the body as the marrow of one's bones to discover one's personal lack of essence (5.63) enables one to be radically open to the other, to look at them directly, and to drink them in with the eyes (5.80). Ironically, the block of wood is able to move as carefully, delicately, and perceptively as a crane or a cat (5.73). She achieves her intended goal precisely because of her 360-degree angle of vision. Perhaps the body, and its special form of "dark consciousness," is especially capable of leading the way in the suspension of intentional subject-object bifurcation.[15] Perhaps the body *qua* block of wood is just alert enough to see what is really important, out there in the suffering world, around and beyond the self.

NOTES

1. All quotes from the *Guide* in this essay are taken from Śāntideva, *The Bodhicaryāvatāra*, trans. Crosby and Skilton.
2. Inami, "The Problem of Other Minds in the Buddhist Epistemological Tradition."

3. Stein, *On the Problem of Empathy.* I came to this work after hearing the Tanner Lectures of Rowan Williams in 2014. See following note.
4. Williams, "The Other as Myself."
5. According to Stein's analysis, we cannot actually experience another's inner state "primordially," but we can use our ability to understand the relation between an effect (facial expression, bodily posture, etc.) and its cause (inner states) in order to discern the suffering of others. But even for Stein, what is crucial is the recognition of similarity to oneself. Stein, *On the Problem of Empathy,* 51–54; 61–63; 75 seq.
6. Stein, *On the Problem of Empathy,* 96–97 seq.
7. Rimer and Masakasu, trans., *On the Art of the Nō Drama,* 80.
8. In *Finding Gems and Gaining the Flower,* in Rimer and Yamazaki, *On the Art of the Nō Drama,* 127–128.
9. Rimer and Yamazaki, *On the Art of the Nō Drama,* 82.
10. Rimer and Yamazaki, *On the Art of the Nō Drama,* 81.
11. Rimer and Yamazaki, *On the Art of the Nō Drama,* 81.
12. Rimer and Yamazaki, *On the Art of the Nō Drama,* 82.
13. Rimer and Yamazaki, *On the Art of the Nō Drama,* 81.
14. Reeves, trans., *The Lotus Sutra,* 367; 373–374.
15. For the notion of dark consciousness see Yuasa, *The Body.*

REFERENCES

Inami, Masahiro. "The Problem of Other Minds in the Buddhist Epistemological Tradition." *Journal of Indian Philosophy* 29 (2001): 465–483.

Reeves, Gene, trans. *The Lotus Sutra.* Boston: Wisdom, 2008.

Rimer, J. Thomas, and Yamazaki Masakasu, trans. *On the Art of the Nō Drama: The Major Treatises of Zeami.* Princeton, NJ: Princeton University Press, 1984.

Śāntideva. *The Bodhicaryāvatāra.* Trans. Kate Crosby and Andrew Skilton. Oxford: Oxford University of Press, 1995.

Stein, Edith. *On the Problem of Empathy.* Trans. Waltraut Stein. Washington, D.C.: ICP Press, 1989.

Williams, Rowan. "The Other as Myself: Empathy and Power." Tanner Lectures on "The Paradoxes of Empathy." Lecture 1 of 3. Delivered at Harvard University and sponsored by the Mahindra Humanities Center, April 8, 2014. https://www.youtube.com/watch?v=v79tL7uYTrA.

Yuasa Yasuo. *The Body: Toward an Eastern Mind-Body Theory.* Albany: State University of New York Press, 1987.

[6]

BODIES AND EMBODIMENT IN THE *BODHICARYĀVATĀRA*

REIKO OHNUMA

While the *Guide to Bodhisattva Practice* (*Bodhicaryāvatāra*, hereafter the *Guide*) is rightly celebrated for its intense focus upon the mind and its careful attention to a complex moral psychology (as many of the essays in this volume will attest), we should not lose sight of the significant role that the *body* and *embodiment* also play within Śāntideva's text. Indeed, throughout Śāntideva's work, the language of the mind cannot stand alone, but is constantly intertwined with and expressed through the language of the body. This should not be surprising if we remember the total interpenetration of the moral and physical orders characteristic of the Buddhist worldview. As Susanne Mrozik has so clearly demonstrated—specifically in connection with Śāntideva's other major work, the *Training Anthology* (*Śikṣāsamuccaya*)—the body and morality are intimately intertwined in Buddhist ethics: moral status is always reflected in the type of physical body one bears, and this body itself constitutes both the necessary condition for further moral development and the means by which such development is brought about, not only for oneself but also for others with whom one interacts.[1] It therefore stands to reason that as Śāntideva guides us along the bodhisattva path, he should pay ample attention to any number of different bodies: the body that should be avoided, the body one needs to advance, the body as a means of such advancement, the bodies that inspire us as we proceed, and the body one finally seeks to achieve. As Mrozik has noted, Śāntideva exists within a world of "corporeal specificity":[2] not all bodies are the same, and the *Guide* thus describes for us various types. As we move along the bodhisattva path, moreover, Śāntideva offers a plethora of techniques to encourage our advance, including attitudes toward the body whose cultivation can be helpful at specific points along the way—and these attitudes too are multiple and constantly shifting. To speak of "embodiment" in the *Guide* therefore involves both the *actual physical bodies* that are involved in the attainment of buddhahood and the *attitudes toward the body* that should be fostered along the path. In this chapter, I seek to offer a succinct account that encompasses both categories. In doing so, I draw freely from the *Guide* (using Crosby and Skilton's elegant translation for the most part),[3] for Śāntideva's statements concerning the body are scattered throughout the text rather than being limited to any single discussion.

THE WORTH AND WORTHLESSNESS OF THE BODY

One of the basic preconditions for following the bodhisattva path, or engaging in any type of moral cultivation at all, is that one must be endowed with a certain type of body—first and foremost, a *human* body, since the human realm is understood to be the realm of rebirth in which moral agency is most robust and spiritual progress can be made. Much of the *Guide* is therefore pervaded by an extreme sense of *urgency*: the urgency of taking full advantage of a fleeting human rebirth. To instill this sense of urgency, Śāntideva frequently engages in scare tactics, painting a gruesome and terrifying portrait of the human body under siege: alive for just an instant yet ever threatened by the imminence of death and the high likelihood of falling into the excruciating tortures of hell. We thereby come to understand the type of body that must be avoided at all costs: the intensely suffering body of a bad rebirth, especially a rebirth in hell. Thus, Śāntideva reminds us that if a bodhisattva does not exercise constant vigilance (*apramāda*) in maintaining *bodhicitta* (the aspiration to buddhahood), he will "repeatedly attain bad rebirths, disease, and death, have limbs cut off, and be cleaved apart,"[4] suffering for many eons "the intolerable roasting of [his] body in hell-fire."[5] If he does not exercise vigor (*vīrya*) in his practice of the path, he will soon find himself "screaming in agony as his entire skin is ripped away by Yama's minions" and "segments of his flesh [are] cleaved away by the hundredfold blows of blazing swords and pikes."[6] So how can he ever be complacent? What will he do when death arrives and he "[hears] the hellish bellowings, quaking, from terror [his] body caked in excrement"?[7] Throughout the *Guide*, Śāntideva uses these repulsive images of a body on the verge of excruciating pain to encourage the bodhisattva to take advantage of the precious opportunity of a human rebirth. For "where shall [he] find such rare circumstances again: the arising of a Tathāgata, faith, the human state itself, the capacity to practise skilful deeds, health, and this day, with food and freedom from disaster?"[8]

In emphasizing the advantages of possessing a human body, however, Śāntideva must walk a careful line—a Middle Way, as it were—between two detrimental attitudes: if one overvalues the body by identifying with it and constantly giving in to its whims and desires, one soon falls into the afflictions of attachment, passion, and lust. But if one undervalues the body by failing to meet its basic needs, one soon falls into a state of physical exhaustion that renders the cultivation of the mind impossible. Seeking to steer the bodhisattva along a path that avoids these two extremes, Śāntideva alternates between two traditional lines of thinking about the body that are both widely represented throughout Buddhist literature.

We might refer to one line of thinking as the *worthlessness* of the body: the body is impure, foul, and disgusting (commonly described as a "wound," a "boil with nine openings," and a "bag of excrement"); afflicted by old age, disease, suffering, and death; transient and impermanent (like a "bubble" or "foam")—yet the body's deceptive wholeness leads to delusions of selfhood, sexual passion for others, and other undesirable consequences that entrap one in the round of rebirth. Negative views of the body thus center around its impurity, its impermanence, its fragility, and its significant role in reinforcing one's passions and delusions. Given these negative qualities, attachment to the body is worthless and futile, and the Buddhist monk is encouraged to overcome such attachment through a variety of body-focused meditations, such as meditation on the thirty-two loathsome parts of the body or the nine stages of decomposition undergone by a corpse. These practices, and the notions that underlie them, both suggest the body's worthlessness.

In contrast, we might refer to the second line of thinking as the *worth* of the body. First and foremost, the body is a necessary locus of awakening; as Bernard Faure has said: "Despite its transcendental claims, awakening is always localized: it needs a locus to 'take place,' and this locus is the body."[9] More than just a passive locus where awakening "takes place," however, the body is also a necessary instrument for the attainment of awakening. Without the physical body, one could not engage in religious practice of any sort; meditation, worship, ritual, and acts of devotion and merit making would all be impossible to perform. Thus, the human body, as both the vehicle for one's spiritual progress and the locus of its ultimate goal, should be adequately cared for and maintained. This second line of thinking finds expression in many different contexts. In the Buddha's own life story, for example, the culminating spiritual progress was made only after he renounced severe mortification of the body and came to understand that the body needed adequate food and maintenance. Proper care for the body was thus an essential element of the Middle Way propounded by the Buddha and distinguished his teaching from some of the other religious movements of his time that engaged overzealously in asceticism. Similarly, the human body is celebrated for the rare opportunity it provides to engage in religious practice, while suicide is frowned upon as a wasteful squandering of this opportunity; food is recommended in moderation; health and physical vitality are extolled; the bodily pleasures of meditation are praised; and so on. In a variety of such ways, the essential worth of the human body and the necessity of caring for it properly are clearly recognized and extolled.[10]

The worthlessness and worth of the body may appear, on the surface, to be contradictory, until we recognize that each view is like a powerful antidote intended to counteract a specific poison, with the worthlessness of the body preventing its overvaluation and the worth of the body preventing its undervaluation. Thus, Śāntideva invokes both views throughout his text, strategically emphasizing one or the other depending upon his purpose. In general, he invokes the worthlessness of the body when speaking of the virtues of a renunciatory lifestyle and the importance of controlling one's mind rather than succumbing to the whims of the body. Using nauseating images of impurity and decay, he asks the bodhisattva, "Why do you guard this festering contraption made of filth?"[11] After all, "you will not eat it, unclean as it is, nor drink the blood, nor suck out the entrails"[12]—so why continue to cater to its every desire? Instead, he advises, you should mentally "pull apart this bag of skin," "loosen the flesh from the cage of bones," and then "work out for yourself what essence (*sāra*) is there."[13] Of course, "searching hard like this, you have found no essence here," so "explain why it is that you still continue to guard the body."[14] If this purely mental dissection proves to be insufficient, the bodhisattva should physically go to the charnel ground and compare "[his own] rotting body with other corpses," reminding himself that "this body of mine will also turn putrid in that way, its stench so vile even the jackals will not slink near."[15] So why continue to cling to a "ghastly impure form" that will only "end up lost in ashes"?[16] The body, in fact, is an already-dead object that does not even appreciate the care one bestows upon it: "Whether protected by me in this way, or devoured by vultures and other scavengers, it feels neither affection nor dislike. Why do I create affection for it?"[17] By thus cultivating a strong sense of the body's worthless and disgusting nature, its impermanence, and its lack of essence, the bodhisattva will loosen the bonds of attachment and clinging, become disengaged from his bodily desires, and prioritize the control of his mind.

Not only should he cultivate such disgust in regard to his own body, however, but he should also cultivate it in regard to the bodies of others, especially those for whom he feels passion or lust—and here Śāntideva's statements about the worthless body take on a distinctively gendered cast. Leading the male bodhisattva through a long meditative exercise, Śāntideva dispenses a particularly powerful antidote to the disease of man's passion for woman. He asks the bodhisattva afflicted by lust to imagine his female lover as a lifeless corpse who is "nothing but bones,"[18] a "pile of meat being devoured by vultures and other scavengers."[19] If he would not embrace her in this state, Śāntideva asks, why was he so intent on doing so before? In fact, imagining his lover's body as a corpse is not even necessary, since even when alive, this body is thoroughly repulsive:

> They produce both spit and shit from the single source of food. You do not want the shit from it. Why are you so fond of drinking the spit? (8.49)
>
> If you have no passion for what is foul, why do you embrace another, a cage of bones bound by sinew, smeared with slime and flesh? (8.52)
>
> If you do not want to touch something such as soil because it is smeared with excrement, how can you long to touch the body which excreted it? (8.58)
>
> If you have no passion for what is foul, why do you embrace another, born in a field of filth, seeded by filth, nourished by filth? (8.59)
>
> Not only are you not disgusted at your own foulness, you glutton for crap, you yearn for other vats of filth! (8.61)
>
> You have plenty of filth of your own. Satisfy yourself with that! Glutton for crap! Forget her, that other pouch of filth! (8.53)[20]

The powerful sense of revulsion and disgust conveyed within these verses suggests that this is far less an objective or detached description of the body than it is a strong medicine for a strong disease: attachment to sensual and sexual pleasures. The role of gender here, moreover, is ambivalent. On the one hand, multiple verses make it clear that *both* male and female bodies should be viewed as "vats of filth." On the other hand, Śāntideva clearly assumes a male (heterosexual) perspective, and his language seems particularly harsh when speaking of the body of a woman. It is possible, in fact, to place these verses within a long Buddhist tradition (well described by Liz Wilson)[21] of viewing the body's impurity primarily in regard to women—reminding us again that not all bodies are equal, as well as reflecting the social environment (celibate, male, and monastic) in which Śāntideva worked.

Cultivating a sense of the worthlessness of one's own and others' bodies can thus help the bodhisattva to eradicate lust and passion, prioritize his mind, and live a renunciatory life. But just as any powerful medicine might have side effects that could be worse than the disease itself, such a view becomes dangerous if it leads the bodhisattva to discount his body altogether—for the body is necessary, as we have seen, and must therefore be cared for and maintained. Śāntideva's invocations of the body's worthlessness are thus counterbalanced at regular intervals by invocations of the body's worth. The concept of worth is particularly appropriate here, as Śāntideva makes use of several economic metaphors that have the effect of instrumentalizing the body and thus attributing to it its legitimate value while still keeping it detached from the bodhisattva himself. At one point, he notes that "this body is like an object on loan"[22]—in other words, something that has been borrowed and must be cared for, yet will never truly belong to the one who possesses it only temporarily. Elsewhere, he likens the body to a servant one has employed, who must be given his proper wages yet should never be overpaid:

> You do not give clothes and such to a servant if you think he is not going to stay. The body will eat and then go. Why do you make the outlay? (5.68)
>
> On that account, having given the body its wages, Mind, now look to your own needs, for a labourer does not receive all of the wealth he creates. (5.69)[23]

By likening the body to an object one has temporarily borrowed or a servant one has temporarily employed, Śāntideva seeks to distance the bodhisattva from his own body, while still ensuring that this body receives the minimal care it needs (such as adequate food, clothing, and shelter) in order to serve as a vehicle of religious practice.

In a Mahāyāna context, moreover, the worth of the body lies not only in its role as a vehicle for bringing about one's own spiritual welfare but also in its role as a vehicle for bringing about the welfare of others. After all, without a physical body, one cannot exercise compassion toward others, do good deeds for them, or work for their welfare—which is the foremost imperative for a bodhisattva. The bodhisattva needs to realize that this "wretched body" (*śarīrakam*) is also his best "implement of action for the benefit of humankind" (*karmopakaraṇaṃ manuṣyāṇāṃ*),[24] and then make such action the body's first priority. He should "apply to the body the notion of a ship" and then "set the body on course to fulfill the needs of beings."[25] Like the object on loan and the servant one employs, the notion of a ship suggests something detached from the bodhisattva himself yet able to be deployed at the bodhisattva's will—in this case, in the service of others. In fact, while the body, as we have seen, can never truly belong to the bodhisattva himself, he should cultivate the view that it "belongs" wholly to other beings: "Therefore," he should tell himself, "without regret, I abandon my body to the benefit of the world."[26] And further:

> I make over this body to all embodied beings to do with as they please.
> Let them continually beat it, insult it, and splatter it with filth. (3.12)
> Let them play with my body; let them be derisive and amuse themselves.
> I have given this body to them. What point has this concern of mine? (3.13)[27]

The irony here is that the more the bodhisattva dedicates his physical body wholly to the service of others, the more he stands to gain for himself—for due to what Stephen Jenkins has described as a "productive paradox" lying at the heart of Mahāyāna thought (and evident throughout Śāntideva's works), self-interest (*svārtha*) and other-interest (*parārtha*) are mutually intertwined: nothing is more beneficial to one's own self-interest than to act solely for the interests of others, and conversely, one cannot be effective in furthering the interests of others without paying due attention to the development of oneself.[28] The bodhisattva must therefore recognize the body's worth both in pursuing his own interests and in pursuing the interests of others—which ultimately amount to the same thing.

Once again, however, Śāntideva must exercise some caution, constantly adjusting the medicine he administers. For when he encourages the bodhisattva to wholly abandon his body to others "to do with as they please"—even to "beat it, insult it, and splatter it with filth"—his self-degrading language swings the pendulum back the other way and veers perilously close to the overly worthless body that is discounted, neglected, and thereby lost. The bodhisattva who takes such language to heart—and who is familiar with the many famous Buddhist stories involving bodhisattvas engaging in gruesome deeds of bodily self-sacrifice[29]—is liable to pursue the welfare of others so zealously that he ends up wastefully throwing his own body away. After all, if the body has been dedicated wholly to the welfare of others, why not just let oneself, for example, be devoured by wild and hungry animals—as the Buddha himself did in many of his previous lives?[30] In order to guard against this kind of mistake, Śāntideva includes several verses that place the act of bodily self-sacrifice within its proper context and ensure that it is not performed prematurely.

To understand Śāntideva's attitude toward the paradigmatic bodhisattva deed of bodily self-sacrifice, we can turn to his other famous work, the *Training Anthology.* As several scholars have noted,[31] this training manual for monastic bodhisattvas organizes the entire path to buddhahood in terms of the three categories of the bodhisattva's body (*ātmabhāva*), enjoyments (*bhoga*), and merit (*puṇya*). It then instructs the bodhisattva to engage in four activities with regard to these three categories: He should protect them (√*rakṣ*), he should purify them (√*śudh*), he should enhance them (√*vṛddh*), and he should give them away (√*dā*). In other words, the ultimate goal of the bodhisattva is to attain awakening by giving away his body, enjoyments, and merit—but in order for such gifts to be effective in accomplishing the welfare of others, these things must *first* be preserved, purified, and enhanced, for only then will they have their proper salutary effect. Once again, we are reminded that not all bodies are the same, and only some bodies are morally transformative for others. Bodily self-sacrifice therefore stands near the end of the bodhisattva path, appropriate only for advanced bodhisattvas, whereas most of the path should rather be focused on protecting, purifying, and enhancing the body one is lucky enough to have.

Thus, at the same time that Śāntideva encourages the bodhisattva to dedicate his body solely to the service of others, he also takes pains to make it clear that "abandoning the body" does *not* mean wastefully throwing it away in a premature and ill-considered act of self-sacrifice. "One should not harm [the body] for some inferior reason," he reminds us, for "[this] body serves the True Dharma"—and treating its disposition thoughtfully "is the only way that one can quickly fulfill the hopes of living beings."[32] He continues (this time, using the Wallace and Wallace translation): "Therefore, when [one's] thought of compassion is impure, one should not sacrifice one's life, but it should be sacrificed when one's thought is unbiased."[33] Here, Prajñākaramati's commentary makes clear that a thought that is "unbiased" (*tulya*) is one that prudently considers how best to secure the welfare of both oneself and others (*svaparahitārtha*) before deciding to engage in self-sacrifice.[34] A gift of one's body that brings about minimal benefit for others at enormous cost to oneself is thereby precluded. For although it is true that self-interest and other-interest ultimately merge together, they do not do so in all immediate circumstances, and the bodhisattva on the earlier stages of the path must act with prudence to preserve and develop his human body until it *becomes* a gift that will truly benefit others.

Śāntideva's cautious treatment of bodily self-sacrifice serves to illustrate a larger point: throughout the *Guide*, Śāntideva must devise a careful therapeutic regimen for the aspiring bodhisattva, sometimes dispensing a dose of the body's worthlessness and sometimes dispensing a dose of the body's worth. The ambiguity surrounding the question of what the "proper" attitude toward the body should be is perhaps best summed up by the juxtaposition of these two consecutive lines: "Therefore, without regret, I abandon my body to the benefit of the world. For this reason, though it has many faults, I carry it as a tool for the task."[35] The same body is both "abandoned" (√*tyaj*) and "carried" (√*dhṛ*)[36]—both full of "many faults" and yet an essential "tool for the task." The bodhisattva must be flexible and learn to cultivate either one attitude or the other, depending upon what is needed at any particular time.

As one cultivates these varying attitudes, moreover, the actual body itself is not just an unchanging blank slate upon which purely mental attitudes are projected. Instead, as the *Training Anthology* has reminded us, mind and body transform together, and the body itself is thus "purified" and "enhanced" by mental attitudes that are skillfully cultivated. Here, we return again to the realm of actual bodies: just as one seeks, at a minimum, to avoid a particular kind of body—the suffering body of a low rebirth—and to take advantage of a particular kind of body—the body of a human being—so also one's ultimate goal is to achieve a particular kind of body: the glorious body of a fully awakened buddha or advanced bodhisattva, a body that paradoxically reverses all of the bodily limitations and deficiencies whose realization helps to bring it about, a body that effortlessly fulfills the interests of both oneself and others. Śāntideva does not describe these "beautiful forms" (*sadvapuṣaḥ*)[37] at any length, but he does recognize their value as inspiring examples, especially at the beginning of the path. Near the beginning of the *Guide*, in his version of the Mahāyāna liturgy known as the "Supreme Worship" (*anuttara-pūjā*), Śāntideva instructs the beginner bodhisattva to worship all buddhas and bodhisattvas through an elaborate meditative offering that includes ample attention to honoring their *bodies*: "I bathe the Tathāgatas and their sons . . . I wipe down their bodies with cloths beyond compare . . . I present them with the finest robes . . . I adorn [them] . . . I anoint [their] bodies . . . I envelop them in heady clouds of incense . . . I make them an offering of foods . . . and many kinds of drink."[38] Here, the body that is so lovingly pampered is not only an object of worship but also the body the bodhisattva himself ultimately seeks to attain.

The bodhisattva's ability to transform his "festering contraption made of filth" into the jewel-like body of a buddha can be explained, as we have seen, by invoking the interpenetration of the moral and physical orders and their gradual, mutual evolution over time. Nevertheless, this transformation must finally strike us as a miracle, a mystery, an unbelievable wonder—one that Śāntideva can only celebrate by likening to the pure magic of alchemy.[39] At the very beginning of the *Guide*, Śāntideva offers us a long litany of praise in honor of *bodhicitta*—the "Awakening Mind" or aspiration to buddhahood that makes all things possible, and the crucial element around which he structures the entire bodhisattva path. He urges us to "grasp tightly" this "quicksilver elixir, known as the Awakening Mind," which transmutes "this base image" (*aśuci-pratimām*)—the human body—into "the priceless image of the Buddha-gem" (*jina-ratna-pratimām anarghām*).[40] For a fuller explanation of this verse, we can turn to the esteemed early twentieth-century Tibetan commentator Kunzang Pelden:

> Here, bodhichitta is described using an example taken from alchemy, the point of comparison being the transformation of something bad into something good. By means of the supreme substance, the elixir of the alchemists (the gold-producing mercury), a single ounce of iron may be transmuted into a thousand ounces of pure gold. In the same way, if, with bodhichitta, one lays hold of this lowly human body composed of numerous impure substances, and if, instead of rejecting it as the Shravakas do, one adopts it throughout the course of many lifetimes in order to secure the welfare of others, this [human] body will itself become the body of the Buddha. It becomes something endowed with unimaginable qualities of excellence: a priceless wish-fulfilling jewel.[41]

This is the miracle made possible by the bodhisattva's compassionate intention toward others, a miracle in which the minimal "worth" of the human body as a necessary evil magically transforms itself into the maximal "worth" of "a priceless wish-fulfilling jewel." This is what allows Śāntideva, in formulating his bodhisattva vows, to speak of his hoped-for body in self-aggrandizing terms that are the very opposite of the self-debasing language used elsewhere in the text—envisioning himself as "the boat, the causeway, and the bridge for those who long to reach the further shore," "a light for those in need of light," "a bed for those in need of rest," "a servant for those in need of service," "the wish-fulfilling jewel, the pot of plenty, the spell that always works, the potent healing herb, the magical tree that grants every wish, and the milch-cow that supplies all wants."[42] The physical nature of these metaphors (bed, jewel, pot, tree, cow) reminds us again that the ultimate goal of buddhahood is not just moral, mental, or spiritual in nature, but also concretely *material*. In other words, it involves a *body:* an unimaginably great body, a body that satisfies everyone, the very best body ever.

WISDOM, COMPASSION, AND THE BODY

Śāntideva's concern in composing the *Guide* was not simply to outline the bodhisattva path, but also to elucidate one of its most crucial elements: the wisdom (*prajñā*) that penetrates the veil of appearances and sees things "the way they really are." As he tells us in the very first verse of the much-heralded chapter 9 (devoted to the bodhisattva's "perfection of wisdom" or *prajñā-pāramitā*), "The Sage taught this entire system for the sake of wisdom."[43] For without the development and perfection of wisdom, the bodhisattva's compassionate intention can never effectively come to fruition. Wisdom consists, for Śāntideva, of seeing reality through the lens of fundamental Buddhist doctrines such as no-self (*anātman*), dependent origination (*pratītya-samutpāda*), and emptiness (*śūnyatā*)—all of which involve the subjection of entities to an acute analysis that finally dissolves them into nothing that can be grasped onto. The body plays a major role within this process, both as an entity whose analysis helps to clarify the absence of any self (*ātman*) and as an entity that can itself be dissolved into essencelessness and thereby serve as a model for the analysis of all such entities.

The first step in this process is to undermine one's inherent belief in a self by considering the self's relationship to the body: if there *is* a self, one should ask, is it identical to the body or distinct from the body? Is it equivalent to the parts of the body, taken singly or as a whole, or does it reside somewhere outside of these parts? The bodhisattva will soon come to realize that none of these options is tenable—for example:

The teeth, hair, or nails are not I, nor is the bone, nor am I the blood, neither the mucus nor the phlegm, not the pus nor the synovial fluid. (9.57)
I am neither the marrow nor the sweat. I am neither the lymph nor the intestines. I am not the rectum, nor am I the excrement or the urine. (9.58)
I am neither the flesh nor the sinews. I am neither heat nor wind. I am neither the orifices nor, in any way, the six consciousnesses. (9.59)[44]

Employing a mode of analysis well known in the Buddhist tradition ever since Nāgasena asked King Milinda to locate his "chariot,"[45] Śāntideva uses the concrete materiality of the body and its different parts to undermine our unshakable conviction in the existence of the self (*ātman*). By attempting to tie the ephemeral self to the physical reality of the body, we come to understand that the "self"—as Nāgasena has told us—is just a name, an appellation, a convenient designation we use to identify the conglomeration of these parts.

Yet even the solidity of the body is deceptive, for in the next step of the process, Śāntideva performs the same analysis on the so-called "body"—reducing it too to nothing more than a temporary label:

The body is not the feet, not the calves, not the thighs . . . not the buttocks . . . not the stomach nor the back . . . nor is it the chest nor arms. (9.78)
. . . What among these, then, is the body? (9.79)
If you argue that the body is present in part in all of these, [our response is that] it is only the parts that are present in the parts, so where does it occur itself? (9.80)
If the body did exist in its entirety in the hands and all these other parts, then there would be just as many bodies as there are hands and other parts. (9.81)
. . . How can the body be in the hands and other parts? It is not separate from the hands and other parts. How, then, is it to be found? (9.82)
So there is no body. Yet, under the influence of delusion, there is the belief in a body regarding the hands and other parts, because of their particular configuration. (9.83)[46]

Having eradicated the self by recourse to the body, Śāntideva now leads us to eradicate the body by recourse to its multiple parts. The body that constitutes perhaps *the* primary physical fact of our experience thus quickly dissolves into multiplicity. But why stop there?

In the same way, since it is an assemblage of toes, which one is the foot? The same goes for a toe, since it is an assemblage of joints. A joint can also be analysed into its own constituents. (9.85)
Even the constituents can be analysed down to atoms. The atom too can be divided according to the directions. The division of a direction, since it is without parts, leaves space. Therefore the atom does not exist. (9.86)
What person who analyses things thoroughly would take delight in a form which, as has been demonstrated, is like a dream? (9.87)[47]

The entire material world around us thus dissolves into a shimmering illusion, "like a dream." And "when neither entity nor non-entity remains before the mind"—Śāntideva states (in the verse during whose recitation legend says he rose into the air and disappeared)—"since there is no other mode of operation, grasping no objects, [the mind] becomes tranquil."[48]

With the body as a basis, Śāntideva thus moves from the early Buddhist notion of no-self (*anātman*) to the more thoroughgoing Mahāyāna assertion of emptiness (*śūnyatā*), or the lack of inherent existence that characterizes all things. The body in this analysis is, I believe, not merely one illustrative example out of many that could have been chosen (like, for example, "chariot"). Instead, since mind and body transform together and in mutual dependence, subjecting the body to this analysis (especially in meditation) ensures that the wisdom one acquires is an *embodied* wisdom and that the body itself is transformed in the process. After all, fully realizing the emptiness of the body—and thus its changeability and endless creative potential—is what makes possible the transformation of the "festering contraption made of filth" into "a priceless wish-fulfilling jewel." The body thus plays a crucial role in Śāntideva's exposition of wisdom.

Yet in spite of the necessity of dissolving both the self and the body under the penetrating gaze of wisdom, Śāntideva never loses sight of the usefulness of these constructs in cultivating the essential counterpart of wisdom: compassion. Thus, at the same time as he seeks to deconstruct "self" and "body" and reveal their illusory nature, Śāntideva also takes advantage of our innate belief in their existence, strategically deploying both notions to encourage our compassion for others. The unity of the body so thoroughly demolished in the verses cited above elsewhere becomes a powerful impetus for compassion when it is imaginatively projected upon all others:

Just as the body, with its many parts from division into hands and other limbs, should be protected as a single entity, so too should this entire

> world which is divided, but undivided in its nature to suffer and be happy. (8.91)
>
> In the same way that the hands and other limbs are loved because they form part of the body, why are embodied creatures not likewise loved because they form part of the universe? (8.114)[49]

Far from dissolving the body down into its parts, as we saw above, here the bodhisattva projects his sense of the body's unity upon all other beings. In this way, he will grow in his compassion for others and work to protect them with as much concern as he protects his own body. The bodhisattva's attachment to his body and constant efforts to protect it, which are ordinarily harmful, become beneficial once their power has been harnessed in the service of others. Again, this is the paradox brought about by compassion for others—as Śāntideva states, "All those who suffer in the world do so because of their desire for their own happiness. All those happy in the world are so because of their desire for the happiness of others."[50]

In a similar manner, rather than eradicating one's sense of a self by questioning its relationship to the body (as we saw above), the bodhisattva can benefit from his sense of a self by placing that self within the bodies of others:

> Through habituation there is the understanding of "I" regarding the drops of sperm and blood of two other people, even though there is in fact no such thing. (8.111)
>
> Why can I not also accept another's body as my self in the same way, since the otherness of my own body has been settled and is not hard to accept? (8.112)
>
> In the same way that, with practice, the idea of a self arose towards this, one's own body, though it is without a self, with practice will not the same idea of a self develop towards others too? (8.115)
>
> Therefore, just as you have formed the notion "I" regarding others' drops of sperm and blood, you must also develop that notion regarding other people. (8.158)[51]

Here, the bodhisattva encourages (rather than eradicating) his innate belief in the self and its connection with the body—but he changes its moral valence by tying this self to the bodies of others. By placing his self in the bodies of others, he will naturally come to work for their welfare just as zealously as he once worked for his own, and he will benefit rather than suffer from his innate belief in a self. He can only perform this maneuver, however, because there is no "self" to begin with, and the "self" can therefore be placed wherever it will be most beneficial. In this way, attitudes that are detrimental from the point of view of wisdom can be cleverly manipulated to become beneficial from the point of view of compassion—yet this manipulation itself is only made possible through the wisdom that realizes emptiness.[52] Wisdom and compassion merge together, self-interest and other-interest become the same, the worthlessness and worth of the body are perfectly balanced—until the miracle of buddhahood is finally attained.

CONCLUSION: THE BODY AS PATH AND GOAL

In spite of the ample attention Śāntideva pays to the primacy of the mind, the body is also crucial to his aims in composing the *Guide*. Yet, as we have seen, to speak of "the body" is not a simple matter, for the "body" in question is multifarious and constantly shifting. At the beginning of the *Guide*, Śāntideva provides a twofold classification of *bodhicitta*—as "the Mind resolved on Awakening and the Mind proceeding towards Awakening"[53]—and the same distinction can perhaps be applied to the body as well: in other words, the body as *goal* and the body as *path*, the body one is aiming for and the body as a tool to get there. Neither of these two conceptions is singular in nature, however, but is presented in multiple ways to appeal to multiple practitioners and to speak to aspiring bodhisattvas at every level of the path.

For the body as goal, the *Guide* affirms a complex hierarchy of different bodily goals, ranging from avoiding the suffering that afflicts the worst kinds of bodies to taking full advantage of the most beneficial body available within samsara, to dissolving the "body" into emptiness, and finally, to acquiring the glorious, golden body of a buddha or bodhisattva. The body is not only the goal, however, but also the path that leads to the desired goal—or, as Śāntideva puts it, an "implement of action" or "tool for the task."[54] Again, the tool is a multipurpose one (a veritable Swiss army knife), for throughout the text, Śāntideva deploys the tool of the body in multifarious ways: the body is worthless and disgusting and should be abandoned; the body is a necessary evil that should be cared for and maintained; the body is a "wish-fulfilling jewel" or "pot of plenty" that leads all beings to full awakening. The body should not be identified with—unless we identify with the bodies of others. The body is a construct that dissolves into emptiness—unless we take all beings as the body itself. Ultimately, however, path and goal merge together—just as mind-and-body transform together—as the successful reader of Śāntideva's text uses the "quicksilver elixir" of *bodhicitta* to change his filthy and "base image" into the "priceless image of the Buddha-gem."[55]

NOTES

1. Mrozik, *Virtuous Bodies.*
2. Mrozik, *Virtuous Bodies,* 34.
3. Śāntideva, *The Bodhicaryāvatāra,* trans. Crosby and Skilton. On two occasions (as indicated in the notes), I have used an alternative translation.
4. *Guide* 4.14. Śāntideva, *The Bodhicaryāvatāra,* trans. Crosby and Skilton, 26.
5. *Guide* 4.25. Śāntideva, *The Bodhicaryāvatāra,* trans. Crosby and Skilton, 27.
6. *Guide* 7.45. Śāntideva, *The Bodhicaryāvatāra,* trans. Crosby and Skilton, 71.
7. *Guide* 7.10. Śāntideva, *The Bodhicaryāvatāra,* trans. Crosby and Skilton, 67.
8. *Guide* 4.15–16. Śāntideva, *The Bodhicaryāvatāra,* trans. Crosby and Skilton, 26.
9. Faure, "Substitute Bodies in Chan/Zen Buddhism," 212.
10. For a fuller discussion of these two lines of thinking regarding the human body, see Ohnuma, *Head, Eyes, Flesh, and Blood,* 201–205.
11. *Guide* 5.61. Śāntideva, *The Bodhicaryāvatāra,* trans. Crosby and Skilton, 39.
12. *Guide* 5.65. Śāntideva, *The Bodhicaryāvatāra,* trans. Crosby and Skilton, 39.
13. *Guide* 5.62–63. Śāntideva, *The Bodhicaryāvatāra,* trans. Crosby and Skilton, 39; Vaidya, ed., *Bodhicaryāvatāra,* 65.
14. *Guide* 5.64. Śāntideva, *The Bodhicaryāvatāra,* trans. Crosby and Skilton, 39.
15. *Guide* 8.30–31. Śāntideva, *The Bodhicaryāvatāra,* trans. Crosby and Skilton, 90.
16. *Guide* 8.178. Śāntideva, *The Bodhicaryāvatāra,* trans. Crosby and Skilton, 104.
17. *Guide* 8.181. Śāntideva, *The Bodhicaryāvatāra,* trans. Crosby and Skilton, 104.
18. *Guide* 8.43. Śāntideva, *The Bodhicaryāvatāra,* trans. Crosby and Skilton, 91.
19. *Guide* 8.47. Śāntideva, *The Bodhicaryāvatāra,* trans. Crosby and Skilton, 92.
20. Śāntideva, *The Bodhicaryāvatāra,* trans. Crosby and Skilton, 92–93. I have quoted these verses out of sequence, but they all appear in a single long passage.
21. Wilson, *Charming Cadavers.*
22. *Guide* 4.16. Śāntideva, *The Bodhicaryāvatāra,* trans. Crosby and Skilton, 26. Here, the translators note: "We have taken the reading *kāyo yācitakopamaḥ,* giving 'The body is like an object on loan,' rather than the *kāyopācitakopamaḥ* of de la Vallée Poussin's edition, for which we see no meaning" (Śāntideva, *The Bodhicaryāvatāra,* trans. Crosby and Skilton, 151).
23. Śāntideva, *The Bodhicaryāvatāra,* trans. Crosby and Skilton, 40.
24. *Guide* 5.66. Śāntideva, *The Bodhicaryāvatāra,* trans. Crosby and Skilton, 39; Vaidya, *Bodhicaryāvatāra,* 65.
25. *Guide* 5.70. Śāntideva, *The Bodhicaryāvatāra,* trans. Crosby and Skilton, 40.
26. *Guide* 8.184. Śāntideva, *The Bodhicaryāvatāra,* trans. Crosby and Skilton, 104.
27. Śāntideva, *The Bodhicaryāvatāra,* trans. Crosby and Skilton, 21.
28. Jenkins, "Benefit of Self and Other."
29. On this genre of Buddhist narrative, see Ohnuma, *Head, Eyes, Flesh, and Blood.*
30. Most famously, perhaps, in the story of the bodhisattva allowing himself to be devoured by a hungry tigress in order to keep her from devouring her own newborn

cubs; this story is related, for example, in the *Jātakamālā*, the *Avadānakalpalatā*, and the *Suvarṇabhāsottama Sūtra*.

31. For example, Mrozik, *Virtuous Bodies*; Mahoney, "Of the Progress of the Bodhisattva"; and Goodman, trans., *The Training Anthology of Śāntideva*. See also Harrison's contribution to this volume.
32. *Guide* 5.86. Śāntideva, *The Bodhicaryāvatāra*, trans. Crosby and Skilton, 41.
33. *Guide* 5.87. Wallace and Wallace, trans., *A Guide to the Bodhisattva Way of Life*, 57. For this verse, I have made use of the translation by Wallace and Wallace rather than that of Crosby and Skilton. In the latter, the first line of the verse reads, "Therefore, one should not relinquish one's life for someone whose disposition to compassion is not as pure"—which suggests that one should consider the recipient's disposition to compassion rather than one's own (Śāntideva, *The Bodhicaryāvatāra*, trans. Crosby and Skilton, 41). I read this line (in agreement with Wallace and Wallace) as referring to the giver's thought of compassion rather than the recipient's. The whole verse reads: *tyajen na jīvitaṃ tasmād aśuddhe karuṇāśaye / tulyāśaye tu tat tyājyam itthaṃ na parihīyate //* (Vaidya, *Bodhicaryāvatāra*, 71). The meaning can be further clarified by considering the explanation of the early twentieth-century Tibetan commentator Kunzang Pelden: "The compassionate attitude of a beginner is not pure. Therefore until one reaches Perfect Joy, the first of the Bodhisattva grounds, one should refrain from actually giving away one's body (one's head or one's limbs), which is the basis for the practice of the sublime Dharma. For it is not certain that such actions will be of benefit to others. It is also possible that one will have regrets, which will in turn create obstacles to the practice of virtue . . . But such sacrifices can be made when they are beneficial for the teaching and for beings in this and future lives, and when they are not an obstacle to virtue." Padmakara Translation Group, trans., *The Nectar of Manjushri's Speech*, 190.
34. Vaidya, *Bodhicaryāvatāra*, 71.
35. *Guide* 8.184. Śāntideva, *The Bodhicaryāvatāra*, trans. Crosby and Skilton, 104.
36. Vaidya, *Bodhicaryāvatāra*, 166.
37. *Guide* 7.44. Śāntideva, *The Bodhicaryāvatāra*, trans. Crosby and Skilton, 71; Vaidya, *Bodhicaryāvatāra*, 126.
38. *Guide* 2.11–16. Śāntideva, *The Bodhicaryāvatāra*, trans. Crosby and Skilton, 15.
39. For a discussion of this image, see Harris, "The Skillful Handling of Poison." The same comparison is made in the *Śikṣāsamuccaya*, as discussed by Mrozik (*Virtuous Bodies* 47–48).
40. *Guide* 1.10. Śāntideva, *The Bodhicaryāvatāra*, trans. Crosby and Skilton, 6; Vaidya, *Bodhicaryāvatāra*, 8.
41. Padmakara Translation Group, *The Nectar of Manjushri's Speech*, 48.
42. *Guide* 3.17–19. Śāntideva, *The Bodhicaryāvatāra*, trans. Crosby and Skilton, 21.
43. *Guide* 9.1. Wallace and Wallace, *Guide to the Bodhisattva Way of Life*, 115. I have used the Wallace and Wallace translation for this verse because I prefer their translation of *prajñā* as "wisdom" over Crosby and Skilton's translation of *prajñā* as "understanding," which strikes me as a bit too weak. Crosby and Skilton's translation of the line in question is: "It is for the sake of understanding that the Sage taught this entire collection of preparations" (Śāntideva, *The Bodhicaryāvatāra*, 115).
44. Śāntideva, *The Bodhicaryāvatāra*, trans. Crosby and Skilton, 121.
45. I am referring, of course, to the famous passage from the Pāli text, the *Questions of King Milinda* (*Milindapañha*), in which the monk Nāgasena explains the Buddhist doctrine of no-self to King Milinda through the analogy of a chariot: Just as

"chariot" is merely a label we use to designate the conglomeration of the wheels, carriage, reins, and so forth, but does not exist independently, the same is also true of the self. For a translation of this passage, see Strong, ed., *The Experience of Buddhism*, 101–104.

46. *Guide* 9.78–83. Śāntideva, *The Bodhicaryāvatāra,* trans. Crosby and Skilton, 123.
47. Śāntideva, *The Bodhicaryāvatāra,* trans. Crosby and Skilton, 124.
48. *Guide* 9.34. Śāntideva, *The Bodhicaryāvatāra,* trans. Crosby and Skilton, 118.
49. Śāntideva, *The Bodhicaryāvatāra,* trans. Crosby and Skilton, 96 and 98.
50. *Guide* 8.129. Śāntideva, *The Bodhicaryāvatāra,* trans. Crosby and Skilton, 99.
51. Śāntideva, *The Bodhicaryāvatāra,* trans. Crosby and Skilton, 98 and 102.
52. For another discussion of this process, see Harris, "Skillful Handling of Poison."
53. *Guide* 1.15. Śāntideva, *The Bodhicaryāvatāra,* trans. Crosby and Skilton, 6.
54. *Guide* 5.66 (*karmopakaraṇa*); *Guide* 8.184 (*karmabhāṇḍa*). Śāntideva, *The Bodhicaryāvatāra,* trans. Crosby and Skilton, 39 and 104; Vaidya, *Bodhicaryāvatāra,* 65 and 166.
55. *Guide* 1.10. Śāntideva, *The Bodhicaryāvatāra,* trans. Crosby and Skilton, 6.

REFERENCES

Faure, Bernard. "Substitute Bodies in Chan/Zen Buddhism." In *Religious Reflections on the Human Body,* ed. Jane Marie Law, 211–229. Bloomington: Indiana University Press, 1995.

Goodman, Charles, trans. *The Training Anthology of Śāntideva: A Translation of the Śikṣā-samuccaya*. New York: Oxford University Press, 2016.

Harris, Stephen E. "The Skillful Handling of Poison: *Bodhicitta* and the *Kleśas* in Śāntideva's *Bodhicaryāvatāra.*" *Journal of Indian Philosophy* 45 (2017): 331–348.

Jenkins, Stephen L. "Benefit of Self and Other: The Importance of Persons and Their Self-Interest in Buddhist Ethics." *Dharma Drum Journal of Buddhist Studies* 16 (2015): 141–169.

Mahoney, Richard. "Of the Progresse of the Bodhisattva: The Bodhisattvamārga in the Śikṣāsamuccaya." M.A. thesis, University of Canterbury, 2002.

Mrozik, Susanne. *Virtuous Bodies: The Physical Dimensions of Morality in Buddhist Ethics*. New York: Oxford University Press, 2007.

Ohnuma, Reiko. *Head, Eyes, Flesh, and Blood: Giving Away the Body in Indian Buddhist Literature*. New York: Columbia University Press, 2007.

Padmakara Translation Group, trans. *The Nectar of Manjushri's Speech: A Detailed Commentary on Shantideva's* Way of the Bodhisattva. Boston: Shambhala, 2010.

Śāntideva. *The Bodhicaryāvatāra*. Trans. Kate Crosby and Andrew Skilton. Oxford World Classics. Oxford: Oxford University Press, 1998.

——. *A Guide to the Bodhisattva Way of Life (Bodhicaryāvatāra).* Trans. Vesna A. Wallace and B. Alan Wallace. Ithaca, NY: Snow Lion, 1997.

Strong, John S., ed. *The Experience of Buddhism: Sources and Interpretations.* 3rd ed. Belmont, CA: Thomson Wadsworth, 2008.

Vaidya, P. L., ed. *Bodhicaryāvatāra of Śāntideva with the Commentary Pañjikā of Prajñākaramati.* Buddhist Sanskrit Texts, No. 12. Darbhanga: Mithila Institute, 1960.

Wilson, Liz. *Charming Cadavers: Figurations of the Feminine in Indian Buddhist Hagiographic Literature.* Chicago: University of Chicago Press, 1996.

[7]

RITUAL STRUCTURE AND MATERIAL CULTURE IN THE *GUIDE TO BODHISATTVA PRACTICE*

Eric Huntington

THE GUIDE *to Bodhisattva Practice* (*Bodhicaryāvatāra*, henceforth *Guide*) is rightly praised as a literary masterpiece of philosophy and ethics, so some modern readers might be surprised to learn of the importance of ritual and devotion both in Śāntideva's own text and in its broader reception in Buddhist history. Indeed, while the *Guide* compellingly portrays the internal struggles of an author, it clearly relies on a framework of common Buddhist practices and even serves as a basis for ritual in and of itself. If nothing else, such rituals provide a structure that reinforces specific progressions along the Buddhist path. Complementing the personal transformations through self-awareness that are foregrounded by the text, these rituals employ faith in higher powers and repetition to bolster the practitioner at critical moments. Accompanying its captivating philosophy and ethics, then, the *Guide* can be read to reveal actual practices of physical and material worship, such as making offerings to artistic images of the Buddha placed on an altar. Such activities are among the most common forms of Buddhist religiosity, and while they are only loosely addressed in Śāntideva's training text, they clearly underlie its composition and practice.

This chapter investigates the overall ritual structure of the *Guide* and describes material practices that correspond to specific passages. As with many aspects of Buddhist tradition, these rituals allow multiple, simultaneous levels of interpretation. In one sense, many of the rituals of the text directly support its well-known goals of mental transformation. Rituals of confession and dedication, in which one repeatedly rejects bad actions and devotes oneself to the benefit of others, may be considered mechanisms for improving the habits of one's mind. Such practices can also be understood in terms of faith and material performance. Confession, for example, depends on the real or imagined presence of a more awakened being to act as recipient and help subjects overcome the negative consequences of their past mistakes. The confession ritual described later in this chapter invokes thirty-five separate buddhas who are frequently depicted in paintings as a visual support for the practice. More elaborate rituals of offering involve not only artistic images of buddhas but also the daily placement of precious substances on altars, recitations, and other activities rarely noted when the *Guide* is treated solely in terms of its doctrines.

In order to address both the broad scope of ritual in the *Guide* and a few specific, material examples, this chapter comprises two distinct halves. The first identifies the overall ritual structure of the *Guide* and introduces two types of ritual central to the text, the unexcelled worship (*anuttara-pūjā*) and the bodhisattva vow (*praṇidhāna*). Structurally speaking, such formalized rituals bookend the *Guide* in its beginning and ending chapters, suggesting that the entire composition can be read within a ritual framework, complementary to its meditational strategies and philosophical arguments. The repetition of certain rituals, including confession and dedication, further suggests a changing significance of these practices as one progresses through stages of personal development. Activities initially performed out of faith in an external Buddha eventually become internalized, modeling the transformation of the practitioner toward awakening.

The second section of the chapter deals with two rituals that are more obliquely revealed in the text but provide a much clearer sense of the specific material objects, art forms, and practices that an adherent might engage alongside philosophical and ethical meditations. Here the focus is not on Śāntideva's own context, but rather on the connections of his text to the major ritual and material traditions of later forms of Himalayan Buddhism, especially rituals of offering (*pūjā*) and confession (*pāpa-deśanā*). Both rituals emphasize not just personal transformation but specific, contrasting relationships between a ritual performer and an awakened other. In offering, one presents good objects as a sign of respect to this other, while in confession, one seeks to abandon bad actions in reliance on the assistance of the other.[1] Both rituals involve artistic images of awakened figures as supports. Offering additionally requires the presentation of various material substances to these supports, including everything from bowls filled daily with water on an altar to representations of the entire cosmos given as a sign of vast devotion.

FRAMEWORKS AND FOUNDATIONS

Just as the *Guide* can be read as a stepwise cultivation of emotional, moral, and intellectual qualities, so too can it be understood in terms of a ritual progression, or even better, as a complementary combination of the two. Śāntideva's text begins with rituals that prepare his mind for the meditations that follow, and it ends with a practice that models the culmination of awakening transformation. In this sense, Śāntideva uses ritual as a tool, a means of habit formation to improve the mind to the point where scripted ritual is no longer necessary. Throughout the *Guide*, these activities emphasize the development of two phases of the awakening mind (*bodhicitta*), the key feature of the Mahāyāna Buddhist path.

Mahāyāna Buddhism prioritizes the ideal of the bodhisattva, a being who desires to become awakened not for their own benefit, but so that they can help all other beings. The mind awakening for the sake of all other beings is understood to arise in two stages, as Śāntideva defines at the outset of the *Guide*:[2]

> The awakening mind should be understood to be of two kinds; in brief: the mind resolved on awakening and the mind proceeding towards awakening. (1.15)
>
> The distinction between these two should be understood by the wise in the same way as the distinction is recognized between a person who desires to go and one who is going, in that order. (1.16)

In other words, the first is the mind intent on awakening; the second is the mind that is actively awakening. Whether the *Guide* is interpreted in terms of philosophy, ethics, or ritual performance, it unequivocally prioritizes the development of the awakening mind at every step.

In broad outline, the first three chapters of the *Guide* establish the mind intent on awakening, with the remaining chapters shifting to develop the mind that is actively awakening (see the chapter by Harrison in this volume).[3] The first chapter praises the awakening mind, with chapters 2 and 3 building on this exaltation to engender the intention for awakening. Chapter 4 argues that one must turn intention into action, in part because abandoning the intention would effectively prevent benefit for other living beings, an inherently bad action. The fifth through ninth chapters develop the actively awakening mind by cultivating six perfections (*pāramitā*), purified behaviors and mental attitudes conducive to complete awakening. In addressing the first two perfections, chapter 5 suggests that the key to success is the improvement of one's mind, a process that culminates in the ninth chapter's perfection of wisdom. Finally, chapter 10 recalls the ritual that concludes chapter 3 to exemplify the awakening mind realized at the completion of the text.

The first three chapters develop one's intention for awakening specifically through the ritual of unexcelled worship, which follows a formulaic procedure even as it promotes a compelling series of mental states. Categorizations of the stages of unexcelled worship differ, but often include several (usually seven) of the following:[4]

a. praise (*vandanā*)
b. worship (*pūjanā*)
c. going for refuge (*śaraṇa-gamana*)
d. confession of misdeeds (*pāpa-deśanā*)
e. rejoicing in merits (*puṇyānumodanā*)
f. request [for the buddhas to teach] (*adhyeṣaṇā*)
g. supplication [for the buddhas to remain] (*yācanā*)
h. dedication [of merit] (*pariṇāmanā*)

Although it is most commonly understood as a separate activity, arousal of the awakening mind (*bodhicittotpāda*) is sometimes also listed as one of the final steps of this sequence.[5] In any case, Śāntideva seems to view arousal of the awakening mind as a natural conclusion to the unexcelled worship process.[6] In psychological terms, praise of the awakening mind establishes it as a worthy goal. Once the awakening mind is respected, the practitioner develops a positive personal relationship with awakened beings by making offerings to them and relying on them for refuge. Comparing their own minds to these ideals, practitioners confess their shortcomings and celebrate the merits of others. Subsequently desiring improvement, they request the teachings of the Buddha and beseech the teachers to remain to continue instruction. Realizing that the desire to improve oneself alone is selfish, they dedicate all the good results of their actions to the benefit of others, setting the stage for arousal of the awakening mind.[7]

The dedication of merit and subsequent arousal of the awakening mind can be understood as a key transformation of the bodhisattva path—devotion to the benefit and awakening of others through the awakening of oneself. Indeed, the dedication and arousal recur in chapter 10, the very culmination of the *Guide* as a whole. Placed at the conclusion, after the meditative practices and philosophical discussions, chapter 10 can be read as exemplifying a new achievement of mental and ethical development, especially if one views the *Guide* in its entirety as a ritual framework for personal transformation.

Admittedly, there are many ways to understand this tenth chapter, not all of which prioritize ritual structure. In the least engaged, it is little more than an anticlimax following the dramatic and philosophically challenging chapter on wisdom (chapter 9) that expresses the full insight of awakening. More judiciously, Jonathan Gold reads the tenth chapter homogeneously with the rest of the text, as an exercise in generating merit (*puṇya*) through good thoughts and deeds (see chapter by Jonathan Gold). Crosby and Skilton alternatively suggest that the tenth chapter reveals something unique in the *Guide*, specifically the accomplishment of Śāntideva's second kind of awakening mind, the mind that is actively awakening.[8] They describe the dedications in chapter 10 as: "on a far grander scale, because [the bodhisattva] can dedicate the far greater merit acquired by putting his resolve for awakening into action. . . . Through his training in the perfections [of the previous chapters] he has become a bodhisattva."[9] In other words, by performing numerous good thoughts and deeds with the actualized intention to help all beings, the practitioner develops significantly greater merit to dedicate to others.

This transformation at the end of the *Guide* can be taken one step further, for the tenth chapter can also be read as transcending questions of personal merit to model the completely awakened mind. In the dedicatory verses in chapters 3 and 10, the grammar shifts noticeably from the first person to the third person, as exemplified in the following parallel passages:

> May I be (*bhaveyaṃ*) [both a doctor and a nurse for the sick] . . . (3.7)
> Let there be (*astu*) [health for the sick] . . . (10.22)[10]

In the latter, the wish is expressed without any wisher, epitomizing a purely selfless compassion generated through the insight into emptiness that is described in the preceding, ninth chapter. Overcoming the false view that one has an essential self makes the intending agent disappear from view, and one becomes completely devoted to the service of others—a condition of true selflessness (compassion for others through lack of self) in which personal merit is no longer at stake.

These competing readings of chapter 10 are not necessarily contradictory, but reflect different descriptions of awakening in Buddhist literature. In some Mahāyāna texts, awakening is understood as a long accumulation of incalculable amounts of merit, allowing the awakened figure to

FIGURE 7.1 Assembly hall shrine. Royal Bhutanese Monastery, Bodh Gaya, India PHOTOGRAPH BY AUTHOR

FIGURE 7.2 Altar with the outer offering. Shankh Monastery, Mongolia PHOTOGRAPH BY AUTHOR

FIGURE 7.3 Treasure mandala offering. Daschan Chokhorling, Mongolia
PHOTOGRAPH BY AUTHOR

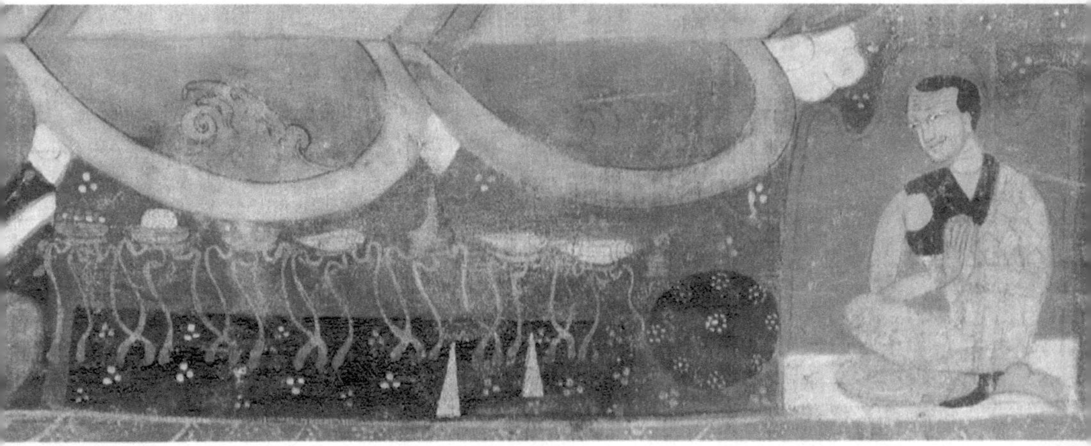

FIGURE 7.4 Detail of offerings in a painting of the Buddha Amitāyus. 11th–12th century, Tibet ROGERS FUND, 1989 (1989.284), THE METROPOLITAN MUSEUM OF ART. IMAGE COPYRIGHT © THE METROPOLITAN MUSEUM OF ART. IMAGE SOURCE: ART RESOURCE, NY

FIGURE 7.5 Mural of the thirty-five Confession Buddhas. Twentieth century, Mak Dhok Aloobari, Darjeeling, India PHOTOGRAPH BY AUTHOR

bring about good results for beings who could not perform great deeds on their own. Perhaps the most famous example is the bodhisattva Dharmākara, who became the Buddha Amitābha. His tremendous efforts as a bodhisattva allowed his adherents to be reborn in his paradise and effortlessly proceed along the path to awakening by having only a few pure thoughts of him.[11] Unlike the vows of Dharmākara, which stress his personal role in creating benefit,[12] the tenth chapter of the *Guide* largely deemphasizes notions of selfhood and personal merit, demonstrating that after the experience of emptiness in chapter 9, the practitioner should emerge with no sense of self at all.

This shift subtly aligns chapter 10 with later tantric rituals in which the practitioner is understood to enact awakening during the performance, with the goal of bringing awakened awareness to everyday life. The few key verses in chapter 10 that do incorporate a concept of self occur mostly at its beginning and end, marking the ritual structure and reminding the practitioner to internalize these transformations as the text closes. The first verses frame the act of dedicating merit as a way of concluding the *Guide* itself:

> By the good that is mine from considering [the *Guide to Bodhisattva Practice*,] the *Bodhicaryāvatāra*, may all people adorn the path to awakening. (10.1)
> Through my merit may all those in any of the directions suffering distress in body or mind find oceans of happiness and delight. (10.2)

The end of the chapter (10.51–58) reaffirms the bodhisattva's commitment, reminding the practitioner to permanently adopt the selfless dedication to others engendered by the *Guide*:

> May my own conduct emulate that of Mañjuśrī, who works to achieve the welfare of all living beings throughout the ten directions of space. (10.54)
> As long as space abides and as long as the world abides, so long may I abide, destroying the sufferings of the world. (10.55)

Of course, ordinary individuals would require significant cultivation to achieve real psychological transformation, but the grammar and structure of the tenth chapter model the development of a truly selfless dedication to others. This compatibility with tantrism may also contribute to the sustained popularity of Śāntideva's text in later traditions, despite its not being tantric in its language or practice.

The rituals of chapters 3 and 10 are not the only ones repeated in the *Guide* to different effects. The confession of misdeeds also occurs in two separate chapters, also representing two stages of development. In chapter 2, confession helps create the intention for awakening and purifies the practitioner before undertaking the bodhisattva vow.[13] In chapter 5 (verse 98),[14] Śāntideva recommends performing the confession of the *Three Heaps* (*Triskandha*) three times every day to overcome downfalls (*āpatti*) along the bodhisattva path, transgressions of the precepts (*saṃvara*) adopted with the bodhisattva vow. In both cases, bad actions are not sins to be judged and forgiven by a higher power, but rather obstacles that can be tempered by the assistance of more awakened beings, the ranks of whom the practitioner intends to join. Rituals like confession are thus not formalities, but tools to achieve specific goals, a requisite foundation for the difficult personal transformations demanded by the text.

Of course, there is no greater example of the ritual as foundation than the bodhisattva vow, the act that defines bodhisattvas and the path they follow. The vow does not simply voice the intention for awakening but repeats a formalized procedure for actualizing that intention. The Buddhist scholar Asaṅga (fourth century CE) describes one version of this rite in the *Bodhisattva Stages* (*Bodhisattvabhūmi*).[15] Essentially, a candidate sits in front of an image of the Buddha and is asked by one who has already taken the vow whether they have also made the aspiration to awakening, wishing to help all other sentient beings and accept the bodhisattva precepts. Three times they are asked, and three times they must agree. The candidate then proclaims their intention in full in the presence of all buddhas.

Outside this formalized ritual structure, Buddhist literature also tells of many important bodhisattvas who took unique vows under special circumstances, including the aforementioned Dharmākara. In this sense, the *Guide* can be understood as a personalized formulation of Śāntideva's own bodhisattva vow. In the context of history, however, it has also come to serve as a liturgical formula for the bodhisattva vows of many others. Indeed, one may perform the bodhisattva vow by reciting just two verses from the third chapter:[16]

> In the same way as bygone Sugatas (buddhas) took up the awakening mind, in the same way as they progressed in the bodhisattva training, (3.22)

> So too, I myself shall generate the awakening mind for the welfare of the world; and just so shall I train in those precepts in due order. (3.23)[17]

The bodhisattva precepts can also be understood both as formalized rules and as excerpts collected from other sources, including the *Three Heaps*, the *Ākāśagarbha Sūtra* (mentioned in *Guide* 5.104), and Candragomin's *Twenty Verses on the Bodhisattva Vow*.[18] These rules include not rejecting the teachings of the Buddha, not stealing from the community of monks and nuns, not giving advanced teachings to the unprepared, and not causing others to give up the Buddhist path. Even if a practitioner develops their own set of bodhisattva vows, then, they embrace these additional proscriptions against the most disastrous downfalls.

Considering such details, the *Guide* hints at both the rigidity and the flexibility of Buddhist ritual systems. Vows can express individuality, but practitioners are encouraged to repeat formulaic actions like dedication and confession to make progress. The last half of this chapter focuses more closely on such standardized performances, especially ones based on material objects and faith in an awakened other.

OBJECTS AND IMAGES

Although it is difficult to describe with certainty the rituals Śāntideva himself performed, specific passages in the *Guide* closely parallel actual material and visual practices of later Himalayan Buddhism. In particular, verses in chapters 2 and 5 describe performances of offering and confession, two phases of the unexcelled worship that involve the presence of an awakened other. By recognizing how these interactions between self and other can be mediated by visual and material objects, we can understand something of the ritual world surrounding the text.

Śāntideva's own words emphasize sumptuous materiality, as he begins chapter 2 with a lavish series of visualized offerings involving jewels, flowers, incense, and more. Eventually imagining himself in the presence of buddhas and bodhisattvas, he describes bathing them,[19] presenting them with robes, anointing them with perfumes, enveloping them with clouds of incense, offering food and drink, and even giving them palaces decorated with jewels and pearl-encrusted umbrellas (*Guide* 2.10–19). Such offerings are not only imagined, however, but are also described in relation to physical subjects:

> May flowers and jewels and other offerings rain down incessantly upon the *caityas*, images, and all the jewels which make up the true dharma. (2.21)
>
> I worship all *caityas* and places associated with the bodhisattva. I bow down to my teachers, and to spiritual aspirants who are worthy of praise. (2.25)

These subjects, including human teachers and artistic images of buddhas and bodhisattvas, provide physical bases for the giving of real, material offerings.

Indeed, Śāntideva's imaginative descriptions accord with the appearance of real shrines and altars, for example at the modern Royal Bhutanese Monastery at Bodh Gaya, India (see fig. 7.1).

In this scene, a central sculpture of the Buddha Śākyamuni sits on a throne wearing colored silks, much like Śāntideva's Buddha who is bathed and offered robes. Similar to the palaces, the shrine includes red pillars adorned with simulated jewels and canopies hanging from the ceiling (decorated with multicolored chevrons). A multitiered silver altar in front of the Buddha holds numerous pleasant substances, including flowers, food, and incense.

The sequence of offerings in verses 2.10–17 can also be understood in terms of a typical collection of Buddhist altar objects, sometimes called the outer offering (*bāhya-pūjā*).[20] This set uses early Indic hospitality practice as a model for showing respect toward deities, thereby including substances like water for washing the dusty feet of a traveler who arrives at one's home. Additional gifts, such as perfume and flowers, please the senses. Practitioners array these materials in rows upon an altar, as can be seen at Shankh Monastery in Mongolia (fig. 7.2).

In this photograph, each row contains two complete sets of the seven items of the outer offering, with additional sets multiplying toward the rear. Reading from left to right, there are containers for:

1. water for drinking or washing the face (*arghya*)
2. water to wash the feet (*pādya*)
3. flowers (*puṣpa*)
4. incense (*dhūpa*)
5. light/lamp (*āloka*/*dīpa*)
6. perfume (*gandha*)
7. food (*naivedya*)

In each row, there is also a second set of the same, for a total of fourteen objects. Looking back at the shrine at Bodh Gaya more closely (see again fig. 7.1), one finds a similar row of fourteen silver bowls on the middle tier of the central altar, representing the same offerings. In circumstances where these substances are difficult to acquire, they can be replaced by filling each bowl with water. Variations on this set also exist, most frequently adding an eighth bowl to symbolize music (*śabda*), another object of sense pleasure mentioned in the *Guide* (at 2.20).

Śāntideva's verses also suggest a more elaborate offering in which one gives all of the valuable substances in the entire world, as in the phrase "all those things unowned within the boundaries and breadth of space" (*Guide* 2.5). This can be understood in relation to another material offering known as the treasure mandala (*ratna-maṇḍala*), which represents a donation of the entire cosmos (fig. 7.3).[21]

Tibetans create this offering by filling metal rings with grain while reciting a liturgy that names the most important geography and treasures of the world, including Mount Sumeru (where the gods dwell), the major inhabited continents, and the treasures of the universal emperor (*cakravartin*). Eventually building up a simulacrum of the complete universe, the practitioner gives the object as a sign of total devotion and the abandonment of material wealth for the far more valuable teachings of the Buddha.

The artistic record provides evidence for the early conjunction of the outer offering and treasure mandala, just a few centuries after Śāntideva's time. A painting of the Buddha Amitāyus attributed to the eleventh–twelfth centuries depicts a monk offering both (fig. 7.4).

The black circle directly in front of him represents the treasure mandala, while beyond that, seven tripod stands hold substances identifiable with the outer offering (with some inside conch shells instead of metal bowls).

Even the entire cosmos is not treasure enough to express the incalculable devotion of the aspirant, however, and Śāntideva continues his worship in excess of the number of discrete objects in a single universe, here substituting bodily action for material wealth: "With as many prostrations as there are atoms in all the Buddha-fields, I throw myself down before the Buddhas of all three times (past, present, and future), before the dharma, and before the highest assembly" (2.24). Such language recalls the famously expansive bodhisattva vows of Samantabhadra, given at the very conclusion of the *Flower Array Sutra* (*Gaṇḍa-vyūha Sūtra*).[22] By rehearsing Samantabhadra's commitment, practitioners not only pay respect to the buddhas and bodhisattvas but also emulate one of the greatest bodhisattvas of Buddhist literature.

Like the offerings, the ritual of confession follows a precise formula of thoughts, words, and actions. As described in the Tibetan version of the *Three Heaps Sutra*,[23] one begins by stating one's name and taking refuge in the three jewels. Asking for aid, the practitioner recites the names of thirty-five different buddhas and bows to them. The subject acknowledges past transgressions and reaffirms the resolve to awakening, finally exalting the buddhas once again. The physical actions of recitation and prostration are not mere gestures but key components of the ritual that strengthen respect for awakened beings and regret of one's transgressions, dramatically increasing the impact of confession. It is also worth noting that the very first transgression mentioned in the liturgy is the theft of wealth from places of offering, the precise inversion of the offering rituals just described.

Confession also involves visualization of the thirty-five buddhas, who are therefore frequent subjects of visual artwork. In some traditions, each of the buddhas has their own unique appearance and special areas of efficacy (fig. 7.5).

The red-skinned Jewel Fire (Ratnāgni, first row, second from right), for example, holds a jewel and a ring of flame in his left and right hands. The jewel symbolizes his excellence, while the fire burns away the obstacles of practitioners. The white-skinned Glorious Light (Prabhāśrī, sixth row, far left) holds a rainbow-filled circle of white light, symbolizing the luminous insight that dispels dark ignorance. By visualizing, naming, and prostrating to each of these figures in turn, practitioners repeatedly work to remedy their own faults, combining ritual activity and faith with deeply personal transformation.

CONCLUSION

With such examples, it is easy to see how much can be missed when reading the *Guide* as a disembodied literary treatment of philosophy and ethics. Without question, intellectual and practical concerns were central to Śāntideva's project, but he also clearly wrote in a context of ritual performance and devotion. Evident in the *Guide* are his own descriptions of worshiping images, practicing daily confession, and presenting offerings. Even for Śāntideva, then, materiality and faith were essential components of the bodhisattva path. Working in tandem with emotional and analytic progressions, the rituals of the *Guide* express nuanced balances between self and other, devotion and transformation, and systematicity and freedom. They further provide an overall structure to the text, especially in the opening and closing chapters that generate and exemplify the all-important awakening mind. In the end, the rituals of the *Guide* combine with its emotional, moral, and intellectual factors to express a more complete view of the Buddhist path to awakening.

NOTES

1. Śāntideva and Kunpal, "Shantideva's Bodhisattva-Charyavatara, the Second Chapter and Commentary," 260.
2. Unless otherwise stated, all translations from the *Guide* and all references to chapter and verse numbers come from Śāntideva, *The Bodhicaryāvatāra*, trans. Crosby and Skilton.
3. Śāntideva, *The Bodhicaryāvatāra*, trans. Crosby and Skilton, 11–12.
4. See also Dayal, *The Bodhisattva Doctrine in Buddhist Sanskrit Literature*, 54–58; Makransky, "Offering (mChod Pa) in Tibetan Ritual Literature," 320.
5. Śāntideva, *The Bodhicaryāvatāra*, trans. Crosby and Skilton, 10.
6. Śāntideva, *The Bodhicaryāvatāra*, trans. Crosby and Skilton, xxxiv, 10–13; Goodman, trans., *The Training Anthology of Śāntideva*, xxviii–xxx.
7. See also Śāntideva, *The Bodhicaryāvatāra*, trans. Crosby and Skilton, 12–13.
8. Śāntideva, *The Bodhicaryāvatāra*, trans. Crosby and Skilton, 133. See also Kajihara, "On the Pariṇāmanā Chapter of the *Bodhicaryāvatāra*," 25–28.
9. Śāntideva, *The Bodhicaryāvatāra*, trans. Crosby and Skilton, 134–135.
10. My rendering of the Sanskrit from Śāntideva, *Bodhicaryāvatāra*, trans. Sharma, 1:71, 2:478.
11. Gómez, *The Land of Bliss*, 27–31.
12. See Gómez, *The Land of Bliss*, 69–76.
13. Notions of ritual purity and impurity are central to Indic ritual traditions, but too complex to address here. See, for example, Gellner, *Monk, Householder, and Tantric Priest*, 105–107.
14. An early version of the *Guide* does not contain this verse. Ishida, "Some New Remarks on the Bodhicaryāvatāra Chap. V," 479.
15. Asaṅga, *The Bodhisattva Path to Unsurpassed Enlightenment*, 260–264.
16. Rinchen, *Atisha's Lamp for the Path to Enlightenment*, 204n6.
17. These verses are 3.22–23 in the Sanskrit, but may appear as 3.23–24 in editions based on the Tibetan.
18. For translations of the latter two texts, see Sakya Pandita Translation Group, "The Ākāśagarbha Sūtra"; and Candragomin, *Difficult Beginnings*.
19. For more on bathing as an act of worship, see Boucher, "Sūtra on the Merit of Bathing the Buddha," 59–68.
20. See Beyer, *The Cult of Tārā*, 148; Makransky, "Offering (mChod Pa) in Tibetan Ritual Literature," 317–318.
21. For more on this offering, see Kongtrul, *The Torch of Certainty*, 92–105; Tharchin, *A Commentary on Guru Yoga and Offering of the Mandala*, 62–83.

22. Cleary, *The Flower Ornament Scripture*, 3:379–394. The liturgy of these vows also existed as an independently circulating text; see Osto, "A New Translation of the Sanskrit *Bhadracarī* with Introduction and Notes," 1–8.
23. Beresford, *Mahāyāna Purification*. There is some indication that the *Three Heaps Sutra* in the Tibetan canon may not be identical to the *Three Heaps* cited in the earliest Mahāyāna literature; see Nattier, *A Few Good Men*, 117–121. For a version of the confession to thirty-five buddhas explicitly known to Śāntideva, see the excerpt from the *Inquiry of Upāli* in Goodman, *The Training Anthology of Śāntideva*, 167–169.

REFERENCES

Asaṅga. *The Bodhisattva Path to Unsurpassed Enlightenment: A Complete Translation of the Bodhisattvabhūmi*. Trans. Artemus B. Engle. Boulder, CO: Snow Lion, 2016.

Beresford, Brian. *Mahāyāna Purification: The Confession Sūtra (Sūtra of Three Heaps) with Commentary by Ārya Nāgārjuna and the Practice of Vajrasattva with Sādhana*. Dharamsala: The Library of Tibetan Works and Archives, 1980.

Beyer, Stephan. *The Cult of Tārā: Magic and Ritual in Tibet*. Berkeley: University of California Press, 1973.

Boucher, Daniel. "Sūtra on the Merit of Bathing the Buddha." In *Buddhism in Practice*, ed. Donald S. Lopez Jr., 59–68. Princeton Readings in Religions. Princeton, NJ: Princeton University Press, 1995.

Candragomin. *Difficult Beginnings: Three Works on the Bodhisattva Path*. Trans. Mark Tatz. Boston: Shambhala, 1985.

Cleary, Thomas. *The Flower Ornament Scripture: A Translation of the Avatamsaka Sutra*. Boston: Shambhala, 1984.

Dayal, Har. *The Bodhisattva Doctrine in Buddhist Sanskrit Literature*. Delhi: Motilal Banarsidass, 1932.

Gellner, David N. *Monk, Householder, and Tantric Priest: Newar Buddhism and Its Hierarchy of Ritual*. Cambridge: Cambridge University Press, 1992.

Gómez, Luis O. *The Land of Bliss: The Paradise of the Buddha of Measureless Light; Sanskrit and Chinese Versions of the Sukhāvatīvyūha Sutras*. Honolulu: University of Hawai'i Press, 1996.

Goodman, Charles, trans. *The Training Anthology of Śāntideva: A Translation of the Śikṣā-samuccaya*. New York: Oxford University Press, 2016.

Ishida, Chikō. "Some New Remarks on the Bodhicaryāvatāra Chap. V." *Journal of Indian and Buddhist Studies* 37, no. 1 (December 1988): 479–476.

Kajihara, Mieko. "On the Pariṇāmanā Chapter of the Bodhicaryāvatāra." *Journal of Indian and Buddhist Studies* 40, no. 2 (March 1992): 25–28.

Kongtrul, Jamgon. *The Torch of Certainty*. Trans. Judith Hanson. Boulder, CO: Shambhala, 1977.

Makransky, John. "Offering (mChod Pa) in Tibetan Ritual Literature." In *Tibetan Literature: Studies in Genre*, ed. José Ignacio Cabezón and Roger R. Jackson. Ithaca, NY: Snow Lion, 1996.

Nattier, Jan. *A Few Good Men: The Bodhisattva Path According to the Inquiry of Ugra (Ugraparipṛcchā)*. Honolulu: University of Hawai'i Press, 2003.

Osto, Douglas. "A New Translation of the Sanskrit Bhadracarī with Introduction and Notes." *New Zealand Journal of Asian Studies* 12, no. 2 (December 2010): 1–21.

Rinchen, Sonam. *Atisha's Lamp for the Path to Enlightenment.* Trans. Ruth Sonam. Ithaca, NY: Snow Lion, 1997.

Sakya Pandita Translation Group. "The Ākāśagarbha Sūtra." *84000: Translating the Words of the Buddha.* Accessed April 18, 2017. http://read.84000.co/#UT22084-066-018/title.

Śāntideva. *Bodhicharyāvatāra.* Trans. Parmananda Sharma. New Delhi: Aditya Prakashan, 1990.

———. *The Bodhicaryāvatāra.* Trans. Kate Crosby and Andrew Skilton. Oxford: Oxford University Press, 1996.

Śāntideva, and Kunpal. "Shantideva's Bodhisattva-Charyavatara, the Second Chapter and Commentary." Trans. Andreas Kretschmar. Accessed April 17, 2017. http://www.kunpal.com/bca2comm.pdf.

Tharchin, Lobsang. *A Commentary on Guru Yoga and Offering of the Mandala.* Ithaca, NY: Snow Lion, 1981.

[8]

BODHICARYĀVATĀRA AND TIBETAN MIND TRAINING (*LOJONG*)

Thupten Jinpa

ALL TIBETAN sources agree that Śāntideva's *Guide to Bodhisattva Practice* (*Bodhicaryāvatāra,* hereafter *Guide*), one of the most celebrated Indian Buddhist texts, constitutes a principal origin for the Tibetan mind training or *lojong* tradition. Mind training refers to a specific genre of instructions and their associated spiritual exercises, which include, among others, the famed practice of *tonglen,* "giving and taking," and traces its immediate origin to the legacy of the Indian Bengali teacher Atiśa, who came to Tibet in the middle of the eleventh century. As in the *Guide,* the central concern of *lojong* is to cultivate Mahāyāna Buddhism's highest spiritual ideal of *bodhicitta* (the altruistic intention to attain enlightenment for the sake of all beings) and to live one's life in accord with that aspiration. The Tibetan term for mind training, *lojong,* is composed of two syllables, with *lo* standing for "mind," "thought," or "attitudes," while *jong* connotes "to purify, cleanse, refine, exercise, or train" (as in sports training). Associated, originally, with the Kadam School of Atiśa (982–1054) and his principal Tibetan disciple Dromtönpa (1005–64), over time, the *lojong* tradition became part of the common heritage of all Tibetan schools.

Today, as Tibetan Buddhism becomes more widely accessible to the world outside Tibet, it is often the *lojong* instructions that the Tibetan teachers share first with their new audiences. For example, when His Holiness the Dalai Lama spoke to a crowd of nearly a hundred thousand in New York's Central Park in 1999, he chose the "Eight Verses on Mind Training" as the basis of his talk. When the Dalai Lama returned to speak once more in Central Park in 2002, he chose as the topic for his talk Atiśa's "Bodhisattva's Jewel Garland," an important source text for *lojong*.

On the surface, the relationship between the *Guide* and Tibetan mind training appears fairly straightforward. First and foremost, there seems to be a direct link, if not an equivalence, between the exchanging of self and others as outlined in chapter 8 of the *Guide* and *lojong*'s "giving and taking" (*tonglen*) meditation, which involves imaginatively taking on others' suffering, misfortune, and negative karma and giving to others one's happiness, good fortune, and positive karma. Second, the *Guide* is listed as one of the "six treatises of Kadam," which also include Śāntideva's *Compendium of Training*.[1] Third, most *lojong* texts, especially since the appearance of Chekawa's "Seven-Point Mind Training" in the twelfth century, seem to contain disproportionately high numbers of citations from the *Guide*. Fourth, Atiśa's explicit acknowledgment of Serlingpa (literally, "the one from the Island of Sumatra") as the principal source for his instruction on generating *bodhicitta*, combined with the fact that Serlingpa's approach is thought to emphasize the exchanging of self and others, suggest the *Guide* to be the direct source of *lojong*'s approach to cultivating *bodhicitta*.[2] Finally, it cannot be a matter of pure coincidence that most Tibetan masters who have been *Guide* enthusiasts were also great advocates of *lojong*. This is true from the earliest Tibetan *lojong* teachers, especially Langri Thangpa (1054–1123) and Chekawa (1101–75), to Ngulchu Thokmé Sangpo (1297–1371) and Tsongkhapa (1357–1419), and from Yongzin Yeshé Gyaltsen in the eighteenth century to Dza Paltrül in the nineteenth century.

That said, a closer examination reveals that the actual relationship between the *Guide* and *lojong* is far more complex. In what follows I shall examine this important question so we might appreciate more accurately how the *Guide* may have shaped the development of this unique Tibetan tradition. My chapter is divided into four sections. Part 1 presents a brief outline of the key features of *lojong* so that its unique characteristics—terminology, outlook, and approach, as well as its spiritual exercises—can be recognized. Then, part 2 sketches a broad outline of the central theme of the *Guide* with specific focus on the unique practice of equalizing and exchanging of self and others as found in its eighth chapter. In part 3 I then correlate the *Guide* with *lojong* and trace the Indian sources, especially in Śāntideva, for the specific features of *lojong* and practice. Finally, in part 4, I conclude with some general observations on the place of the *Guide* in today's pluralistic world, and how it (and by extension Tibetan mind training) could play an influential role in the growing emergence of

Buddhist-derived contemplative practices in the shared public domain, especially in the West.

1

Although the usage of the word *lojong* could be traced to the Kadam master Potowa (1027–1105), the earliest Tibetan texts that actually include the word *lojong* in their titles are Langri Thangpa's "Eight Verses on Mind Training"[3] and Chekawa's "Seven-Point Mind Training."[4] Based on these two short works, we can obtain a good idea of the basic structure of *lojong* as well as its central themes. Structurally, *lojong* organizes its entire instruction and spiritual exercises around three broad headings: (1) the preliminaries; (2) the main practice; and (3) complementary or "branch" practices. The first includes such general preparatory practices as reflection on the value of human existence, contemplation on death and impermanence, karma and its effects, and contemplation of the suffering within the cycle of existence (*saṃsāra*). Second, the main practice is framed in terms of the cultivation of the two awakening minds (*bodhicitta*): conventional *bodhicitta* (*saṃvṛtibodhicitta*), which is the altruistic aspiration to seek enlightenment for the sake of all beings, and ultimate *bodhicitta* (*paramārthabodhicitta*), which is the realization of the ultimate nature of things in terms of emptiness, especially of one's own mind. In *lojong* the cultivation of conventional *bodhicitta* is done primarily on the basis of its unique practice of *tonglen*, with the twin acts of "giving and receiving" often correlated with cycles of exhalation and inhalation. The "Seven-Point Mind Training" describes this: "Train in the two—giving and taking—alternately. Place the two astride your breath."[5] All remaining *lojong* practices are, in one way or another, aimed at enhancing, reinforcing, and complementing the main practice of the two awakening minds. From the twelfth century on, Chekawa's "Seven-Point Mind Training" effectively became the central or the root text of *lojong*.[6] This short work organizes *lojong* instructions in terms of the following seven points:

1. The preliminaries
2. Training in the two awakening minds
3. Taking adversities onto the path
4. Presenting a lifetime's practice in summary
5. The measure of having trained the mind
6. The commitments of mind training
7. The precepts of mind training.

Within the threefold structure, the first of the seven points belongs to the preliminary practice while the second belongs to the main practice, and points 3 through 7 belong to the category of branch practices. These branch practices, the domain in which *lojong* instructions excel in their unique down-to-earth approach, entail dealing with practical challenges posed by embracing *bodhicitta* and implementing its ideal in everyday life. First and foremost, there is the transforming of one's basic attitude toward fellow sentient beings, training to see them as "more precious than a wish-granting jewel."[7] As in the *Guide*, this transformation of outlook involves working on one's attitudes toward difficult people by learning to view them as one's "most sublime spiritual teachers." There is a somewhat oblique line in the "Seven-Point Mind Training"—"There are three objects, three poisons, and three roots of virtue"—which encapsulates the central task of the *lojong* practitioner.[8] In transforming one's outlook and attitudes, one needs to pay special attention to three types of people in one's life: spiritual teachers, loved ones, and those difficult to deal with. One needs to regulate, be vigilant toward, and counter the three poisons of the mind (attachment, anger, and ignorance) and transform them into the three roots of virtue: nonattachment, nonhatred, and wisdom. Implementing this above injunction involves maintaining a radical self-awareness (or vigilance) in everyday life—when eating, walking, speaking, even when thinking, and so on—such that every aspect of one's life comes to be permeated by the sentiments and perspectives of universal compassion, by *bodhicitta*, and by the view of emptiness. The "Seven-Point Mind Training" articulates this approach in the following: "Relate whatever you can to meditation right now," (a variant reading has "Relate whatever you encounter to your meditation right now") and "When the world and its inhabitants boil with negativity, transform adverse conditions into the path of enlightenment."[9] The *lojong* text speaks of taking both misfortune as well as good fortune onto the path, both sickness and health, both pain and joy, so that no ups and down in one's life have the power to dislodge one from one's practice of the altruistic ideal. In this way, one is able to make true the *lojong* instruction, "Cultivate constantly the joyful mind alone."[10]

2

Ever since its appearance in India in the eighth century, the *Guide* seems to have enjoyed great popularity among Mahāyāna Buddhists. In Tibet in particular, the *Guide* attracted a large number of commentarial expositions,[11] shaped the tradition's understanding of the bodhisattva path, and profoundly informed its compassion cultivation practices as well as Mahāyāna Buddhist ethics. In general, the *Guide* presents the Mahāyāna path to enlightenment on the basis of the bodhisattva ideal and its implementation through the six perfections—generosity, moral discipline, forbearance, diligence, meditation, and wisdom. Of its ten chapters, the first three pertain primarily to generating *bodhicitta*: chapter 1 presents the benefits of *bodhicitta*; chapter 2 the means by which one could eliminate the obstacles to generating *bodhicitta*, such as through purification of one's negative karma; and chapter 3 presents how to actually generate *bodhicitta* and uphold it. Chapters 4 and 5, on conscientiousness and meta-awareness, present the perfection of moral discipline, and 6–9 present the remaining perfections: forbearance, diligence, meditation, and wisdom. The final, tenth chapter presents a series of deeply felt aspirations dedicating the entirety of one's being—body, speech, mind, good karma—toward the welfare of all beings. In the Tibetan tradition this tenth chapter came to be treated as an independent text and used as a popular Mahāyāna prayer, recited often at funeral ceremonies and other important occasions.

The part of the *Guide* that is most relevant for our discussion of its relationship with *lojong* is chapter 8, especially verses 90–187.[12] The first part of the chapter presents, in extensive detail, the various elements of the practice of meditation, aimed at the cultivation of single-pointedness of mind. This first part then concludes with the following statement:

Having reflected on the virtues of solitude
In ways such as those outlined above,
And with distracted thoughts being calmed,
One should now develop the awakening mind. (8.89)[13]

The actual development of *bodhicitta* (awakening mind) in the *Guide* takes the form of two main practices: *equalizing* self and others (8.90–112) and *exchanging* self and others (8.113–184).[14] Three concluding verses (185–187) reconnect with earlier themes, presented especially in chapter 4, of conscientiousness and the importance of countering the obstacles to single-pointed practice of *bodhicitta*.

On the surface, the *Guide* itself (8.90) and its Indian commentaries are clear that, between the two practices, the equalizing should be done first, thus preparing the way for the more challenging practice of exchanging self and others.[15] With the two lines, "Since both are equal with regard to happiness and suffering, I should look after all as I do myself" (8.90cd), the

Guide defines this equality of self and others in terms of the fundamental fact that, just as one desires happiness and does not want to suffer, the same is true of others as well. Śāntideva then goes on to explain how recognition of this equality is not only possible but in fact logically appropriate to cultivate. The *Guide* points out that the reason one cannot tolerate one's own suffering is because of one's identification with one's own self (see Gyatso's essay in this volume). This means that by expanding one's identification and embracing others within it, one could learn not to tolerate others' suffering as well. In any case, the *Guide* argues that, if suffering is to be removed, then it should not matter whose suffering it is, that of oneself or others (8.102). The section on equalizing concludes with the point that, through habituation, one can learn to identify with others' bodies and feel their pains as if they were one's own (8.112cd). This then opens the way to the discussion of the next practice, that of exchanging of self and others.

The *Guide* defines the exchanging of self and others in terms of changing one's self-identification—viewing others as self and one's self as other. This is not simply a matter of changing one's attitude, but more radically, entails renouncing one's self-identity and viewing others as one's own self. The well-known Indian expositor of the *Guide*, Prajñākaramati, glosses 8.113cd thus: "Renouncing one's own body means to view oneself as the other person, while embracing other people means to view others in terms of one's own self."[16] So the essence of exchanging involves switching one's identity so that one learns to view and feel others' suffering as one's own. This switching of identification is further explained in terms of "embracing others" (8.114–120), "renouncing one's own identity" (8.121–125), "disadvantages and benefits of viewing self versus others as primary" (8.126–130), "the downfall of not engaging in such exchanging of identity" (8.131–135), and concluding observations (8.136–139).[17] In speaking of embracing others, as part of such an exchange we find the following memorable verse:

> Whosoever longs to protect quickly,
> Both oneself and others,
> Should practice the supreme secret:
> The exchanging of self and others. (8.120)

In *Guide* 8.140–158, Śāntideva presents an intriguing thought experiment where, having switched the two identities of self and others, one then turns to look upon one's former "self" with the all too human attitudes of "envy toward the higher, competitiveness toward the equal, and contempt toward the lower." Having "turned" oneself into another self, this other looks at oneself, and the new self, which is in fact another, then generates envy of this new self's good fortune, prestige, fame, and so on. One enters into similar contemplations with regard to competitiveness and pride. These thought experiments are then followed by instructions on how to actually implement the exchanging of self and others, including exchanging one's happiness with others' suffering, in everyday life (8.159–184).

3

Now that we have the broad outlines of both *lojong* and the *Guide*, let us return to the question of their relationship. First there is *lojong*'s framing of its main practice as the cultivation of the two awakening minds. To my knowledge, nowhere does the *Guide* or its principal early Indian commentaries even use the language of conventional *bodhicitta* and ultimate *bodhicitta*, to say nothing of framing the main subject matter in such terms. In *lojong*, however, the earliest exposition of Chekawa's "Seven-Point Mind Training" equates the generation of conventional *bodhicitta* with exchanging self and others. It seems that by the time the Tibetans developed their own exposition of the *Guide*, the tradition was already established to impose this two-*bodhicitta* framework upon the subject matter of the text. For example, the influential fourteenth-century Tibetan exponent of the *Guide* as well as *lojong*, Thokmé Sangpo, interprets the *bodhicitta* section of chapter 8 in terms of the two *bodhicitta* or awakening minds, with the final verse (8.187) as presenting ultimate *bodhicitta*.[18] To appreciate the Tibetan interpretation of the *Guide*, the following summary by the Indian commentator Kṛṣṇapa (eleventh century) appears crucial:

> Therefore, thus having generated the [awakening] mind, beginning with the line "*The son of the Conqueror who has adopted*" (4.1a) up to the line "*To them emptiness shall be taught*" (9.167d), the six chapters (4–9) present the practice of moral discipline, forbearance, diligence, meditation, and wisdom. Similarly, one should engage in the practice of generosity tempered by the aspirations as outlined in the prayer chapter (10). These then constitute [the practice of] engaging *bodhicitta* for they enhance the preceding [aspirational awakening] mind. Furthermore, the chapter that presents the perfection of wisdom is referred to as [presenting] the ultimate *bodhicitta*, while the other nine chapters are described as presenting the conventional *bodhicitta*. Thus the two awakening minds are present here

> [in the *Guide*]. . . . In view of the above, we should recognize this work, *Bodhicaryāvatāra,* which expounds the path as well as its results for all the bodhisattvas, including its chapter on wisdom, to be like the mother of the entire scriptural basket of the bodhisattva path.[19]

In brief, although Śāntideva himself, and his early commentators, did not frame the *Guide* in terms of the practice of the two awakening minds, a later Indian commentarial tradition's reading of the *Guide* as doing so seems to have been adopted by Tibetans as their received approach to the text. This reading of the *Guide* shaped *lojong*'s characterization of its main practice as the cultivation of the two awakening minds.

A second important issue is the relationship between the *Guide*'s exchanging of self and others and *lojong*'s giving and taking (*tonglen*) practice. On this matter too, although *lojong* authors such as Chekawa explicitly present exchanging of self and others on the basis of *tonglen* (giving and taking) practice, the *Guide*'s definition of the exchange seems quite different from the one envisioned in *tonglen*. As explained earlier, in the *Guide,* the essence of the exchange consists in switching one's identification—self as the other and others as the self—and the shift in attitudes resulting from this. In contrast, *tonglen*'s imaginative taking on others' suffering, misfortune, and bad karma and giving to others one's happiness, good fortune, and virtuous deeds does not appear to entail the switching of one's personal identity. Although the *Guide* does speak of exchanging one's happiness with others' suffering, it seems quite different from *lojong*'s giving and taking. The *Guide*'s version involves adopting the perspective of a neutral observer and then taking everything good it sees in one's body and so on, and using them for the benefit of others (8.159), not just in imagination, but in actual practice. If anything, the strongest *Guide* source, perhaps inspiration, for *lojong*'s giving and taking practice of *tonglen* seems to be the following verse found in the dedication chapter:

> Whatever suffering there is of sentient beings,
> May it all be realized upon me;
> And through the virtues of the bodhisattvas,
> May all beings enjoy happiness. (10.56)

These lines powerfully echo the following passage from Nāgārjuna's *Precious Garland* (*Ratnāvalī*): "May the fruits of their non-virtuous deeds ripen upon me,/And may the fruits of my virtuous deeds ripen upon them" (5.84cd).[20] These words are often cited as an authoritative Indian source for *tonglen*. Although today *tonglen* is understood almost exclusively in terms of the imaginative act of visualization, Chekawa in fact speaks of three forms: giving and taking in thought (through imagination), in action, and through aspiration.[21]

Given this above difference, how is it that *lojong* masters came to view *tonglen* as representing the *Guide*'s exchanging of self and others? The answer to this crucial question lies in hermeneutics—namely how the Tibetan commentators read key lines of the *Guide* on the exchange, especially 8.113, 120, 131, and 136. As already stated earlier, all known Indian commentaries understand the *Guide*'s exchange literally in terms of switching of identity, which leads to a shift in attitudes toward self and others. They all speak of "renouncing self-grasping (or self-identification)" and "adopting others as oneself." In contrast, to my knowledge no Tibetan *Guide* commentators interpret the exchange in terms of such a radical switching of identity. Rather, they understand it in terms of an attitudinal shift, renouncing the habitual attitude of cherishing oneself and embracing the attitude of cherishing others. In other words, the exchange entails a fundamental reorientation of one's perspectives and attitudes, switching from habitual self-centeredness to other-centeredness so that one cares for others and their welfare—not changing one's very personal identity as such. Both Thokmé Sangpo and Gyaltsap Jé, two influential Tibetan commentators on the *Guide*, use the crucial term "cherishing" (*gces 'dzin*) and explain that it is "self-cherishing" (*rang gces 'dzin*) that needs to be renounced and "other-cherishing" (*gzhan gces 'dzin*) that should be embraced.[22] This interpretation offers the perfect basis for *tonglen*'s taking others' suffering upon oneself and giving to others one's own happiness. What we see in this Tibetan interpretation is an important distinction drawn between self-grasping (*bdag tu 'dzin pa*) and self-cherishing (*rang gces 'dzin*), the renouncing of the former requiring the more radical approach of the wisdom of no-self and emptiness.

Recognizing these differences between the *Guide*'s exchange and *lojong*'s *tonglen* helps shed some light on certain obscure statements found in the early *lojong* texts. For example, there is the comment about how Serlingpa, the principal source of Atiśa's own instructions on *bodhicitta*, is said to have upheld a philosophical view closer to that of the non-Buddhist schools, and how the *lojong* instruction stemming from Serlingpa through Atiśa in fact proceeds from not renouncing self-identification. As support for this, the following statement from *Teachings of Vimalakīrti* is often cited: "The self-view based on the perishable composite is the seed of the Tathāgata."[23] According to Chekawa, Serlingpa uses self-grasping (or self-identity), without having to relinquish it, as the very basis for training. Elaborating this point, Chekawa says:

> Just as a lotus does not grow out of well-leveled soil but from the mire, in the same way the awakening mind (*bodhicitta*) is not born in the hearts of disciples in whom the moisture of attachment has dried up. It grows instead in the hearts of ordinary sentient beings who possess in full all the fetters of bondage. Therefore, in dependence on self-grasping, it is possible to cultivate the awakening mind that exchanges self and others, which is the uncommon cause for attaining buddhahood. This very self-grasping is, therefore, the "bone" of the buddhas.[24]

The Tibetan sources also speak of three distinct lineages for Atiśa's "secret" *lojong* teachings—each associated with a specific Indian master—and how, of these three, Serlingpa is said to have taught the approach of generating *bodhicitta* that proceeds immediately with exchanging, rather than starting first with equalizing of self and others, as suggested in the *Guide*. The Kadam master Chengawa's approach is said to involve proceeding first with equalizing of self and others, which is believed to be in the tradition of Maitriyogi, one of the three supposed *lojong* sources of Atiśa.[25] Given the dominant influence of Chekawa's "Seven-Point Mind Training," almost all subsequent *lojong* texts adopt this approach of proceeding directly from exchanging of self with others. Surprisingly, very little attention, if any, is paid to the first component of the *Guide*'s instruction on generating *bodhicitta*, namely the equalizing of self and others. When Tibetan masters do address this, most tend to do so not in the context of *lojong* but mainly in *lamrim* (stages of the path), another dominant lineage of teachings that stems from Atiśa.

To sum up, there is no doubt that the *Guide*'s exchanging of self and others, as well as the aspirational prayers wishing that others' suffering befall oneself and that others enjoy the fruits of one's own good karma, do constitute a powerful source for *lojong*'s principal practice of *tonglen*.[26] There also seems to be a close connection between Śāntideva's characterization of exchanging self and others as "the supreme secret" (*Guide* 8.120d) and the Tibetan sources' characterization of *lojong* as representing Atiśa's "teachings that were taught in secret."[27] That said, the practice of *tonglen* itself, especially as it is defined in *lojong*, appears to be a Tibetan innovation, with its first appearance in Langri Thangpa's "Eight Verses on Mind Training." This *tonglen* practice was further refined by Chekawa's innovation that involved correlating the twin activity of giving and taking with the process of breathing—taking on others' suffering as one breathes in and giving one's happiness to others as one breathes out. Subsequent *lojong* works, such as Sangyé Gompa's *Public Explication* as well as its *Supplement* by Könchok Gyaltsen, further elaborate this giving and taking, in terms of the diversity of their targets and objects exchanged, as well as in the diversity of visualizations that could be practiced.

To me, the area where the *Guide*'s influence on *lojong* is most discernable is the highly practical and personal nature of its approach in dealing with everyday challenges posed by living up to the ideals of *bodhicitta*. Whether in *lojong*'s "taking adversities onto the path" or its commitments and the precepts, echoes of the *Guide* can be heard unmistakably in "Seven-Point Mind Training" injunctions such as: "Do not speak of defects [of others]"; "Discard all expectations of reward"; "Whichever of the two [success or failure] arises, be patient"; "Engage in the principal practices right now"; and "Train with decisiveness."[28] Similarly, as observed earlier, there is a direct link between the "Eight Verses on Mind Training" instruction to view one's enemy as the most sublime teacher and the *Guide*'s (6.107) admonition to view one's enemy as a precious treasure. Thus, at the heart of one's approach to everyday life recommended in both the *Guide* and *lojong*, there is the admonition to maintain a high degree of self-awareness through constant application of mindfulness. Through this, nothing will have the power to undermine one's spiritual practice and everything that one encounters in life—good, bad, or neutral—can be transformed into conditions that would only enhance one's practice on the path to awakening. It is perhaps this highly practical and deeply personal style of the *Guide* that explains, to a large extent, why Āryasura's *Compendium of the Perfections* (*Pāramitāsamāsa*)—in fact a more tightly woven text composed in an authoritative style—never attained a status and influence comparable to that of the *Guide*.

In brief, despite the complexities outlined above, it is clear that key figures in the development of Tibetan *lojong* did view the *Guide* to be a principal source for *lojong* instructions and their associated spiritual exercises, as presented in such classic works as the "Eight Verses on Mind Training" and the "Seven-Point Mind Training." Many in fact understood the meaning of the word *lojong* (mind training) as a shorthand for Mahāyāna Mind Training (*thegs pa chen po blo sbyong*), and that also in terms of training the mind in the cultivation of *bodhicitta* according to the *Guide*'s exchanging of self and others. Furthermore, this unique approach to generating *bodhicitta* or awakening mind, as outlined in the *Guide*, is seen to be traceable all the way to the great master Nāgārjuna, an approach that is contrasted to another lineage of cultivating *bodhicitta* stemming from Maitreyanātha and Asaṅga. To put it succinctly, I am convinced that, without the *Guide*, the Tibetan tradition of *lojong* simply wouldn't have emerged.

4

In concluding this chapter, I would like to draw attention to the novel and creative ways the Tibetan inheritors of the *Guide*, especially the pioneers in the development of *lojong*, have engaged with it, thus making the insights and teachings of the *Guide* resonate powerfully with a Tibetan audience. Thanks to the Tibetan tradition's entry into the contemporary world, primarily as a consequence of Tibet's tragic twentieth-century history, the *Guide* as a living text and tradition, supported by *lojong*, has today become part of the global spiritual heritage. To date there are at least five different translations of the *Guide* available in English, and large numbers of instructional texts on *lojong* are becoming widely available. Many of the features that made this particular Indian Buddhist work so appealing to the Tibetans—its deeply personal tone, the lucidity of its verses (except for the philosophical section, wisdom chapter), the amazing practicality in its approach, and, most importantly, the deep insights it offers on basic human psychology—remain potent for the contemporary reader. As Tibetan Buddhism's encounter with contemporary cultures and global societies deepens, I am convinced that the *Guide* (and by extension *lojong*) will play a critical role in these cross-cultural encounters. Already I see three important areas where Śāntideva's *Guide* is playing a role as an important resource.

One is the Dalai Lama's advocacy of what he calls "secular ethics," a universal approach to understanding and promoting fundamental values and ethics that are rooted in the appreciation of our shared humanity. A central premise of the Dalai Lama's approach is to embrace the fundamental equality of all humans: He often says, "Just like me, everyone wishes to be happy and nobody wants suffering." This is clearly an expression of the *Guide*'s equalizing of self and others. This acceptance of shared humanity then serves as the basis for the appreciation of our natural instincts of empathy and compassion as the foundation for the ethical norms that guide our conduct, especially in relation to our fellow humans. We can discern unmistakable echoes of the *Guide* in the Dalai Lama's advocacy of secular ethics, in the grounding of his ethics and in offering specific sets of practical instructions on how to live in accord with them.[29]

The second domain where the *Guide* is capable of making an important impact is in the emerging, Buddhist-derived secular protocols on cultivating compassion using contemplative techniques, such as meditation. For two of the more well-known protocols, Stanford's CCT (Compassion Cultivation Training) and Emory's CBCT (Cognitive-Based Compassion Training), the *Guide* (*lojong* as well) is a primary source for contemplative techniques integral to programs.[30] What makes the *Guide*'s approach so appropriate for these secularized programs is that, unlike other traditional Buddhist techniques for cultivating compassion, its cogency and potency are not contingent upon concepts such as rebirth and the theory of karma across lifetimes. It is based primarily in the recognition of shared humanity—equality with regard to happiness and suffering—and insights into human psychology that bear on universal facts of our human condition. For this reason, secular adaptations of techniques from the *Guide*, such as cultivating and enhancing compassion, can proceed with greater ease while retaining the poignancy of the profound human and spiritual aspects of the *Guide*'s approach.

Finally, the *Guide*'s detailed psychological analysis of the character, function, and effects of our habitual patterns of self-centeredness, and how the adoption of a more other-oriented outlook with respect to one's own identity as well as to one's fellow humans, has the potential to inform the ongoing explorations of the role of altruism within our basic nature as human beings. I am convinced that there are still more chapters to be written when it comes to the amazing story of the *Bodhicaryāvatāra*, an Indian Buddhist text written by a simple monk some thirteen hundred years ago.

NOTES

1. For a succinct explanation of the rationale for the choice of these six texts and how they are grouped into three sets of two, including their specific roles in the development of the practitioner on the path, see Kapstein, "Stoics and Bodhisattvas," 102 and note 3.
2. On Serlingpa (Dharmakīrti) and Atiśa's relationship with him, including the legend of the latter's travel to the island of Sumatra to receive *bodhicitta* instructions from Serlingpa, see Shönu and Gyaltsen, eds., *Mind Training*, introduction as well as "The Story of Atiśa's Voyage to Sumatra," 57–70. On the identity of Serlingpa, see Chattopadaya, *Atiśa in Tibet*, 84–95.
3. For lucid commentary on Langri Thangpa's "Eight Verses on Mind Training," see the Dalai Lama, *Transforming the Mind*.
4. There are in fact numerous later texts bearing the words "mind training" in their titles. On the usage of the term in general, and more specifically its use to name a unique genre, see my introduction in Shönu and Gyaltsen, eds., *Mind Training*.

5. This and other quotations from the "Seven-Point Mind Training" here are from my own translation as found in Shönu and Gyaltsen, eds., *Mind Training*, 83–85.
6. Shönu and Gyaltsen, eds., *Mind Training*, 9–13. Chekawa's "Seven-Point" itself is not an original work in the contemporary sense. Rather, it seems to be primarily a collation of assorted sayings attributed to Atiśa, organized within the framework of seven points.
7. For a translation of Langri Thangpa, "Eight Verses on Mind Training," see Shönu and Gyaltsen, eds., *Mind Training*, 275–276.
8. Shönu and Gyaltsen, eds., *Mind Training*, 83.
9. Shönu and Gyaltsen, eds., *Mind Training*, 83–84.
10. Shönu and Gyaltsen, eds., *Mind Training*, 84.
11. Gendun Chopel, for example, speaks of seeing the names of many older Tibetan commentaries of the *Guide* among the texts that belonged to the Chim masters at Narthang Monastery, a major center of learning for the Kadam School. Chopel, *Grains of Gold*, 53.
12. In Kṛṣṇapa's commentary, the practice of equalizing and exchange of self and others is found in the chapter on diligence, not in the one on meditation, where the cultivation of *bodhicitta* is presented as the object of the bodhisattva's diligent effort. Kṛṣṇapa, *Spyod 'jug gi rnam par bshad pa* (Tengyur, vol. 61, p. 1792) in fact accuses other commentators who assert that the practice of equalizing and exchange should be presented later, in the meditation chapter, of being at odds with Śāntideva himself. This suggests that he was working from a version that differs from the canonical version. (All classical Indian texts cited here from the Tengyur are from the Comparative Edition, China, 2000).
13. Unless otherwise stated, all translations of classical Indian and Buddhist sources in this essay, including those from the *Guide*, are mine.
14. Although Śāntideva, *The Bodhicaryāvatāra*, trans. Crosby and Skilton, 80, asserts this practice of equalizing self and others to be passages cited from the *Tathāgataguhya Sūtra* in *Compendium of Training*, Harrison, "The Case of the Vanishing Poet," 219, has shown that those passages are in fact not from that sūtra.
15. The influential commentary *Bodhicaryāvatārapañjikā* of Prajñākaramati (Tengyur, vol. 61, p. 1343), for example, reads: "Therefore, in order to counter that [grasping at self], first or at the beginning, one should meditate on the equality of self and others. Later one should then do the exchanging. This is the meaning." Although the *Guide* itself and Prajñākaramati do not use the more active word "equalizing," Vairocanarakṣita (Tengyur, vol. 62, p. 335) prefaces the explanation of *Guide* 8.90 with the following: "Given that without equalizing self and others one cannot cultivate *bodhicitta*."
16. *Bodhicaryāvatārapañjikā* 1357.
17. This division of the section elaborating the exchange practice is based on Thokmé Sangpo's commentary, *Ocean of Excellent Utterances* (*Legs bshad rgya mtsho* in *rgyal sras kyi spyod pa la 'jug pa'i chos skor*) (Delhi: Institute of Tibetan Classics, 2006).
18. Thokmé Sangpo, *Ocean of Excellent Utterances*, 142. The Tibetan version of the *Guide* contains an extra verse at the end of chapter 8, thus making the total number 187, instead of 186 as found in the current Sanskrit version.
19. Kṛṣṇapa, *Presenting the Difficult Points of Bodhicaryāvatāra*, 242. The translator's colophon states that the work was translated into Tibetan by the author himself with the Tibetan translator Chökyi Sherap (eleventh century).

20. For an alternative translation of these lines, see *The Precious Garland*, trans. Dunne and McClintock, 85.
21. Shönu and Gyaltsen, eds., *Mind Training*, 287.
22. Thokmé Sangpo, *Ocean of Excellent Utterances*, 134; Gyaltsap Jé, *Entrance of the Bodhisattvas* (*rgyal sras 'jug ngogs*), 112:b6, reads *Guide* 8.136 in the following: "Given that renouncing others and cherishing one's own self is the source of all unwanted problems, in order to prevent causing harm to one's own self and to bring benefit to others, one should relinquish cherishing oneself. One should, for the sake of all sentient beings, give oneself away and hold others as dear as your own self."
23. Shönu and Gyaltsen, eds., *Mind Training*, 88.
24. Shönu and Gyaltsen, eds., *Mind Training*, 88.
25. Shönu and Gyaltsen, eds., *Mind Training*, 89. On these three *lojong* sources of Atiśa, and especially the problems concerning the identity of Dharmarakṣita (the other two being Serlingpa and Maitriyogi), see the introduction by Michael Sweet and Leonard Zwilling in Lhundub Sopa et al., *Peacock in the Poison Grove*.
26. Against the near universal popularity of the *Guide*'s exchange practice as well as *lojong*'s giving and taking in Tibet, an important dissenting voice was Kyopa Jikten Gönpo (1143–1217), the founder of the Drigung Kagyu School. His *Single Viewpoint*, as written down by Sherap Jungné (381) contains a short passage where he asserts that, unless one is skilled (possibly meaning an advanced bodhisattva), engaging in this exchange practice is an error—a statement later critiqued by Sakya Paṇḍita in his *Clarifying the Sage's Intent*, 476.
27. Prajñākaramati (*Bodhicaryāvatārapañjikā* 1359) writes: "It is a supreme secret in that it is something that could cause terror for those who are not so inclined; so to prevent such fear and potential loss of faith from such individuals, this should be kept very much as a secret." On *lojong* as Atiśa's secret teachings, see my introduction to Shönu and Gyaltsen, eds., *Mind Training*, esp. 7.
28. These quotations are from the "Seven-Point Mind Training," in Shönu and Gyaltsen, eds., *Mind Training*, 83–85.
29. The Dalai Lama's views on secular universal ethics are developed, specifically, in *Ethics for the New Millennium* and *Beyond Religion: Ethics for a Whole World*.
30. See, for example, my recent book *A Fearless Heart*.

REFERENCES

Chattopadaya, Alaka. *Atiśa in Tibet*. Delhi: Motilal Banarsidass, 1967.

Chekawa (1101–75). *Seven-Point Mind Training*. In Shönu and Gyaltsen, eds., *Mind Training: The Great Collection*, trans. Thupten Jinpa, 83–85. Boston: Wisdom, 2006.

Chopel, Gendun. *Grains of Gold: Tales of a Cosmopolitan Traveler*. Trans. Thupten Jinpa and Donald S. Lopez. Chicago: University of Chicago Press, 2014.

Dalai Lama. *Ethics for the New Millennium*. New York: Riverhead, 1999.

——. *Transforming the Mind*. Trans. Geshe Thupten Jinpa. London: Thorson, 2000.

——. *Beyond Religion: Ethics for a Whole World*. New York: Houghton Mifflin, 2011.

Gyaltsap Jé (1364–1432). *Entrance of the Bodhisattvas* (*rgyal sras 'jug ngogs*). Collected Works, Kumbum Edition, vol. *nga*.

Harrison, Paul. "The Case of the Vanishing Poet: New Light on Śāntideva and the *Śikṣāsamuccaya*." In *Indica et Tibetica: Festschrift für Michael Hahn, Zum 65. Geburtstag von Freunden und Schülern überreicht*, ed. Konrad Klaus & Jens-Uwe Hartmann,

215–248. Vienna: Arbeitskreis für tibetische und buddhistische Studien Universität Wien, 2007.

Jinpa, Thupten. *A Fearless Heart: How the Courage to Be Compassionate Can Transform Our Lives.* New York: Avery Penguin, 2015.

Kapstein, Matthew T. "Stoics and Bodhisattvas: Spiritual Exercise and Faith in Two Philosophical Traditions." In *Philosophy as a Way of Life: Ancient and Moderns, Essays in Honor of Pierre Hadot*, ed. Michael Chase, Stephen R. L. Clark, and Michael McGhee, 99–115. Oxford: Blackwell, 2013.

Kṛṣṇapa (circa eleventh century). *Spyod 'jug gi rnam par bshad pa.* Tengyur, Comparative Edition, vol. 61, 1686–1836. China, 2000.

——. *Presenting the Difficult Points of Bodhicaryāvatāra* (*Byang chub sems dpa'i spyod pa la 'jug pa'i rtogs par dka' ba'i gnad gtan la dbabs pa*). Tengyur, Comparative Edition, vol. 62, 242–243. China, 2000.

Langri Thangpa (1054–1123). *Eight Verses on Mind Training.* In Shönu and Gyaltsen, eds., *Mind Training: The Great Collection*, trans. Thupten Jinpa, 275–276. Boston: Wisdom, 2006.

Lhundub Sopa, Geshe, Michael Sweet, and Leonard Zwilling, eds. *Peacock in the Poison Grove: Two Buddhist Texts on Training the Mind.* Boston: Wisdom, 2001.

Nāgārjuna (second century). *The Precious Garland: An Epistle to a King.* Trans. John Dunne and Sara McClintock. Boston: Wisdom, 1997.

Prajñākaramati (circa tenth century). *Bodhicaryāvatārapañjikā (Byang chub kyi spyod pa la 'jug pa'i dka' 'grel*). Tengyur, Comparative Edition, vol. 61, 1049–1641. China, 2000.

Sakya Paṇḍita (1182–1251). *Clarifying the Sage's Intent.* Trans. David P. Jackson. In *Stages of the Buddha's Teachings: Three Key Texts*, 383–602. Boston: Wisdom, 2015.

Śāntideva. *Bodhicaryāvatāra.* Trans. Kate Crosby and Andrew Skilton. New York: Oxford University Press, 1998.

Sé Chilbu (1121–89). *A Commentary on the "Seven-Point Mind Training."* Shönu and Gyaltsen, eds., *Mind Training: The Great Collection*, trans. Thupten Jinpa, 87–132. Boston: Wisdom, 2006.

Sherap Jungné (1187–1241). *The Single Viewpoint: A Root Text.* In *Mahāmudrā and Related Instructions: Core Teachings of the Kagyü Schools*, trans. Peter Alan Roberts, 379–400. Boston: Wisdom, 2011.

Shönu Gyalchok and Könchok Gyaltsen, eds. *Mind Training: The Great Collection.* Trans. Thupten Jinpa. Library of Tibetan Classics. Boston: Wisdom, 2006.

Thokmé Sangpo (1295–1369). *Ocean of Excellent Utterances* (*Legs bshad rgya mtsho* in *rgyal sras kyi spyod pa la 'jug pa'i chos skor*), 9–188. Delhi: Institute of Tibetan Classics, 2006.

Vairocanarakṣita (circa tenth century). *Bodhisattvacaryāvatārapañjikā* (*Byang chub sems pa'i spyod pa la 'jug pa'i dka' 'grel*). Tengyur, Comparative Edition, vol. 62, 248–399. China, 2000.

[9]

TAMING ŚĀNTIDEVA

TSONGKHAPA'S USE OF THE *BODHICARYĀVATĀRA*

Roger Jackson

As Jonathan Gold points out in his introduction to this volume, Śāntideva's *Guide* is a "classic," a text that speaks so deeply to common human concerns that it can resonate with people born into cultures far removed in time and space from that of the author. A classic is, in short, "universal"—or nearly so. For all our human commonalities and interconnections, however, even in the twenty-first century we live in a profoundly plural world, so to be truly meaningful in a wide variety of settings, hence fulfill the definition of a "classic," a text must not only achieve excellence of form and content and touch on "timeless" questions but also be, in the language of theologian David Tracy, plural and ambiguous.[1] That is, it must overflow with possible meanings and uses, while avoiding any straightforward statement as to which of these meanings and uses is definitive or final. It is safe to say that religious texts such as the Bible, the Qur'ān, and the *Bhagavad Gītā*, or the literary works of Dante, Shakespeare, and Rumi, would never have become classics had they been open only to a single interpretation; it is precisely *because* they are plural and ambiguous that they could appeal to people in various times and places. Put another way, a classic is a "wild" text, resistant to domestication, impossible to fully subdue or contain. Yet to be human is to seek to tame the wild, whether encountered as natural forces, our fellow creatures, or the intractable meanings we seek to wrest from the world.

As a classic, the *Guide* is plural, ambiguous—and "wild." It is plural because it may be read as a ritual manual, a guide to meditation, an inquiry into ethics, a treatise on metaphysics, a psychological self-interrogation, a great devotional poem—or all of the above. It is ambiguous because its precise meaning, especially in its philosophical passages, was debated for centuries in India, for a millennium (and counting) among Tibetans, and now is contested by academics and Buddhist practitioners in the West. And it is, uncontestably, wild. Granted, it is systematic to a degree, more or less following the course of a bodhisattva's training as crystallized in the six perfections (*pāramitā*). Just as often, however, it is marked by Śāntideva's improvisational approach to the topics that interest him, as shown, for instance, in the way he will proffer one set of meditative reflections, then suggest a different tack, and another—not in an attempt to establish a rigid contemplative sequence but to provide himself and the reader with a set of possibilities, at least one of which is bound to be effective. In this way, the *Guide* is resistant to highly ramified commentary—yet that is precisely the treatment it has received from scholastic traditions, especially in Tibet, where for a thousand years or more it has shaped understanding of what it means to be a bodhisattva, working toward full awakening for the sake of all beings. Despite the *Guide*'s occasional unruliness, its sheer poetic, philosophical, and psychological brilliance—not to mention its influence in India—made it impossible to ignore, so scholastics within the developing monastic orders of second-millennium Tibet set out to "tame" it, to routinize its charisma, by bringing it under their intellectual and institutional control.[2]

This chapter will examine one such attempt to tame the *Guide*, that of Tsongkhapa Losang Drakpa (Tsong kha pa Blo bzang grags pa, 1357–1417), the forefather of the Geluk (*dge lugs*) order of Tibetan Buddhism, the monastic lineage that would give Tibet the institution of the Dalai Lamas and dominate Tibetan politics from the mid-seventeenth to the mid-twentieth century. Tsongkhapa was one of the most influential figures in Tibetan Buddhist history, at once a visionary mystic, a brilliant and controversial philosopher, a dogged monastic reformer, and a founder of religious institutions that have lasted down to the present day. Our primary focus will be on Tsongkhapa's treatment of the *Guide* in his 1402 magnum opus, *The Great Treatise on the Stages of the Path to Awakening* (*Byang chub lam rim chen mo*),[3] but we also will cast a backward glance at Indian and Tibetan thinkers preceding him and touch on developments in Geluk tradition after his time.

There are two primary ways Tibetan scholastics managed the *Guide*: commentary and selective incorporation. Between the eleventh and twentieth centuries, they composed over a hundred full-fledged *Guide* commentaries, all of which, to one degree or another, approach the poem with a classic scholastic tool, developed in India and brought to perfection in Tibet: a highly detailed and elaborate topical outline (*sa bcad*).[4] These commentaries, found in all the major Tibetan Buddhist orders, served as the basis for concerted study of the *Guide*, which formed an important part of the scholastic curriculum at monasteries large and small, and was, like other major texts, often committed to memory. As impressive as the number of Tibetan *Guide* commentaries may be, it is dwarfed by the myriad of original Tibetan treatises that selectively incorporated passages from the *Guide* into their argument, typically as a proof text for points their authors wished to make, whether about cosmology, psychology, ethics, metaphysics, or some other matter. The *Great Treatise* typifies the second type of management, in that it weaves perspectives and quotations from the *Guide* into its lengthy, original exposition of various ways of progressing along the spiritual path. It is arguably the most influential such exposition in Tibetan Buddhist literature, and certainly a key to understanding the Geluk perspective on the world.[5]

The *Great Treatise* is an example of the Tibetan literary genre called stages of the path (*lam rim*), which seeks to outline, in greater or lesser detail, the entire path to awakening contained in the sūtras, commentaries, and treatises of nontantric Indian Buddhism, utilizing textual citations, reasoning, and meditation instruction to give the reader a basis for putting the vast resources of the tradition into actual practice. Prototypes of this genre may be found in Indian texts like Buddhaghosa's *Path of Purity* (*Visuddhimagga*, fifth century CE), Āryaśūra's *Concise Presentation of the Perfections* (*Pāramitāsamāsa*, d.u.), and the three *Stages of Meditation* (*Bhāvanākrama*) texts of Kamalaśīla (eighth century)—as well the *Guide* itself and Śāntideva's other great overview of the path, the *Training Anthology* (*Śikṣāsamuccaya*)[6]—but it was in Tibet that stages-of-the-path literature flourished. Examples are found in all the extant Tibetan religious orders, a fact that in part reflects the influence exerted on all post-1000 Buddhist schools by Atiśa (982–1054) and his successors in the Kadam (*bka' gdams*) tradition, whose writings focused on the bodhisattva's mind training (*blo sbyong*) and the sequence of "stages of the doctrine" (*bstan rim*); from the latter, the stages-of-the-path literature developed.[7] The influence of the *Guide* is evident in both mind-training and stages-of-the-doctrine texts, where it is quoted frequently, especially in discussions of the development of the key Mahāyāna Buddhist attitude, *bodhicitta*, the awakening mind or spirit of enlightenment.[8]

By the fourteenth century the Kadam had nearly disappeared, but Tsongkhapa saw himself as renewing the tradition, to the point where in its early period, the Geluk sometimes was referred to as the Neo-Kadam. Tsongkhapa explicitly took Atiśa's *Lamp on the Path to Enlightenment* (*Bodhipathapradīpa*) as the model for the *Great Treatise*, echoing Atiśa's threefold division of people into (1) those of small spiritual capacity, who only aspire to high rebirths; (2) those of medium capacity, who as practitioners of the "Lesser" Vehicle, the Hīnayāna, solely seek their own liberation from rebirth in samsara, and (3) those of great capacity, Mahāyāna bodhisattvas, who aspire to full buddhahood so as to be able to benefit all sentient beings to the greatest possible degree.[9] Given the importance of the *Guide* for Atiśa and other Kadampas, it is not surprising that Tsongkhapa incorporates it into his text in a significant way. Indeed, the *Great Treatise*'s 145 citations of the *Guide*, covering 213 of the poem's 914 verses[10] wholly or in part, make it, by a considerable margin, the text Tsongkhapa quotes most often. *Guide* quotations are scattered throughout the *Great Treatise*, but are particularly concentrated in the sections that introduce the being of great capacity, outline meditations for the development of *bodhicitta*, and detail the perfections of generosity, patience, and joyous perseverance. In what follows, I will briefly survey the ways Tsongkhapa uses the *Guide* in these and other parts of the *Great Treatise*, noting when possible the points where he departs (or doesn't) from Śāntideva's original context or meaning.

In the first section of the *Great Treatise*—which extols the greatness of the teaching handed down by Atiśa and explains how to find a proper spiritual teacher, treat them with respect, and study and contemplate their teachings—Tsongkhapa hardly uses the *Guide* at all, simply citing two verses that compare practicing the Dharma as an antidote for our afflictions to taking medicine for an illness (2.55, 5.109).[11] As basic as the spiritual teacher is for Tsongkhapa and many Tibetan Buddhists, and as significant as his teachers must have been for Śāntideva, the figure of the guru does not loom large in the *Guide*. The insistence by Tsongkhapa and others that the guru is the "root of the path" no doubt reflects the degree to which Tibetan Buddhism was infused by tantric perspectives, which probably were known to Śāntideva but were not as prominent in his day as they became in the later versions of Indian Buddhism that were transmitted to Tibet.

In his ensuing discussion of people of lower and medium capacity, who self-centeredly aim, respectively, at higher rebirths and liberation from samsara, Tsongkhapa cites the *Guide* twenty-nine times, drawing on every chapter but the tenth. He most often quotes chapters 4 and 5, which, with their focus on mental and ethical self-scrutiny, are especially germane to persons of lower and medium capacity. Addressing the importance, for spiritual progress, of taking advantage of a human life of leisure and opportunity, he cites passages that stress the usefulness of a human rebirth (5.69, 8.14)[12] and the stupidity of squandering it—which we surely will regret when we end up in a hell realm (e.g., 4.23–27, 4.17–21).[13] Reflecting on the inevitability of death, he cites verses that remind his readers that at death they can't take their possessions with them, but that their karma will follow them to the next life (2.34, 2.40).[14] Considering the uncertainties to be faced in a future life, he cites verses emphasizing the incentive for good behavior provided by suffering and fear (6.12cd, 6.21, 4.18)[15] and the need to find a reliable source of protection outside of samsara (2.50ab, 2.46–48).[16] Underlining the importance of refuge in the Triple Gem, he cites one of the *Guide*'s most famous verses, which likens our ever-so-rare opportunity to learn how to cultivate virtue from a buddha to a flash of lightning in the dark of night (1.5).[17] Mulling the vagaries of karma, Tsongkhapa cites verses that lay out the dire consequences of negative actions, especially anger (6.1, 1.34),[18] and encourages constant reflection on the results of our deeds (2.63, 7.40).[19] Detailing the various types of suffering to which sentient beings are prey, he cites verses emphasizing the rarity of rebirth in a higher realm (9.156),[20] the importance of performing religious acts with an undistracted mind (5.16),[21] and the necessity to detach ourselves from worldly hindrances, including loved ones (8.32–33).[22] Seeking the origins of suffering, he cites a series of verses that locate the source not in external foes but in our internal enemies, the afflictions (4.28–33).[23] Outlining the three trainings (in ethics, meditation, and wisdom) that help us transcend suffering, he similarly focuses on the importance, for all three, of overcoming our greatest enemy, the afflictions (4.43–46, 4.20, 4.39, 8.60).[24]

As noted above, the supporting verses cited by Tsongkhapa in his discussion of the being of lesser capacity are drawn from throughout the *Guide*, though especially from chapters 4 and 5. This tells us that while Śāntideva held and espoused views common to all Buddhist traditions, including the "Hīnayāna" intended for persons of lesser and medium capacity, he did not choose to concentrate them in a single place as part of a sequence that led from "lower" to "higher" ideas and practices, instead applying them throughout the text as the subject matter warranted. The *Guide* does display an overall progressive sequence, but it is very much within a Mahāyāna frame, moving from the initial chapters on the awakening mind and mental and moral discipline through the six perfections of a bodhisattva, which culminate in the perfection of wisdom.

In introducing the person of great capacity, the bodhisattva, who strives for perfect buddhahood for the sake of all sentient beings, Tsongkhapa follows long-standing tradition by defining the ideal Mahāyāna practitioner in terms of their possession of *bodhicitta*, and in so doing cites the *Guide* ten times, mostly from chapter 1, which is famous for its eloquent celebration and explanation of the awakening mind. When, near the beginning of the *Great Treatise*, he first describes the person of great capacity, Tsongkhapa uses passages from the *Guide* to underscore the rarity of *bodhicitta*, as well as the way possession of it makes one a "child of the Buddha" (1.9abc, 1.24)[25]—a status underlined, near the outset of the section on the bodhisattva's attitude and training, by an additional *Guide* verse (3.26cd).[26] In going on to celebrate the greatness of *bodhicitta*, Tsongkhapa draws extensively on the *Guide*, citing verses that describe it as a "jewel of the mind" and "the quintessential butter churned from milk of the sublime teaching" (1.36ab, 3.31cd),[27] and asserting its immeasurable virtue, its unconquerable power to overcome negative actions, and its capacity to bear spiritual fruit unceasingly (1.30bcd, 1.66cd, 1.14ab, 1.21–22, 1.12).[28] As before, however, Tsongkhapa's placement and sequencing differ from Śāntideva's: the discussion of the awakening mind comes at the very beginning of the *Guide*, but does not really make its entrance in the *Great Treatise* until a third of the way through the text, at the point where the focus shifts from Hīnayāna to Mahāyāna.

Arguably, Tsongkhapa's most original contribution to the discussion of *bodhicitta* comes in his all-important exposition of the way to develop the awakening mind, which he analyzes into two practices. The first is the "seven cause-and-effect personal instructions," which he traces back primarily to Atiśa, and before him such masters as Candragomin and Kamalaśīla; these instructions focus on recognizing all sentient beings as having been, in one or another rebirth, our devoted mother, and developing love, compassion, and *bodhicitta* toward all beings on that basis.[29] We begin by developing equanimity toward all beings, then contemplating the seven points:

1. Recognizing that that all beings have been our mothers
2. Remembering our mothers' kindness
3. Wishing to repay our mothers' kindness
4. Cultivating love toward all beings

5. Cultivating compassion toward all beings
6. Cultivating the special resolve to attain awakening for the sake of all beings
7. Generating *bodhicitta*.

Since this particular meditative sequence is traced to masters other than Śāntideva, Tsongkhapa does not cite the *Guide* much here (he quotes Kamalaśīla most often); the two exceptions are a series of verses focused on the ritual vow undertaken by a bodhisattva (3.23–26)[30] and a verse explaining the difference between aspirational and engaged *bodhicitta*, which are to be understood as analogous to intending to go somewhere and actually making the journey (1.15).[31]

The second way to develop *bodhicitta* is "exchanging self and other," a practice that Tsongkhapa traces primarily to Śāntideva, with a nod to Nāgārjuna before him. This involves a willingness to take on the sufferings of others and giving them our own happiness, through (a) undercutting our sense of separateness from others, (b) recognizing the faults of self-cherishing thought, and (c) an exercise in which we deliberately see ourselves as others see us.[32] Tsongkhapa's presentation of exchanging ourselves with others—which focuses on (a) and (b) but omits (c)—contains thirteen *Guide* citations, almost all of them from the last half of chapter 8, where Śāntideva explores the topic in considerable detail.

Tsongkhapa's presentation begins with the famous *Guide* verse in which Śāntideva announces that if we wish to protect ourselves and others, we must practice the supreme secret: exchanging ourselves for others (8.120).[33] He goes on to cite the verses in which the *Guide* insists that all the misery we experience in samsara is a result of cherishing ourselves at the expense of others, while all our happiness derives from putting others ahead of ourselves (8.129–131).[34] In encouraging himself and his readers to undertake the exchange, Tsongkhapa cites several *Guide* verses that ask us to overcome our natural reluctance, for instance, by recognizing that the physical "I" with which we identify is made up of physical substances contributed by others (our parents) (8.112cd, 8.111),[35] and conversely, that the mental "I" to which we are so attached is impossible to find, so that we are in fact interrelated with all beings, and the suffering of "another" is really no different from "my" suffering (8.99, 8.101).[36] Describing the actual meditation on exchanging ourselves with others, Tsongkhapa cites the *Guide* copiously, focusing on verses in which Śāntideva further emphasizes the relation between self-cherishing and suffering on the one hand and other-cherishing and happiness on the other (8.154c–155, 8.157),[37] admonishes his own mind to cherish others (8.137–138, 8.167–172, 8.136cd),[38] and points out that we should be as grateful to sentient beings as we are to buddhas, since we "achieve a buddha's qualities" through both (6.113).[39] Through the development of these understandings and attitudes, we will be able to generate *bodhicitta*. Tsongkhapa also cites the *Guide* several times in his discussion of how to maintain *bodhicitta* once it has been developed, focusing in particular on verses that stress that attaining *bodhicitta* is like "a blind person finding a jewel in a heap of garbage" and involves a promise to all sentient beings, the breaking of which entails the direst karmic consequences (4.5–6, 3.27).[40]

Once again, Tsongkhapa takes verses from the *Guide* out of their original context and inserts them into his own version of the path to awakening. The setting in which Śāntideva addresses the development of *bodhicitta* is near the end of the long chapter on the perfection of meditation (or meditative stabilization) (*dhyānapāramitā*), which typically focuses on the development of concentration. In that eighth chapter, the discussion of *bodhicitta* is preceded by long passages promoting detachment from sense desires (including the verses, problematic to many moderns, that expound on the defects of the female body), and describing the physical and psychological conditions required for a meditation retreat. It is not entirely clear why the last part of the chapter on meditation is focused on *bodhicitta* practices; perhaps *bodhicitta* itself is to be taken as the main object of concentration. What is clear is that, unlike many other authors, Śāntideva does not utilize his discussion of the perfection of meditation to describe the standard details and techniques of attaining serenity or concentration, especially as found in the works of the Indian philosopher Asaṅga. For his part, Tsongkhapa lifts the *Guide*'s description of how to develop *bodhicitta* out of its original context and places it near the beginning of his own discussion of the path of the bodhisattva. By the same token, his later chapters on the perfection of meditative stabilization and serenity meditation focus either generally or in great detail on precisely those details and techniques of concentration practice ignored by Śāntideva.

The *Great Treatise*'s ensuing exposition of the six Mahāyāna perfections (*pāramitā*) draws on the *Guide* to a greater or lesser degree in defining and explaining each transcendent virtue. The chapter on the perfection of generosity (*dānapāramitā*) quotes the *Guide* six times, drawing from chapters 3 and 5. Near the outset, Tsongkhapa cites a key verse that identifies the perfection of generosity *not* with the elimination of all material needs but with a state of mind: it is "the attitude of giving away to all beings" (5.9–10).[41] Other verses cited in relation to generosity encourage giving away our body and resources and all our merit, and assert that doing so will lead us to nirvana (3.10–11).[42] With regard to giving up our body, however, Tsongkhapa quotes the *Guide*'s admonition not to sacrifice it if we are psychologically unprepared to do so (5.86–87);[43] more broadly, he cites Śāntideva's suggestion that, when considering whether to give something, we should weigh the overall benefit and loss for sentient beings—there will be times when we should *not* give, because to do so will harm our own spiritual practice and hence be to the long-term detriment of beings (5.83c).[44] The chapter on the perfection of ethical discipline (*śīlapāramitā*) quotes the *Guide* only once, for definitional purposes: ethical discipline is said to be "an attitude of abstention" (5.11),[45] and in this sense, it is "psychologized" much as the perfection of generosity is. Because both the *Guide* and the *Great Treatise* more or less explicitly deal with the six perfections, more or less in sequence, it is here that Tsongkhapa's and Śāntideva's programs overlap to the greatest degree. At the same time, while Śāntideva covers all six perfections, he devotes separate chapters (6–9) only to the last four; his discussions of generosity and ethical discipline must be drawn out of earlier chapters. Hence the range of the *Guide* contexts from which Tsongkhapa draws in discussing the first two perfections, and perhaps too the relative paucity of his *Guide* citations.

In contrast, Tsongkhapa's discussion of the next two perfections, patience (*kṣānti*) and joyous perseverance (*vīrya*), is based almost entirely on Śāntideva's treatment of these topics. The patience chapter includes thirty-four *Guide* citations, all but one from chapter 6, 40 percent of whose verses are cited. In keeping with tradition, Tsongkhapa divides patience into patience in the face of physical or verbal abuse, patience in the face of general suffering, and patience with our spiritual practice. In addressing patience in the face of physical or verbal abuse, Tsongkhapa draws on the *Guide* abundantly in considering our natural reaction to such abuse, namely anger. He cites numerous verses that emphasize the terrible psychological, social, and karmic consequences of anger (6.1, 6.3–5),[46] while at the same time extolling patience as an antidote that will bring us happiness in this and future lives (5.12–14, 6.6cd, 6.2).[47] In reviewing particular techniques for disarming anger, Tsongkhapa cites numerous *Guide* verses to make the point that those who harm us physically should *not* be hated or blamed, because:

- They are at the mercy of the afflictions, hence lack the self-control that would make them culpable (6.31, 6.33–34, 6.37);[48]

- Whether human nature is evil or good, evildoers cannot be blamed, for in the former case it is who they are, and in the latter case it is *not* who they are (6.39);[49]
- It is not a weapon or even a person that harms us, but the hostile mind that impels the action, and *that*, if anything, should be the target of our anger (6.41);[50]
- Those who harm us are really just instruments for the fruition of our own negative karma (6.42, 6.45–47, 6.73, 6.43–44);[51] and
- Both those who harm us and we ourselves are subject to afflictions, so "who is blameless and who is to blame?" (6.67).[52]

Tsongkhapa goes on to encourage patience with those who undermine our sense of self-worth through verbal abuse, arguing on the basis of the *Guide* that the praise, fame, and honor we crave bring us neither merit nor health and in fact distract us from more important matters (6.90–91b, 6.93, 6.98);[53] indeed, not only does verbal abuse not harm our bodies or our minds, but also we ought to be grateful to those who insult us, because they keep us from obsession with selfish concerns that may entail negative consequences for us (6.52–53, 6.54, 6.99–101)[54]—after all, none of the praise we garner will go with us at death, while the deeds we perform with body, speech, and mind will continue as karmic seeds (6.55–59).[55]

In the final sections of the patience chapter, Tsongkhapa uses the *Guide* to make a number of further points. First, if we have adopted *bodhicitta* as our central outlook, we should not be angry at beings or resentful of their successes and happiness (6.80–84, 6.87–89).[56] Second, we must be willing to endure suffering, for it is far more common than happiness (6.12ab),[57] "If there is a remedy, Why be displeased? If there is no remedy, Why be displeased?" (6.10),[58] and suffering helps us to build good qualities, including disenchantment, compassion, and a determination to be free (6.12cd, 6.31, 6.74–75).[59] Finally, we must be courageous in the face of suffering, for, as the *Guide* reminds us, it is possible to build up our endurance: beginning with small problems, we train ourselves to the point where even the terrors of hell can be borne for the sake of sentient beings (6.14, 6.17–18b).[60] Tsongkhapa goes on to explain briefly the third type of patience, related to spiritual practice, but does not quote the *Guide*.

While Tsongkhapa does not follow the precise ordering of topics in Śāntideva's chapter on patience—for he is guided above all by the classic threefold division of patience, which the *Guide* does not employ—he mines it thoroughly for supporting citations, leaving no major argument unacknowledged and utilizing quotations in an order and a manner that any student of the *Guide* will recognize as quite consonant with Śāntideva's own general approach to a given topic. Nevertheless, Tsongkhapa's organization of material from the patience chapter under scholastic rubrics provides further evidence that he is "taming" the *Guide* for his own particular purposes, regardless of how Śāntideva may have intended his text to be used.

The joyous perseverance (*vīrya*) chapter contains thirty-five *Guide* quotations, all from chapter 7—a remarkable 60 percent of whose verses are cited. As with most other perfections, Tsongkhapa draws his definition from the *Guide*: "joyous perseverance . . . is delight in virtue" (7.2a).[61] He goes on to discuss the method for developing joyous perseverance, first, with the help of the *Guide*, identifying the factors that prevent its arising: laziness, adhering to the ignoble, and self-contempt (7.2bcd, 7.3).[62] Tsongkhapa rails against procrastination, then argues against adherence to the ignoble with the help of a *Guide* verse that asks rhetorically how we could be drawn away from "the source of infinite joy" to "delight in distractions and amusements" that only cause suffering (7.15).[63] He argues against self-contempt by citing a verse that reminds us that we should not be discouraged, because all beings will attain buddhahood—and that as humans following the bodhisattva path, we have it within our grasp (7.17–19).[64] Tsongkhapa goes on to assure us that the difficulties we face are bearable because we grow accustomed to them gradually, such that our capacity to give away a simple vegetable eventually becomes the capacity to give away our body (7.20–7.26).[65] In fact, Śāntideva reminds us, as bodhisattvas we are accumulating vast amounts of merit and knowledge, so our body and mind, mounted on the steed of *bodhicitta*, will "proceed from joy to joy," with discouragement left far behind (7.27–28, 7.30).[66]

Tsongkhapa's analysis of joyous perseverance continues with a discussion of the four powers favorable to perfecting it: aspiration, steadfastness, joy, and relinquishment. His sections on all of these draw heavily on the *Guide* for support. The power of aspiration is developed through reflection on the importance of aspiring to attain spiritual goals, rooted in prior recognition of "karma's fruitional effects" (7.39–40)[67] and a consideration of the terrible waste involved if we fail to use this human rebirth for our own and others' higher purposes (7.33–36).[68] The power of steadfastness is developed through confidence in our own ability to begin a project and follow it through to completion, and the resolve to liberate sentient beings who do not have the ability or the will to free themselves (7.47–50).[69] In striving to liberate others, we should avoid arrogance toward those whom we help while maintaining pride in our own talent, determination, and readiness to overcome obstacles (7.51cd, 7.55, 7.52–54).[70] The power of joy is developed through relishing the work of helping others: bodhisattvas are passionate about any activity they undertake, embracing it as "an elephant, scourged by the midday sun,/comes upon a pond and plunges in" (7.62–64, 7.65).[71] The power of relinquishment is developed through recognition that there are times when our capacity reaches its limit and we must step back, postponing completion of the task for another day (7.66).[72] Finally, in terms of the mindset with which the bodhisattva's work must be approached, Tsongkhapa draws from the *Guide* the insight that we must perform all actions with great mindfulness, lest we lapse in our commitment to the task of freeing beings. Indeed, we must be as alert as a person engaged in a sword fight, or a person carrying mustard oil that must not be spilled on pain of death, or a person on whose lap a poisonous snake is coiled (7.67–73).[73] In short, we must approach all our work conscientiously, allowing ourselves to be driven by enthusiasm as cotton is blown by the wind (7.74–75).[74]

It is, then, in their treatment of the perfection of joyous perseverance that Śāntideva and Tsongkhapa most closely align: Tsongkhapa quotes most of the chapter, and in precisely the order set forth by the *Guide*. In this sense, the *Great Treatise*'s joyous perseverance chapter is more or less a straightforward commentary on Śāntideva's chapter on the same topic—and in this, it is unique.

As prominent as the *Guide* is in the *Great Treatise*'s treatment of the perfections of patience and joyous perseverance, Tsongkhapa cites it only once in his brief analyses of the perfections of meditation (*dhyāna*) and wisdom (*prajñā*); he simply quotes a verse to the effect that the perfection of joyous perseverance issues naturally in the practice of meditation (8.1ab).[75] By the same token, he cites it quite sparingly in the *Great Treatise*'s lengthy final sections on serenity (*śamatha*) and insight (*vipaśyanā*). In the serenity section, he quotes the *Guide* to make several points, to the effect that "religious" practices are pointless if performed with an unconcentrated mind (5.16), serenity meditation is vital because our afflictions are destroyed only when our insight into reality is based on a concentrated mind (8.4), and an important part of serenity meditation is constant awareness of what is happening in our body and mind (5.108).[76] The insight section, which sometimes is regarded as an independent treatise on emptiness, quotes the *Guide*'s ninth chapter, on wisdom, but a single time, on the importance of ascertaining the object of negation before refuting it (9.140ab).[77] Although Tsongkhapa considered Śāntideva a Prāsaṅgika Mādhyamika just like him, he supports his own arguments in the insight section mostly on the basis of the works of Nāgārjuna and Candrakīrti, which Tibetan thinkers regarded as foundational to an understanding of Madhyamaka thought, and which Tsongkhapa saw as the true sources of the Prāsaṅgika perspective.

Tsongkhapa discussed the bodhisattva path in numerous other works, including shorter stages-of-the-path texts,[78] and the influence of the *Guide* is explicit or implicit in each. He also is said by later Geluk tradition to have handed down a Ganden Ear-Whispered Tradition (*dga' ldan snyan brgyud*) of teachings on such topics as *mahāmudrā* meditation, *guru-yoga* practice, and *bodhicitta* that he received in visions from the wisdom bodhisattva, Mañjughoṣa. Restricted for centuries, these instructions eventually were written down by such masters as Panchen Losang Chökyi Gyaltsen (Paṇ chen Blo bzang chos kyi rgyal mtshan, 1570–1662), Kachen Yeshé Gyaltsen (Dka' chen Ye shes rgyal mtshan, 1713–93), and, more recently, Pabongkha Dechen Nyingpo (Pha bong kha Bde chen snying po, 1878–1941). One of the essential *bodhicitta* practices of this tradition, said to have been transmitted from the time of Tsongkhapa, combines the seven-point cause-and-effect instruction and exchanging self with others—which are separate procedures in the *Great Treatise*—into a single eleven-point meditation:[79]

1. Developing equanimity
2. Recognizing that that all beings have been our mothers
3. Remembering our mothers' kindness
4. Wishing to repay our mothers' kindness
5. Equalizing ourselves with others
6. Considering the faults of self-cherishing
7. Considering the virtues of cherishing others
8. Compassionately taking over the sufferings of others
9. Lovingly giving to others our own virtues and attainments
10. Cultivating the special resolve to attain awakening for the sake of all beings
11. Generating *bodhicitta*.[80]

The eighth and ninth points, which cover compassion and love respectively, entail the practice of giving and taking (*gtong lan*), a way of exchanging self for other that typically involves visualizing the inhalation of other beings' defilements and sufferings in the form of dark smoke, and the exhalation of our own happiness and attainments toward those beings in the form of white light. So far as I am aware, Tsongkhapa's writings do not describe this practice, but it was prominent in the writings of the Kadam masters who inspired him.[81] They, in turn, regarded giving and taking as the key to effectuating Śāntideva's ideal of exchanging self and others—even though it never is mentioned in the *Guide*.[82] Whatever its antiquity, the eleven-point meditation, with giving and taking as its key technique, has become the standard Gelukpa method for developing *bodhicitta*.

In conclusion, we can see that Tsongkhapa utilized the *Guide* extensively in his *Great Treatise on the Stages of the Path to Enlightenment*, finding apposite quotations to support his own distinctive articulation of the sequence of reflections and practices we must follow if we are to make the Buddha's teaching our own. In the process, he selected many vital passages from the *Guide* while ignoring others, and arranged the verses he did select according to his own programmatic needs. In the process, something of Śāntideva's originality and insight was inevitably lost, some of his charisma routinized, some of his wildness tamed. Tsongkhapa was not alone: whether in commentaries, independent works, or oral transmissions, Tibetan masters took the unique poetry and perspectives of the *Guide* and molded them to their own intellectual, institutional, and pedagogical purposes—even at the cost of straitjacketing a philosophical and psychological classic that is subtler than the scholastic mind can fully fathom. This seems, however, to be the price a work must pay to become a classic, for a text stays fresh and relevant only by continual, creative appropriation by men and women in times and places distant from those of the author. Thus, whatever our ambivalence about the scholastic project in general and its application to the *Guide* in particular, we must be grateful to those Tibetan teachers who sought to bring Śāntideva's masterwork alive in their own time—and to those who do so in our own.

NOTES

1. See Tracy, *Plurality and Ambiguity*.
2. For a thoughtful collection of reflections on the theory and practice of scholasticism, see Cabezón, ed., *Scholasticism*; of special note are Cabezón's introduction (1–17) and the essay by Paul Griffiths ("Scholasticism: The Possible Recovery of an Intellectual Practice," 201–235).
3. Tibetan edition: Tsong kha pa, *sKyes bu gsum gyi rnyams su blang ba'i rim pa thams cad tshang bar ston pa'i byang chub lam gyi rim pa/ Byang chub lam rim che ba*; English translation: Tsong-kha-pa, *The Great Treatise on the Stages of the Path to Enlightenment*, trans. Lamrim Chenmo Translation Committee. For a helpful gloss on the *Great Treatise*, see Yangsi Rinpoche, *Practicing the Path*. For background on the stages of the path, see David Seyfort Ruegg's introduction to Tsong-kha-pa, *Great Treatise*, vol. I, 17–32.

4. For English-language versions of *Guide* commentaries that employ such an outline, see Gyatso, *Meaningful to Behold*; and Pelden, *Nectar of Manjushri's Speech*.
5. My own teacher, Geshe Lhundub Sopa, taught the *Great Treatise* in and around Madison, Wisconsin, over the course of more than two decades; in my experience, he almost never began a discourse on Tsongkhapa's text without first quoting from memory, then commenting upon, a verse from the *Guide*. For his commentary, see Sopa, *Steps on the Path*.
6. For the *Visuddhimagga*, see, e.g., Buddhaghosa, *The Path of Purification (Visuddhimagga)*; for the *Pāramitāsamāsa*, see Meadows, *Arya-Śūra's Compendium of the Perfections*; for the *Bhāvanākramas*, see, e.g., Beyer, *The Buddhist Experience*, 99–115; H.H. the Dalai Lama, *Stages of Meditation*, trans. Geshe Lobsang Jordhen et al.; for the *Śikṣāsamuccaya*, see Goodman, trans., *The Training Anthology of Śāntideva*; for a facing-page Sanskrit and Tibetan edition of the *Guide*, see Bhattacharya, ed., *Bodhicaryāvatāra of Śāntideva*; for a fine translation of the Tibetan version of the *Guide*, see Shantideva, *The Way of the Bodhisattva*, trans. Padmakara Translation Committee.
7. For Atiśa, see, e.g., Atīśa, *A Lamp for the Path and Commentary*, and *The Complete Works of Atiśa*, trans. Sherburne. For mind training, see, especially, Shönu and Gyaltsen, eds., *Mind Training: The Great Collection*, trans. Jinpa, and Jinpa in this volume; for stages of the doctrine, see, e.g., Jackson, "The *bsTan rim* ('Stages of the Doctrine') and Similar Graded Expositions of the Bodhisattva's Path," 229–243.
8. See, e.g., Shönu and Gyaltsen, eds., *Mind Training*; and Gampopa, *The Jewel Ornament of Liberation*, trans. Khenpo Konchog Gyaltsen Rinpoche. On *bodhicitta*, see, especially, Wangchuk, *The Resolve to Become a Buddha*.
9. For Atiśa's *Lamp*, which has been translated multiple times, see, e.g. Atīśa, *A Lamp for the Path and Commentary*; for Tsongkhapa's indebtedness to Atiśa, see Tsong-kha-pa, *Great Treatise*, vol. I, 35–43.
10. This, in any case, is the number of verses in the standard, post-1000 CE Tibetan translation of the *Guide*. This version, which has been the basis for almost all Tibetan discussion of the text, was brought into final form in the eleventh century by the Indian pundit Sumatikīrti and the Tibetan scholar Ngok Loden Sherab (Rngog blo ldan shes rab, 1059–1109); for details, see Shantideva, *Way of the Bodhisattva*, 171. An earlier, and significantly different, Tibetan version of the *Guide*, apparently unknown to later Tibetans, was discovered early in the twentieth century in the cave complex at Dunhuang, China; see Śāntideva, *The Bodhicaryāvatāra*, trans. Crosby and Skilton, xxxii–xxxiv.
11. Tsong-kha-pa, *Great Treatise*, vol. I, 59, 61.
12. Tsong-kha-pa, *Great Treatise*, vol. I, 123–124.
13. Tsong-kha-pa, *Great Treatise*, vol. I, 122, 125.
14. Tsong-kha-pa, *Great Treatise*, vol. I, 146, 150.
15. Tsong-kha-pa, *Great Treatise*, vol. I, 162, 174.
16. Tsong-kha-pa, *Great Treatise*, vol. I, 162, 175.
17. Tsong-kha-pa, *Great Treatise*, vol. I, 178.
18. Tsong-kha-pa, *Great Treatise*, vol. I, 235.
19. Tsong-kha-pa, *Great Treatise*, vol. I, 247.
20. Tsong-kha-pa, *Great Treatise*, vol. I, 266.
21. Tsong-kha-pa, *Great Treatise*, vol. I, 272.
22. Tsong-kha-pa, *Great Treatise*, vol. I, 287.

23. Tsong-kha-pa, *Great Treatise*, vol. I, 302.
24. Tsong-kha-pa, *Great Treatise*, vol. I, 348–349, 352–353.
25. Tsong-kha-pa, *Great Treatise*, vol. I, 134, 135.
26. Tsong-kha-pa, *Great Treatise*, vol. II, 16, where 1.9abc is cited again as well.
27. Tsong-kha-pa, *Great Treatise*, vol. II, 20.
28. Tsong-kha-pa, *Great Treatise*, vol. II, 20–21.
29. Tsong-kha-pa, *Great Treatise*, vol. II, 35–49. For an excellent summary of this meditation, which identifies it as an "intuitive" or "emotional" approach to *bodhicitta*, see Tsering, *The Awakening Mind*, 33–50.
30. Tsong-kha-pa, *Great Treatise*, vol. II, 46.
31. Tsong-kha-pa, *Great Treatise*, vol. II, 48–49.
32. Tsong-kha-pa, *Great Treatise*, vol. II, 51–60; see also Tsering, *Awakening Mind*, 51–78, where it is identified as an "intellectual" or "rational" approach to *bodhicitta*; and Jinpa's chapter in this volume.
33. Tsong-kha-pa, *Great Treatise*, vol. II, 51.
34. Tsong-kha-pa, *Great Treatise*, vol. II, 52.
35. Tsong-kha-pa, *Great Treatise*, vol. II, 52–53.
36. Tsong-kha-pa, *Great Treatise*, vol. II, 54.
37. Tsong-kha-pa, *Great Treatise*, vol. II, 155.
38. Tsong-kha-pa, *Great Treatise*, vol. II, 56.
39. Tsong-kha-pa, *Great Treatise*, vol. II, 57.
40. Tsong-kha-pa, *Great Treatise*, vol. II, 74.
41. Tsong-kha-pa, *Great Treatise*, vol. II, 115.
42. Tsong-kha-pa, *Great Treatise*, vol. II, 119, 116.
43. Tsong-kha-pa, *Great Treatise*, vol. II, 131.
44. Tsong-kha-pa, *Great Treatise*, vol. II, 134.
45. Tsong-kha-pa, *Great Treatise*, vol. II, 144.
46. Tsong-kha-pa, *Great Treatise*, vol. II, 154, 158.
47. Tsong-kha-pa, *Great Treatise*, vol. II, 153, 154, 159.
48. Tsong-kha-pa, *Great Treatise*, vol. II, 162.
49. Tsong-kha-pa, *Great Treatise*, vol. II, 163.
50. Tsong-kha-pa, *Great Treatise*, vol. II, 163.
51. Tsong-kha-pa, *Great Treatise*, vol. II, 164–165.
52. Tsong-kha-pa, *Great Treatise*, vol. II, 165.
53. Tsong-kha-pa, *Great Treatise*, vol. II, 167.
54. Tsong-kha-pa, *Great Treatise*, vol. II, 168–169. Interestingly, Tsongkhapa does not cite the famous set of verses (6.99–111) in which Śāntideva expresses his gratitude to his enemies, who help him develop patience, hence complete the path to buddhahood.
55. Tsong-kha-pa, *Great Treatise*, vol. II, 170.
56. Tsong-kha-pa, *Great Treatise*, vol. II, 170–171.
57. Tsong-kha-pa, *Great Treatise*, vol. II, 172.
58. Tsong-kha-pa, *Great Treatise*, vol. II, 173.
59. Tsong-kha-pa, *Great Treatise*, vol. II, 174–175.
60. Tsong-kha-pa, *Great Treatise*, vol. II, 176.
61. Tsong-kha-pa, *Great Treatise*, vol. II, 182.
62. Tsong-kha-pa, *Great Treatise*, vol. II, 187.
63. Tsong-kha-pa, *Great Treatise*, vol. II, 188.
64. Tsong-kha-pa, *Great Treatise*, vol. II, 188–189.

65. Tsong-kha-pa, *Great Treatise*, vol. II, 190–191.
66. Tsong-kha-pa, *Great Treatise*, vol. II, 192.
67. Tsong-kha-pa, *Great Treatise*, vol. II, 195.
68. Tsong-kha-pa, *Great Treatise*, vol. II, 196.
69. Tsong-kha-pa, *Great Treatise*, vol. II, 197.
70. Tsong-kha-pa, *Great Treatise*, vol. II, 198–199.
71. Tsong-kha-pa, *Great Treatise*, vol. II, 200.
72. Tsong-kha-pa, *Great Treatise*, vol. II, 201.
73. Tsong-kha-pa, *Great Treatise*, vol. II, 202–205.
74. Tsong-kha-pa, *Great Treatise*, vol. II, 206.
75. Tsong-kha-pa, *Great Treatise*, vol. II, 210.
76. Tsong-kha-pa, *Great Treatise*, vol. III, 21, 23, 61.
77. Tsong-kha-pa, *Great Treatise*, vol. III, 126.
78. See, e.g., Wangyal, *The Door of Liberation*, 135–212.
79. Although tradition insists that the eleven-point meditation was given to Tsongkhapa by Mañjughoṣa and that it continued as part of the Ganden Ear-Whispered Tradition from his time on, I am not aware of any textual evidence for the practice until the time of Panchen Losang Chökyi Gyaltsen, who spelled it out in *The Easy Path* (*Bde lam*) and suggested it in his *Offering to the Guru* (*Bla ma mchod pa*); see Jampa, *The Easy Path*, 179; Donald S. Lopez Jr., "A Prayer to the Lama," 384–385 [verses 60–70].
80. For discussion, see, e.g., Jampa, *The Easy Path*, 179–96; Pabongka, *Liberation in the Palm of Your Hand*, 609; Tsering, *Awakening Mind*, 78–81.
81. See, e.g., Shönu and Gyaltsen, eds., *Mind Training*, 83, 94–96, 258–259, 335–355, 426–428, 487–494; and Jinpa's chapter in the present volume. Many of these instructions are based on two of the fifty-odd "slogans" in the *Seven-Point Mind Training* (*Blo sbyong don bdun ma*) of Chekawa Yeshe Dorje (Che ka wa ye shes rdo rje, 1101–75): "Train in the two—giving and taking—alternately. Place the two astride your breath." Chekawa, in turn, drew on a set of slogans that is typically, if questionably, traced back to Atiśa; see Shönu and Gyaltsen, eds., *Mind Training*, 71.
82. However, the practice is usually traced to the *Guide* verse 8.131: "If I do not interchange/My happiness for others' pain,/Enlightenment will never be attained,/And even in saṃsāra, joy will fly from me" (Shantideva, *The Way of the Bodhisattva*, 128).

REFERENCES

Atiśa. *A Lamp for the Path and Commentary*. London: George Allen & Unwin, 1983.

——. *The Complete Works of Atiśa*. Trans. Richard Sherburne. 2nd ed. Delhi: Adiya Prakashan, 2006.

Beyer, Stephan. *The Buddhist Experience: Sources and Interpretations*. Encino and Belmont, CA: Dickenson, 1974.

Bhattacharya, Vidhisekhara, ed. *Bodhicaryāvatāra of Śāntideva*. Biblioteca Indica no. 280. Calcutta: The Asiatic Society, 1960.

Buddhaghosa, Bhadanta. *The Path of Purification (Visuddhimagga)*. Trans. Bhikkhu Ñāṇamoli. 2 vols. Berkeley, CA: Shambhala, 1976.

Cabezón, José Ignacio, ed. *Scholasticism: Cross-Cultural and Comparative Perspectives*. Albany: State University of New York Press, 1998.

Dalai Lama, H.H. [XIV]. *Stages of Meditation*. Trans. Geshe Lobsang Jordhen et al. Ithaca, NY: Snow Lion, 2001.

Gampopa. *The Jewel Ornament of Liberation*. Trans. Khenpo Konchog Gyaltsan Rinpoche. Ithaca, NY: Snow Lion, 1998.

Goodman, Charles, trans. *The Training Anthology of Śāntideva: A Translation of the Śikṣā-samuccaya*. New York; Oxford: Oxford University Press, 2016.

Gyatso, Geshe Kelsang. *Meaningful to Behold: View, Meditation and Action in Mahayana Buddhism*. Trans. Tenzin Norbu. Ed. Jonathan Landaw. Ulverston, Cumbria, England: Tharpa Publications, 1980.

Jackson, David. "The *bsTan rim* ("Stages of the Doctrine") and Similar Graded Expositions of the Bodhisattva's Path." In *Tibetan Literature: Studies in Genre*, ed. José Ignacio Cabezón and Roger R. Jackson, 229–243. Ithaca, NY: Snow Lion, 1996.

Jampa, Gyumed Khensur Lobsang. *The Easy Path: Illuminating the First Panchen Lama's Secret Instructions*. Ed. Lorne Ladner. Boston: Wisdom, 2013.

Shönu Gyalchok and Könchok Gyaltsen, eds. *Mind Training: The Great Collection*. Trans. Thupten Jinpa. Library of Tibetan Classics. Boston: Wisdom, 2006.

Lopez Jr., Donald S. "A Prayer to the Lama." In *Religions of Tibet in Practice*, ed. Donald S. Lopez Jr., 376–386. Princeton, NJ: Princeton University Press, 1997.

Meadows, Carol. *Arya-Śūra's Compendium of the Perfections: Text, Translation and Analysis of the Pāramitāsamāsa*. Bonn: Indica et Tibetica Verlag, 1986.

Pabongka Rinpoche. *Liberation in the Palm of Your Hand: A Concise Discourse on the Path to Enlightenment*. Ed. Trijang Rinpoche. Trans. Michael Richards. Boston: Wisdom, 1997.

Pelden Kunzang. *Nectar of Manjushri's Speech: A Detailed Commentary on Shantideva's* Way of the Bodhisattva. Trans. Padmakara Translation Committee. Ithaca, NY: Snow Lion, 2010.

Śāntideva. *The Bodhicaryāvatāra*. Trans. Kate Crosby and Andrew Skilton. Oxford; New York: Oxford University Press, 1996.

Shantideva. *The Way of the Bodhisattva: A Translation of the* Bodhicaryāvatāra. Trans. Padmakara Translation Committee. Boston and London: Shambhala, 2006.

Sopa, Geshe Lhundub. *Steps on the Path: A Commentary on Tsongkhapa's Lamrim Chenmo*. 5 vols. Boston: Wisdom, 2004–17.

Tracy, David. *Plurality and Ambiguity: Hermeneutics, Religion, Hope*. Chicago: University of Chicago Press, 1985.

Tsering, Geshe Tashi. *The Awakening Mind*. The Foundations of Buddhist Thought, vol. 4. Boston: Wisdom, 2008.

Tsong kha pa. *sKyes bug sum gyi rnyams su blang ba'i rim pa thams cad tshang bar ston pa'i byang chub lam gyi rim pa/Byang chub lam rim che ba*. Zi-ling (Xining): Tso Ngön (mTsho sngon) People's Press, 1985.

Tsong-kha-pa. *The Great Treatise on the Stages of the Path to Enlightenment*. Trans. Lamrim Chenmo Translation Committee. 3 vols. Ithaca, NY: Snow Lion, 2000–2002.

Wangchuk, Dorji. *The Resolve to Become a* Buddha*: A Study of the* Bodhicitta *Concept in Indo-Tibetan Buddhism*. Studia Philologica Buddhica Monograph Series XXIII. Tokyo: The International Institute for Buddhist Studies, 2007.

Wangyal, Geshe. *The Door of Liberation: Essential Teachings of the Tibetan Buddhist Tradition*. Boston: Wisdom, 1995.

Yangsi Rinpoche. *Practicing the Path: A Commentary on the Lamrim Chenmo*. Boston: Wisdom, 2003.

[10]

THE MIDDLE WAY OF THE BODHISATTVA

Douglas S. Duckworth

Śāntideva is commonly associated with a particular interpretation of the Middle Way philosophy in Tibet, the Prāsaṅgika-Madhyamaka or "Consequence School of the Middle Way." Why might this be the case? Śāntideva's *Guide* (*Bodhicaryāvatāra*) clearly does not address a difference between the two types of argument, *reductios* and independent probative arguments, that form the etymological basis of what distinguishes a Prāsaṅgika ("one who uses consequences") from a Svātantrika ("one who uses independent probative arguments"). So why is Śāntideva's composition considered by Tibetans to be a Prāsaṅgika text?

An answer can be found in how one influential Tibetan author, Künzang Sönam (1823–1905), explains the issue in his nearly 1,000-page commentary on the *Guide*. In short, he says that "the basis of the debate between Svātantrika and Prāsaṅgika is whether or not there is something that exists on its own" (*rang mtshan kyis grub pa*).[1] This chapter discusses the role and implications of "existing on its own" as the main principle guiding Künzang Sönam's interpretation of Śāntideva's *Guide*. For him, this particular feature of the Middle Way conveys the thoroughgoing interdependence that is essential for reaching a proper understanding of Śāntideva's text. In particular, he holds that it is through this interpretation of the Middle Way that Śāntideva maintains a view of emptiness that is compatible with an altruistic ethic.

ŚĀNTIDEVA AS A PRĀSAṄGIKA-MĀDHYAMIKA

In his explanation of the ninth chapter of Śāntideva's *Guide,* Künzang Sönam outlines three meanings of interdependence, which can be a useful rubric to position some of the challenging philosophical content of the ninth chapter within the context of the entire text. The three meanings are: "meeting" (*phrad*), "relying" (*ltos*), and "depending" (*brten*). The first, "meeting," connotes dependent arising that is part of the general grammar of Buddhism. Dependent arising is a feature of causal processes, the way there are regularities without substances: "when this is present, that arises, then this ceases, that ceases." Indeed, Śāntideva links his work with this central feature of Buddhist doctrine. That things arise based on causes is a central part of dependent arising, which Śāntideva uses in his analysis of anger in the sixth chapter on patience.

> I feel no anger toward bile and the like, even though they cause intense suffering. Why am I angry with the sentient? They too have reasons for their anger. (6.22)
>
> As this sharp pain wells up, though unsought for, so, though unsought for, wrath wells up against one's will. (6.23)
>
> A person does not get angry at will, having decided "I shall get angry," nor does anger well up after deciding "I shall well up." (6.24)[2]

Continuing a few verses down, he says: "In this way everything is dependent upon something else. Even that thing upon which each is dependent is not independent. Since, like a magical display, phenomena do not initiate activity, at what does one get angry like this?" (6.31).

With these lines, not only does Śāntideva embed his work within the framework of Buddhist doctrine in general, but his argument uncovers an *ethical* component to dependent causality. That is, the objects of our aggression are not isolated individuals but part of an impersonal causal chain.

The notion of dependent arising also extends from causal processes, or chains of events, to spatial relationships as well. This is where we find a second meaning of dependent arising, "relying." Here, dependent arising is interpreted to connote the interdependent relationship of wholes and parts. This meaning also has a major role to play in Buddhist thought in general, where singular persons or selves, like chariots, are critiqued as lacking singular, autonomous existence. Where Śāntideva says: "Teeth, hair, and nails, are not I, nor is the bone, nor I the blood" (9.57), he makes a case for there being no real self. Śāntideva takes up this analysis in the eighth and ninth chapters when he deconstructs the notion of personal identity with an analysis respectively of the body, feelings, the mind, and phenomena: "Just as the trunk of a banana tree is nothing when split into pieces, in the same way too, the 'I' is not a real entity when hunted out analytically" (9.74).

And,

> In the same way, since it is an assemblage of toes, which one is the foot? The same goes for a toe, since it is an assemblage of joints. A joint can also be analysed into its own constituents. (9.85)
>
> Even the constituents can be analysed down to atoms. The atom too can be divided according to the directions. The division of a direction, since it is without parts, leaves space. Therefore the atom does not exist. (9.86)
>
> What person who analyses things thoroughly would take delight in a form which, as has been demonstrated, is like a dream? And since the body, as demonstrated, does not exist, then what woman or what man is there? (9.87)

We find this kind of reductive analysis here with reference to the self and the body. He also uses this analysis of the interdependence of parts and whole later in the ninth chapter to critique notions of a singular agent that is efficacious, such as a creator God (*īśvara*), as well as the notion that there is a singular principle of the world, such as materiality (*prakṛti*), that has multiple qualities.

Śāntideva poetically evokes the absence of true identity when he repeats with emphasis the way that the body is not its constituent parts. It is not the nose, left ear, ankle, spleen, or heart. Rather, it is simply a label designating the collective. Yet the collective, Śāntideva contends, is not a natural unit but an arbitrary one, and has no real boundary around which a self can be demarcated as really separate from others:

> First, just in your mind, pull apart this bag of skin. With the knife of wisdom loosen the flesh from the cage of bones. (5.62)
>
> Cracking open the bones, too, look at the marrow within. Work out for yourself what essence is there. (5.63)
>
> Searching hard like this, you have found no essence here. Now explain why it is that you still continue to guard the body. (5.64)

From the fact that nothing with spatial extension is truly singular—all is dependent on component parts—he again draws an ethical conclusion from the argument of dependent arising: the self is not independent, so there is no reason I am singularly important; hence, I should take care of others as I take care of myself. We find this argument in the eighth chapter on meditative concentration: "If you think it is for the person who has the pain to guard against it, a pain in the foot is not of the hand, so why is the one protected by the other?" (8.99).

And,

> The continuum of consciousness, like a queue, and the combination of constituents, like an army, are not real. The person who experiences suffering does not exist. To whom will that suffering belong? (8.101)
> Without exception, no sufferings belong to anyone. They must be warded off simply because they are suffering. Why is any limitation put on this? (8.102)

Acknowledging that things are dependent on parts (and parts, in turn, are dependent on wholes) is a general feature of the Middle Way view.

The last and subtlest view is found in the third of the three connotations of dependent arising, "depend." That things exist in dependence upon linguistic and conceptual designation is another feature of a Middle Way view. Yet that things do not exist otherwise, *even conventionally*, is a unique feature of Prāsaṅgika as explained by Künzang Sönam—where all things without exception are conceptually or linguistically designated.

While Künzang Sönam interprets Prāsaṅgika as repudiating objective existence, even conventionally, he also holds that Prāsaṅgikas maintain valid sources of knowledge to establish the ultimate and conventional truths. Thus he rejects that the ultimate truth is not an object of knowledge. Yet Śāntideva's claim in the second verse of the ninth chapter that the ultimate truth "is beyond the range of the mind" (9.2) appears to be an explicit rejection of cognitive access to an ultimate truth, not to mention any systematic formulation of it. This is a reason other traditions in Tibet have aligned Śāntideva with Prāsaṅgika. Also, a cognitively delimited ultimate truth is difficult to reconcile with Śāntideva's later statement in the ninth chapter, at the pivotal point in the text where he was said to float away and dissolve into space as the following words resounded: "When entities and non-entities do not exist before the mind, there is nothing else: there is complete pacification without referent object" (9.34).[3]

Śāntideva's words further suggest, *contra* an interpretation of the Middle Way as consistently holding an object in mind and an accompanying thesis, that even emptiness is not really the correct view of things, when he states:

> Without contacting an imputed entity, one cannot apprehend the
> absence of this entity. Therefore, the absence of an unreal entity is
> clearly unreal, too. (9.139)
> Thus, when one's child dies in a dream, the thought "he does not exist"
> Counters the thought of his existence, yet this too is unreal. (9.140)[4]

That is, Śāntideva's verses here indicate that emptiness is unreal; they suggest that it is derivative and thus only a corrective or purgative, not the final view. Künzang Sönam mentions how these verses have been glossed in two distinct ways, reflecting two kinds of interpretation of the ultimate (respectively, as a determinate emptiness of true existence and as an undetermined, nonconceptual emptiness) along two dominant lines of interpreting Prāsaṅgika in Tibet.[5] To avoid the slippery slope of relativism and self-contradiction with a claim that the ultimate truth is completely unknowable, Künzang Sönam emphatically asserts that the ultimate truth is knowable, that it is an absence of intrinsic nature.

With this kind of insistence on maintaining that the correct view of the ultimate is a mere absence of intrinsic existence, his interpretation may be seen as weak on characterizing the transcendence of ultimate truth—which Śāntideva depicts as beyond the range of the mind. Yet by consistently denying that anything exists on its own *even conventionally*, his interpretation is particularly strong with regard to representing conventional truth without reification (and by implication, ultimate truth without reification as well). Since the conventional and ultimate truths are not really different for him, a misunderstanding of one entails a misunderstanding of the other. Thus, his interpretation not only emphasizes that nothing exists on its own, ultimately and conventionally, but also offers a robust account of the complementarity of the two truths. Within this complementarity he positions emptiness and compassion as mutually supportive, and through it emptiness becomes a basis for Śāntideva's altruistic ethic.

Since the issue of the Prāsaṅgika's treatment of the ultimate in the *Guide* has been discussed elsewhere,[6] I will focus here on the status of conventional truth in Śāntideva's text, with particular attention to the status of conventional truth in relation to assertions unique to Prāsaṅgika.

THE CONVENTIONAL TRUTH OF PRĀSAṄGIKA

Since all conventions are like illusions for proponents of the Middle Way, we may wonder how distinctions can be maintained between correct and incorrect views regarding the conventional world. Bodies imagined in dreams and bodies encountered when awake can be said to be equally existent conventionally and equally nonexistent ultimately. There is no ontological priority for either because both rise and fall dependently, based on conditions, and neither is independently real.

Yet as Künzang Sönam claims, in contrast to Prāsaṅgika, an alternative interpretation, Svātantrika, accepts a distinction between correct and incorrect conventional truths. The reason, he says, is because they accept that conventional truth exists on its own (*rang gi mtshan nyid kyis grub pa*); Prāsaṅgikas do not accept this because "whatever is conventional necessarily does not exist the way it appears."[7] Thus, Prāsaṅgikas need not make a distinction between correct or incorrect conventional truths. In this context, Künzang Sönam adds that "correct" (*yang dag pa*) effectively means "on its own" (*rang gi mtshan nyid kyis grub pa*).[8]

Künzang Sönam claims that accepting the difference between the respective existence and nonexistence of a real body and an illusory one does not conflict with a Prāsaṅgika not accepting correct or incorrect conventional truths.[9] For a Prāsaṅgika, the difference between a conventional illusion (e.g., a rope-snake) and a conventional reality (e.g., a rope) can be and is drawn, but it is not a difference that is drawn *objectively*:

> Since the difference in the status of the existence of these two cannot be differentiated from the side of the object itself (*yul de'i rang ngos nas*), one must draw a fine line (*'jog mtshams phra mo*) by means of differentiating whether or not it is undermined by another conventional cognition. This has been said again and again to be a consummate essential point of the Prāsaṅgika view that is difficult to understand.[10]

In other words, the essential point of the Prāsaṅgika view is that distinctions within the conventional—between truth and falsity, existence and nonexistence, real and unreal—are not objective; that is, they are not determined from objects themselves. Conventional distinctions between what is real and unreal are made *in terms of the world*. These distinctions are not made based on any real differences in objects themselves; rather, what constitutes real and unreal is *intersubjective*. Significantly, what is intersubjective necessarily incorporates a subjective dimension.

One might think that if a Prāsaṅgika does not accept objective distinctions, then this position would be no different from a kind of subjective idealism commonly characterized as "Mind Only." Rather than claim that the mind is independently real in contrast to unreal external objects, like a subjective idealist, Śāntideva explicitly affirms the interdependency of minds and objects (9.110–113). Künzang Sönam further describes how minds and external objects are equally existent in worldly convention (and in Abhidharma) and equally nonexistent when their nature is sought in analysis (and in a sublime being's meditative equipoise). He goes on to say that Prāsaṅgikas accept external objects conventionally because the coextensive presence and absence of objects and cognitions undermines the claim that even conventionally there are no external objects. That is, when there are external objects there are internal cognitions, and when there are internal cognitions there are external objects; cognitions and objects rise and fall together—they are paired. He reiterates this point by saying that not only does no *conventional* analysis negate external objects, but also conventional analysis invalidates the absence of externality.[11]

Elaborating on the difference between the Middle Way and Mind Only, Künzang Sönam says that "the distinction of whether or not external objects are asserted or not conventionally comes down to the acceptance of something existing on its own (*rang mtshan gyis grub pa*)."[12] Once again this is the main issue for his interpretation. He argues that proponents of Mind Only are not satisfied with assenting to the external world as it is proclaimed by the world; they think that if there were external objects, they would have to be the types of things that would be findable upon analysis and existing separately from cognition.[13] Yet since there are no such things, they deny them. Prāsaṅgikas, in contrast, assert external objects without these criteria, namely, without there being any objective basis of designation for these claims. Thus, Prāsaṅgikas simply assent to external objects in accord with the ways of the world, and this is due once again to the fact that they do not accept anything existing on its own (*rang mtshan gyis grub pa*), neither an external or an internal world, even conventionally.[14]

Künzang Sönam clarifies the Prāsaṅgika's acceptance of the empirical reality of external objects by arguing that it is not at all like the claim of those who come to posit the reality of external objects based on ontological analysis. This is because Prāsaṅgikas reject the kind of realism that is implicated by the acceptance of an analytically determined external world. Rather, Prāsaṅgikas simply accept external objects (conventionally) in accord with the ways of the world, without (ontological) analysis.[15] There is a subtle distinction to be made here that can easily be overlooked. That is, Prāsaṅgikas are not external realists despite claiming the reality of an external world because they acknowledge that the external world does not stand on its own, even conventionally; like minds and objects, an external world rises and falls together with an internal world.

As Śāntideva states in chapter 5 of his *Guide*, the instruments of torture in hell and hell itself are products of an evil mind (5.7–8). Thus, neither hell realms nor human worlds are external, but that does not necessarily mean that they are simply mental projections that are "all in your head." It is important to see that a Prāsaṅgika's affirmation of an external world is not an assertion from her own perspective that there is an external world in reality; it is only an assent to the intersubjective agreement determined by mundane convention. Ultimately, there is no external world for Prāsaṅgikas, so while they may not be idealists, they are certainly not external realists.

There is a tendency to attribute external realism to the tradition of Prāsaṅgika described by Künzang Sönam. Perhaps some in this tradition may fall into this camp, but Künzang Sönam does not. Rather than "idealist" or "realist," we might call his brand of Prāsaṅgika "constructivist" or "nominalist." This "constructivist" form of Prāsaṅgika contrasts with the more radical strands of skepticism in other interpretations of Prāsaṅgika, for which the ultimate truth is cognitively inaccessible and there is no ultimate truth to be established.

In any case, the reason Künzang Sönam understands Śāntideva's Prāsaṅgika to negate objective foundations like reflexive awareness (9.17–24), the dependent nature (*gzhan dbang*), and the basic consciousness (*kun gzhi*) comes down again to the same issue: there is nothing that exists on its own even conventionally. He claims that "Svātantrikas think that if such a [conventional] objective reality (*rang mtshan*) is negated, then one will not be able to posit anything conventionally."[16] Thus, he says: "In the system of Svātantrika, a conventionally existent object, like a sprout, is posited to exist by the force of its appearance to cognition in accord with its own mode of being (*rang gi sdod lugs ltar*). Moreover, prior to cognition's ascription, the cognized sprout is held to first exist with an objective mode of being (*rang ngos kyi sdod lugs*)."[17]

The realism of the purported Svātantrika contrasts sharply with the Prāsaṅgika, for whom no ascribed object is held to objectively exist whatsoever apart from what is ascribed mentally, linguistically, and/or conceptually.[18] This "constructivist" interpretation of Prāsaṅgika is a type of radical (albeit collective) nominalism. In this interpretation, the world is not objective, nor is it subjective; it is relationally constituted or dependently originated. In other words, the world is intersubjective.

Nevertheless, that conventional truth is intersubjective, that it "accords with the world," should not be confused with a view of relativism: the fact that things are empty and that the process of causality (karma) is incontrovertible are non-negotiable in Künzang Sönam's interpretation. Despite being established by consensus, the world as understood by ordinary beings is always wrong in a fundamental way, as Śāntideva says:

> Even the objects of direct perception, such as visible form, are only established by popular consensus and not by a valid means of knowledge.
> That consensus is wrong, like, for example, the popular view that impure things are pure. (9.6)

Künzang Sönam explicitly says that for Prāsaṅgikas, being a mistaken cognition (*'khrul shes*) does not contradict being a valid source of knowledge (*tshad ma*).[19] In this way, valid sources of knowledge for conventional truths can be held to be right and wrong pragmatically (or intersubjectively) while being mistaken in terms of the ontological status of these truths when they appear as if they were truly existent. For this reason, an ordinary being's conventional truth is superseded by a perspective of higher knowledge, for which the way things appear does not conflict with the way things are, namely, when things are seen as illusionlike, empty of true existence.

Śāntideva clearly says that the world of ordinary beings is superseded by yogis when he states:

> The world of ordinary beings is invalidated by that of yogis. (9.3)
> Among yogis as well, those with higher intelligence supersede the others. (9.4)[20]

For Künzang Sönam, the "yogis" are the Prāsaṅgikas or the ones on their way to understanding the Prāsaṅgika view—that things do not exist on their own, even conventionally. Yet in his interpretation, there remains a tension between what is represented as correct truth *for the world*, as an intersubjective truth, and what is held to be the correct truth for anyone (as an objective truth): emptiness (as a non-negotiable ultimate truth) and the undeviating causal process of karma (as a non-negotiable conventional truth).[21] In his tradition, valid sources of knowledge come into play to keep the radical dialectic of Prāsaṅgika within the boundaries of Buddhist doctrine and in service of defending Buddhist claims of emptiness and the causal process. Despite an ordinary being's conventional sources of knowledge always being wrong about the way things are, they are seen to deliver objects that correspond to objects in the world; thus, they are necessary, at least as long as the conditions for their existence (i.e., ignorance) are present. In other words, partly correct and partly distorted conventional sources of knowledge continue to function until the ultimate is realized, just as an illusion continues as long as the conditions for its appearance remain, as Śāntideva said (9.10).

CONCLUSION

Tibetan interpreters of Śāntideva like Künzang Sönam understand his *Guide* as a Prāsaṅgika text. The key to the placement in this category, in this case, is that Śāntideva is seen to support the idea that nothing exists on its own even conventionally. Thereby, Śāntideva has no need to ground conventions in any deeper foundation. Without the need for conventional foundations, like a dependent nature or a basic consciousness, he needs no ultimate foundations, either, as if a *real* ultimate were needed to ground *unreal* conventions. As Śāntideva said, an illusory Buddha works just as well as a truly existent one (9.9). When there is nothing but groundless conventions—all the way up and all the way down—the ultimate and the conventional are no longer separate; the two truths are none other than two aspects of the same thing. For this reason, the two truths are not only without contradiction but also mutually supportive, and this is key for Künzang Sönam's interpretation of Śāntideva as a Prāsaṅgika, as well as the way he maintains emptiness to be a metaphysical "basis" for an altruistic ethic.

NOTES

1. Künzang Sönam, *Overview of the Wisdom Chapter,* 788; English trans. in *The Profound Reality of Interdependence,* 211. For further discussion of this topic, see Duckworth, *Tibetan Buddhist Philosophy of Mind and Nature,* 84–86.
2. Translations from the *Guide,* unless otherwise noted, are from Śāntideva, *Bodhicaryāvatāra,* trans. Kate Crosby and Andrew Skilton.
3. Translation mine.
4. Translation mine.
5. Künzang Sönam, *Word Commentary on the Wisdom Chapter,* 629. On these two lines of Prāsaṅgika interpretation, see Williams, *Altruism and Reality,* 80–93.

6. See Sweet, "*Bodhicaryāvatāra* 9.2 as a Focus for Tibetan Interpretations of the Two Truths in the Prāsaṅgika Mādhyamika," 79–89; see also Williams, *Altruism and Reality*.
7. Künzang Sönam, *Overview of the Wisdom Chapter*, 665; English trans. in *The Profound Reality of Interdependence*, 51.
8. Künzang Sönam, *Overview of the Wisdom Chapter*, 665–667; English trans. in *The Profound Reality of Interdependence*, 51–54.
9. Künzang Sönam, *Overview of the Wisdom Chapter*, 684; English trans. in *The Profound Reality of Interdependence*, 76.
10. Künzang Sönam, *Overview of the Wisdom Chapter*, 683; English trans. in *The Profound Reality of Interdependence*, 75.
11. Künzang Sönam, *Overview of the Wisdom Chapter*, 706–707; English trans. in *The Profound Reality of Interdependence*, 103–105.
12. Künzang Sönam, *Overview of the Wisdom Chapter*, 707; English trans. in *The Profound Reality of Interdependence*, 105.
13. Künzang Sönam, *Overview of the Wisdom Chapter*, 707; English trans. in *The Profound Reality of Interdependence*, 105.
14. Künzang Sönam, *Overview of the Wisdom Chapter*, 707; English trans. in *The Profound Reality of Interdependence*, 105.
15. Künzang Sönam, *Overview of the Wisdom Chapter*, 707; English trans. in *The Profound Reality of Interdependence*, 105.
16. Künzang Sönam, *Overview of the Wisdom Chapter*, 672; English trans. in *The Profound Reality of Interdependence*, 61.
17. Künzang Sönam, *Overview of the Wisdom Chapter*, 682; English trans. in *The Profound Reality of Interdependence*, 73.
18. Künzang Sönam, *Overview of the Wisdom Chapter*, 682; English trans. in *The Profound Reality of Interdependence*, 74.
19. Künzang Sönam, *Overview of the Wisdom Chapter*, 665; English trans. in *The Profound Reality of Interdependence*, 52.
20. Translation mine.
21. Also, the status of the highest mind, the Buddha mind, as having deceptive, yet "correct" content remains a theological (not a pragmatic) concern for many Tibetan interpreters of the *Guide*. Yet as the tenor of Śāntideva's text remains pragmatic—it does not directly participate in these scholastic concerns; it only ever is pulled into these issues by doxographers ("Buddhist theologians") who want to co-opt it to support a particular agenda, such as to interpret Buddhism as a seamless whole.

REFERENCES

Duckworth, Douglas S. *Tibetan Buddhist Philosophy of Mind and Nature*. New York: Oxford University Press, 2019.

Künzang Sönam (*kun bzang bsod nams, thub bstan chos kyi grags pa*). *Overview of the Wisdom Chapter* (*spyod 'jug shes rab le'u'i spyi don rim par phye ba zab mo rten 'byung gi de kho na nyed yang gsal sgron me*). In Tupten Chödrak (*thub bstan chos kyi grags pa*), *spyod 'jug gi 'grel bshad rgyal sras yon tan bum bzang*, 2nd ed., 645–829. Beijing: China's Tibet Publishing House, 2007.

——. *The Profound Reality of Interdependence: An Overview of the Wisdom Chapter of the "Way of the Bodhisattva."* Trans. and introduced by Douglas S. Duckworth. New York: Oxford University Press, 2019.

——. *Word Commentary on the Wisdom Chapter* (*spyod 'jug shes rab le'u'i gzhung 'grel zab mo rten 'byung gi de kho na nyid gsal ba'i sgron me*). In Tupten Chödrak (*thub bstan chos kyi grags pa*), *spyod 'jug gi 'grel bshad rgyal sras yon tan bum bzang*, 2nd ed., 549–643. Beijing: China's Tibet Publishing House, 2007.

Śāntideva. *Bodhicaryāvatāra*. Trans. Kate Crosby and Andrew Skilton. Oxford: Oxford University Press, 1995.

Sweet, Michael. "*Bodhicaryāvatāra* 9.2 as a Focus for Tibetan Interpretations of the Two Truths in the Prāsaṅgika Mādhyamika." *Journal of Indian Philosophy* 2, no. 2 (1979): 79–89.

Williams, Paul. *Altruism and Reality: Studies in the Philosophy of the Bodhicaryāvatāra*. New York: Routledge, 1998.

[11]

SEEING SENTIENT BEINGS

ŚĀNTIDEVA'S MORAL PHENOMENOLOGY

Jay L. Garfield

WHY MORAL PHENOMENOLOGY?

What do we gain from reading Śāntideva as a moral phenomenologist? For one thing, we avoid the procrustean strategy of locating him in the standard Western doxography of ethical positions comprising areteic, deontological, and consequentialist ethics, and then having to explain away all of the differences between his views and the doctrines central to everyone else in each of those philosophical systems (*siddhāntas*). I have argued elsewhere for this understanding,[1] and will not repeat those arguments here. More importantly, we open ourselves to a very different way of thinking about the content of ethics and moral development than those dominant in Western ethical thought, and we find in classical Indian ethics a way of responding to some important contemporary moral issues.

In this chapter, I will first explore a bit more deeply the idea of moral phenomenology and Śāntideva's account of moral cultivation. I will then turn to the use to which we can put moral phenomenology in thinking about phenomena like implicit bias, and conclude with a few remarks about how to imagine the bodhisattva vows in the contemporary world.

When I use the term "moral phenomenology," I have in mind an approach to ethics in which the principal object of concern and of moral evaluation is the way one *experiences* the world, including oneself, other moral agents, and especially other moral patients. This contrasts with assessing dispositions to act, motivations for actions, or the consequences of actions as basic moral goods, or with any focus on an agent's own well-being. When we approach ethics phenomenologically, we aim to foster ethical growth not by instilling a sense of duty, teaching people to focus on the consequences of their actions, or accustoming them to *do* things, but by training people to *see* themselves and others in a better way, with the confidence that that experience will not only be more accurate but also yield more effective engagement with the world in a host of situations. All of this might look like a straightforward particularism of the kind advocated by Dancy,[2] according to which there are simply no general conditions for moral assessment and no general properties that determine moral value. But this would be the case only if one focuses only on actions, principles, or states of character. Which of these is most salutary, or skillful, will indeed vary dependent on circumstances, and from the standpoint of standard Western ethical viewpoints they will appear irreducibly unpatterned.

Despite being particularist in this sense, however, there is a single principle of a sort that induces the variety that otherwise defies comprehension by any tight description: the proper way to act in any given situation, the proper rule to apply, and the proper emotion to experience are those that flow from the right kind of experience of that situation.[3] This of course involves two rather optimistic theses about human psychology, *viz.*, that to see the world aright leads naturally to appropriate action, and that it is possible to transform our perceptual experience through practice. It also involves a commitment to a certain metaphysical view about reality that explains what the content of that correct vision is, *viz.*, the Madhyamaka position. Any of these could be wrong, and we will talk a bit about the second. But I want to take them each for granted here to see where the doctrine takes us.

Moral phenomenology as an approach to ethics harmonizes very well with the path structure of Buddhist ethics generally and with that of the Mahāyāna tradition in particular, and with Buddhist psychology. From the beginning, Buddhist practice has been guided by the metaphor of path, with practice designed to advance one from an initial state to a goal of perfection. That initial state of samsara is one of bondage by psychopathological confusion about one's own nature and the nature of the world around one, pathological attraction and egoism, and corresponding pathologies of aversion, manifested in hostility, fear, and dysfunctional reaction. The path culminates (shorn of grandiose cosmology and hyperbolic accounts of the superhuman) in a state of awakened existence. That state is grounded in an understanding of one's own nature as a selfless, interdependent being and of the world as a matrix of interdependence in which one is inextricably embedded—an understanding so internalized that it transforms one's perceptual experience, just as disciplinary expertise transforms the way one sees objects in one's domain of knowledge or skill. This transformed perception and skilled engagement reduces the sense of being at the center of the universe and dislodges the pathologies of egoistic attraction and hostile aversion, allowing one to become less atavistically reactive and more humanely responsive. The path to liberation is hence simultaneously a path out of individual suffering and a path that allows one to become the agent of others' well-being.

The Mahāyāna version of the path to liberation that structures the *Guide* adumbrates progress as the development of six moral perfections: generosity, morality, patience, perseverance, meditative skill, and wisdom. Each is characterized in the text as a mode of skilled engagement, a way of being in the world. The path of the bodhisattva is a path to liberation in a very specific sense: liberation from psychopathology to psychological health, with wisdom as the crowning achievement that permits the internalization of understanding so as to permit spontaneous engagement.

These analyses of the path to perfection are underwritten by a distinctive psychology developed in detail in the Abdhidharma literature and taken for granted in all Buddhist ethical thought. That is a psychology with no center, no individual agent, but rather a constantly evolving set of interdependent perceptual, conceptual, and conative processes that can be shaped and impaired by error and illusion, or shaped and improved by training, and made increasingly effective. Perceptual processes, on this account, are already pregnant with purpose, intention, conceptualization, affective response, and action readiness. Anyone familiar with the psychology of Tolman or Gibson, Sellarsian epistemology, or the phenomenology of Bhattacharyya, Merleau-Ponty, or Heidegger will recognize this account of perceptual experience as deeply implicated with embodiment, attention, desire, and intention, and as quite distinct from passive reception of data to be passed on to independent cognitive processes.[4] Recent literature on implicit bias provides striking confirmation of this view, and of its moral significance.

Moral phenomenology fits perfectly with this account of psychology and of path. The moral phenomenologist sees ethical achievement as the achievement of a set of perceptual and action skills, as a transformation of the nature of embodied experience and the replacement of instinctive reaction with spontaneous responsiveness. This is precisely what Buddhist psychology claims distinguishes the bondage of samsara from the liberation of nirvana and precisely the kind of change that characterizes the path, the possibility of which is explained by Abhidharma psychology.

Consequentialist and deontological ethical theory, on the other hand, see moral development in terms of coming to know and to conform to obligations—either obligations given by universal maxims or by utility calculations. While conforming to moral principles or maximizing utility may sometimes be the right thing to do, they are not always the most skillful ways to navigate morally charged situations, and they do not exhaust the moral domain. Moreover, one still needs the skill to *see* when these considerations are called for and how to bring them to bear, as well as a motivation and personal comportment that will enable one to be effective. And each of these frameworks implicates a sense of the autonomy and unity of the moral agent that a Buddhist psychology suggests is illusory.[5] An areteic account emphasizes the active, the objective, and does not do the same justice to the subjective or perceptual aspect of moral development, while subordinating morality to individual flourishing as opposed to the benefit to the world at large. It is natural, therefore, that Śāntideva advances a moral phenomenology.

Śāntideva's emphasis on the role of introspective attention and vigilance regarding one's mental states (*smṛti* and *samprajaña*), jointly constituting what has come to be known as mindfulness, is a central aspect of his moral phenomenology. Ethical practice, he emphasizes at the beginning of chapter 5, is grounded in the ability to monitor and to sustain salutary states of mind (as opposed to dispositions to act or commitments to duty, to utility, etc.):

> One who wishes to guard his training
> Should carefully guard his mind.
> If the mind is not guarded,
> It is impossible to guard one's training. (5.1)
> Wild mad elephants do not
> Cause as much harm as
> The elephant of the mind
> Causes in Avici hell! (5.2)[6]
> But if the elephant of the mind
> Is restrained by the rope of attention,
> Then all fear vanishes
> And all virtues develop. (5.3)[7]

In these three opening verses, Śāntideva emphasizes the central role of cognitive states in vice and in virtue, and the clear assertion that the fundamental moral practice is the attainment of control over one's mind, which in turn presupposes some prior moral accomplishment. Mental control and other kinds of moral development, Śāntideva emphasizes, go hand in hand and are mutually reinforcing, entailing that achieving mental control is an ethical achievement. He emphasizes the central role of the deliberate transformation of experience and attitude in ethical life a few verses later, taking first generosity and then patience as examples. Each of these might be thought, *ab initio,* to be virtues manifested primarily in action and in speech. But Śāntideva insists that they are instead states of mind and modes of experience:

> If the perfection of generosity
> Eliminates all poverty,
> Given that there is still so much destitution,
> How could it be that the protectors perfected it? (5.9)
> The perfection of generosity is said
> To be the intention to give everything
> Along with the fruits of that act, to all beings.
> Therefore, it is simply a state of mind. (5.10)
>
> Where is there enough leather
> To cover the surface of the earth?
> But the entire earth is covered
> Just by the leather of my shoes. (5.13)
> Just so, I am unable
> To control external phenomena;
> But if I can control my own mind,
> Why would I need to control anything else? (5.14)

These last two verses are particularly apposite. To put on my shoes instead of covering the earth is simply to change the way I experience and hence respond to the world, instead of changing the world. The centrality to moral practice of such control of experience is the hallmark of the Buddhist moral phenomenology Śāntideva recommends.

ASPIRATIONAL AND ENGAGED *BODHICITTA*

The distinction between aspirational and engaged *bodhicitta* that Śāntideva draws early in chapter 1 reflects this orientation. Aspirational *bodhicitta* is the attitude of one at the beginning of the bodhisattva path, when emptiness and selflessness are not yet realized. It is the attitude that enables one to begin the transformation of one's consciousness from an experience of the world in which one is the egoistic center of experience and agency and others are reduced to objects whose interests are subordinate to one's own into an experience that is decentered, absent self-grasping. When one sees the world that way, others are experienced as of equal subjective standing with oneself, in the attitude of nonegocentricity or impartiality (*upekṣā*) that enables beneficence (*maitrī*), care (*karuṇā*), and rejoicing in the success and virtue of others (*muditā*). Only when this state of mind is cultivated does one achieve *engaged bodhicitta.*

Śāntideva characterizes this difference by distinguishing between one who has an intention to act and one engaged in activity. It is useful to connect this to the familiar Buddhist distinction between two epistemic modes of engagement with the world—the conceptual and the perceptual. The former is indirect and even somewhat misleading; the latter is veridical and enables effective engagement. This connection leads to the idea that Śāntideva is thinking of this distinction in phenomenological terms, as the difference between a conceptual and a perceptual engagement with the world and with others:

> In brief, one should understand that
> *Bodhicitta* has two aspects:
> Aspirational *bodhicitta*
> And engaged *bodhicitta.* (1.15)
> The wise understand these two,
> Just as one understands the difference
> Between one who desires to travel and one who is traveling,
> Recognizing the differences between them and the order in which they arise. (1.16)
>
> Aspirational *bodhicitta* brings about great results,
> Even as we continue to circle within saṃsāra;
> Yet it does not bring about a ceaseless stream of merit,
> For that requires engaged *bodhicitta.* (1.17)

One who has cultivated aspirational *bodhicitta* knows conceptually what kinds of perceptual states she aims to achieve; one who has thoroughly cultivated engaged *bodhicitta* perceives the world directly through emptiness and its ethical corollaries. Śāntideva expands on this theme at the opening of the eighth—the meditation—chapter. Here, he argues that the fundamental psychopathologies of egoism, aversion to others, and confusion about the nature of reality, one's own nature, and one's position in the world arise naturally when one is distracted, and that they can be eliminated by meditative practice.

> Having thus increased one's efforts,
> One should place one's mind in meditation.
> For if one's mind is distracted
> One lies in the fangs of psychopathology (*kleśa*). (8.1)
>
> By secluding the mind and body,
> Distraction is prevented from arising.
> Therefore, one should, abandoning the world,
> Completely relinquish conceptual thought. (8.2)
>
> Because of such things as desire and attachment,
> The world is not renounced.
> Therefore, in order to renounce these,
> The wise practice as follows: (8.3)
>
> Having understood that one can completely destroy psychopathology
> By deep insight achieved in mental tranquility,
> One should first seek tranquility and then
> Relinquish desire for the world. (8.4)

The reason that meditation is an ethical pursuit and that such a long chapter in the *Guide* is devoted to meditation is that it is the central method of moral cultivation. The reason for this distinctive positioning of meditation—not seen in any principal Western ethical system—is that meditation is the technique by means of which one can transform what one *knows* into what one *sees*, conviction into experience. And moral experience constitutes the engaged *bodhicitta* in which the path to moral perfection consists. The extent to which this is possible is far from clear, but if it is possible, this kind of transformation can have far-reaching implications.[8]

MORAL PERCEPTION AND IMPLICIT BIAS

The psychological demonstration of the pervasiveness of implicit bias, its resistance to introspection, and the possibility—albeit the difficulty—of its extirpation is one of the most important empirical discoveries about our moral psychology ever made. By now the data are familiar, so I will merely recall some of the most important facts in brief. In the United States, when people perceive African American faces and Caucasian faces on a screen, they have a much more difficult time responding with a positive evaluation to a pleasant object when the response key is on the side shared by the African American face, and a much harder time assigning a negative response when the negative key is on the Caucasian side than when the faces are reversed.[9] Objects are more likely to be perceived as threatening (guns, as opposed to keys) when in the hands of African Americans than when in the hands of Caucasians.[10] There are many tests for implicit bias, and their results converge powerfully.

For present purposes, a few further disturbing facts deserve note. First, the pervasiveness of implicit bias is overwhelming.[11] Second, it develops very early.[12] Third, it is present every bit as much in those ideologically committed to and involved in antiracism issues and social justice movements as in those not so committed, and it is entirely invisible to introspection;[13] taking an implicit bias test can be a sobering experience, one I recommend to everyone who has not done so. Finally, although it is possible to mitigate implicit bias with training, it is difficult, and if training is not repeated regularly, the effects appear to be only short-lived.[14]

The impact of implicit bias is also pervasive and disturbing. It shows up in policing, in often fatal ways when African Americans are perceived as armed or as threatening in much greater proportion than are Caucasians.[15] It shows up in the judicial system: African Americans are much more readily perceived as guilty, are perceived as responsible for criminal behavior to a much higher degree than are Caucasian suspects against whom similar evidence is adduced, and receive disproportionately longer sentences than do Caucasian defendants.[16] It shows up in the medical system: African American patients are much less likely to be prescribed painkillers than Caucasian patients, and much less likely to be offered experimental treatments.[17] It shows up in the educational system, in which African American students are more likely to be seen as impaired or disruptive and less likely to be seen as gifted than white students of comparable ability who exhibit comparable learning styles and behavior.[18] And it shows up in employment when identical resumés are treated differently if the name at the top is apparently African American.[19] You and I have undoubtedly behaved unjustly many times in the past because of implicit bias.[20]

Why am I talking about implicit bias in this context? Because, while explicit racist (or sexist, or homophobic, or . . . fill in the blank) ideology plays a very great role in social oppression and immorality, implicit bias probably plays the greatest role and is the most invisible and most recalcitrant source. But for present purposes, the reasons to focus on implicit bias are twofold. First, it makes clear just why moral phenomenology is so important and fundamental to ethical training and to ethical theory, and second, because, as Śāntideva saw correctly, it operates at the level of *perception*—before we engage in any conscious deliberation or engage our explicit beliefs, we have committed ourselves to wrong view and the roots of wrong action in our spontaneous perceptual engagement with the world.

In previous work I emphasized the role that fear plays in moral motivation in the opening chapters of the *Guide.*[21] Śāntideva argues throughout the second chapter that fear—and in particular, fear of *death*—motivates vice. (See esp. 2.32–2.50.)[22] The amelioration of fear through meditation that embeds the view of selflessness is, he argues, the path to virtue. *And,* he emphasizes, that fear is universal, and hard to notice; *and,* its content, while psychologically powerful, runs counter to our explicit beliefs about ourselves and our lives. Now, Śāntideva is not talking explicitly about implicit bias: he is worried about our innate and unconscious fear of death and its role in motivating self-grasping, and he is as worried about the explicit psychopathologies to which we are as heir as he is about the implicit one.[23] Nonetheless, Śāntideva is identifying a more general moral psychological phenomenon of which implicit bias is an important instance: the driving of our conscious behavior, speech, and thought by unconscious but morally charged perceptual judgments.[24]

Perceptual processes themselves involve appraisal, which is not morally neutral; moreover, it constitutes the affective and conative horizon of confusion, attraction, and aversion that grounds all other immorality. That is why moral phenomenology is the most important level of moral intervention and the most important locus of moral practice, and why there is hope, as indicated by studies that show some effectiveness of meditative and other practices for ameliorating implicit bias.[25]

That is also why the fifth chapter—the mindfulness chapter—and the eighth chapter—the meditation chapter—are so important in the project of the *Guide.* Mindfulness and meditation are not part of the Western moral landscape in *any* major moral tradition, and that is because of the West's general inattention to moral phenomenology. Even Hume, that great sentimentalist, can recommend "carelessness and inattention" as salutary attitudes. But if you think that how we *see* makes a great difference in our moral lives, then the cultivation of moral responsiveness requires first a cultivation of awareness, then a cultivation of responsiveness, followed by control of those very automatic perceptual processes, and that requires the cultivation of mindfulness and meditative discipline, focused on the eradication of egoism and partiality. And if you think that implicit bias is an important issue, you have to take seriously the task of reorganizing your perceptual processes; and if you take that task seriously, mindfulness is important.

In chapter 5, following the introductory verses discussed earlier, Śāntideva recommends the following mental discipline directed to resisting the impulses deriving from psychopathological sets or reactions:

When one sees that one's mind
Is desirous or angry,
One should neither act nor speak.
One should remain like a block of wood. (5.48)

When one's mind is
Agitated, deprecatory,
Arrogant, vain,
Or deceitful . . . (5.49)

When one is devoted to self-promotion,
And the deprecation of others,
When one is abusive or scornful,
One should remain like a block of wood. (5.50)

When one seeks profit, honors, or fame,
Or desires to have servants,
Or wants others to venerate one,
One should remain like a block of wood. (5.51)

When one's concern for others' ends vanishes,
And concern for advancing one's own ends grows,
When the desire to speak arises,
One should remain like a block of wood. (5.52)

When impatient, lazy, or fearful,
Impudent or rude,
Or partial to oneself,
One should remain like a block of wood. (5.53)

To remain like a block of wood is to pause, to refrain from acting on the basis of psychopathology, on motives that one recognizes as immoral and explicitly renounces. But the first step to this achievement is recognition of those motives, and of the ways of seeing that generate them. That is why this passage occurs in the fifth chapter. Any of the attitudes Śāntideva repudiates here can be an unconscious mental set that frames the way we perceive others and drives our behavior, speech, and reasoning in ways of which we are unaware, as an implicit bias. Although Śāntideva does not mention racial or gender prejudice explicitly—kinds of prejudice hardly thematized as problematic in eighth-century India—the deprecation of others, scorn, and fear certainly are central components of that kind of prejudice. Only rigorous attention to our own phenomenology can prepare the way for the task of transforming our mode of engagement with the world, a task that is of paramount importance.

COGNITIVE ILLUSION AND INTROSPECTION

Earlier in chapter 5, Śāntideva emphasizes that this kind of awareness of our own cognitive and affective states, while crucial to moral development, is not easy. As he notes, anticipating the data concerning the pervasiveness and cognitive opacity of implicit bias, even those who are deeply committed to morality and are really smart fail to make moral progress due to inattention to their own cognitive processes and affective states. This is precisely the kind of failure that we now know makes implicit bias so hard to detect and so hard to remediate.

> Even scholars with faith
> And great perseverance
> Through the vice of introspective distraction (*asaṃprajanya*)
> Fall into unfortunate states. (5.26)
>
> Having been robbed by the thief of introspective distraction
> (*asaṃprajanya*)
> As a consequence of the fall from attention (*smṛti*),
> Even if one has accumulated merit,
> That theft makes life in a fortunate realm impossible. (5.27)
>
> Therefore, one should never remove
> Introspective attention (*smṛti*) from the doorway.

And if it has gone, with hell in mind,
One should restore it to its place. (5.29)[26]

But it is not only the sheer difficulty of introspecting the deeply buried and only implicit that stands in the way of moral progress. Cognitive illusion is also an obstacle, and a feature of our phenomenological structure that is, although pervasive, difficult to appreciate and acknowledge.[27] It is not a specifically moral failing, Śāntideva notes:

Since some harm because of delusion, and
Others become angry when deluded,
Who should we say are guiltless,
And who should we say are guilty? (6.67)

Who is guiltless? Who is guilty? Everyone and no one. Cognitive illusion, like optical illusion, is pervasive, built into the very structure of human subjectivity, and impossible to escape entirely. Just as we are convinced perceptually that the two lines of the Müller-Lyer illusion are of unequal length, we can be convinced introspectively of our own impartiality (*upekṣā*), or of our own immunity to implicit bias. Nonetheless, although we cannot be faulted for succumbing to the visual illusion of taking the lines perceptually to be unequal, we are responsible for knowing that that is just an illusion and for believing them to be equal, and for engaging that belief, not the illusory appearance, in our reasoning and action.

In the same way, although we cannot be faulted for misperceiving our own cognitive, affective, and conative states in introspection, we are responsible for becoming aware of the cognitive illusion that pervades our introspective awareness, hiding our own implicit bias and its effects from us, and for forming a more accurate survey of our own psychology, through reflection and consultation with others or taking online implicit bias tests, and for using that more accurate survey, as much as we can, to guide our actions, speech, and deliberations.[28] Knowing that we live like fish, in the fangs of delusion, Śāntideva admonishes us, it is both irrational and immoral to do nothing about it.

Since you are terrified
Of living like a captive fish,
How much more suffering will you experience,
When you end up in hell due to vice? (7.11)

And what we are called upon to do is not to *act* differently, adopt different *principles*, or transform our *character*, at least not primarily. We are called upon to work first to understand how we see the world, then to correct for the distortions we know we impose upon our perception of ourselves and others, and finally, to transform the nature of that experience. For all else flows from our spontaneous experience.

THE BODHISATTVA VOW

The *Guide* closes with an extended version of the bodhisattva vow.[29] In light of this analysis of Śāntideva's approach to ethics as moral phenomenology, it is worth reflecting on some of the content of that vow. Śāntideva begins by resolving to recollect, or to attend to (*smṛti, dran pa*) past lives, that is, to maintain and be guided by an accurate awareness of the determinants of his cognitive state. He then vows to maintain strength and resolves to *see* Mañjughoṣa in all of his deeds, that is, to experience the world through insight and discernment, not through delusion. Finally, he vows to take the suffering of the world to ripen on himself—that is, to genuinely *experience* the suffering of others, not merely conceptualize it, and so be *moved* by it in virtue of an absence of egocentricity, for attitudes of care, love, sympathetic joy, and impartiality will emerge from coming to see the world not as one's object but as one's home. That resolution to transform experience is the entrance to the bodhisattva path. As I have suggested, aspirational *bodhicitta* may require that we take immediate action to transform our experience.

NOTES

1. Garfield, "What Is It Like to Be a Bodhisattva"; Garfield, "Mindfulness and Ethics"; Garfield, "Buddhistische Ethiks"; Garfield, *Engaging Buddhism*.
2. Dancy, *Ethics Without Principles*.
3. There are obvious intriguing affinities here to the views of the British sentimentalists, especially Hutcheson, Shaftesbury, Adam Smith, and Hume. I explore these in Garfield, "Hume as a Western Mādhyamika". But there are also unexplored affinities to Wittgenstein's "Lecture on Ethics," a suggestive essay that deserves more attention.
4. See Thompson, *Mind in Life*, Thompson, *Waking, Dreaming, Being*, or Garfield, *Engaging Buddhism*, for more detail.
5. See Garfield, "Just Another Word for Nothing Left to Lose," for a discussion of Buddhist agency in the absence of a free agent.
6. Avici hell is the lowest and most painful of the hell realms.
7. All translations of the *Guide* are my own, from the Tibetan.

8. The textual history of the *Guide* is complex, and it is clear that chapter 7 moved as the text evolved, and that a considerable amount of material was added as the text achieved its present form. But I here read the text as we have it, not as it originated. See Cowherds, *Moonpaths,* for more on this issue.
9. This is not unique to the United States. Implicit bias effects are found everywhere, differing from one another in response to divergent cultural norms. Dovidio et al., "On the Nature of Prejudice."
10. Blascovich et al., "Perceived Threat in Social Interactions with Stigmatized Others." Kubota et al., "The Role of Expression and Race in Weapons Identification." Gawronski et al., "Implicit and Explicit Evaluation."
11. Hart et al., "Differential Response in the Human Amygdala to Racial Outgroup vs Ingroup Face Stimuli."
12. Castelli et al., "The Transmission of Racial Attitudes Within the Family."Newheiser et al., "White and Black American Children's Implicit Intergroup Bias."Rutland et al., "Social Norms and Self-Presentation."
13. Ashburn-Nardo et al., "Black Americans' Implicit Racial Associations and Their Implications for Intergroup Judgment."
14. Burgess et al., "Reducing Racial Bias Among Health Care Providers." Dasgupta et al., "On the Malleability of Automatic Attitudes." Joy-Gaba et al., "The Surprisingly Limited Malleability of Implicit Racial Evaluations."
15. Correll et al., "The Police Officer's Dilemma." Plant et al., "The Consequences of Race for Police Officers' Responses to Criminal Suspects."
16. American Bar Association, "ABA Panel Examines Impact of Implicit Bias on Judicial System." Bennett, "Unraveling the Gordian Knot of Implicit Bias in Jury Selection." Clemons, "Blind Injustice." Eberhardt et al., "Looking Deathworthy." Sommers et al., "White Juror Bias."
17. Betancourt, "Not Me!" Blair et al., "An Investigation of Associations Between Clinicians' Ethnic or Racial Bias and Hypertension Treatment, Medication Adherence and Blood Pressure Control." Haider et al., "Unconscious Race and Class Bias."
18. Hannon et al., "The Relationship Between Skin Tone and School Suspension for African Americans."
19. Ross, *Everyday Bias.* Sen, "How Judicial Qualification Ratings May Disadvantage Minority and Female Candidates."
20. Beattie, et al., "An Exploration of Possible Unconscious Ethnic Biases in Higher Education."
21. Garfield, "What Is It Like to Be a Bodhisattva," 327–351, and Garfield, *Engaging Buddhism.*
22. To be sure, he also argues that we can mobilize the fear of death as a motivator to practice, recognizing both the finitude of our lives and the uncertainty of our postmortem fate. But that is a more awakened response to death. In chapter 2, he is also calling our attention to the degree to which our lives, and in particular, our vice, are driven by the subconscious fear of death, which, when it rises to consciousness, can then be transformed into a motivator for virtue. Śāntideva, *A Guide to the Bodhisattva Way of Life,* 2.32–2.50.
23. It is useful in this context to consider the iconography of the *Bhavacakra* (Wheel of Existence), an image Śāntideva would have encountered on his way to work every morning. In that icon, our eyes are drawn to the six realms of transmigration (or affective states) and their dangers, and to the three root pathologies at the center around which beings are cycling between them. But only when we stand back and

broaden our gaze do we see that all of this is conditioned by the fear of death symbolized by the jaws of Yama, present in the image only at the periphery, just as the awareness of our own death and the persistent terror it inspires is generally pushed to the periphery of our consciousness.

24. For similar thoughts in the modern medical community see Teal et al., "Helping Medical Learners Recognize and Manage Unconscious Bias Toward Certain Patient Groups."
25. Although, as noted above, there is reason to think that these interventions must be repeated regularly in order to be effective. Of course,long-term meditative practice of the kind that Śāntideva has in mind may have far greater effect, and that effect may be more durable. Kang et al., "The Non-Discriminating Heart." Xiao et al., "Individuation Training with Other-race Faces Reduces Preschoolers' Implicit Racial Bias."
26. The term "mindfulness" in contemporary discourse is used sometimes to translate *saṃprajanya* (Tib: *shes bzhin*), sometimes to translate *smṛti* (Tib: *dran pa*), and sometimes to indicate a kind of amalgam of the two. *Saṃprajanya* suggests a kind of determined vigilance, holding the mind in place; *smṛti* denotes memory or attention, keeping something in mind. In Śāntideva's thought, they are intimately related.
27. Nisbett et al., "Telling More Than We Can Know."
28. See also Fitzgerald, "A Neglected Aspect of Conscience."
29. Śāntideva, *A Guide to the Bodhisattva Way of Life*, 10.51–56.

REFERENCES

American Bar Association. "ABA Panel Examines Impact of Implicit Bias on Judicial System." *ABA News*, August 12, 2014. *http://www.americanbar.org/news/abanews/aba-news-archives/2014/08/aba_panel_examinesi/.*

Ashburn-Nardo, L., M. L. Knowles, and M. J. Monteith. "Black Americans' Implicit Racial Associations and Their Implications for Intergroup Judgment." *Social Cognition* 21, no. 1(2003): 61–87.

Banaji, M. R., and A. G. Greenwald. *Blindspot: Hidden Biases of Good People*. New York: Delacorte Press, 2013.

Beattie. G. *Our Racist Heart? An Exploration of Unconscious Prejudice in Everyday Life*. London: Routledge, 2013.

Beattie, G., D. Cohen, and L. McGuire. "An Exploration of Possible Unconscious Ethnic Biases in Higher Education: The Role of Implicit Attitudes on Selection for University Posts." *Semiotica* 197 (2013): 171–201.

Bennett, M. W. "Unraveling the Gordian Knot of Implict Bias in Jury Selection: The Problem of Judge-Dominated *Voir-Dire*, the Failed Promise of *Batson*, and Proposed Solutions." *Harvard Law and Policy Review* 4, no. 1 (2010): 149–171.

Betancourt, J. R. "Not Me!: Doctors, Decisions, and Disparities in Health Care." *Cardiovascular Reviews and Reports* 25, no. 3 (2004): 105–109.

Blair, I. V., R. Hanratty, D. Price, W. Fairclough, S. Daugherty, and E. Havranek. "An Investigation of Associations Between Clinicians' Ethnic or Racial Bias and Hypertension Treatment, Medication Adherence and Blood Pressure Control." *Journal of General Internal Medicine* 29, no. 7 (2014): 987–995.

Blascovich, J., W. Mendes, S. Hunter, B. Lickel, and N. Kowai-Bell. "Perceived Threat in Social Interactions with Stigmatized Others." *Journal of Personality and Social Psychology* 80, no. 2 (2001): 243–267.

Burgess, D., M. van Ryn, J. Dovidio, and S. Saha. "Reducing Racial Bias Among Health Care Providers: Lessons from Social-Cognitive Psychology." *Journal of General Internal Medicine* 22, no. 6 (2007): 882–887.

Castelli, L., C. Zogmaiseter, and S. Tomaselli. "The Transmission of Racial Attitudes Within the Family." *Developmental Psychology* 45, no. 2 (2009): 586–591.

Clemons, J. T. "Blind Injustice: The Supreme Court, Implicit Racial Bias, and the Racial Disparity in the Criminal Justice System." *American Criminal Law Review* 51 (2014): 689–713.

Correll, J., S. Hudson, S. Guillermo, and D. Ma. "The Police Officer's Dilemma: A Decade of Research on Racial Bias in the Decision to Shoot." *Social and Personality Psychology Compass* 8, no. 5 (2014): 1314–1329.

Cowherds. *Moonpaths: Ethics and Emptiness*. New York: Oxford University Press, 2016.

Dancy, J. *Ethics Without Principles*. New York: Oxford University Press, 2006.

Dasgupta, N., and A. Greenwald. "On the Malleability of Automatic Attitudes: Combatting Automatic Prejudice with Images of Admired and Disliked Individuals." *Journal of Personality and Social Psychology* 81, no. 5 (2001): 800–814.

Dovidio, J., K. Kawakami, C. Johnson, B. Johnson, and A. Howard. "On the Nature of Prejudice: Automatic and Controlled Processes." *Journal of Experimental Social Psychology* 33 (1997): 510–540.

Eberhardt, J., P. Davies, and V. Purdie-Vaughns. "Looking Deathworthy: Perceived Stereotypicality of Black Defendants Predicts Capital Sentencing Outcomes." *Psychological Science* 17, no. 5 (2006): 383–386.

Fitzgerald, C. "A Neglected Aspect of Conscience: Awareness of Implicit Attitudes." *Bioethics* 28, no. 1 (2014): 24–32.

Garfield, J. "What Is It Like to Be a Bodhisattva: Moral Phenomenology in Śāntideva's *Bodhicaryāvatāra*." *Journal of the International Association of Buddhist Studies* 33, no. 1–2 (2010/2011): 327–351.

——. "Mindfulness and Ethics: Attention, Virtue and Perfection." *Thai International Journal of Buddhist Studies* 3 (2012): 1–24.

——. "Buddhistische Ethiks." *Polylog* 97 (2012): 98–110.

——. "Just Another Word for Nothing Left to Lose: Freedom, Agency and Ethics for Mādhyamikas." in M. Dasti and E. Bryant, eds., *Freedom of the Will in a Cross-Cultural Perspective*, ed. M. Dasti and E. Bryant, 164–185. New York: Oxford University Press, 2014. Reprinted in *Buddhism and Free Will*, ed. R. Repetti,45–58. London: Routledge, 2016.

——. *Engaging Buddhism: Why It Matters to Philosophy*. New York: Oxford University Press, 2015.

——. "Hume as a Western Mādhyamika: The Case from Ethics." In *Ethics Without Self, Dharma Without Atman: Western and Buddhist Philosophical Traditions in Dialogue*, ed. Gordon F. Davis. Sophia Studies in Cross-cultural Philosophy of Traditions and Cultures. Basingstoke: Springer Nature, 2018.

Gawronski, B., and G. Bodenhaus. "Implicit and Explicit Evaluation: A Brief Review of the Associated Propositional Evaluation Model." *Social and Personality Compass* 8, no. 8 (2014): 448–462.

Haider, A., E. Schneider, N. Sriram, D. Dosick, V. Scott, S. Swoboda, and L. Cooper. "Unconscious Race and Class Bias: Its Association with Decision Making by Trauma and Acute Care Surgeons." *Journal of Trauma Acute Care Surgery* 77, no. 3 (2014): 409–416.

Hannon, L., R. DeFina, and S. Bruch. "The Relationship Between Skin Tone and School Suspension for African Americans." *Race and Social Problems* 5, no. 4 (2013): 281–295.

Hart, A., P. Whalen, L. Shin, S. McInenry, H. Fischer, and S. Rauch. "Differential Response in the Human Amygdala to Racial Outgroup vs Ingroup Face Stimuli." *Neuroreport* 11, no. 11 (2000): 2351–2355.

Joy-Gaba, J., and B. Nosek. "The Surprisingly Limited Malleability of Implicit Racial Evaluations." *Social Psychology* 41, no. 3 (2010): 137–146.

Kang, Y., J. Gray, and J. Dovidio. "The Non-Discriminating Heart: Lovingkindness Meditation Training Decreases Implicit Intergroup Bias." *Journal of Experimental Psychology* 143, no. 3 (2014): 1306–1313.

Kubota, J., and T. Ito. "The Role of Expression and Race in Weapons Identification." *Emotion* 14, no. 6 (2014): 1115–1124.

Newheiser, A., and K. Olson. "White and Black American Children's Implicit Intergroup Bias." *Journal of Experimental Social Psychology* 48, no. 1 (2012): 264–270.

Nisbett, R., and T. Wilson. "Telling More Than We Can Know: Verbal Report on Mental Processes." *Psychological Review* 84, no. 3 (1977): 231–259.

Plant, E., and B. Peruche. "The Consequences of Race for Police Officers' Responses to Criminal Suspects." *Psychological Science* 16, no. 3 (2005): 180–183.

Ross, H. *Everyday Bias: Identifying and Navigating Unconscious Judgments in Our Daily Lives.* Lanham, MD: Rowman and Littlefield, 2014.

Rutland, A., L. Cameron, L. Milne, and P. McGeorge. "Social Norms and Self-Presentation: Children's Implicit and Explicit Intergroup Attitudes." *Child Development* 76, no. 2 (2005): 451–466.

Śāntideva. *A Guide to the Bodhisattva Way of Life.* Trans. Vesna A. Wallace and B. Alan Wallace. Ithaca, NY: Snow Lion, 1997.

Śāntideva and rGyal tshab dar ma rin chen. *Byang chub sems pa'i spyod pa la 'jug pa'i rnam bshad rgyal sras 'jug ngogs.* Sarnath: Gelukpa Student Welfare Committee, 1999.

Sen, M. "How Judicial Qualification Ratings May Disadvantage Minority and Female Candidates." *Journal of Law and Courts* 2, no. 1 (2014): 33–65.

Sommers, S., and P. Ellsworth. "White Juror Bias: An Investigation of Prejudice Against Black Defendants in the American Courtroom." *Psychology, Public Policy, and Law* 7, no. 1 (2001): 201–229.

Teal, C., A. Gill, A. Green, and S. Crandall. "Helping Medical Learners Recognize and Manage Unconscious Bias Toward Certain Patient Groups." *Medical Education* 41, no. 1 (2012): 80–88.

Thompson, E. *Mind in Life.* Cambridge, MA: Harvard University Press, 2007.

——. *Waking, Dreaming, Being.* New York: Columbia University Press, 2014.

Wittgenstein, L. "Lecture on Ethics." *The Philosophical Review* 74, no. 1 (1965): 3–12.

Xiao, W., G. Fu, P. Qin, J. Tanaka, O. Pascalis, and K. Lee. "Individuation Training with Other-race Faces Reduces Preschoolers' Implicit Racial Bias: A Link Between Perceptual and Social Representation of Faces in Children." *Developmental Science* (2014): 1–9.

[12]

ŚĀNTIDEVA'S ETHICS OF IMPARTIAL COMPASSION

Charles Goodman

THE INSIGHT and eloquence found in Śāntideva's *Guide to Bodhisattva Practice* (*Bodhicaryāvatāra,* hereafter *Guide*) have made the text an influential source of ethical guidance and inspiration to many generations of Buddhists. We today may be able to learn something about ethics from the text as well; but in order to do so successfully, we must understand how its normative concepts function and how they hang together. To many interpreters, engagement with the ethics of the *Guide* also means trying to classify the overall view of the text, or at least some particular aspects of its view, in terms familiar to Westerners who write about ethics today. Not all scholars agree about whether it is appropriate to attempt to use our modern categories to understand South Asian Buddhist views about how to live. But for those who wish to engage seriously and respectfully with the Buddhist tradition as philosophy, it would be very helpful if it were possible to ascertain where Śāntideva's ethical views might fit, if they fit at all, in the space of ethical theories that are defended today.

ŚĀNTIDEVA AND ACT-UTILITARIANISM

Western philosophers often discuss a form of motivation known as "impartial benevolence," by which they mean a motivation to promote the welfare of all sentient beings without exception, and with the interests of each being taken into account equally. Such a motivational state may or may not exist in practice, but even if it does not, it may still be able to function as a regulative ideal. Many Buddhist texts, meanwhile, including the *Guide* and the *Training Anthology* (*Śikṣāsamuccaya*, hereafter *Anthology*), strongly emphasize a set of emotions called the Four Divine Abidings or the Four Immeasurables. Of these, loving-kindness (*maitrī*) is traditionally defined as a sincere wish for others to be happy. Compassion (*karuṇā*), in its most basic and fundamental aspect, is a wish for others to be free from suffering. Equanimity (*upekṣā*) is a complex concept in Buddhism, but its most relevant function here is to extend loving-kindness and compassion to all beings equally, without preference or prejudice.[1] Taken together, these three emotions include the whole meaning of impartial benevolence—at least as regards the happiness of sentient beings. (Many philosophers have held that there are other components of the good life than happiness.)

Śāntideva thinks that, ideally, everyone should cultivate impartial benevolence and put it into practice.[2] He recognizes that not everyone is on the bodhisattva path now, and he urges his audience to show appropriate respect to followers of other Buddhist paths and to rejoice in the virtues those other Buddhists have cultivated. It is likely that he thinks that other ways of practicing, including non-Buddhist spiritual traditions, may be the most appropriate way to live for certain people at certain times, given the abilities they possess and the limitations they face in their particular life situation.[3] At the same time, though, he finds it appropriate at numerous places in the *Guide* and the *Anthology* to wish, and quote texts that express the wish, that everyone were on the bodhisattva path. In *Guide* 10.1, for example, he dedicates the goodness (Skt. *puṇya*) from his composition of the *Guide* to this wish: "may all people adorn the path to Awakening." Similar passages can be found at *Anthology* 33 and at several other places therein. Apparently his view is that as things stand now, and for a long time to come, there are people whose efforts should best be directed at some other spiritual goal; but ideally, everyone would seek buddhahood for the welfare of the world.

Entire ethical theories can be and have been built on the sole basis of impartial benevolence. We can refer to the claim that the best act is the one that is most effective at promoting the welfare of sentient beings as "the principle of utility." An act-utilitarian is an ethicist who holds that in every situation, we should act out of impartial benevolence and directly follow the principle of utility, choosing among the options available to us the one that would most effectively promote the welfare of sentient beings. For an act-utilitarian, whenever we fail to do our best to promote the good, we act wrongly. Act-utilitarianism is a member of a large and diverse class of theories called act-consequentialism, according to which we should always act so as to bring about the best consequences on the whole—or perhaps, given our limited knowledge of what would in fact happen, the best probability distribution of expected consequences.

Several passages in the *Guide*—and many in the *Anthology*—recommend that difficult moral choices be made by assessing the net overall consequences of each alternative for the welfare of sentient beings. One especially clear example is the famous pair of verses on the gift of the body:

> The body serves the True Dharma. One should not harm it for any inferior reason. For it is the only way that one can quickly fulfill the hopes of living beings. (5.86)
>
> Therefore one should not relinquish one's life for someone whose disposition to compassion is not as pure. But for someone whose disposition is comparable, one should relinquish it. That way, there is no overall loss. (5.87)[4]

Many Buddhist texts—including some quoted in the first chapter of the *Anthology*—praise spectacular, and sometimes also gruesome, acts of generosity that often involve the death of the bodhisattva donor. Some of these texts seem actually to emphasize how little benefit the recipient gains: the point seems to be to display and to cultivate further the donor's attitude of renunciation and indifference to the world. But for Śāntideva, fatal acts of generosity should be performed only when they bring about good consequences that outweigh the loss of the bodhisattva's body. This certainly seems similar to utilitarian reasoning.

Śāntideva on Rules: Consequentialist Indirection and Deontology

Śāntideva has nuanced and interesting views about the rules of moral discipline that structure a Buddhist life. These views are relevant to the assessment of whether Śāntideva could be read as supporting a deontological account of ethics, or perhaps some indirect version of consequentialism. To begin with, we need to understand what deontology is and how it differs from utilitarianism.

Ethicists in the deontological tradition do not agree that bringing about good consequences is the only consideration we should have in view when making ethical choices; indeed, they hold that the action that would have the best consequences is often the wrong choice. This is because, for deontologists, there are moral principles that should not be violated, even if breaking them would make the outcome better. Contemporary deontologists often hold that rational beings such as humans have a number of rights and duties, and that these are the source of obligations that often override the reasons we have to promote the good. So, to take one famous example, a deontologist would not be willing to push a man off a bridge, thereby killing him, even if that person's body would stop an out-of-control trolley and thereby save the lives of five people. The man on the bridge has the right not to be killed without his consent, and the fact that five other people's lives are at stake is not enough to override the moral importance of this right. Most people intuitively agree with this assessment of the case, which can therefore serve as an argument against act-consequentialism and in favor of a deontological constraint against harming others to promote the good.

Many philosophers in the utilitarian tradition have not accepted the straightforward act-utilitarian account of how we should make choices in practical life. It has been quite common for utilitarian ethicists to defend various indirect versions of their view, in which the primary locus of appraisal is not the direct consequences of particular acts. The most common form of indirect utilitarianism is rule-utilitarianism, which in one influential version tells us to identify a set of rules that would be optimal for our society if most people tried to follow them, and then to follow those rules ourselves. On this view, even if the particular circumstances of our choices are such that noncompliance with the rules would have better results in this particular case, we should still follow the rules. Thus rule-utilitarian views typically avoid at least some of the disturbing implications of direct consequentialist theories.

A more subtle and nuanced indirect theory would be two-level utilitarianism. A two-level utilitarian thinks of what Mill called "subordinate principles"—that is, moral rules more specific than the principle of utility—as providing practical guidance in situations of uncertainty and protecting us from our own tendencies to misinterpret and misapply the principle of utility in actual cases. Thus, for example, it may be very easy for me to convince myself that embezzling from my employer in order to provide a better life for my children will have better consequences on the whole than honesty. But even as this seductive line of reasoning seems appealing, I may also be able to recognize that in the past, stealing has usually shown a very strong tendency to make things worse for everyone. Considering my own ignorance, emotional confusion, and susceptibility to various irrational biases and cognitive distortions, I may choose to trust a subordinate principle such as "don't steal" or "honesty is the best policy" more than my own sadly fallible judgment. I should be especially vigilant if I am subject to a compulsive emotional need to see myself as special, for in that case, I should be quite skeptical of any judgment of mine to the effect that the current situation, in which I am the central actor, is a special exception to one or more generally acknowledged, subordinate, but usually sound and binding moral principles. Unless I have quite compelling evidence that this case really is a genuine exception, I should follow the rules that I would expect everyone else to follow.

There is therefore an important contrast between the subordinate principles accepted by two-level utilitarians and true deontological constraints. Ethicists from the deontological tradition hold that there are moral principles that should be followed even if doing so will certainly make the outcome worse. These principles derive their validity from the rights of others or from a universal moral law such as Kant's categorical imperative, and so typically do not depend on anything about the agent, such as her motivation or the reliability of her judgments. Two-level consequentialists advocate following rules, even though it seems to us that doing so might make the outcome worse, when and to the extent that the rule is a more reliable guide to what will bring about good consequences than our own judgment would be.

Does Śāntideva accept any constraints that might restrain the practice of impartial benevolence, and if so, what kind of constraints are they?[5] Śāntideva often emphasizes the importance of the rules of Buddhist moral discipline, such as the *prātimokṣa* code of conduct for monastic practitioners. In understanding his attitude toward these rules, the key passage is *Guide* 5.84cd: "Even what is proscribed is permitted to a compassionate person who sees it will be of benefit." The permission that Śāntideva endorses here seems to have been quite carefully worded. The practitioner must be someone who sees, and not merely guesses, that the rule violation will be beneficial. Moreover, the permission depends on the motivational state of the agent. Those who are genuinely compassionate can make exceptions to any and all of the rules when doing so will make the outcome better. Those whose motivations are less elevated and pure have to follow the rules. These aspects of the verse constitute evidence that Śāntideva understands the rules of moral discipline as something like utilitarian subordinate principles.

But although the rules of moral discipline should not, for Śāntideva, be understood as deontological constraints, there is a candidate for a deontological constraint that he might have accepted. It is possible to understand Śāntideva as holding that a bodhisattva should never harm anyone for any reason at all, unless there will be compensating benefits to that same person in the long term.

For a contemporary Western deontologist, that constraint would be far too simple; it would rule out many types of responses to the wrongdoing of others, such as self-defense, other-defense, and punishment, that are seen as entirely appropriate by the common sense of most societies and by the vast majority of deontological theorists. But for a traditional Buddhist such as Śāntideva, the doctrines of rebirth and karma have implications that could transform the practical upshot of such a constraint.

For example, if a pirate is about to commit a terrible act of aggression—say, murdering the passengers on a boat to steal their meager possessions—and a bodhisattva knows the pirate's intentions, then by preemptively killing the pirate, the bodhisattva would not merely save the passengers from an early death but would also actually benefit the pirate by protecting him from the horrifying, eons-long suffering that would be the natural karmic result of successfully completing the action.[6] So the constraint "never harm anyone," as qualified above, would permit the use of violence in defense of innocent others—at least in cases as extreme, and as clear, as this one.

In *Guide* 3.14, Śāntideva expresses one of his aspirations in this way: "Let there never be harm to anyone on account of me."[7] We cannot say with certainty whether he intends this aspiration to be an inviolable constraint on his actions or whether he merely hopes that he will never be placed in a situation where it would be necessary to harm anyone. But given his Buddhist worldview, based on karma and rebirth, such a constraint would be more reasonable for him than it would be for someone who believes that death is the end of all our journeys.

ŚĀNTIDEVA, VIRTUES, AND VIRTUE ETHICS

Some Western ethicists have thought that moral value was not primarily something an agent should try to *promote* but rather something an agent should try to *embody*. In the tradition flowing from Aristotle, ethicists ask in the first instance not "What should I do?" but "What kind of person should I be?" The answer to the latter question typically involves identifying particular traits of character as virtues to be cultivated.

Any reader of Buddhist texts, including the *Guide*, will gather very quickly that they are deeply interested in the cultivation of character and the development of enumerated virtues. Śāntideva frequently uses words that refer to what we in English call "virtues." These include *guṇa*, a highly general term for virtues that can also refer to a person's abilities or to the advantages anything might have, and *kuśala*, a subtle technical term that refers to choices and inner states that lead in the direction of freedom from cyclic existence. The Six Perfections (generosity, morality, patience, perseverence, meditation, and wisdom), a list that plays a crucial role in the overall structure of the *Guide* (it contributes the themes and titles of ch. 6–9, for example), is naturally understood as a classification of virtues that a bodhisattva needs to develop. Śāntideva repeatedly expresses a deep reverence for the virtues developed by the Buddhas: "If a virtue appears anywhere which is even an atom of those who are a unique mass of the very essence of virtue, then even the three worlds are not adequate for the purpose of worshipping it" (6.117).

Could such passages indicate that Śāntideva is best understood as some kind of virtue ethicist?[8]

One natural way to understand Buddhist views as forms of virtue ethics is to think of enlightenment, or awakening (Skt. *bodhi*) as an unconditional, absolute value playing a structural role analogous to that played by eudaimonia, "happiness" or "human flourishing," in the thought of Aristotle.[9] On such a reading, we might wonder: does the importance of liberation from cyclic existence supersede impartial benevolence? Alternately, is the value of liberation, for Śāntideva, incommensurable with that of the welfare of sentient beings?[10] This seems to be a possible interpretation of the views of many, or even most, Buddhist authors. But, somewhat surprisingly, Śāntideva answers this question unequivocally in the negative, in a line that occurs both in the concluding verses of the *Training Anthology* and at *Guide* 8.108: "What would be the point in a liberation without sweetness?"[11] On the natural reading of this rhetorical question, the normative importance of liberation for the life of the one who becomes free is that liberation represents the end of suffering and the beginning of true, lasting happiness.

Textual evidence from the *Guide* may be insufficient to settle the question of the viability of a virtue ethics interpretation of Śāntideva, but there are passages from the *Training Anthology* that can be used to critique such a reading. The most important is a complex passage at *Training Anthology* 145–146, of which the most relevant portion is: "Suppose that he fails to discard what is wholesome of his own in order to bring about what is wholesome for other bodhisattvas. Well, if he fears the suffering of the lower realms for himself, what others fear is also suffering. If he is indifferent, thinking 'That suffering has nothing to do with me,' then as the sūtras say, he undergoes a downfall."[12]

This passage states very clearly that the bodhisattva must be willing to sacrifice his own wholesome (*kuśala*) states—or as we might say, his virtues—when doing so would be for the greater benefit of others. A theorist who advocates the cultivation of virtue as the foundation of ethics could advocate sacrificing wealth, blood, limbs, even life itself; but such an ethicist could never support taking an action that would result in the agent herself being less virtuous than she otherwise would have been. Thus this passage represents an interpretive difficulty for the virtue ethics reading.

One particular type of virtue ethics interpretation of Śāntideva, though, may have a satisfactory answer.[13] Clearly, for Śāntideva, not all virtues are equal. One quality in particular, *bodhicitta*, is such a central concern of both of his texts that it can plausibly be regarded as a "sovereign virtue." Numerous passages could be cited in support of such a reading, including the beautiful, poetic praise of *bodhicitta* that occupies much of chapter 3 of the *Guide*. Still more on point is the discussion of *bodhicitta* at *Anthology* 5–7, which quotes several texts claiming that "like a summary, it collects together all of a bodhisattva's practices and aspirations."[14] Two pages later, at *Anthology* 9, we read that "the diamond gem of [*bodhicitta*,] even when divided from earnest practice, outshines the golden ornaments that are the abilities of the Disciples and Solitary Sages."[15] Since disciples can possess almost all of the virtues that Buddhism recommends, this statement amounts to a striking and comprehensive affirmation of the superiority of *bodhicitta* even to centrally important qualities such as mindfulness, loving-kindness, and meditative stability.

If it is granted that *bodhicitta* is the most important and comprehensive of all virtues, then the virtue theorist can offer a slightly strained but potentially admissible interpretation of the *Anthology* passage quoted above. Though virtue ethics could never recommend that an agent make herself less virtuous on the whole, it could tell her to sacrifice virtues of lesser importance in order to achieve others of greater importance. Thus a virtue ethicist might suggest to Oskar Schindler that he become less honest and develop proficiency in bribing corrupt officials so as to save the lives of persecuted Jews and thus more fully embody the virtue of benevolence. In the same way, one might suggest that if a bodhisattva were to sacrifice some of the less important virtues in order to benefit others, in doing so she would be more fully cultivating and embodying the sovereign virtue of *bodhicitta*, and thus becoming more virtuous overall.

Now suppose that a bodhisattva found herself in a position where she could lead ten other sentient beings to adopt *bodhicitta*, but only through some course of action that would lead her to lose or forget her own *bodhicitta*. What should she do then? This is a difficult question, one that Śāntideva never answers; he may not believe that such a situation could ever arise. But it differentiates the two interpretations: a utilitarian would say that the bodhisattva should sacrifice her own *bodhicitta* for the sake of others, whereas a virtue ethicist would say that she should not, that she should never do anything that would prevent her from embodying the greatest of all virtues, even for the sake of others.

In this connection we might appeal to one of the most frequently discussed of all of Śāntideva's arguments:

> When happiness is dear to me and others equally, what is so special about me, so that I strive after happiness only for myself? (8.95)
> When fear and suffering are disliked by me and others equally, what is so special about me, so that I protect myself and not the other?[16] (8.96)

In our imagined disagreement, the utilitarian might say: What is so special about me, so that the continuation of my own *bodhicitta* is more important than inspiring *bodhicitta* in ten other sentient beings?

Here we run straight into one of the most difficult interpretive disagreements among scholars interested in Śāntideva today. The verses just given form part of a passage, *Guide* 8.90–103, articulating what some writers now call the Ownerless Suffering Argument. If we could take this argument as a whole at face value, it would simply rule out the virtue ethics interpretation. But it is not clear that we can interpret it as a serious expression of Śāntideva's philosophical commitments.[17]

A crucial move in the Ownerless Suffering Argument is the rejection of any real relation of personal identity:

> The continuum of consciousnesses, like a queue, and the combination of constituents, like an army, are not real. The person who experiences suffering does not exist. To whom will that suffering belong? (8.101)
> Without exception, no sufferings belong to anyone. They must be warded off simply because they are suffering. Why is any limitation put on this? (8.102).

By deploying a radical critique of personal identity to support the rationality of altruism, this text anticipates central aspects of one of the most important and celebrated works of recent analytic philosophy: Derek Parfit's *Reasons and Persons*.[18] The trouble is that this critique seems to depend on the reductionist Buddhist philosophy known as the Abhidharma. And this is not Śāntideva's final view; he follows the Madhyamaka school, which holds that suffering is just as empty as persons are. How, then, can he rely on this argument? Is there any way to make the argument cogent, even within a Madhyamaka view? This is the deepest and most difficult question facing the utilitarian interpretation.

CONCLUSION

We have seen some arguments and evidence that could be used to show that Śāntideva's ethics should be understood as a form of utilitarianism, as well as some reasons to think that other interpretations might also be viable. Even if we do support the utilitarian interpretation, it is important to recognize that Śāntideva's view does differ in some respects from that of classical utilitarians such as Bentham, Mill, and Sidgwick, even beyond those differences induced in obvious ways by his endorsement of Buddhist descriptive beliefs not shared by nineteenth-century Englishmen. These important differences do not block the utilitarian interpretation, but they suggest that we should regard Śāntideva's views as belonging to a somewhat different subclass of utilitarianism from the "classical" type represented by the authors just mentioned.

Classical utilitarians regarded it as very important to make room for a wide variety of forms of life, each with its own conception of how to be happy. Their view was well suited, in many respects, to be used for public deliberation in a pluralistic society, since it already incorporates into its fundamental structure a certain kind of neutrality between different conceptions of how to live. It also abandons all pretensions to specialized and esoteric moral knowledge, since on the classical view, normative questions can reliably be answered using just two kinds of information: about the empirical results of social science and about the subjective feelings of individuals.[19]

By contrast, Śāntideva is fully committed to a particular vision of the good life, which he regards as superior to all other possible ways of living and in which he sees a central role for rare and exceptional forms of wisdom. These features of his view may make Śāntideva immune to some important objections against classical utilitarianism. They also make his position, if taken unmodified and at full strength, quite unsuitable for the purposes of policy design, political deliberation, and legal reform that the classical utilitarians had in mind. Śāntideva's ethical view was designed for the monastery, the meditation hall, and the forest; Buddhists will have to water it down considerably if they wish to bring it into the public sphere.

NOTES

1. The fourth divine abiding, joy (*pramuditā*), is traditionally understood to involve rejoicing in the good fortune and moral goodness of others.
2. The question of whether, according to Śāntideva, impartial benevolence should be practiced by everyone is raised in Harris, "On the Classification of Śāntideva's Ethics in the Bodhicaryāvatāra," 257. The question is also raised in Barnhart, "Theory and Comparison in the Discussion of Buddhist Ethics."
3. This certainly seems to be the message of *Anthology* 325, which quotes the *Holy Teaching of Vimalakīrti* as saying that bodhisattvas "accept ordination/In all the strange cults of the world,/And so help to mature/Those sentient beings who have developed various false views." Goodman, trans., *Training Anthology.*
4. All *Guide* translations, unless otherwise noted, are from Śāntideva, *The Bodhicaryāvatāra,* trans. Crosby and Skilton.
5. For this question, see Harris, "On the Classification of Śāntideva's Ethics in the Bodhicaryāvatāra," 257.
6. This is, of course, a famous Buddhist story, derived from the *Sūtra on Skill in Means* (*Upāyakauśalyasūtra.*) See Tatz, trans., *The Skill in Means,* 73–74.
7. Śāntideva, *The Bodhicaryāvatāra,* trans. Crosby and Skilton, 21.
8. As suggested by Harris, "On the Classification of Śāntideva's Ethics in the Bodhicaryāvatāra."
9. This is the core idea of Keown, *The Nature of Buddhist Ethics.*
10. See Barnhart, "Theory and Comparison in the Discussion of Buddhist Ethics," 26.
11. Skt. *mokṣeṇa-arasikena kiṃ*. I am following Śāntideva, *The Bodhicaryāvatāra,* trans. Crosby and Skilton, 97. Part of Prajñākaramati's commentary on this verse is unfortunately lost, but what we do have seems to support this translation and interpretation, especially his gloss of *prāmodya-sāgarāḥ* as *saṃtuṣṭi-samudrāḥ*. See Tripathi, ed., *Bodhicaryāvatāra of Śāntideva with the Commentary Pañjikā of Prajñākaramati,* 167.
12. Goodman, trans., *Training Anthology,* 141.
13. Thanks to Matthew Kapstein for pointing out to me the possibility of this reading and how it could answer the argument based on *Anthology* 146.
14. Goodman, trans., *Training Anthology,* 6–7.
15. Goodman, trans., *Training Anthology,* 11.
16. Translation slightly altered from Śāntideva, *The Bodhicaryāvatāra,* trans. Crosby and Skilton, 96.
17. See Harris, "On the Classification of Śāntideva's Ethics in the Bodhicaryāvatāra."
18. See especially ch. 15 of Parfit, *Reasons and Persons.*
19. For these differences, see Barnhart, "Theory and Comparison in the Discussion of Buddhist Ethics," 22–23.

REFERENCES

Barnhart, Michael. "Theory and Comparison in the Discussion of Buddhist Ethics." *Philosophy East and West* 62, no. 1 (2012): 16–43.

Clayton, Barbra. "Śāntideva, Virtue, and Consequentialism." In *Destroying Māra Forever: Buddhist Ethics Essays in Honor of Damien Keown*, ed. John Powers and Charles S. Prebish. Ithaca, NY: Snow Lion, 2009.

Goodman, Charles. "Consequentialism, Agent-Neutrality, and Mahāyāna Ethics." *Philosophy East and West* 58, no. 1 (2008): 17–35.

——. *Consequences of Compassion: An Interpretation and Defense of Buddhist Ethics.* New York: Oxford University Press, 2009.

——, trans. *The Training Anthology of Śāntideva: A Translation of the Śikṣā-samuccaya.* New York: Oxford University Press, 2016.

Harris, Stephen. "On the Classification of Śāntideva's Ethics in the Bodhicaryāvatāra." *Philosophy East and West* 65, no. 1 (2015): 249–275.

Keown, Damien. *The Nature of Buddhist Ethics.* London: Macmillan, 2001.

Parfit, Derek. *Reasons and Persons.* Oxford: Oxford University Press, 1984.

Śāntideva. *The Bodhicaryāvatāra.* Trans. Kate Crosby and Andrew Skilton. Oxford World Classics. New York: Oxford University Press, 1995.

Tatz, Mark, trans. *The Skill in Means (Upāyakauśalya) Sūtra.* Delhi: Motilal Banarsidass, 1994.

Tripathi, Sridhar, ed. *Bodhicaryāvatāra of Śāntideva with the Commentary Pañjikā of Prajñākaramati.* Darbhanga: Mithila Institute, 1988.

[13]

ŚĀNTIDEVA AND THE MORAL PSYCHOLOGY OF FEAR

Bronwyn Finnigan

In chapters 2 and 7 of the *Guide to Bodhisattva Practice* (*Bodhicaryāvatāra*, hereafter *Guide*), Śāntideva provides a series of provocative verses aimed at inciting fear to motivate taking refuge in the bodhisattvas, the "Conquerors" (2.48) and "mighty Protectors of the world" (2.48), and thereby achieve fearlessness. My aim in this chapter is to investigate the moral psychology involved in this transition. Prima facie, it is rather puzzling. Why would one purposely incite fear if one's goal is its elimination? In logical terms, why generate p if the goal is ~p? Śāntideva writes:[1]

> Night and day, without respite, more of life is lost. It never gets longer. Surely, will I not die? (2.40)
>
> Though here laid on my bed, though in the midst of family, it is alone that I must endure the agony of the throes of death. (2.41)
>
> Even someone taken away today to have a limb cut off writhes, throat parched, gaze wretched. He sees the world in a completely different way. (2.44)
>
> But that is nothing to the feverish horror which grips me, covered in my own uncontrolled excrement, as Death's terrifying messengers stand over me. (2.45)
>
> When Death is sizing you up and at every turn the way is blocked, How can it please you to eat? How can you sleep? How make love? (7.6)[2]

> Realizing you are like a captive fish, how right it is for you to be afraid right now?

How much more so when you have committed evil actions and are faced
with the intense agonies of hell? (7.11)

With cowering glances, I search the four directions for deliverance.
What saint will deliver me from this great fear? (2.46)

Right now I go for refuge to the mighty Protectors of the world,
Who have undertaken the care of the world, the Conquerors who
remove all fear. (2.48)

Trembling with fear I give myself to Samantabhadra and
Again, freely I give myself to Mañjughoṣa. (2.50)

I have transgressed your command. Now, at seeing the danger, terrified
I go to you for refuge. Destroy the danger quickly. (2.54)

I give myself wholly to the Conquerors and to their sons . . .
You take possession of me. I become fearless. (2.8–9)

How are we to understand the moral psychology underlying Śāntideva's incitement of fear, and how does it relate to that involved in taking refuge and becoming fearless?

The task is one of rational reconstruction. Śāntideva does not himself provide this analysis. Śāntideva is also a Madhyamaka Buddhist, and Mādhyamikas tend not to have a lot to say about the nature and structure of specific kinds of mental state. This leaves two options: utilize some other Buddhist framework or draw on some contemporary Western framework. This chapter will adopt both approaches. It will appeal to Abhidharma views on the general nature of mental states to analyze the nature of fear, and will draw on Karen Jones's theory of trust to provide an original analysis of the underlying psychology of taking refuge.[3] It will unify these two accounts to provide an original explanation of how Śāntideva's incitement of fear may relate to taking refuge and becoming fearless.

Although this account will appeal to Abhidharma views on the general nature of mental states, the task remains one of reconstruction. While Abhidharma thinkers analyze the general nature and structure of mental states, they do not provide a detailed analysis of fear in particular. There are also subtle differences among Ābhidharmikas in their general accounts as well as interpretive issues about how they are best understood. Resolving all the relevant issues is too much for one chapter. It will thus make some interpretive choices and provide an original analysis of fear (and taking refuge) informed by these choices. It is also too much for one chapter to provide a fully articulated and defended analysis of fear or taking refuge. Each, alone, would be sufficient subject matter for an independent article. This chapter aims merely to provide enough of a sketch of such an analysis that it can be used to help explain the moral psychology underlying Śāntideva's views on fear, taking refuge, and the transition to fearlessness.

There are four parts to my reconstruction. First, I structurally analyze fear in terms that are grounded in, and expand upon, an Abhidharma Buddhist analysis of mind. I contend that fear is a complex intentional attitude and will analyze the object of fear into four aspects. Second, I structurally analyze "taking refuge in the bodhisattvas" as a form of trust that ameliorates some aspects of the object of fear. Third, I consider some objections to this analysis. I then close by considering a more refined analysis of the transition from fear, to taking refuge, to fearlessness that aims to avert these objections.

AN ABHIDHARMA-INSPIRED STRUCTURAL ANALYSIS OF FEAR

The Abhidharma philosophical tradition is widely understood as an attempt to comprehensively and exhaustively map mental and physical phenomena.[4] It conceived of the mind in terms of individual moments of phenomenal awareness. Mental states or events are distinguished from other kinds of events by "being aware" or cognizant (√*jñā*). Of what are they aware? Of the objects that are present to them. For Abhidharma, apprehension of an object (i.e., intentionality in the Brentano sense) is a defining characteristic of awareness, mind, or consciousness. All mental states are intentional in the sense of apprehending an object. The Abhidharma tradition can be understood to analyze the intentionality of the mental into two necessary aspects:

a. *citta* (or *vijñāna*, awareness): the bare function of being aware of, or presencing, an object
b. *caitasika* (or determining factors): the function of determining the qualitative nature of this awareness (viz., the kind of object it presences and its particular characteristics)

Prominent Abhidharma thinkers appear to agree on the necessity of these two aspects or constituents of mental states but disagree on the number and types of each. Consider (b). Vasubandhu identifies 46 determining factors, of which 10 are held to be omnipresent or "universally conjoined" in all mental states.[5] Asaṅga, however, identifies 52 determining factors, of which only 5 are held to be omnipresent.[6]

I will focus my analysis on Asaṅga's list of five omnipresent determining factors. They are: feeling (*vedanā*), discernment (*saṃjñā*), intention (*cetanā*), attention (*manasikāra*), and contact (*sparśa*). While these determining factors are easy to list, it is difficult to specify their precise nature. Consider "feeling" (*vedanā*). The claim that *vedanā* is an omnipresent factor of all mental states could be taken to mean that they have a feeling tone or affective dimension. This might be taken to imply, in the first instance, that every mental state or event has phenomenal qualities. Abhidharma thinkers also maintain that these phenomenal qualities are valenced as pleasant, unpleasant, and neutral.[7] This valenced categorization is not to be understood as the product of reflective judgment but rather is an aspect of conscious experience.

Just as important is intention (*cetanā*), or the orientation of the mental state with respect to an object. There is much dispute about what this means, and this is not the place to lay out the details. For our purposes, *cetanā* is neither a volition (of intending to do some action) nor the mere presencing of an intentional object (which is a function of *citta*). It is also not motivationally neutral. Rather, *cetanā* is an orientation or attitude toward an object that is influenced by its valenced affective dimension and is subject to moral evaluation. This orientation can be, and often is, qualified in various ways. Attraction, aversion, and care are examples of qualified orientations with respect to the object of awareness. They are responsive to variations in the valenced feeling-tone (pleasure or pain) as regards the object; aversion generally couples with pain, attraction with pleasure. It is also subject to moral evaluation, as it gives rise to the kinds of volitional behavior that accrue karmic consequences.

To finish off the set: Asaṅga presents discernment (*saṃjñā*) as the capacity to distinguish the particular qualities of the intentional object—the kind of object it is as well as its characteristics.[8] Attention (*manasikāra*) is presented as the capacity to focus the mental factors on the object. Contact (*sparśa*) is taken to refer to the causal factors that determine the arising of the mental state.

Two key insights can be derived from this fivefold analysis of mental events. First, it implies that mental events are multicompositional in the sense that they have these five features or qualities. Second, they are intentional in the sense that they involve awareness of objects.

As mentioned, Abhidharma philosophers do not specifically analyze the nature and structure of fear. However, the above can serve as a general framework for the construction of such an account. Qua mental event, we might say that fear is a multicompositional intentional attitude that comprises the above five determining factors. Moreover, the way these factors are determined is what individuates fear from other kinds of mental event. That is, fear is distinguished as fear (rather than, say, anger or compassion or equanimity, etc.) relative to its typical kinds of intentional object, its typical modes of bodily-behavioral orientation to such objects, its typical kinds and degrees of valenced apprehension, and typical modes of contact as triggering cause.

It is beyond the scope of this chapter to provide a detailed and fully articulated analysis of how these determining factors pertain to fear. But here is a suggestion. In typical cases, the kind of valenced apprehension involved in fear is negative and experienced as unpleasant or disturbing feelings of various degrees of intensity. And the typical modes of bodily-behavioral orientation are aversive and manifest in subtle or overt varieties of freeze, flight, or fight modes of behavior and physiological response. In many cases, a fearing subject may not be aware of all these elements and their typical modes of manifestation. But this need not imply that they are not necessary constituents. Instead, one might argue that they are masked in some way.

There is one element of this complex analysis of fear that is not adequately captured by the fivefold account sketched thus far: namely, whether the intentional object of fear has some general nature or structure. This is not to propose that all events of fear have a single intentional object. That would be absurd; we are afraid of all kinds of things, and not all necessarily of the same kinds of things. But is there a general structure that all objects of fear have in common? I propose that there is and that it is useful to explicate in order to understand how taking refuge can lead to fearlessness. I propose that the intentional object of fear is determined in four ways. It is experienced as:

1. *Possible.* This is a modal notion that is tied to anticipation and expectation but distinct from the actual triggering cause of fear. Some event may occasion or trigger the arising of fear (hearing the barking of a dog). *What* one fears, however, the object of fear, is something that *could* occur (being harmed by the dog) rather than what *is* occurring. The more probable the possible occurrence is assumed to be, the more intense the valenced dimension of this mental state. This is a

phenomenological claim, about how the object is experienced, which holds irrespective of whether the anticipated event is, in fact, metaphysically or logically possible.

2. *Unwanted.* The relevant possibility is appraised negatively. This appraisal manifests in a negative valence (unpleasant, disturbing feelings) and aversive bodily and behavioral responses.
3. *Uncertain in susceptibility to agential control.* There is a sense in which it is not entirely up to the agent to foreclose this unwanted possibility as a mere matter of will or choice. This connects to a sense of vulnerability in the face of a wider world of agents and causal laws that are outside the subject's personal control. The less perceived agential control, the more probable and unwanted the occurrence, the more intensely the state is experienced.
4. *Matters.* It matters to the subject whether it occurs, where this manifests values, needs, interests, goals, or attachments of the subject. This fourth criterion is the measure or reason why the relevant possibility is unwanted.

In sum, the more some possible occurrence matters, the less perceived agential control over its occurrence, the greater its probability, the more it is unwanted, the more intensely will the mental state be experienced; i.e., its valence will be heightened, aversive bodily and behavioral responses will be more extreme, and the object will be more obvious and focal to attention.

I propose that the transition to fearlessness implied by Śāntideva's verses involves a change in some or all these four dimensions of the intentional object of fear. What is the relevant possibility that is feared? According to the verses cited earlier, it is death. Śāntideva elsewhere discusses illness and impending suffering, more generally, and so there is reason to think the argument has more general application. However, I will focus on the example offered in the verses we are considering. Death is a possible occurrence, probable to the point of certainty, which no act of will or choice can circumvent in a given lifetime. Why does its occurrence matter, and why is it thus unwanted in Śāntideva's view? Śāntideva offers two possibilities. First, death involves suffering; "the agony of the throes of death" (2.41). Second, death marks the point at which suffering is likely to arise; "faced with the intense agonies of hell" (7.11). The latter is relevant to our analysis. It is to circumvent this "danger" (2.54) that the subject turns to the bodhisattvas for protection. What is the cause of this danger? It is the negative karmic consequences of having committed evil actions (7.11) and of transgressing the Buddha's moral teachings (2.54).

What is Śāntideva's purpose for inciting this fear of the karmic consequences of our actions? Presumably, to motivate a desire to do something about it. Śāntideva goes to great lengths to emphasize the great probability of these intense sufferings occurring. He writes that at the moment of death, we are "faced with" (7.11) the agonies that lie ahead; it is a danger toward which we are drawn "night and day, without respite" (2.40). His graphic descriptions of the relevant kinds of sufferings not only emphasize their undesirability but aim to physiologically arouse a high degree of fear. The presupposition seems to be that the more graphically described this unwanted possibility, the more physiologically aroused the fear and the stronger the desire to avert its occurrence. If this is right, what is the role of taking refuge in the bodhisattvas in this transition? And why is *this* Śāntideva's response to the fear thus incited? To answer this question, we need a psychological analysis of "taking refuge."

A STRUCTURAL ANALYSIS OF "TAKING REFUGE IN THE BODHISATTVAS"

How might we understand "taking refuge in the bodhisattvas" in moral psychological terms? One way to understand it is as a form of trust. Philosophers offer competing accounts of trust. According to one view, it is a two-place relationship between a truster and a trustee (singular or collective), where the relationship is best understood as a certain attitude held by the former toward the latter. Inspired by the recent work of Karen Jones,[9] this attitude can be understood as one of optimism or confidence that the trustee is:

a. relevantly *competent* to do a certain act (they *can* do it), and
b. *responsive* to the confidence of the truster (they *will* do it because they are being counted on to do so).

To take refuge in the bodhisattvas in the face of negative karmic consequences is thus to adopt an attitude of profound optimism and confidence that the bodhisattvas both can and will prevent the occurrence of negative karmic consequences after one dies. What reason has one to adopt this attitude? A belief in the bodhisattvas' great compassion for the suffering of all sentient beings (of which set one is a member). How is this a remedy for fear? It ameliorates the first of the four aspects of the object of fear, namely, the sense of these karmic consequences being possible. When one takes refuge in the bodhisattvas, one trusts that they can and will ensure that this possibility won't actualize. The greater the trust, the less probable these sufferings appear. One becomes fearless because assured that these occurrences are no longer a possibility for oneself.

OBJECTIONS

I will now turn to consider a couple of objections that might be raised against this analysis.

First, one might wonder why taking refuge in the bodhisattvas is the proposed response to fear of karmic consequences rather than, for instance, acting morally. Reference to karmic consequences is often made in Buddhist literature to motivate the self-interested person to act morally. Many consider moral action to be an antidote to negative karmic consequences. It might seem, however, that nothing particularly moral follows from the above analysis. It might even be consistent with immorality; so long as the bodhisattvas can and will prevent these negative consequences, the agent might otherwise act as they please.

One response to this objection is to simply say that taking refuge *is* a moral action. It would thus follow that fear of karmic consequences *does* motivate moral action in the above analysis, albeit a moral action of only one kind. For this to be plausible, however, it would need to be supplemented with an account of the criteria for moral action. One might attempt to argue that the reasoning is consequentialist, but the only negative consequences forgone are those that accrue to the agent. No plausible version of consequentialism accommodates such a high degree of partiality.

This relates to a further, and perhaps more fundamental, objection. It might appear that taking refuge in the bodhisattvas is fundamentally egoistic. One enters this trusting relationship to foreclose an unwanted possibility occurring to oneself, which matters for reasons grounded in one's own personal interest and values. If it did not matter *to whom* these karmic consequences occurred, the subject might perform various other acts to avoid its occurrence. By taking refuge in the bodhisattvas, the subject trusts that they can be counted on to save *them*, the trusting agent, from this outcome. According to the teachings of the Buddha, however, egoistic self-concern is not only at the root of many kinds of mental afflictions, including fear, it also manifests ignorance of the fact that there is no self (*anātman*), that everything that exists is dependently originated (*pratītyasamutpāda*) and thereby impermanent (*anitya*). If this is right, one might object that the motivation for taking refuge in the bodhisattvas is fundamentally flawed and manifests a subtle mental defilement.

A MORE REFINED ANALYSIS

I close by considering a more refined analysis of the transition from fear to fearlessness by means of taking refuge that aims to avert the above objections.

As with the original analysis, Śāntideva incites fear to motivate taking refuge in the bodhisattvas and thus entering a relationship of trust. Why does Śāntideva do this? I now propose that it is part of a more complex strategy to promote taking refuge in the Buddha's teachings, the Buddhadharma, an important aspect of which concerns his teaching of no-self. Some support for this claim might be derived from the fact that the ninth chapter of the *Guide* is devoted to a dialectical debate between two interlocutors on the metaphysics of self.

If this is Śāntideva's eventual aim, why does he initially motivate taking refuge in the bodhisattvas? According to this more refined analysis, he understands that his audience is likely to be concerned for their own well-being and, since taking refuge in the bodhisattvas engages this self-concern, understands that they are likely to be motivated by this advice. But (and this is the refinement) taking refuge in the bodhisattvas brings the agent in close contact with the teachings of the Buddha. This provides for a new possibility, namely, openness to learning about the Buddha's teachings, the Buddhadharma, and thereby the possibility of realizing their truth. But why take this route? The Buddha's teachings challenge core beliefs, particularly about the nature and status of self. Agents are often resistant to changing their core beliefs. Inciting intense fear is an effective strategy to motivate this difficult process of reflection and revision.

If this is plausible, then "taking refuge," when applied to the Buddhadharma, can't be the same as when applied to the bodhisattvas. This is because it is no longer a two-place relationship between agents. This refined sense of "taking refuge" might instead be understood as an attitude of "openness to the truth" of what the Buddha says. This is not to say one necessarily accepts the Buddha's teachings *as* true. Rather, this second sense of "taking refuge" marks the beginning of a process rather than its culmination. It takes the Buddha's teachings as a complex hypothetical, the truth of which one is open to realizing and affirming.

What is the culmination of this process? How does this more refined sense of "taking refuge" contribute to the achievement of fearlessness, as Śāntideva proposes? The answer to this question depends on how one interprets the nature of the Buddhadharma; in particular, the Buddha's teaching of no-self (*anātman*). There are (at least) two possible answers to this final question that reflect two distinct positions on this teaching.

◈ ◈ ◈

No Object View: Śāntideva is a Buddhist in the Mādhyamika philosophical tradition. For several prominent Madhyamaka thinkers, to realize the truth of no-self is to remove all conception of "I, me, mine" (*ahaṃkāra*). According to the *No Object View*, the realization of this metaphysical truth has direct bearing on one's psychology; it removes a crucial presupposition that underpins negative mental states. It also has direct bearing on one's phenomenology by removing any sense of self from the scope of experience. This might help explain the transition from fear to fearlessness by removing the object of value and thus the basis of concern presupposed by fear. When subjects fear the karmic consequences of their actions and seek refuge in the protection of the bodhisattvas, it matters to them whether these consequences occur. If they did not care, the consequences would not be an object of fear. This self-concern is grounded in a value for personal well-being. Realizing the truth of no-self involves realizing that this concern does not have a proper object. A genuine and deep understanding of this point thus results in the cessation of self-concern and thus of those mental states for which this self-concern is a necessary presupposition. If there is no self, there is no proper object that could be threatened by anticipated possibilities and relative to which these possibilities are unwanted. If there is no self, there is no one for whom these unwanted possibilities matter—i.e., the sufferings that occur at the point of, and after, death. Taking refuge in the teachings of the Buddha thus leads to fearlessness by eliminating an essential constituent of fear.

This seems like a plausible reading of Śāntideva. One might nevertheless have (at least) two concerns with the *No Object View*. First, it assumes that mattering is necessarily egoistic. This is because it infers a denial of ego from the denial of self, a denial of egoism from the denial of ego, and a denial of mattering from the denial of egoism. In this way, it undermines the object of fear and suggests a transition to fearlessness. One might object, however, that mattering is not necessarily egoistic. An unwanted possibility can matter to subjects in ways that reflect their values, but without being necessarily in their interest. Consider, for instance, observing an unknown child teetering on the edge of a pool. It seems possible to fear the child drowning without necessarily presupposing self-concern. If this is right, then realizing the truth of no-self does not necessarily undermine the possibility of an unwanted possibility mattering to a subject and leaves open the possibility of fear.

Second, one might object that the *No Object View* is too coarse-grained with unwanted implications. It undermines egoism by eliminating the ego. However, it would seem to also and thereby undermine all forms of prudential reasoning (such as brushing one's teeth, putting on sunblock, buying groceries for one's evening meal) grounded in a reasonable degree of self-concern. It would also seem to undermine the distinction between self and other assumed by such bodhisattva virtues as compassion (*karuṇā*), great compassion (*mahākaruṇā*), and the accomplishment of *bodhicitta* (the commitment to serve beings until their suffering is alleviated). If there is no self, then there is also no other. If fear is eradicated by removing the object of concern (the self), a similar argument can be mobilized against the object of concern (the other) presupposed by compassion and other-directed virtues.

◈ ◈ ◈

Dependent Self View: There is a second possible answer that might avoid both of the above problems. According to the *Dependent Self View*, the positive counterpart to realizing the metaphysical truth of no-self does not entail a psychological and phenomenological eradication of all notions of self. Rather, it entails their revision in view of the Buddha's teaching of dependent origination (*pratītyasamutpāda*). On this view, one retains a phenomenological distinction between self and other but gains a deep understanding that, metaphysically, this distinction is a mere convention used to pick out objects that are not essentially distinct but exist dependently. Reflecting on the conventional nature of these distinctions, one might realize that there is no good reason to privilege the interests of a merely conventional self. Rather than eliminating the object of concern, it could be argued that this realization gives reason to expand its scope, from egoistic self-concern to altruistic self-other concern. As we have argued, concern or mattering always manifests values that are local to a subject. However, the relevant value need not be egoistic but may extend to all relevant subjects. What makes a subject a relevant object of concern? The fact that they experience suffering.

By retaining a (revised) distinction between self and other, the *Dependent Self View* is consistent with Śāntideva's endorsement of the bodhisattva virtues, *bodhicitta*, and ordinary forms of prudential reasoning. It thereby averts the second problem raised in response to the *No Object View*. It might, however, appear to be much worse off with respect to the first problem raised against this view. It was objected that it leaves open the possibility of fear by failing to undermine certain unwanted possibilities mattering to a subject in terms that qualify them as objects of fear. One might worry, however, that the *Dependent Self View* not only also admits these possibilities but additionally *expands* the scope of unwanted possibilities that are feared. Rather than simply fearing the possible unwanted sufferings that are likely to occur to oneself, grounded in an egoistic sense of value, this solution seems to entail that one now fears the possible unwanted sufferings *wherever* they might occur, to *whomever* they might occur. Rather than leading to fearlessness, it might seem that this solution leads to the (potentially limitless) *expansion* of fear. How can *this* approach lead to fearlessness?

The solution, I propose, involves contextualizing this analysis in relation to *bodhicitta*, the goal of the bodhisattva ideal at the heart of the *Guide*. *Bodhicitta* is standardly articulated as a commitment to bring about the cessation of suffering of all sentient beings. The purpose of inciting fear is to motivate agents to action, to avert the object of fear from eventuating. The relevant object of fear is suffering, wherever and to whomever it may occur. When the scope of evaluative concern is properly extended, we might think of fear as motivating the very best kinds of altruistic action. Taking refuge in the Buddha's teaching, we might argue, transforms fear from an egoistic motivation, grounded in a concern with personal well-being, to an altruistic self-other motivation that is grounded in a disvalue of suffering wherever it occurs. How does this lead to fearlessness? When all sufferings are eradicated, when all unwanted possibilities of this kind are foreclosed, then and only then is fearlessness achieved. This appears to be concurrent with achieving the objective of *bodhicitta*: namely, the cessation of suffering of all sentient beings. On closer inspection, however, it is actually concurrent with the cessation of all future, potential, possible sufferings, not merely those that are occurrent. This strengthened objective is *bodhicitta*, properly understood.

CONCLUSION

Why would one purposely incite fear if one's goal is its elimination? And how are we to understand the role of taking refuge in making this transition? I have argued that Śāntideva incites fear in subjects with an aim of transforming egoistic self-concern into altruistic self-other concern. This is achieved by provoking their self-interest and motivating them to take refuge in the protection of the bodhisattvas. This puts subjects in proximity to the Buddha's teachings and thereby the possibility of realizing their truth. These teachings challenge core beliefs, which subjects are typically reluctant to change. Śāntideva's incitement of fear thus serves a secondary role: it motivates subjects to engage in the difficult task of belief revision. This may, in turn, lead subjects to revise their understanding of the nature of self and other, inspire an altruistic concern for the sufferings of others and thereby the arising of *bodhicitta*, a commitment to remove all sufferings wherever they occur. In the medium term, this entails an expanded set of unwanted possibilities that matter to them and thus are feared. Fearlessness is achieved at the culmination of the progressive achievement of the goal of *bodhicitta*, which shapes the life of a bodhisattva.

NOTES

1. Translations are from Śāntideva, *Bodhicaryāvatāra*, trans. Crosby and Skilton.
2. This is not one continuous passage but a series of passages selected and ordered for the purposes of this chapter.
3. Jones, "Trustworthiness."
4. Thompson and Dreyfus, "Asian Perspectives: Indian Theories of Mind."
5. Vasubandhu, *Abhidharmakośabhāṣya*, 1.2.3:189.
6. Asaṅga, *Abhidharmasamuccaya*, 1.1.1:8–9.
7. Asaṅga, *Abhidharmasamuccaya*, 1.1.1:6.
8. Asaṅga, *Abhidharmasamuccaya*, 1.1.1:6.
9. Jones, "Trustworthiness."

REFERENCES

Asaṅga. *Abhidharmasamuccaya.* French trans. W. Rahula. English trans. S.Boin-Webb. Berkeley, CA: Asian Humanities Press, 2001.

Dreyfus, G. and E. Thompson. "Asian Perspectives: Indian Theories of Mind." In *Cambridge Handbook of Consciousness*, ed. P. D. Zelazo, M. Moscovitch, and E. Thompson. Cambridge: Cambridge University Press, 2007.

Jones, K. "Trustworthiness." *Ethics* 123, no. 1 (2012) :61–85.

Śāntideva. *Bodhicaryāvatāra*. Trans. Kate Crosby and Andrew Skilton. Oxford World Classics. New York: Oxford University Press, 1998.

Vasubandhu. *Abhidharmakośabhāṣya*. French trans. L. de La Vallée Poussin. English trans. L. M. Pruden. Berkeley, CA: Asian Humanities Press, 1990.

[14]

INNATE HUMAN CONNECTIVITY AND ŚĀNTIDEVA'S CULTIVATION OF COMPASSION

John D. Dunne

A FUNDAMENTAL QUESTION about humans is simply this: why are we so different from other primates, especially the nonhuman great apes or hominids? If we adopt an evolutionary perspective and consider a very long-term view of history, the great apes—chimpanzees, bonobos, orangutans, and gorillas—are our not-so-distant relatives, yet in many of our abilities we humans far exceed them. Some of the latest scientific research in multiple disciplines suggests that the difference lies in a fundamental capacity for a behavior that many primates exhibit but only humans have brought to its highest level: the ability to cooperate.[1] None of our near relatives in the primate world can cooperate in the way that we can, and among the various capacities required for the heightened level of cooperation that humans exhibit, perhaps the most important is the ability to work toward a common goal by connecting to others, in part by extending our sense of self into a broader social group that shares that objective. When that goal is understood to be the universal human aim of relieving suffering and achieving authentic happiness, Śāntideva's *Guide to Bodhisattva Practice* (*Bodhicaryāvatāra,* hereafter *Guide*) becomes highly relevant to these scientific considerations, especially in terms of approaches to cultivating compassion. Likewise, the science of human cooperation and its evolutionary development illuminates certain aspects of Śāntideva's approach to developing compassion.

While various interpretations of Śāntideva's method for cultivating compassion exist, the one proposed here differs from some of the more recent scholarly interpretations.[2] Inspired in part by certain strands of the scientific literature on the evolution of cooperative cognition, I argue that Śāntideva assumes that his audience has an innate capacity for compassion that is inhibited by a self-other distinction that involves a false sense of self. Thus, enhancing compassion for others is not a matter of increasing one's feelings of love, warmth, or care for others; indeed, Śāntideva almost entirely avoids any such "warm fuzzy" language. Nor does compassionate connection with others result from being convinced by an argument that this is the only rational way to behave. Instead, for Śāntideva the cultivation of compassion in relatively inexperienced practitioners is a matter of disrupting the cognitive models that inhibit their innate capacity to sense and respond to all suffering, including the suffering of others. As we will see, this interpretation helps to resolve some puzzling issues in the *Guide* and points to some practical implications for further research on the cultivation of compassion.

GLEANINGS FROM THE SCIENCE OF COOPERATION

Although a growing literature on compassion and its cultivation can be found in current psychology,[3] my interpretation of Śāntideva's approach will draw instead on a few elements within the interdisciplinary study of the emergence of highly complex cooperation as a distinctively human capacity. In a rather selective way, in this section I will discuss current theories in research in two general areas: the innate tendency for humans to connect to other humans and the ways that humans also disconnect from others.

Human Connectivity

The current scientific consensus maintains that, while our nearest primate relatives have a capacity for rudimentary social cognition, they are not observed to cooperate in the complex and rich way that humans do. On this account, our primate relatives do not exhibit those cooperative behaviors primarily because they lack the mental capacity for them. As Michael Tomasello puts it, "In general, humans are able to coordinate with others, in a way that other primates seemingly are not, to form a 'we' that acts as a kind of plural agent to create everything from a collaborative hunting party to a cultural institution."[4] For example, our nearest primate relatives are the chimpanzees, and as with humans, at least some bands of chimpanzee hunt other animals. When humans hunt, they can engage in a kind of "shared intentionality," such that each member of the hunting party adopts distinct roles so that the group as a whole may succeed. In contrast, the most straightforward interpretation of chimpanzee behavior is that they engage in a kind of "parallel hunting," where each one seeks to capture the prey for himself (only males hunt). Thus, although a limited degree of cooperation occurs, chimpanzees do not cooperate in the robust way that humans do.[5] And for scientists such as Tomasello, chimpanzees and other great apes cannot attain a human level of cooperation precisely because they lack the capacity for the type of complex social cognition that enables humans to bond closely together through a shared sense of "we."[6]

The capacities for social cognition that enable humans to cooperate at such a high level permit us to engage in amazing feats of joint action, such as farming vast acres of land, performing symphonies, and flying to the moon. Yet all this comes at a price: to engage in that level of social cognition, humans need unusually large brains. For various reasons, this means that human infants come into the world in a highly vulnerable state, and in comparison to other animals, tremendous resources are required to raise human infants to the point that they can contribute productively to their families and communities. This resource-burden is so great that, unlike chimpanzees and other great apes, a human mother cannot possibly raise her child without significant assistance from others. Human child rearing thus requires the kind of cooperation that only humans exhibit. More importantly, this also means that human infants must have an innate capacity to connect emotionally to multiple human caretakers, not just their mothers.[7]

When all this is examined from an evolutionary perspective, an intriguing interconnection emerges. On the one hand, our robust capacity for cooperation is clearly a tremendous evolutionary advantage: we have been remarkably successful as a species. On the other hand, in order to have enough resources to develop the brain capacity for that level of cooperation, human infants must have the ability to connect readily to multiple caretakers to a degree that chimpanzees and other great apes do not. There are thus converging forces that drive a profound capacity for social connectivity in humans: some come from the mental abilities needed to cooperate, which provide an evolutionary advantage, and others come from the capacities that enable a vulnerable human infant to bond emotionally with other humans, which is evolutionarily necessary for the infant's survival. The upshot of this evolutionary story is that, at birth, we already connect deeply with others in a way that enables us to eventually engage in a level of cooperation that is unique to humans. As the neuroscientist Jim Coan puts it, the human brain *expects* to connect socially to others.[8]

Learning Disconnection

On the account sketched above, humans come into the world with an innate capacity for a high level of social and emotional connectivity that results from various evolutionary forces, yet as they develop, humans also learn to disconnect. Although a matter of some debate, it appears that young infants initially do not clearly distinguish themselves from others; instead, this self/other distinction develops over time, so that a reliable ability to attribute emotional states and beliefs to others requires three or more years to develop.[9] This self/other distinction results in part from expected patterns of brain development, but it is also highly dependent on contextual factors, such as family dynamics and culture. As proponents of Attachment Theory argue, this means that as infants learn to differentiate self from other, they can develop various styles of relating to others, and because they are largely learned, these attachment styles can also change in adulthood, perhaps even through a therapeutic process.[10]

Drawing on the science of social cognition, another mode of disconnection concerns not the basic self/other distinction but rather the distinction between an "in-group" and an "out-group." This distinction relates directly to cooperation; that is, an "in-group" includes those humans with whom one is ready to cooperate toward the achievement of shared goals, while one is not poised to cooperate with members of an "out-group," often because they do not share those goals or are even opposed to them. Since the degree of social connection with others depends on this distinction, one's attention and responsiveness to others' states also depends on whether they are part of one's in-group. One's sensitivity to another's pain, for example, and responsiveness to others' needs both vary in dependence on this distinction, such that one is usually far more sensitive and responsive to the pain and emotional states of one's in-group.[11]

Three features of the in-group/out-group distinction are especially relevant to Śāntideva's approach to cultivating compassion. First, in a way that echoes a human infant's bonds with its caregivers, it seems likely that we are sensitive and responsive to members of our in-group because our own sense of self actually extends to the in-group. Thus, something that harms my in-group is in some sense also harming me, to the point that my neural representations of my own pain closely resemble the neural representations that occur when I see pain being experienced by someone in a close relationship to me.[12] This "inclusion of the self in other" is especially clear in close relationships, but it also applies to more distant members of my in-group.[13]

Second, this in-group/out-group distinction is highly dependent on cultural and contextual influences. As the infamous Stanford Prison Experiment shows, one can create this distinction just by assigning different forms of dress and roles to arbitrary groups of people. And once the distinction has been induced, the sensitivity to the needs or pain of the in-group—and insensitivity or even callousness toward the outgroup—are quickly exhibited in behavior.[14] This contextual nature of the distinction points to the possibility to manipulate in-group/out-group configurations.

Third, and in a more positive vein, in many cases the in-group/out-group distinction can be eliminated or at least reduced through training or experimental manipulations.[15] In relation to Śāntideva's approach, an especially intriguing finding is that maintaining an in-group/out-group distinction, even unconsciously, appears to require some cognitive effort. Thus, when David Rand and colleagues asked experimental subjects to consider an act of generosity toward a stranger (i.e., someone who is not a member of one's in-group), the subjects were *more* generous when they had *less* time to think. In other words, in a way that reflects the fundamental social connectivity of humans, the default behavior tends toward being helpful and generous, an experimental finding that is "consistent with work demonstrating spontaneous helping behavior in young children."[16] The intriguing suggestion here is that enhancing one's caring attitude toward others may be achieved simply by inhibiting the learned tendency to not care as much for "strangers," namely, those who are not part of our in-group. If we can unlearn or suspend this exclusion of others, then by default they become part of the socially extended sense of self—and the extended sphere of care—that is our default state.

ŚĀNTIDEVA'S APPROACH

Turning now to Śāntideva's approach to compassion, one might immediately wonder, "Why bother with all this science?" This question points to a key assumption that I bring to the text, namely, that Śāntideva is writing from the standpoint of his own experience, and he is conveying to "those of similar propensities" (*matsamadhātu*) techniques that will work for them because they have worked for him in the past. When he speaks, for example, of the fear of rebuke from a teacher as a powerful motivator for mindfulness (*Guide* 5.30), or when he berates himself for being lazy (7.14), the flavor of the text is highly practical and experiential. In this sense, the *Guide* can often be read as a record of the tips and tricks that have helped Śāntideva over the course of his contemplative career.

With this assumption in place, the foray into science that began this chapter makes good sense because it can help us to understand various aspects of the practices he recommends, especially his approach to cultivating compassion. Specifically, focusing on a particular line of scientific interpretation, we have gleaned that over the course of our evolution, we humans have developed a deep and innate capacity to connect to other humans in a way that often involves extending our sense of self to them, such that a harm to these others is experienced as a harm to self. When we do not care for others, it is due to their exclusion in an out-group, their identification as "other" and not part of "self." This type of distinction, however, is to a great extent learned, and it also requires some cognitive resources to maintain, such that if those cognitive structures or resources are disrupted, our default tendency for caring generally emerges. If we use this scientific lens to examine Śāntideva's techniques for cultivating compassion, we have a clearer picture of his approach, for if we can assume that somehow Śāntideva discovered a set of contemplative techniques that helped him to care more for others, the science may provide some insight as to why those techniques worked for him.

In any case, as recent scholarship demonstrates,[17] the text as it stands has been a source of considerable confusion and debate. For our purposes, the most problematic passage consists in a set of contemplations for the cultivation of the type of compassion required of the bodhisattva. This passage is found in the chapter on meditation (*bhāvanā*) beginning at verse 90 and proceeding to at least verse 139, although the entire rest of the chapter can be conceived as providing additional contemplations connected to cultivating compassion. In the main passage, two issues have puzzled interpreters: first, the text contains various arguments, but these are much less consistent than one would expect of Śāntideva, whose capacity for sharp and rational debate becomes clear in the subsequent chapter that focuses on wisdom (*prajñā*). Second, to the extent that a clear philosophical argument forms part of the contemplation, it does not reach the level of analysis expected of Śāntideva, whose final position is the Madhyamaka philosophy of emptiness. In other words, the arguments in the compassion contemplation appear to be contradicted by the philosophy of emptiness articulated in the wisdom chapter. As it turns out, these two puzzles are the product of a failure to appreciate several contextual features of the compassion contemplation, so before examining that contemplation itself, let us examine its overall context.

The Context

Three aspects of the context for Śāntideva's techniques for contemplating compassion are especially important: the pragmatic use of compassion as an aid to generating wisdom; the notion that there are multiple levels of conventional reality; and the explicit use of certain kinds of afflictive mental states (*kleśa*), especially confusion (*moha*), as a practical method for advancing on the bodhisattva path.

The pragmatic use of compassion as an aid to generating wisdom emerges clearly from Śāntideva's own statement at the beginning of the wisdom chapter, which immediately follows the contemplation on compassion. In the very first verse of the wisdom chapter, Śāntideva states, "The sage [i.e., the Buddha] taught this entire collection for the sake of wisdom. Therefore, with the desire to eliminate suffering, one should generate wisdom" (*Guide* 9.1). As the Sanskrit commentator Prajñākaramati makes clear, Śāntideva is here referring to the entire contents of the text up to that point. Those contents, conceptualized as the first five "perfections" (*pāramitā*) for a bodhisattva's training, are understood to be the "method" (*upāya*) for obtaining complete awakening or buddhahood, and compassion itself is the final and crucial element.[18] As noted elsewhere in this volume, the motivation for engaging in the practice of these various methods is *bodhicitta,* the aspiration to achieve buddhahood for the purpose of eliminating the suffering of all sentient beings. As was well known to Śāntideva, and as Prajñākaramati attests, compassion and the other methods on the bodhisattva path cannot themselves eliminate suffering; this can be accomplished only through wisdom, specifically the wisdom that knows all persons and things to be empty of essence or fixed identity. Nevertheless, compassion and the other methods are necessary prerequisites for cultivating the wisdom of emptiness in a way that enables one to achieve complete awakening.[19]

With all this in mind, it should be obvious that the philosophical context of the compassion contemplation cannot be the wisdom of emptiness. Śāntideva is quite clear that compassion is an aid to realizing emptiness, not the other way around, and given the order of the chapters, it is also clear that the compassion contemplation is directed at the practitioner who has not yet generated that wisdom.[20] Thus, to the extent that Śāntideva deploys arguments in the compassion contemplation, they are pragmatically aimed at inducing the kind of compassion that will serve as a support for generating wisdom.

This pragmatic approach to the use of argumentation and analysis is also explicitly endorsed by Śāntideva in the wisdom chapter when he discusses the well-known rubric of the "two realities" (*satyadvaya*) (*Guide* 9.2–4). He speaks of the ultimate reality (*paramārthasatya*), which Prajñākaramati, following standard Madhyamaka theory, identifies as "essencelessness" (*niḥsvabhāvatā*) or simply "emptiness" (*śūnyatā*); he likewise speaks of the conventional reality (*saṃvṛtisatya*). Śāntideva then notes that there are levels of conventional reality; the most basic level is the world of ordinary, untrained beings (*prākṛtako lokaḥ*), and as Prajñākaramati notes, the conventional reality at this lowest level is what these ordinary beings take to be truly real from the standpoint of their deeply confused minds.[21] Then, in a way that echoes other Buddhist thinkers, Śāntideva notes that there is a higher level of conventional reality, namely, the world as it appears to contemplatives, whom Prajñākaramati identifies specifically as Buddhist practitioners. Śāntideva continues to assert further levels of conventional reality from the perspectives of contemplatives who are at further stages of development. Finally, at this point, Śāntideva makes a key statement. He notes that to help someone on a lower level move to a higher level, the world as experienced from the lower level of conventional reality must be refuted from the standpoint of the higher level. To do so, one employs "examples accepted by both"—i.e., by both the person on the lower level and the one on the higher level—"*without analysis, for the sake of the goal*" (*dṛṣṭāntenobhayeṣṭena kāryārtham avicārataḥ*, *Guide* 9.4cd).

Without getting into the technical aspects of Mādhyamika philosophy, we can simply note that, with this final phrase, Śāntideva is pointing to a well-known issue for all Madhyamaka thinkers.[22] Suppose that a Madhyamaka philosopher is debating with another Buddhist philosopher who maintains that matter in the form of atoms truly and ultimately exists. From the Madhyamaka perspective, that other Buddhist philosopher is at a lower level of understanding (and thus inhabits a lower level of conventional reality) because according to the Madhyamaka, atoms actually do not exist. However, "for the sake of the goal," which is to convince the other thinker that there are no atoms, the Madhyamaka philosopher must find a way to talk about things like atoms in a provisional way; otherwise, communication will be impossible. To do so, the Madhyamaka philosopher suspends "analysis" (*vicāra*) just enough to allow him to communicate with that confused person. Otherwise, if the Madhyamaka philosophers simply argue from the highest level of conventional reality, persons at lower levels will not be able to understand; they cannot simply jump to the highest level directly.

This pragmatic approach to argument appears in many contexts, and in academic work it is described as adopting "levels of analysis." These levels of analysis are often articulated in terms of Buddhist philosophical schools that are hierarchically ranked, and in one mode of training, practitioners deliberately start at a lower level and then move to a higher one, precisely because the higher one is not immediately accessible to them.[23] The basic idea is that philosophical perspectives at a lower level include more confusion (*moha*), and this is what makes it difficult to move immediately to the highest level. Instead, one proceeds through levels of analysis that gradually peel away layers of confusion until one finally reaches the highest level, which for Śāntideva is the Madhyamaka philosophy of emptiness.

As Stephen Jenkins notes,[24] confusion (*moha*) plays a central role in Śāntideva's account of compassion. The special role of confusion is related to a more general aspect of Śāntideva's method: the use of *kleśa*s or afflictive mental states as a means to progress on the spiritual path. He says:

> I will be relentless in slaughtering the *kleśa*s!
> I will be tenacious in this, and girded with enmity, I will wage war,
> Except not against those *kleśa*s that are useful for killing *kleśa*s. (*Guide* 4.42cd–43)

These verses themselves illustrate their own point, for here a kind of hostility, which is itself a *kleśa*, is being directed toward the *kleśa*s themselves. The point, in any case, is that even though all *kleśa*s must eventually be eliminated because they necessarily cause suffering, one can still provisionally make use of certain *kleśa*s. This technique is especially useful for practitioners near the start of the bodhisattva path, since their minds are still very much filled with *kleśa*s. And it is even more useful in the case of confusion itself, for confusion—also known as ignorance (*avidyā*)—persists to at least some degree until one has attained complete buddhahood.[25] Thus, *every* bodhisattva has some degree of confusion, so it is not surprising that Śāntideva might find use for it on the path.

The bodhisattva's use of confusion is introduced by Śāntideva in the wisdom chapter when he raises an objection, "If no sentient being exists, then for whom is there compassion?" (*Guide* 9.76ab).[26] In other words, according to Madhyamaka philosophy, sentient beings do not ultimately exist; in that case, compassion seems problematic—how could one have compassion for someone who does not really exist?

In response, Śāntideva says that one has compassion for "the one who is conceptualized through confusion that has been provisionally adopted for the sake of the goal" (*Guide* 9.76cd). Here again we see this important phrase: "for the sake of the goal" (*kāryārtham*). Just as Madhyamakas may provisionally suspend a certain level of analysis so as to engage with others who are stuck at a lower level of conventional reality, so too they may provisionally accept the existence of sentient beings by using confusion in a way that will enable them to achieve the goal of complete awakening or buddhahood. To clarify even further, Śāntideva adds another objection: "But if there is no sentient being, for whom is the goal?" (*Guide* 9.77a). That is, one provisionally accepts confusion so as to achieve the goal of complete buddhahood, but if there are no sentient beings, then who benefits from the goal? And who achieves it? Śāntideva answers in a similar way: "For the sake of ending suffering, confusion about the goal is not eliminated" (*Guide* 9.77cd). From the ultimate Madhyamaka perspective, there are no beings, and there are also no goals. Yet our confused notion that beings and goals exist can nevertheless be useful on the path.

Cultivating Compassion: Redrawing the In-Group, Disrupting the Self

The context of Śāntideva's instructions for cultivating compassion points to three key features. First, the bodhisattva's compassion involves at least some degree of confusion, so we should not expect these instructions to presuppose that the practitioner can operate from the final, ultimate standpoint of buddhahood. Second, and along these same lines, the practical aim of these instructions is to induce compassion as an aid to cultivating the wisdom articulated in the next chapter, so it would be odd for Śāntideva to expect his audience to already be able to operate from the ultimate standpoint of wisdom. And third, Śāntideva explicitly endorses the use of provisionally accepted arguments that actually do not hold up in the long run, as long as they are useful for the practical goal of moving practitioners along the path.

With these contextual issues in place, Śāntideva's actual instructions point to an intriguing possibility: they are primarily targeting the self/other distinction and the notion of self altogether, such that it is primarily by altering or disrupting these conceptualizations that compassion will emerge. And if we assume that this type of contemplation is what actually worked for Śāntideva, a psychological account of why it worked emerges from our previous discussion about the innate connectivity that humans share.

As Garfield, Jenkins, and Priest have pointed out,[27] the core of Śāntideva's contemplation is found in verses 90–103 of the meditation chapter. Several reliable translations already exist,[28] and rather than reproduce these verses here, I will summarize their content and point to two themes: the notion that self and other are the same in a way that extends self into other, and the critique of the self concept. These two themes conflict, but keeping in mind the context of this compassion practice, we can treat these two strands of argumentation as pragmatic attempts at inducing compassion while working at different levels of analysis. In that case, the conflict between them is not problematic.

The first theme, the equality of self and other, is the main emphasis in verses 90 to 96, although it surfaces to some degree in the second half of this section. This theme points specifically to the problematic nature of the self/other distinction in the context of suffering (*duḥkha*) and happiness (*sukha*), which can also be translated as pain and pleasure. A central motif is that others are "like me" (*ātmavat*) in that they also wish to be happy and do not wish to suffer. He thus begins the contemplation by saying that "All are equal in [their experience of] suffering and happiness, and I should protect them all, just as I do myself" (*Guide* 8.90).[29] Śāntideva next likens the distinction between self and other to the distinctions that differentiate the parts of one's own body, such as hands and feet. The clear implication here is that, just as the sense of self extends to the whole body, so too it can extend to include others. The next two verses then show that our common goal of avoiding suffering and achieving happiness is rooted in the same fundamental problem of self-attachment (*ātmasneha*), with the clear implication that we should work together to overcome it. Finally, verse 94 is perhaps the peak of this part of the contemplation:

> I should eliminate the suffering of others, just like my own suffering.
> I should care for others because they are sentient beings, just as I am a sentient being. (*Guide* 8.94)

If taken as a rational argument that is meant to persuade a skeptic by force of reason, the first four verses of the contemplation seem rather inadequate. If, however, they are read in light of the innate psychological traits and capacities that bind humans together, these verses could be very effective. By putting us all in the same metaphorical boat of suffering and happiness, they resonate with our impulse for cooperation, and with the refrain of "like me," they invite us to extend our sense of self to an in-group that includes all sentient beings who are in this predicament together. Likewise, simply by referring to suffering, these verses prime us for the kind of spontaneous responsivity to others' suffering that generally characterizes the default state that is arguably manifest starting in infancy. In a way that simply may have been intuitive for Śāntideva, this part of the contemplation clearly could be effective in evoking a compassionate stance toward others by drawing on our innate tendencies. In essence, Śāntideva has created a type of psychological manipulation that alters our in-group by drawing on our connectivity in relation especially to both cooperation and suffering. As noted above, such manipulations are known to be effective.

The next part of the contemplation involves two verses that can be read as transitioning from the breakdown of the self/other distinction to the critique of the self concept. With the previous verses inducing the sense that all sentient beings are members of our in-group, these verses point out that we are not behaving appropriately toward that in-group, which itself draws on the kinds of expectations that arise with in-group identities. These verses basically ask, what is special about me that I am not caring for these other beings, who are effectively part of my in-group? The verses thus continue the motif of reconfiguring one's sense of in-group, but they also begin an inquiry about the nature of one's self.

The inquiry into one's concept of self is the uniting theme for the remainder of the verses in this core section of the contemplation, and this inquiry is best interpreted as a "leveling up" in terms of the philosophical context for the verses. In the beginning of the contemplation, the sense of self was left untouched, in part so that one could see others as "just like me." Now, moving to a higher level of analysis, the very notion of self is critiqued. From a philosophical perspective, this shift can seem problematic, since it appears to undermine the sense of self assumed at the start of the contemplation, but as a step in a psychological process of inducing compassion it has great potential. As noted earlier, it appears that the in-group/out-group distinction requires some cognitive effort, and also that it emerges from a more basic self-other distinction. Thus, critiquing the sense of self with a philosophical argument could erode that distinction and promote compassion in two ways simultaneously. On the one hand, by undermining the sense of self, the critique removes the foundation for distinguishing an in-group from an out-group, which depends on a more basic separation of self from other. On the other hand, creating a cognitive load that is intensified by the counterintuitive notion that the self does not truly exist disrupts the effort to maintain the self/other and in-group/out-group distinctions to at least some degree. The kind of caring that emerges from our innate psychological tendencies, and which has been primed by the start of the contemplation, might thus have a chance to express itself more fully.

CONCLUSION: SOME IMPLICATIONS

On the interpretation offered here, I have assumed that Śāntideva's instructions for cultivating compassion are based upon his own experience. In other words, Śāntideva believed that this contemplation actually increased his own compassion, and he thus taught this approach to others. With this assumption in place, the obvious question is: why did this work? If read as a purely rational argument, Śāntideva's contemplation seems rather inadequate, especially in comparison to the far sharper arguments presented in the wisdom chapter. It is hard to believe that he would have found them philosophically or rationally persuasive from the standpoint of his highest level of analysis, where not only the self but even the basic psychophysical constituents that are mistakenly apprehended as a self actually do not exist. I have instead proposed that, deliberately or not, Śāntideva came up with an approach to compassion that effectively manipulates our own innate tendencies in a way that could be highly effective in enhancing and broadening our compassionate attitudes and behaviors, and given the overall context of the compassion contemplation, this interpretation seems preferable to one that attempts to render it as a philosophically persuasive argument.

At the same time, Śāntideva's approach raises some questions for ongoing research in multiple domains. Within the study of Buddhism, a key question is the applicability of this analysis to other contexts: do we see similar inductions of compassion elsewhere? More broadly, did Buddhists over the centuries develop other manipulations that were effective in changing attitudes and behaviors, and might it be fruitful to examine them from the standpoint of contemporary theories in psychology, cognitive science, and other such domains? Finally, for researchers in the various scientific disciplines involved in the study of compassion and empathy, there are also intriguing implications. In particular, Śāntideva's strong emphasis on cognitive—rather than affective or emotional—manipulations may suggest that, for at least some people, the key to cultivating compassion has more to do with the way we think than the way we feel.

NOTES

1. The most developed evolutionary argument, along with a review of the relevant literature, is found in Tomasello, *A Natural History of Human Thinking.*
2. See especially Garfield, Jenkins, and Priest, "The Śāntideva Passage"; Jenkins, "Waking Into Compassion"; Garfield, "Buddhist Ethics in the Context of Conventional Truth."
3. See Goetz, Keltner, and Simon-Thomas, "Compassion"; for a review of clinical outcomes, see Shonin et al., "Buddhist-Derived Loving-Kindness and Compassion Meditation for the Treatment of Psychopathology"; for a broader view that integrates compassion practice into an overall framework, see Dahl, Lutz, and Davidson, "Reconstructing and Deconstructing the Self."
4. Tomasello, *A Natural History of Human Thinking*, 3.
5. Tomasello, *A Natural History of Human Thinking*, 33–38.
6. Tomasello, *A Natural History of Human Thinking*, 80–123; Tomasello and Carpenter, "Shared Intentionality"; Hrdy, "Development+ Social Selection in the Emergence of 'Emotionally Modern' Humans."
7. This line of thought has been articulated most prominently by Sarah Hrdy; see especially Hrdy, *Mothers and Others.*
8. Coan et al., "Meaning and Method"; see also Coan and Sbarra, "Social Baseline Theory"; Beckes and Coan, "Social Baseline Theory."
9. Lewis, "Emotional Development and Consciousness."
10. Marvin, Britner, and Russel, "Normative Development"; Cassidy, Shaver, and Slade, "Attachment and Adult Psychotherapy," 771–772.
11. Cikara and Van Bavel, "The Neuroscience of Intergroup Relations."
12. Hein and Singer, "I Feel How You Feel but Not Always."
13. Aron, Aron, and Norman, "Self-Expansion Model of Motivation and Cognition in Close Relationships and Beyond."
14. Blass et al., "Reflections on the Stanford Prison Experiment." For a less well-known but also less controversial study that covers much of the same ground, see Sharif et al., *Intergroup Conflict and Cooperation.*
15. Olsson and Phelps, "Social Learning of Fear"; Olsson et al., "The Role of Social Groups in the Persistence of Learned Fear."
16. Rand, Greene, and Nowak, "Spontaneous Giving and Calculated Greed," 429; see also Rand, "Cooperation, Fast and Slow."
17. See especially The Cowherds, eds., *Moonpaths.*
18. Prajñākaramati, "*Bodhicaryāvatārapañjikā*," 168–170.
19. Prajñākaramati, "*Bodhicaryāvatārapañjikā*," 168.
20. This point is well argued by Jenkins, "Waking Into Compassion."
21. Prajñākaramati, "*Bodhicaryāvatārapañjikā*," 170–171.
22. This issue is the focus of the excellent work by Dreyfus and McClintock, *The Svātantrika-Prāsaṅgika Distinction.*
23. Dunne, *Foundations of Dharmakīrti's Philosophy*; Dunne, "Buddhism, Schools of"; McClintock, *Omniscience and the Rhetoric of Reason*; Dreyfus, *Recognizing Reality.*
24. Jenkins, "Waking Into Compassion," 102–108.
25. Dunne, "Buddhism, Schools of."
26. With a few small variations, my analysis of this material follows Jenkins, "Waking Into Compassion," 102–111.

27. Garfield, Jenkins, and Priest, "The Śāntideva Passage."
28. I especially recommend the translation by Wallace and Wallace: Śāntideva, *A Guide to the Bodhisattva Way of Life.*
29. Translations in this section are based on Wallace and Wallace, sometimes with considerable modification.

REFERENCES

Aron, Arthur, Elaine N. Aron, and Christina Norman. "Self-Expansion Model of Motivation and Cognition in Close Relationships and Beyond." In *Blackwell Handbook of Social Psychology: Interpersonal Processes*, ed. Garth J. O. Fletcher and Margaret S. Clark, 478–501. Oxford: Blackwell, 2003.

Beckes, Lane, and James A. Coan. "Social Baseline Theory: The Role of Social Proximity in Emotion and Economy of Action." *Social and Personality Psychology Compass* 5, no. 12 (2011): 976–988.

Blass, Thomas, Philip G Zimbardo, Christina Maslach, and Craig Haney, eds. "Reflections on the Stanford Prison Experiment: Genesis, Transformations and Consequences." In *Obedience to Authority: Current Perspectives on the Milgram Paradigm*, 193–237. Mahwah, NJ: Lawrence Erlbaum, 2000.

Cassidy, Jude, Phillip R. Shaver, and Arietta Slade, eds. "Attachment and Adult Psychotherapy: Theory, Research, and Practice." In *Handbook of Attachment, Third Edition: Theory, Research, and Clinical Applications*, 759–79. New York: Guilford, 2016.

Cikara, Mina, and Jay J. Van Bavel. "The Neuroscience of Intergroup Relations: An Integrative Review." *Perspectives on Psychological Science* 9, no. 3 (May 1, 2014): 245–274. https://doi.org/10.1177/1745691614527464.

Coan, James A., and David A. Sbarra. "Social Baseline Theory: The Social Regulation of Risk and Effort." *Current Opinion in Psychology* 1 (2015): 87–91.

Coan, Jim, Paul Condon, Brooke Dodson-Lavelle, John D. Dunne, and John Makransky. "Meaning and Method: Scientific and Contemplative Perspectives on Compassion." Conference panel presented at the 2016 International Symposium for Contemplative Studies, San Diego, CA, November 11, 2016.

Cowherds. *Moonpaths: Ethics and Emptiness*. New York: Oxford University Press, 2016.

Dahl, Cortland J., Antoine Lutz, and Richard J. Davidson. "Reconstructing and Deconstructing the Self: Cognitive Mechanisms in Meditation Practice." *Trends in Cognitive Sciences* 19, no. 9 (September 2015): 515–523. https://doi.org/10.1016/j.tics.2015.07.001.

Dreyfus, Georges. *Recognizing Reality: Dharmakīrti's Philosophy and Its Tibetan Interpretations*. Albany: State University of New York Press, 1997.

Dreyfus, Georges B. J., and Sara L McClintock, eds. *The Svātantrika-Prāsaṅgika Distinction: What Difference Does a Difference Make?* Studies in Indian and Tibetan Buddhism. Boston: Wisdom, 2003.

Dunne, John D. *Foundations of Dharmakīrti's Philosophy*. Boston: Wisdom, 2004.

——. "Buddhism, Schools of: Mahāyāna Philosophical Schools of Buddhism." In *Encyclopedia of Religion*, ed. Lindsay Jones, 2nd ed., 2:1203–13. Detroit: Macmillan Reference USA, 2005.

Garfield, Jay L. "Buddhist Ethics in the Context of Conventional Truth: Path and Transformation." In *Moonpaths: Ethics and Emptiness*, ed. The Cowherds, 77–95. New York: Oxford University Press, 2016.

Garfield, Jay L., Stephen Jenkins, and Graham Priest. "The Śāntideva Passage: *Bodhicaryāvatāra* VIII.90–103." In *Moonpaths: Ethics and Emptiness*, ed. The Cowherds, 54–76. New York: Oxford University Press, 2016.

Goetz, Jennifer L., Dacher Keltner and Emiliana Simon-Thomas. "Compassion: An Evolutionary Analysis and Empirical Review." *Psychological Bulletin* 136, no. 3 (2010): 351–75.

Hein, Grit, and Tania Singer. "I Feel How You Feel but Not Always: The Empathic Brain and Its Modulation." *Current Opinion in Neurobiology*, Cognitive neuroscience, 18, no. 2 (2008): 153–158. https://doi.org/10.1016/j.conb.2008.07.012.

Hrdy, Sarah B. *Mothers and Others: The Evolutionary Origins of Mutual Understanding.* Cambridge: Belknap Press, 2011.

——. "Development+ Social Selection in the Emergence of 'Emotionally Modern' Humans." In *New Frontiers in Social Neuroscience*, 57–91. New York: Springer, 2014. http://link.springer.com/chapter/10.1007/978-3-319-02904-7_5.

Jenkins, Stephen. "Waking Into Compassion: The Three *Ālambana* of *Karuṇā*." In *Moonpaths: Ethics and Emptiness*, ed. The Cowherds. New York: Oxford University Press, 2016.

Lewis, Michael. "Emotional Development and Consciousness." In *Handbook of Child Psychology and Developmental Science, Theory and Method*, ed. Richard M. Lerner, Willis F. Overton, and Peter C. M. Molenaar, 7th ed., 1:407–451. Hoboken, NJ: Wiley, 2015.

Marvin, Robert S., Preston A. Britner, and Beth S. Russel. "Normative Development: The Ontogeny of Attachment in Childhood." In *Handbook of Attachment, Third Edition: Theory, Research, and Clinical Applications*, ed. Jude Cassidy and Phillip R. Shaver, 273–290. New York: Guilford, 2016.

McClintock, Sara L. *Omniscience and the Rhetoric of Reason: Śāntarakṣita and Kamalaśīla on Rationality, Argumentation, and Religious Authority.* Boston: Wisdom, 2010.

Olsson, Andreas, Jeffrey P. Ebert, Mahzarin R. Banaji, and Elizabeth A. Phelps. "The Role of Social Groups in the Persistence of Learned Fear." *Science (New York, N.Y.)* 309, no. 5735 (July 29, 2005): 785–787. https://doi.org/10.1126/science.1113551.

Olsson, Andreas, and Elizabeth A. Phelps. "Social Learning of Fear." *Nature Neuroscience* 10, no. 9 (September 2007): 1095–1102. https://doi.org/10.1038/nn1968.

Prajñākaramati. "*Bodhicaryāvatārapañjikā*." In *Bodhicaryāvatāra of Śāntideva with the Commentary Pañjikā of Prajñākaramati*, ed. P. L. Vaidya. Buddhist Sanskrit Texts, No. 12. Darbhanga, India: The Mithila Institute, 1960.

Rand, David G. "Cooperation, Fast and Slow: Meta-Analytic Evidence for a Theory of Social Heuristics and Self-Interested Deliberation." *Psychological Science* 27, no. 9 (September 1, 2016): 1192–1206. https://doi.org/10.1177/0956797616654455.

Rand, David G., Joshua D. Greene, and Martin A. Nowak. "Spontaneous Giving and Calculated Greed." *Nature* 489, no. 7416 (September 2012): 427. https://doi.org/10.1038/nature11467.

Śāntideva. *A Guide to the Bodhisattva Way of Life*. Trans. Vesna A. Wallace and B. Alan Wallace. Ithaca, NY: Snow Lion, 1997.

Sharif, Muzafer, O. J. Harvey, Jack White, William R. Hood, and Carolyn W. Sherif. *Intergroup Conflict and Cooperation: The Robbers Cave Experiment.* 1954; reprint, Norman: University of Oklahoma Institute of Group Relations, 1961.

Shonin, Edo, William Van Gordon, Angelo Compare, Masood Zangeneh, and Mark D. Griffiths. "Buddhist-Derived Loving-Kindness and Compassion Meditation for the Treatment of Psychopathology: A Systematic Review." *Mindfulness* 6, no. 5 (October 1, 2015): 1161–1180. https://doi.org/10.1007/s12671-014-0368-1.

Tomasello, Michael. *A Natural History of Human Thinking*. Cambridge, MA: Harvard University Press, 2014.

Tomasello, Michael, and Malinda Carpenter. "Shared Intentionality." *Developmental Science* 10, no. 1 (January 1, 2007): 121–125. https://doi.org/10.1111/j.1467-7687.2007.00573.x.

Appendix 1

A GUIDE TO *GUIDE* TRANSLATIONS: ADVICE FOR STUDENTS AND INSTRUCTORS

THIS VOLUME is dedicated to the memory of Luis O. Gómez (1943–2017), a distinguished scholar and translator of Buddhism, who was a cherished colleague, mentor, and friend to many of its contributors. Among Prof. Gómez's signature accomplishments is a magisterial 1999 review essay, "The Way of the Translators: Three Recent Translations of Śāntideva's *Bodhicaryāvatāra*," *Buddhist Literature* 1, 262–354. The essay takes the opportunity of the coincidental appearance (in 1996 and 1997) of three English translations of the *Guide* as an invitation to range widely, over ninety-two pages, across various topics in the theory and practice of Buddhist translation. Through a careful study of selected verses from the new translations, Gómez considers problems of grammar, idiom, rhetoric, and cultural context facing translators of a work like the *Guide* (and of the *Guide*, specifically). In the process, he analyzes and pronounces upon the assets and defects of several modern scholarly translations.

Gómez's stated opinion is that, although all three of the new translations are useful, and it is possible to consider one of the three the best (he prefers the one by the Padmakara Translation Group), none of them has surpassed the translations already available in French, German, and English. A surprising claim is that the 1909 translation by Lionel D. Barnett, in spite of its outdated diction, its error-filled introduction, and its Christian doctrine-inspired terminological choices, is *still* "the best English rendition in terms of accuracy, clarity, and elegance." He points out that Barnett, for all his failures, understood the Sanskrit, and was not too proud to depend upon the excellent scholarship of Louis de La Vallée

Poussin. For this reason, Gómez recommends that all serious students consult the translations by La Vallée Poussin, Louis Finot, Richard Schmidt, and Ernst Steinkellner, and he recommends that *all instructors* should keep Barnett at hand (and, if they can, use Steinkellner for the philosophy).

In the twenty years since Prof. Gómez's article, many new translations into modern languages have continued to appear, the most exciting being a series of translations of Tibetan commentaries. Among translations of the *Guide* alone, one stands out as a major addition to the field for scholarly use: in 2015, Gómez published his own complete translation of the *Guide* (excepting a few sections from chapter 9) as a section of the *Norton Anthology of World Religions: Buddhism*. As expected, Gómez's translation meets a new standard for expressive, idiomatic English that preserves an impressive degree of accuracy, nuance, and textual insight.

Gómez's concerns notwithstanding, each of the three English translations from 1996–1997 also have their excellences, and your authors recommend all of them for their various strengths. As readers of the volume will notice, different authors have each chosen either to rely upon the Crosby and Skilton, Wallace and Wallace, or Padmakara Translation Group translations, or to translate the verses themselves. Each of them resonates in a different key, but the *Guide*'s distinct music may be heard in them all. In the spirit of openness to the multiplicity of readings that constitute any classic, readers should feel free to seek their own preferences.

Our volume's most cited translation is the one by Kate Crosby and Andrew Skilton, which appears in the Oxford World Classics series. Worries about its linguistic elegance and precision are amply offset by the translators' careful attention to structure and consistency, and above all by their informed, insightful introductions to the *Guide* as a whole as well as to each of its chapters. The combination of these introductions amounts to a readable, sophisticated monograph on the *Guide*, whose influence can be felt throughout current Mahāyāna scholarship.

Gómez preferred the Padmakara Translation Group's translation for its accuracy in reading and expressing the meaning of the *Guide*, remarkably in spite of the fact that it is a translation of the canonical Tibetan translation, not of the Sanskrit original. Often traditional Tibetan translators, who always worked together with Indian scholars, were privy to implicit meanings unnoticed by readers of the Sanskrit today, and the result was sometimes a rich expression of the point, rather than the literal meaning, of a verse. If the goal is not a representation of the original Sanskrit but an entryway into the import of the inherited text that has influenced Tibet, and through Tibetans the world, this is an excellent place to begin.

Several of our authors also quite appreciate the Wallace and Wallace translation for its unusually fluid language and its reliability. Wallace and Wallace are not as consistent in representing the Sanskrit grammar as Crosby and Skilton, but the benefit of this is that they are often able to emphasize the deeper meaning of a given verse; their translation can therefore be used fruitfully to rectify obscure readings and missteps in other translations.

RECOMMENDED ENGLISH TRANSLATIONS

Gómez, Luis O., trans. "How to Be a Bodhisattva: Introduction to the Practice of the Bodhisattva Path (*The Bodhicaryāvatāra*)." In *Norton Anthology of World Religions: Buddhism*, 395–441. New York: Norton, 2015.

Padmakara Translation Group, trans. *The Way of the Bodhisattva*. Boston and London: Shambhala Translation Group, 1997. (Note: This translation has superseded the 1979 translation from Tibetan by Stephen Batchelor, much beloved as it was and remains. Time to renew your memorization project.)

Śāntideva. *The Bodhicaryāvatāra*. Trans. Kate Crosby and Andrew Skilton. Oxford World's Classics. Oxford & New York: Oxford University Press, 1996.

Śāntideva. *A Guide to the Bodhisattva Way of Life*. Trans. Vesna Wallace and B. Alan Wallace. Ithaca, NY: Snow Lion, 1997.

RECOMMENDED FOR CONSULTATION (BY GÓMEZ)

For Accurate Reading of Sanskrit:

Barnett, Lionel D., trans. *The Path of Light: Rendered from the Bodhi-caryāvatāra of Sānti-deva: A Manual of Mahāyāna Buddhism*. Wisdom of the East Series. 1909; reprint, London: John Murray, 1947, 1959.

For Word Choice:

Finot, Louis, trans. *La marche à la lumière: Bodhicaryāvatāra*. Les classiques de l'Orient vol. 2. Paris: Éditions Bossard, 1920.

For Philosophy:

Schmidt, Richard, trans. *Der Eintritt in den Wandel in Erlechtung (Bodhicaryāvatāra). Von Śāntideva. Ein buddhistisches Lehrgedicht des VII. Jahrhunderts n. Chr.* Aus dem Sanskrit übersetzt. Dokumente der Religion vol. 5. Paderborn: Ferdinand Schöning, 1923.

Steinkellner, Ernst, trans. *Śāntideva, Eintritt in das Leven zur Erleuchtung (Bodicharyāvatār). Lehrgedicht des Mahāyāna aus dem Sanskrit übersetzt.* Diederichs gelbe Reihe, 34. Indien. Düsseldorf-Köln: Eugen Diederichs Verlag, 1981.

For All of the Above:

de La Vallée Poussin, Louis, trans. *Bodhicaryāvatāra: Introduction à la pratique de la sainteté bouddhique (bodhi) par Çantidéva.* Chapitres I, II, III, IV et X. Texte et traduction. *Le Museon* 11, no. 1 (1892): 68–82; 11, no. 2 (1892): 87–109. [This is the source for chapter 10, which is missing from the 1907 reprint.]

de La Vallée Poussin, Louis, trans. *Bodhicaryāvatāra. Introduction à la pratique des futurs bouddhas, poème de Çāntideva.* Traduit du sanscrit et annoté par Louis de La Vallée Poussin. Paris: Librairie Bloud, 1907. [This reprint contains all but chapter 10.]

Appendix 2

INDEX OF *GUIDE* VERSES CITED

Citation numbers below generally refer to the standard (La Vallée Poussin) Sanskrit edition. In some areas in the *Guide* (esp. 2.32–66, 7.62–76, and 8.25–51), this Sanskrit numbering differs by one verse from standard Tibetan editions, a numeric shift that is also, naturally, reflected in English translations based on the Tibetan. Our authors have, very occasionally, cited Tibetan numbering when appropriate to context. Note, especially, references to 8.187. The Sanskrit version of Chapter 8 has only 186 verses, whereas in Tibetan there is an additional verse, 8.186, the penultimate verse of the chapter, not found in the Sanskrit.

The manuscript versions discovered at Dunhuang are also in Tibetan, but they differ greatly from standard Sanskrit and Tibetan editions, so citations therefrom are listed in a separate section.

CHAPTER 1

entire chapter 5, 29, 36, 134–135

1.1 29, 33, 233

1.2 2, 8, 29, 79n21, 102

1.3 2, 7, 29, 79n19, 102

1.4 102

1.5 101, 108, 166

1.7 101

1.9 2, 167, 177n26
1.10 2, 102, 130n40, 131n55
1.11 2
1.12 167
1.14 39, 167
1.15 3, 131n53, 134, 168, 197
1.16 3, 134, 197
1.17 3, 197
1.18 4
1.19 4
1.20 39
1.21 101, 167
1.22 167
1.24 101, 167
1.25 101
1.27 101
130 167
1.34 166
1.36 167
1.66 167

CHAPTER 2

entire chapter 5, 36, 42n7, 48, 134–135
2.7 102
2.8 102, 222
2.9 102, 222
2.10–17 140
2.10–19 139
2.11–16 130n38
2.20 141
2.21 140
2.24 141
2.25 140
2.32–50 200
2.32 49
2.33 49
2.34 166
2.40 166, 221, 227
2.41 221, 226

2.42 102
2.43 50
2.44–45 49, 221
2.45–66 80n29
2.46 166, 222
2.47 166
2.48 166, 221, 222
2.50 166, 222
2.54 222, 226, 227
2.55 165
2.63 166

CHAPTER 3

entire chapter 5, 36, 42n7, 50, 52, 134–135
3.1–3 50
3.6 50
3.7–23 50
3.7 136
3.10 170
3.11 42n18, 170
3.12 103, 120
3.13 103, 120
3.14 214
3.17–19 130n42
3.22 138, 143n17
3.23 139, 143n17
3.23–26 168
3.26 80n29, 167
3.27 80n29, 169
3.31 167

CHAPTER 4

entire chapter 5, 36, 51, 134
4.1 152
4.2–4.4 80n28
4.5 169
4.6 51, 169

4.11 51, 80n29
4.14 129n4
4.15 51, 129n8
4.16 129n8, 129n22
4.17–21 166
4.18 51, 166
4.20 43n30, 103, 166
4.21 103
4.22 51
4.23–27 166
4.23 51
4.25 103, 129n5
4.27 69
4.28–33 166
4.28–34 54
4.28 74–75, 103
4.29 74–75, 81n34
4.39 52, 166
4.40 52
4.42 243
4.43–46 166
4.43 54, 243
4.47 68

CHAPTER 5

entire chapter 5–6, 36, 48, 53–55, 134
5.1 195
5.2 53, 195
5.3 53, 54, 195
5.4 53
5.7 187
5.8 187
5.9 170, 196
5.10 46, 170, 196
5.11 46, 170
5.12 58n6, 170
5.13 58n6, 170, 196
5.14 58n6, 170, 196
5.15 58n6, 170

5.16 43n30, 166, 173
5.18 6
5.20 56
5.23 54
5.26 55, 202
5.27 55, 80n28, 202
5.29 54–55, 202–203
5.30 59n16, 239
5.31 55, 59n16
5.32 55
5.33 55
5.34 55, 103
5.35 112
5.39 112
5.46 112
5.48 55, 103, 201
5.49 55, 56, 201
5.50 55, 56, 201
5.51 55, 56, 201
5.52 55, 56, 201
5.53 55, 56, 201
5.54 56
5.55 112
5.60 56, 68
5.61 56, 69, 103, 129n11
5.62 56, 69, 103, 129n13, 182
5.63 56, 103, 112, 129n13, 182
5.64 56, 103, 129n14, 182
5.65 103, 129n12
5.66 103, 129n24, 131n54
5.68 119
5.69 119, 166
5.70 129n25
5.73 112
5.80 112
5.83 170
5.84 213
5.86 130n32, 170, 211
5.87 130n33, 170, 211
5.88–95 43n30

5.98 138
5.103 39
5.104 31, 38, 39, 42n9, 139
5.105 31, 37, 38, 39, 42n9
5.106 31, 38, 39, 42n9
5.108 173
5.109 165

CHAPTER 6

entire chapter 5–6, 15, 36, 56–57, 134
6.1 166, 170
6.2 6, 170
6.3–5 170
6.6 170
6.7 16
6.10 16, 171
6.12 166, 171
6.13 17
6.14 171
6.17 171
6.18 171
6.20 17
6.21 57, 166
6.22 181
6.23 181
6.24 57, 181
6.25 56, 57
6.26 56, 57
6.27 56
6.28 56
6.29 56
6.30 56
6.31 56, 57, 170, 171, 181
6.32 56
6.33 170
6.34 57, 170
6.37 170
6.39 171

6.41 171
6.42 171
6.43 171
6.44 171
6.45 171
6.46 171
6.47 103, 171
6.52 171
6.53 171
6.54 171
6.55 171
6.56 171
6.57 171
6.58 171
6.59 171
6.67 171, 203
6.73 171
6.74 171
6.75 171
6.80 171
6.81 106, 171
6.82 171
6.83 171
6.84 171
6.87 171
6.88 171
6.89 171
6.90 171
6.91 171
6.92
6.93 106, 171
6.98 171
6.99–111 177n54
6.99 171
6.100 171
6.101 171
6.107 156
6.112 43n20
6.113 169

6.117 215
6.123 80n27

CHAPTER 7

entire chapter 5–6, 36, 134, 205n8
7.1 6
7.2 172
7.3 172
7.6 221
7.10 129n7
7.11 203, 221–222, 226, 227
7.14 240
7.15 172
7.17 172
7.18 172
7.19 172
7.20 172
7.21 172
7.22 172
7.23 172
7.24 172
7.25 45, 172
7.26 45, 172
7.27 172
7.28 172
7.30 172
7.33 172
7.34 172
7.35 172
7.36 172
7.39 172
7.40 166, 172
7.44 130n37
7.45 129n6
7.46 39
7.47 172
7.48 172
7.49 172

7.50 172
7.51 173
7.52 173
7.53 173
7.54 173
7.55 173
7.62 80n27, 173
7.63 173
7.64 173
7.65 173
7.66 173
7.67–75 173

CHAPTER 8

entire chapter 5–6, 23n20, 36, 57, 134, 150
8.1 6, 173, 198
8.2 198
8.3 198
8.4 173, 198
8.14 166
8.30 129n15
8.31 129n15
8.32–33 166
8.43 129n18
8.47 129n19
8.49 118
8.50 70
8.51 70
8.52 70–72, 118
8.53 71, 118
8.54 72
8.55 72–73
8.56 72–73
8.57 74
8.58 118
8.59 118
8.60 166

8.61 118
8.70–84 61
8.70 62
8.73–77 63
8.80 63
8.81–100 67
8.85 61
8.86 61–62, 106
8.89 104, 150
8.90–103 217, 245
8.90–112 150
8.90–139 240
8.90–184 67
8.90–187 150
8.90 104, 150–151, 159n15, 245
8.91 57, 126–127
8.92 104
8.93 104
8.94 104, 245
8.95 104, 217
8.96 217
8.97 104
8.99 57, 168, 183
8.101 168, 183, 217
8.102 151, 183, 217
8.105 104
8.106 43n30
8.108 215
8.111 127, 168
8.112 127, 151, 168
8.113–184 150
8.113 151
8.114 127, 151
8.115 57, 105, 127, 151
8.116 151
8.117 151
8.118 43n30, 111, 151
8.119 151
8.120 100, 105, 151, 155, 168
8.121 151

8.122 151
8.123 151
8.124 151
8.125 151
8.126 151
8.127 105, 151
8.128 151
8.129 131n50, 151, 168
8.130 151, 168
8.131 151, 168, 178n82
8.132 151
8.133 151
8.134 151
8.135 151
8.136 151, 169
8.137 151, 169
8.138 169
8.139 151
8.140–158 151
8.140 67, 105
8.141–154 105
8.141 67, 105
8.142 67, 105
8.146 106
8.149 107
8.150 107
8.151 107
8.152 107
8.153 80n23, 107
8.154 110, 168
8.155 108, 168
8.156 108
8.157 168
8.158 67, 127
8.159–184 152
8.159 153
8.160 108
8.163 108
8.164 108
8.165 107

8.166 80n23
8.167 169
8.168 108, 169
8.169 108, 169
8.170 169
8.171 109, 169
8.172 169
8.174 109
8.178 129n16
8.181 129n17
8.184 129n26, 130n35, 131n54
8.185–187 150
8.187 152

CHAPTER 9

entire chapter 5–7, 9, 14, 22n11, 36, 40, 85–86, 95n7, 134–135
9.1 6, 124, 130n43, 241
9.2 87, 183, 242
9.3 87, 242
9.4 87, 188, 242
9.6 188
9.9 189
9.10 189
9.15 89
9.17–23 90
9.17 43n30, 89
9.24 91, 96n27
9.26 93–94
9.34 9, 10, 28, 94, 126, 131n48, 183
9.57 125, 181
9.58 125
9.59 125
9.74 182
9.76 243–244
9.77 244
9.78 125, 131n46
9.79 125, 131n46
9.80 125, 131n46

9.81 125, 131n46
9.82 125, 131n46
9.83 125, 131n46
9.85 126, 182
9.86 126, 182
9.87 126, 182
9.110–113 186
9.139 184
9.140 173, 184
9.156 166
9.167 152

CHAPTER 10

entire chapter 6, 36, 40, 43n25, 136, 137, 150
10.1 137, 210
10.2 137
10.6 64
10.7 64–65
10.11–16 111
10.22 136
10.28 43n30
10.30 22n4
10.51–56 204, 206n29
10.51–58 137
10.54 137
10.55 11, 137
10.56 153

DUNHUANG [***GUIDE$_1$***]

1.20 39
4.90 30, 42n9
4.91 31, 42n9

BIBLIOGRAPHY

American Bar Association. "ABA Panel Examines Impact of Implicit Bias on Judicial System." *ABA News*, August 12, 2014. http://www.americanbar.org/news/abanews/aba-news-archives/2014/08/aba_panel_examinesi/.

Aron, Arthur, Elaine N. Aron, and Christina Norman. "Self-Expansion Model of Motivation and Cognition in Close Relationships and Beyond." In *Blackwell Handbook of Social Psychology: Interpersonal Processes*, ed. Garth J. O. Fletcher and Margaret S. Clark, 478–501. Oxford: Blackwell, 2003.

Asaṅga. *Abhidharmasamuccaya*. French trans. W. Rahula. English trans. S.Boin-Webb. Berkeley, CA: Asian Humanities Press, 2001.

——. *The Bodhisattva Path to Unsurpassed Enlightenment: A Complete Translation of the Bodhisattvabhūmi*. Trans. Artemus B. Engle. Boulder: Snow Lion, 2016.

Ashburn-Nardo, L., M. L. Knowles, and M. J. Monteith. "Black Americans' Implicit Racial Associations and Their Implications for Intergroup Judgment,. *Social Cognition* 21, no. 1 (2003): 61–87.

Atīśa. *A Lamp for the Path and Commentary*. London: George Allen & Unwin, 1983.

——. *The Complete Works of Atiśa*. Trans. Richard Sherburne. 2nd ed. Delhi: Adiya Prakashan, 2006.

Banaji, M. R., and A. G. Greenwald. *Blindspot: Hidden Biases of Good People*. New York: Delacorte Press, 2013.

Barnhart, Michael. "Theory and Comparison in the Discussion of Buddhist Ethics." *Philosophy East and West* 6, no. 1 (2012): 16–43.

Barstow, Geoffrey. *Food of Sinful Demons: Meat, Vegetarianism, and the Limits of Buddhism in Tibet*. New York: Columbia University Press, 2017.

Beattie, G. *Our Racist Heart? An Exploration of Unconscious Prejudice in Everyday Life*. London: Routledge, 2013.

Beattie, G., D. Cohen, and L. McGuire. "An Exploration of Possible Unconscious Ethnic Biases in Higher Education: The Role of Implicit Attitudes on Selection for University Posts." *Semiotica* 197 (2013): 171–201.

Beckes, Lane, and James A. Coan. "Social Baseline Theory: The Role of Social Proximity in Emotion and Economy of Action." *Social and Personality Psychology Compass* 5, no. 12 (2011): 976–988.

Bendall, Cecil, ed. *Çikshāsamuccaya: A Compendium of Buddhistic Teaching* (*Bibliotheca Buddhica I*). St. Petersburg: Imperial Academy, 1897–1902. Reprinted Delhi: Motilal Banarsidass, 1971.

Bendall, Cecil, and W. H. D. Rouse, trans. *Śikshā-samuccaya: A Compendium of Buddhist Doctrine*. London: John Murray, 1922. Reprinted Delhi: Motilal Banarsidass, 1971]

Bennett, M. W. "Unraveling the Gordian Knot of Implict Bias in Jury Selection: The Problem of Judge-Dominated *Voir-Dire*, the Failed Promise of *Batson*, and Proposed Solutions." *Harvard Law and Policy Review* 4, no. 1 (2010): 149–171.

Beresford, Brian. *Mahāyāna Purification: The Confession Sūtra (Sūtra of Three Heaps) with Commentary by Ārya Nāgārjuna and the Practice of Vajrasattva with Sādhana*. Dharamsala: The Library of Tibetan Works and Archives, 1980.

Betancourt, J. R. "Not Me!: Doctors, Decisions, and Disparities in Health Care." *Cardiovascular Reviews and Reports* 25, no. 3 (2004): 105–109.

Beyer, Stephan. *The Cult of Tārā: Magic and Ritual in Tibet*. Berkeley: University of California Press, 1973.

——. *The Buddhist Experience: Sources and Interpretations*. Encino and Belmont, CA: Dickenson, 1974.

Bhattacharya, Vidhisekhara, ed. *Bodhicaryāvatāra of Śāntideva*. Biblioteca Indica no. 280. Calcutta: The Asiatic Society, 1960.

Blair, I. V., R. Hanratty, D. Price, W. Fairclough, S. Daugherty, and E. Havranek. "An Investigation of Associations Between Clinicians' Ethnic or Racial Bias and Hypertension Treatment, Medication Adherence and Blood Pressure Control." *Journal of General Internal Medicine* 29, no. 7 (2014): 987–995.

Blascovich, J., W. Mendes, S. Hunter, B. Lickel, and N. Kowai-Bell. "Perceived Threat in Social Interactions with Stigmatized Others.," *Journal of Personality and Social Psychology* 80, no. 2 (2001): 243–267.

Blass, Thomas, Philip G. Zimbardo, Christina Maslach, and Craig Haney, eds. "Reflections on the Stanford Prison Experiment: Genesis, Transformations and Consequences." In *Obedience to Authority: Current Perspectives on the Milgram Paradigm*, 193–237. Mahwah, NJ: Lawrence Erlbaum, 2000.

Bloom, Harold. 1998. *Shakespeare: The Invention of the Human*. New York: Riverhead.

Boucher, Daniel. "Sūtra on the Merit of Bathing the Buddha." In *Buddhism in Practice*, ed. Donald S. Lopez Jr., 59–68. Princeton Readings in Religions. Princeton, NJ: Princeton University Press, 1995.

Brentano, Franz. *Psychology from an Empirical Standpoint*. Trans. Antos C. Rancurello, D. B. Terrell, and Linda L. McAlister. International Library of Philosophy and Scientific Method. London: Routledge & Kegan Paul, 1973.

Brough, John. *The Gāndhārī Dharmapada: edited with an introduction and commentary*. London: Oxford University Press, 1962.

Brunnhölzl, Karl. *The Center of the Sunlit Sky: Madhyamaka in the Kagyü Tradition*. Ithaca, NY: Snow Lion, 2004.

Buddhaghosa, Bhadanta. *The Path of Purification (Visuddhismagga)*. Trans. Bhikkhu Ñāṇamoli. 2 vols. Berkeley, CA: Shambhala, 1976.

Burgess, D., M. van Ryn, J. Dovidio, and S. Saha. "Reducing Racial Bias Among Health Care Providers: Lessons from Social-Cognitive Psychology." *Journal of General Internal Medicine* 22, no. 6 (2007): 882–887.

Cabezón, José Ignacio, ed. *Scholasticism: Cross-Cultural and Comparative Perspectives.* Albany: State University of New York Press, 1998.

Candragomin. *Difficult Beginnings: Three Works on the Bodhisattva Path.* Trans. Mark Tatz. Boston: Shambhala, 1985.

Carpenter, Amber. *Indian Buddhist Philosophy.* New York: Routledge, 2014.

Cassidy, Jude, Phillip R. Shaver, and Arietta Slade, eds. "Attachment and Adult Psychotherapy: Theory, Research, and Practice." In *Handbook of Attachment, Third Edition: Theory, Research, and Clinical Applications*, 759–779. New York: Guilford, 2016.

Castelli, L., C. Zogmaiseter, and S. Tomaselli. "The Transmission of Racial Attitudes Within the Family." *Developmental Psychology* 45, no. 2 (2009): 586–591.

Chattopadaya, Alaka. *Atiśa in Tibet.* Delhi: Motilal Banarsidass, 1967.

Chekawa (1101–75). *Seven-Point Mind Training.* in Shönu and Gyaltsen, eds. *Mind Training*, 83–85.

Chopel, Gendun. *Grains of Gold: Tales of a Cosmopolitan Traveler.* Trans. Thupten Jinpa and Donald S. Lopez. Chicago: University of Chicago Press, 2014.

Cikara, Mina, and Jay J. Van Bavel. "The Neuroscience of Intergroup Relations: An Integrative Review." *Perspectives on Psychological Science* 9, no. 3 (May 1, 2014): 245–274. https://doi.org/10.1177/1745691614527464.

Clayton, Barbra. *Moral Theory in Śāntideva's* Śikṣāsamuccaya*: Cultivating the Fruits of Virtue.* New York: Routledge, 2007.

——. "Śāntideva, Virtue, and Consequentialism." In *Destroying Māra Forever: Buddhist Ethics Essays in Honor of Damien Keown*, ed. John Powers and Charles S. Prebish. Ithaca, NY: Snow Lion, 2009.

Cleary, Thomas. *The Flower Ornament Scripture: A Translation of the Avatamsaka Sutra.* Boston: Shambhala, 1984.

Clemons, J. T. "Blind Injustice: The Supreme Court, Implicit Racial Bias, and the Racial Disparity in the Criminal Justice System." *American Criminal Law Review* 51 (2014): 689–713.

Coan, James A., and David A. Sbarra. "Social Baseline Theory: The Social Regulation of Risk and Effort." *Current Opinion in Psychology* 1 (2015): 87–91.

Coan, Jim, Paul Condon, Brooke Dodson-Lavelle, John D. Dunne, and John Makransky. "Meaning and Method: Scientific and Contemplative Perspectives on Compassion." Conference Panel presented at the 2016 International Symposium for Contemplative Studies, San Diego, CA, November 11, 2016.

Cooper, John, ed. *Plato: Complete Works.* Indianapolis: Hackett, 1997.

Correll, J., S. Hudson, S. Guillermo, and D. Ma. "The Police Officer's Dilemma: A Decade of Research on Racial Bias in the Decision to Shoot." *Social and Personality Psychology Compass* 8, no. 5 (2014): 1314–1329.

Cowherds, The, eds. *Moonpaths: Ethics and Emptiness.* New York: Oxford University Press, 2016.

Dahl, Cortland J., Antoine Lutz, and Richard J. Davidson. "Reconstructing and Deconstructing the Self: Cognitive Mechanisms in Meditation Practice." *Trends in Cognitive Sciences* 19, no. 9 (September 2015): 515–523. https://doi.org/10.1016/j.tics.2015.07.001.

Dalai Lama. *Transforming the Mind.* Trans. Geshe Thupten Jinpa. London: Thorson, 2000.

——. *Stages of Meditation.* Trans. Geshe Lobsang Jordhen et al. Ithaca, NY: Snow Lion, 2001.

——. *Practicing Wisdom.* Boston: Wisdom, 2005.

——. *Mind in Comfort and Ease: The Vision of Enlightenment in the Great Perfection.* Boston: Wisdom, 2007.

Dancy, J. *Ethics Without Principles.* New York: Oxford University Press, 2006.

Dasgupta, N., and A. Greenwald. "On the Malleability of Automatic Attitudes: Combatting Automatic Prejudice with Images of Admired and Disliked Individuals." *Journal of Personality and Social Psychology* 81, no. 5 (2001): 800–814.

Dayal, Har. *The Bodhisattva Doctrine in Buddhist Sanskrit Literature.* Delhi: Motilal Banarsidass, 1932.

Dovidio, J. K. Kawakami, C. Johnson, B. Johnson, and A. Howard. "On the Nature of Prejudice: Automatic and Controlled Processes." *Journal of Experimental Social Psychology* 33 (1997): 510–540.

Dreyfus, Georges. *Recognizing Reality: Dharmakīrti's Philosophy and Its Tibetan Interpretations.* Albany: State University of New York Press, 1997.

——. "Tibetan Monasticism." In *The Sound of Two Hands Clapping: The Education of a Tibetan Buddhist Monk,* 32–53. Berkeley: University of California Press, 2003.

Dreyfus, G., and E. ThompsonE. "Asian Perspectives: Indian Theories of Mind." In *Cambridge Handbook of Consciousness,* ed. P. D. Zelazo, M. Moscovitch, and E. Thompson. Cambridge: Cambridge University Press, 2007.

Dreyfus, Georges B. J., and Sara L McClintock, eds. *The Svātantrika-Prasangika Distinction: What Difference Does a Difference Make?* Studies in Indian and Tibetan Buddhism. Boston: Wisdom, 2003.

Duckworth, Douglas S. *Tibetan Buddhist Philosophy of Mind and Nature.* New York: Oxford University Press, 2019.

Dunne, John D. *Foundations of Dharmakīrti's Philosophy.* Boston: Wisdom, 2004.

——. "Buddhism, Schools of: Mahāyāna Philosophical Schools of Buddhism." In *Encyclopedia of Religion,* ed. Lindsay Jones, 2nd ed., 2:1203–1213. Detroit: Macmillan Reference USA, 2005.

Eberhardt, J., P. Davies, and V. Purdie-Vaughns. "Looking Deathworthy: Perceived Stereotypicality of Black Defendants Predicts Capital Sentencing Outcomes." *Psychological Science* 17, no. 5 (2006): 383–386.

Eimer, Helmut. "Suvarṇadvīpa's 'Commentaries' on the *Bodhicaryāvatāra.*" In *Studien zum Jainismus und Buddhismus: Gedenkschrift für Ludwig Alsdorf,* ed. Klaus Bruhn and Ambrecht Wezler, 73–78. Wiesbaden: Franz Steiner Verlag, 1981.

Engle, Artemus B. *The Bodhisattva Path to Unsurpassed Enlightenment, A Complete Translation of the Bodhisattvabhūmi.* Boulder, CO. Snow Lion, 2016.

Faure, Bernard. "Substitute Bodies in Chan/Zen Buddhism." In *Religious Reflections on the Human Body,* ed. Jane Marie Law, 211–229. Bloomington: Indiana University Press, 1995.

Fitzgerald, C. "A Neglected Aspect of Conscience: Awareness of Implicit Attitudes." *Bioethics* 28, no. 1 (2014): 24–32.

Frankfurt, Harry G. *Demons, Dreamers, and Madmen: The Defense of Reason in Descartes's* Meditations. Princeton, NJ and Oxford, Princeton University Press, 2008.

Gadamer, Hans-Georg. *Truth and Method.* 1974; reprint, London and New York: Bloomsbury Academic, 2013.

Gampopa. *The Jewel Ornament of Liberation.* Trans. Khenpo Konchog Gyaltsan Rinpoche. Ithaca, NY: Snow Lion, 1998.

Garfield, Jay L. "What Is It Like to Be a Bodhisattva: Moral Phenomenology in Śāntideva's *Bodhicāryāvatāra*." *Journal of the International Association of Buddhist Studies* 33, no. 1–2 (2010/2011): 327–351.

——. "Buddhistische Ethiks." *Polylog* 97 (2012): 98–110.

——. "Mindfulness and Ethics: Attention, Virtue and Perfection." *Thai International Journal of Buddhist Studies* 3 (2012): 1–24.

——. *Engaging Buddhism*. New York: Oxford University Press, 2014.

——. "Just Another Word for Nothing Left to Lose: Freedom, Agency and Ethics for Mādhyamikas." In *Freedom of the Will in a Cross-Cultural Perspective*, ed. M. Dasti and E. Bryant, 164–185. New York: Oxford University Press, 2014. Reprinted in *Buddhism and Free Will*, ed. R. Repetti, 45–58. London: Routledge, 2016.

——. "Buddhist Ethics in the Context of Conventional Truth: Path and Transformation." In *Moonpaths: Ethics and Emptiness*, ed. The Cowherds, 77–95. New York: Oxford University Press, 2016.

——. "Hume as a Western Mādhyamika: The Case from Ethics." In *Ethics Without Self, Dharma without Atman: Western and Buddhist Philosophical Traditions in Dialogue*, ed. Gordon F. Davis. Sophia Studies in Cross-cultural Philosophy of Traditions and Cultures. New York: Springer Nature, 2018.

Garfield, Jay L., Stephen Jenkins, and Graham Priest. "The Śāntideva Passage: *Bodhicaryāvatāra* VIII.90–103." In *Moonpaths: Ethics and Emptiness*, ed. The Cowherds, 54–76. New York: Oxford University Press, 2016.

Gawronski, B., and G. Bodenhaus. "Implicit and Explicit Evaluation: A Brief Review of the Associated Propositional Evaluation Model." *Social and Personality Compass* 8, no. 8 (2014): 448–462.

Gellner, David N. *Monk, Householder, and Tantric Priest: Newar Buddhism and Its Hierarchy of Ritual*. Cambridge: Cambridge University Press, 1992.

Gethin, R.M.L. *The Buddhist Path to Awakening*. Classics in Religious Studies. Oxford: Oneworld, 2001.

Goetz, Jennifer L., Dacher Keltner, and Emiliana Simon-Thomas. "Compassion: An Evolutionary Analysis and Empirical Review." *Psychological Bulletin* 136, no. 3 (2010): 351–375.

Gómez, Luis. *The Land of Bliss: The Paradise of the Buddha of Measureless Light: Sanskrit and Chinese Versions of the Sukhāvatīvyūha Sutras*. Honolulu: University of Hawai'i Press, 1996.

——. "The Way of the Translators: Three Recent Translations of Śāntideva's *Bodhicaryāvatāra*." *Buddhist Literature* 1 (1999): 262–354.

——. "How to Be a Bodhisattva: Introduction to the Practice of the Bodhisattva Path (*The Bodhicharyavatara*)." In *The Norton Anthology of World Religions: Buddhism*, ed. Donald S. Lopez Jr., 395–441. New York: Norton, 2015.

Goodman, Charles. "Consequentialism, Agent-Neutrality, and Mahāyāna Ethics," *Philosophy East and West* 58, no. 1 (2008): 17–35.

——. *Consequences of Compassion*. New York: Oxford University Press, 2009.

——. *The Training Anthology of Śāntideva: A Translation of the* Śikṣā-samuccaya. New York: Oxford University Press, 2016.

Gyaltsap Jé (1364–1432). *Entrance of the Bodhisattvas* (*rgyal sras 'jug ngogs*), Collected Works, Kumbum Edition, vol. *nga*.

Gyatso, Geshe Kelsang. *Meaningful to Behold: View, Meditation and Action in Mahayana Buddhism*. Trans. Tenzin Norbu. Ed. Jonathan Landaw. Ulverston, Cumbria, England: Tharpa Publications, 1980.

Hahn, Michael. "Carpaṭi's Avalokiteśvarastotra: Critical Edition of the Sanskrit Text and Its English Translation." In *Buddhist Texts From Kashgar and Nepal*, ed. I. P. Minayeff and S. Oldenburg, 11–22. New Delhi: International Academy of Indian Culture, 1983.

Haider, A., E. Schneider, N. Sriram, D. Dosick, V. Scott, S. Swoboda, and L. Cooper. "Unconscious Race and Class Bias: Its Association with Decision Making by Trauma and Acute Care Surgeons." *Journal of Trauma Acute Care Surgery* 77, no. 3 (2014): 409–416.

Hallisey, Charles. *Therigatha: Poems of the First Buddhist Women*. Murty Classical Library of India. Cambridge, MA: Harvard University Press, 2015.

Hannon, L., R. DeFina, and S. Bruch. "The Relationship Between Skin Tone and School Suspension for African Americans." *Race and Social Problems* 5, no. 4 (2013): 281–295.

Harris, Stephen. "On the Classification of Śāntideva's Ethics in the Bodhicaryāvatāra." *Philosophy East and West* 65, no. 1 (2015): 249–275.

——. "The Skillful Handling of Poison: *Bodhicitta* and the *Kleśas* in Śāntideva's *Bodhicaryāvatāra*." *Journal of Indian Philosophy* 45 (2017): 331–348.

Harrison, Paul. "Mediums and Messages: Reflections on the Production of Mahāyāna Sūtras." *The Eastern Buddhist* 35, no. 1/2 (2003): 115–151.

——. "The Case of the Vanishing Poet: New Light on Śāntideva and the *Śikṣāsamuccaya*." In *Indica et Tibetica: Festschrift für Michael Hahn, Zum 65. Geburtstag von Freunden und Schülern überreicht*, ed. Konrad Klaus and Jens-Uwe Hartmann, 215–248. Vienna: Arbeitskreis für tibetische und buddhistische Studien Universität Wien, 2007.

——. "Verses by Śāntideva in the *Śikṣāsamuccaya*: A New English Translation." In *Evo ṣuyadi: Essays in Honor of Richard Salomon's 65th Birthday*, ed. Carol Altman Bromberg, Timothy J. Lenz, and Jason Neelis, 87–103 (Bulletin of the Asia Institute, New Series, Vol. 23, 2009) [actual year of publication 2013].

Hart, A., P. Whalen, L. Shin, S. McInenry, H. Fischer, and S. Rauch. "Differential Response in the Human Amygdala to Racial Outgroup vs Ingroup Face Stimuli." *Neuroreport* 11, no. 11 (2000): 2351–2355.

Harvey, Peter, trans. "Extract from the *Kālāma Sutta*." In *Buddhist Philosophy: Essential Readings*, ed. William Edelglass and Jay L. Garfield, 177–178. New York: Oxford University Press, 2009.

Hein, Grit, and Tania Singer. "I Feel How You Feel but Not Always: The Empathic Brain and Its Modulation." *Current Opinion in Neurobiology, Cognitive Neuroscience* 18, no. 2 (2008): 153–158. https://doi.org/10.1016/j.conb.2008.07.012.

Hrdy, Sarah B. *Mothers and Others: The Evolutionary Origins of Mutual Understanding*. Cambridge, MA: Belknap Press, 2011.

——. "Development+ Social Selection in the Emergence of 'Emotionally Modern' Humans." In *New Frontiers in Social Neuroscience*, 57–91. New York: Springer, 2014. http://link.springer.com/chapter/10.1007/978-3-319-02904-7_5.

Inami, Masahiro. "The Problem of Other Minds in the Buddhist Epistemological Tradition." *Journal of Indian Philosophy* 29 (2001): 465–483.

Ishida, Chikō. "Some New Remarks on the Bodhicaryāvatāra Chap. V." *Journal of Indian and Buddhist Studies* 37, no. 1 (December 1988): 479–476.

Jackson, David. "The *bsTan rim* ("Stages of the Doctrine") and Similar Graded Expositions of the Bodhisattva's Path." In *Tibetan Literature: Studies in Genre*, ed. José Ignacio Cabezón and Roger R. Jackson, 229–243. Ithaca, NY: Snow Lion, 1996.

Jackson, Roger R. *Tantric Treasures: Three Collections of Mystical Verse from Buddhist India*. Oxford: Oxford University Press, 2004.

Jamgon Mipham and the Padmakara Translation Group. *The Wisdom Chapter: Jamgön Mipham's Commentary on the Ninth Chapter of the Way of the Bodhisattva*. Boulder, CO: Shambhala, 2017.

Jampa, Gyumed Khensur Lobsang. *The Easy Path: Illuminating the First Panchen Lama's Secret Instructions*. Ed. Lorne Ladner. Boston: Wisdom, 2013.

Jenkins, Stephen L. "Benefit of Self and Other: The Importance of Persons and Their Self-Interest in Buddhist Ethics." *Dharma Drum Journal of Buddhist Studies* 16 (2015): 141–169.

——. "Waking Into Compassion: The Three *Ālambana* of *Karuṇā*." In *Moonpaths: Ethics and Emptiness*, ed. The Cowherds. New York: Oxford University Press, 2016.

Joglekar, K. M. *Bhartrihari: Niti and Vairagya Shatakas*. Bombay: Oriental Publishing Company, 1911.

Johnson, W. J., trans. *The Bhagavad Gīta*. Oxford World Classics. Oxford: Oxford University Press, 1994.

Jones, K. "Trustworthiness," *Ethics* 123, no. 1 (2012): 61–85.

Joy-Gaba, J., and B. Nosek. "The Surprisingly Limited Malleability of Implicit Racial Evaluations." *Social Psychology* 41, no. 3 (2010): 137–146.

Kajihara, Mieko. "On the Pariṇāmanā Chapter of the Bodhicaryāvatāra." *Journal of Indian and Buddhist Studies* 40, no. 2 (March 1992): 25–28.

Kang, Y., J. Gray, and J. Dovidio. "The Non-Discriminating Heart: Lovingkindness Meditation Training Decreases Implicit Intergroup Bias." *Journal of Experimental Psychology* 143, no. 3 (2014): 1306–1313.

Kapstein, Matthew T. 2001. *Reason's Traces: Identity and Interpretation in Indian and Tibetan Buddhist Thought*. Boston: Wisdom Publications.

——. "Spiritual Exercise' and Buddhist Epistemologists in India and Tibet." In *The Blackwell Companion to Buddhist Philosophy*, ed. Steven Emmanuel, 270–289. Oxford: Blackwell, 2013.

——. "Stoics and Bodhisattvas: Spiritual Exercise and Faith in Two Philosophical Traditions." In: *Philosophy as a Way of Life: Ancients and Moderns—Essays in Honor of Pierre Hadot*, ed. Michael Chase, Stephen R. L. Clark, and Michael McGhee, 99–115. Hoboken, NJ: Wiley-Blackwell, 2013.

——. "Buddhist Idealists and Their Jain Critics on Our Knowledge of External Objects." In *Philosophical Traditions*, ed. Anthony O'Hear, 123–148. Royal Institute of Philosophy Supplements 74. Cambridge: Cambridge University Press, 2014.

——. "Interpreting Indian Philosophy: Three Parables." In *The Oxford Handbook of Indian Philosophy*, ed. Jonardon Ganeri, 15–31. New York: Oxford University Press, 2016.

Keown, Damien. *The Nature of Buddhist Ethics*. London: Macmillan, 2001.

Khenchen Kunzang Pelden and Minyak Kunzang Sonam. *Wisdom: Two Buddhist Commentaries*. Trans. Padmakara Translation Group. St. Leon sur Vezere, France: Editions Padmakara, 1999.

Khoroche, Peter, and Herman Tieken. *Poems on Life and Love in Ancient India: Hāla's Sattasaī*. Albany: State University of New York Press, 2009.

Kongtrul, Jamgon. *The Torch of Certainty*. Trans. Judith Hanson. Boulder, CO: Shambhala, 1977.

Kṛṣṇapa (circa eleventh century). *Spyod 'jug gi rnam par bshad pa*. Tengyur, Comparative Edition, vol. 61, 1686–1836. China, 2000.

——. *Presenting the Difficult Points of Bodhicaryāvatāra (Byang chub sems dpa'i spyod pa la 'jug pa'i rtogs par dka' ba'i gnad gtan la dbabs pa)*. Tengyur, Comparative Edition, vol. 62, 242–243. China, 2000.

Kubota, J., and T. Ito. "The role of Expression and Race in Weapons Identification." *Emotion* 14, no. 6 (2014): 1115–1124.

Künzang Sönam (*kun bzang bsod nams, thub bstan chos kyi grags pa*). *Overview of the Wisdom Chapter (spyod 'jug shes rab le'u'i spyi don rim par phye ba zab mo rten 'byung gi de kho na nyed yang gsal sgron me)*. In Tupten Chödrak (*thub bstan chos kyi grags pa*), *spyod 'jug gi 'grel bshad rgyal sras yon tan bum bzang*, 2nd ed., 645–829. Beijing: China's Tibet Publishing House, 2007.

——. *Word Commentary on the Wisdom Chapter (spyod 'jug shes rab le'u'i gzhung 'grel zab mo rten 'byung gi de kho na nyid gsal ba'i sgron me)*. In Tupten Chödrak (*thub bstan chos kyi grags pa*), *spyod 'jug gi 'grel bshad rgyal sras yon tan bum bzang*, 2nd ed., 549–643. Beijing: China's Tibet Publishing House, 2007.

——. *The Profound Reality of Interdependence: An Overview of the Wisdom Chapter of the Way of the Bodhisattva*. Trans. Douglas Duckworth. New York: Oxford University Press, 2019.

de La Vallée Poussin, Louis, ed. *Madhyamakāvatāra*. St. Pétersbourg: Impr. de l'Académie impériale des sciences, 1912.

——. *Bodhicaryāvatārapañjikā: Prajñākaramati's Commentary to the Bodhicaryāvatāra of Śāntideva*. Calcutta: Asiatic Society, 1901–1914.

Langri Thangpa (1054–1123). *Eight Verses on Mind Training*. In Shönu and Gyaltsen, eds., *Mind Training*, 275–276.

Lewis, Michael. "Emotional Development and Consciousness." In *Handbook of Child Psychology and Developmental Science, Theory and Method*, ed. Richard M. Lerner, Willis F. Overton, and Peter C. M. Molenaar, 7th ed., 1:407–451. Hoboken, NJ: Wiley, 2015.

Lhundub Sopa, Geshe, Michael Sweet, and Leonard Zwilling, eds. *Peacock in the Poison Grove: Two Buddhist Texts on Training the Mind*. Boston: Wisdom, 2001.

Li Xuezhu. "*Madhyamakāvatāra-kārikā* Chapter 6." *Journal of Indian Philosophy* 43 (2015): 1–30.

Liland, Fredrik. "The Transmission of the *Bodhicaryāvatāra*: The History, Diffusion and Influence of a Mahāyāna Buddhist Text." M.A. thesis, University of Oslo, 2009.

Lindtner, Christian. "Mātṛceta's *Praṇidhānsaptati*." *Asiatische Studien/Études asiatiques* 38 (1984): 100–128.

Lopez, Jr., Donald S. "A Prayer to the Lama." In *Religions of Tibet in Practice*, ed. Donald S. Lopez, Jr., 376–386. Princeton, NJ: Princeton University Press, 1997.

Mahoney, Richard. "Of the Progress of the Bodhisattva: The Bodhisattvamārga in the Śikṣāsamuccaya." M. A. thesis, University of Canterbury, 2002.

Makransky, John. "Offering (mChod Pa) in Tibetan Ritual Literature." In *Tibetan Literature: Studies in Genre*, ed. José Ignacio Cabezón and Roger R. Jackson. Ithaca, NY: Snow Lion, 1996.

Marvin, Robert S., Preston A. Britner, and Beth S. Russel. "Normative Development: The Ontogeny of Attachment in Childhood." In *Handbook of Attachment, Third Edition: Theory, Research, and Clinical Applications*, ed. Jude Cassidy and Phillip R. Shaver, 273–290. New York: Guilford, 2016.

Mayeda, Sengaku. *A Thousand Teachings: The* Upadeśasahasrī *of Śaṅkara*. Albany: State University of New York Press, 1992.

McClintock, Sara L. *Omniscience and the Rhetoric of Reason: Śāntarakṣita and Kamalaśīla on Rationality, Argumentation, and Religious Authority.* Boston: Wisdom, 2010.

McCrea, Lawrence J. *The Teleology of Poetics in Medieval Kashmir.* Cambridge, MA: Harvard University Press, 2008.

McCumber, John. *The Politics of Reason in the Early Cold War.* Chicago: University of Chicago Press, 2016.

McGinn, Bernard. "The Language of Inner Experience in Christian Mysticism." *Spiritus: A Journal of Christian Spirituality* 1, no. 2 (2001): 156–171.

Meadows, Carol. *Arya-Śūra's Compendium of the Perfections: Text, Translation and Analysis of the Pāramitāsamāsa.* Bonn: Indica et Tibetica Verlag, 1986.

Mercer, C. "The Methodology of the *Meditations*: Tradition and Innovation." In *Cambridge Companion to Descartes'* Meditations, ed. D. Cunning, 23–47. Cambridge: Cambridge University Press, 2014.

Minayeff, Ivan Pavlovich, ed. "Çāntideva: `Bodhicaryāvatāra'." In *Zapiski Vostochnago Otdeleniya Imperatorskago Russkago Arkheologicheskago Obshchestva* (Transactions of the Oriental Section of the Royal Russian Archeological Society) 4 (1889): 153–228. Retrieved from "Bibliotheca Polyglotta," February 2017. http://www2.hf.uio.no/common/apps/permlink/permlink.php?app=polyglotta&context=volume&uid=433c2dda-4412-11df-870c-00215aecadea.

Mrozik, Susanne. *Virtuous Bodies: The Physical Dimensions of Morality in Buddhist Ethics.* New York: Oxford University Press, 2007.

Nagao, Gadjin M. *Mādhyamika and Yogācāra.* Trans. Leslie S. Kawamura. Albany: State University of New York Press, 1991.

Nāgārjuna (second century). *The Precious Garland: An Epistle to a King.* Trans. John Dunne and Sara McClintock. Boston: Wisdom, 1997.

Ñāṇamoli, Bhikkhu. 2010. *The Path of Purification: Visuddhimagga by Bhadantācariya Buddhaghosa.* 4th ed. Kandy: Buddhist Publication Society.

Nance, Richard. 2013. "The Voice of Another: Speech, Responsiveness, and Buddhist Philosophy of Language." In *A Companion to Buddhist Philosophy,* ed. S. Emmanuel. Hoboken, NJ: Wiley-Blackwell.

Nattier, Jan. *A Few Good Men: The Bodhisattva Path According to the Inquiry of Ugra (Ugraparipṛcchā).* Honolulu: University of Hawai'i Press, 2003.

Newheiser, A., and K. Olson. "White and Black American Children's Implicit Intergroup Bias." *Journal of Experimental Social Psychology* 48, no. 1 (2012): 264–270.

Nisbett, R., and T. Wilson. "Telling More Than We Can Know: Verbal Report on Mental Processes." *Psychological Review* 84. no. 3 (1977): 231–259.

Norman, K. R. *The Elders' Verses I: Theragāthā.* London: Pali Text Society, 1969.

Ohnuma, Reiko. *Head, Eyes, Flesh, and Blood: Giving Away the Body in Indian Buddhist Literature.* New York: Columbia University Press, 2007.

Olivelle, Patrick. "Review of Trautmann, Thomas R., *Elephants and Kings: An Environmental History.*" *H-Asia, H-Net Reviews,* August 2016.

Olsson, Andreas, Jeffrey P. Ebert, Mahzarin R. Banaji, and Elizabeth A. Phelps. "The Role of Social Groups in the Persistence of Learned Fear." *Science (New York, N.Y.)* 309, no. 5735 (July 29, 2005): 785–787. https://doi.org/10.1126/science.1113551.

Olsson, Andreas, and Elizabeth A. Phelps. "Social Learning of Fear." *Nature Neuroscience* 10, no. 9 (September 2007): 1095–1102. https://doi.org/10.1038/nn1968.

Osto, Douglas. "A New Translation of the Sanskrit Bhadracarī with Introduction and Notes." *New Zealand Journal of Asian Studies* 12, no. 2 (December 2010): 1–21.

Pabongka Rinpoche. *Liberation in the Palm of Your Hand: A Concise Discourse on the Path to Enlightenment.* Ed. Trijang Rinpoche. Trans. Michael Richards. Boston: Wisdom, 1997.

Parfit, Derek. 1984. *Reasons and Persons.* Oxford: Oxford University Press.

Pelden Kunzang. *Nectar of Manjushri's Speech: A Detailed Commentary on Shantideva's* Way of the Bodhisattva. Trans. Padmakara Translation Committee. Ithaca, NY: Snow Lion, 2010.

Pezzali, Amalia. *Śāntideva: mystique bouddhiste des VIIe et VIIIe siècles.* Firenze: Vallechi Editore, 1968.

Plant, E., and B. Peruche. "The Consequences of Race for Police Officers' Responses to Criminal Suspects." *Psychological Science* 16, no. 3 (2005): 180–183.

Pollard, Natalie. *Speaking to You: Contemporary Poetry and Public Address.* Oxford: Oxford University Press, 2012.

Prajñākaramati (circa tenth century). *Bodhicaryāvatārapañjikā (Byang chub kyi spyod pa la 'jug pa'i dka' 'grel).* Tengyur, Comparative Edition, vol. 61, 1049–1641. China, 2000.

Prajñākaramati. "*Bodhicaryāvatārapañjikā.*" In *Bodhicaryāvatāra of Śāntideva with the Commentary Pañjikā of Prajñākaramati*, ed. P. L. Vaidya. Buddhist Sanskrit Texts 12. Darbhanga: Mithila Institute, 1960.

Rand, David G. "Cooperation, Fast and Slow: Meta-Analytic Evidence for a Theory of Social Heuristics and Self-Interested Deliberation." *Psychological Science* 27, no. 9 (September 1, 2016): 1192–1206. https://doi.org/10.1177/0956797616654455.

Rand, David G., Joshua D. Greene, and Martin A. Nowak. "Spontaneous Giving and Calculated Greed." *Nature* 489, no. 7416 (September 2012): 427. https://doi.org/10.1038/nature11467.

Reeves, Gene. trans. *The Lotus Sutra.* Boston: Wisdom, 2008.

Rimer, J. Thomas, and Yamazaki Masakasu, trans. *On the Art of the Nō Drama: The Major Treatises of Zeami.* Princeton, NJ: Princeton University Press, 1984.

Rinchen, Sonam. *Atisha's Lamp for the Path to Enlightenment.* Trans. Ruth Sonam. Ithaca, NY: Snow Lion Publications, 1997.

Robertson, Duncan. 2011. *Lectio Divina: The Medieval Experience of Reading.* Cistercian Studies Series 238. Collegeville, MN: Liturgical Press.

Rorty, A. O. "Experiments in Philosophic Genre: Descartes' Meditations" *Critical Inquiry*, 9, no. 3 (1983): 545–564

Ross, H. *Everyday Bias: Identifying and Navigating Unconscious Judgments in Our Daily Lives.* Lanham, MD: Rowman and Littlefield, 2014.

Rutland, A., L. Cameron, L. Milne, and P. McGeorge. "Social Norms and Self-Presentation: Children's Implicit and Explicit Intergroup Attitudes." *Child Development* 76, no. 2 (2005): 451–466.

Saitō Akira. "A Study of Akṣayamati (=Śāntideva)'s *Bodhisattvacaryāvatāra* as Found in the Tibetan Manuscripts from Tun-huang." Unpublished project report. Tsu, Japan: Miye University, 1993.

——. "A Study of the Dūn-huáng Recension of the *Bodhisattvacaryāvatāra.*" Unpublished project report. Tsu, Japan: Mie University, 2000.

——. "Notes on the Interpretation of *Bodhi(sattva)caryāvatāra* V.104–106." In *Gedenkschrift J. W. de Jong*, ed. H. W. Bodewitz and Minoru Hara, 135–147. Studia Philologica Buddhica, Monograph Series, XVII. Tokyo: The International Institute for Buddhist Studies, 2004.

——. "Facts or Fictions: Reconsidering Śāntideva's Names, Life, and Works." *Journal of the International College for Postgraduate Buddhist Studies* 22 (2018): 1–20.

Sakya Paṇḍita (1182–1251). *Clarifying the Sage's Intent.* Trans. David P. Jackson In *Stages of the Buddha's Teachings: Three Key Texts*, 383–602. Boston: Wisdom, 2015.

Sakya Pandita Translation Group. "The Ākāśagarbha Sūtra." *84000: Translating the Words of the Buddha.* http://read.84000.co/#UT22084–066-018/title.

Śāntideva. *The Bodhicaryāvatāra.* Trans. Kate Crosby and Andrew Skilton. Oxford World Classics. New York: Oxford University Press, 1995.

Śāntideva. *The Bodhicaryāvatāra.* Trans. Kate Crosby and Andrew Skilton. Oxford: Oxford University Press, 2008.

Śāntideva. *Bodhicharyāvatāra.* Trans. Parmananda Sharma. New Delhi: Aditya Prakashan, 1990.

Śāntideva. *A Guide to the Bodhisattva Way of Life (Bodhicaryāvatāra).* Trans. Vesna A. Wallace and B. Alan Wallace. Ithaca, NY: Snow Lion, 1997.

Śāntideva and Kunpal. "Shantideva's Bodhisattva-Charyavatara, the Second Chapter and Commentary." Trans. Andreas Kretschmar. http://www.kunpal.com/bca2comm.pdf.

Śāntideva and rGyal tshab dar ma rin chen. *Byang chub sems pa'i spyod pa la 'jug pa'i rnam bshad rgyal sras 'jug ngogs.* Sarnath: Gelukpa Student Welfare Committee, 1999.

van Schaik, Sam. "The Original *Bodhicaryāvatāra.*" 2014. Retrieved from "early Tibet," https://earlytibet.com/2014/02/04/the-original-bodhicaryavatara/.

Schmithausen, Lambert. *Maitrī and Magic: Aspects of the Buddhist Attitude Toward the Dangerous in Nature.* Vienna: Verlag der Osterreichischen Akademie der Wissenschaften, 1997.

Schopen, Gregory. *Buddhist Nuns, Monks, and Other Worldly Matters: Recent Papers on Monastic Buddhism in India.* Honolulu, University of Hawai'i Press, 2014.

Sé Chilbu (1121–1189). *A Commentary on the "Seven-Point Mind Training."* In Shönu and Gyaltsen, eds., *Mind Training*, 87–132.

Sen, M. "How Judicial Qualification Ratings May Disadvantage Minority and Female Candidates." *Journal of Law and Courts* 2, no. 1 (2014): 33–65.

Shabkar [Tsokdruk Rangdrol]. *Food of Bodhisattvas: Buddhist Teachings on Abstaining from Meat.* Trans. the Padmakara Translation Group. Boston: Shambhala, 2004.

Shantideva. *The Way of the Bodhisattva: A Translation of the* Bodhicaryāvatāra. Trans. the Padmakara Translation Committee. Boston and London: Shambhala, 2006.

Sharif, Muzafer, O. J. Harvey, Jack White, William R. Hood, and Carolyn W. Sherif. *Intergroup Conflict and Cooperation: The Robbers Cave Experiment.* Norman: University of Oklahoma Institute of Group Relations, 1961.

Shaw, Sarah. *The Jatakas: Birth Stories of the Bodhisatta.* New York: Penguin, 2006.

Sherap Jungné (1187–1241). "The Single Viewpoint: A Root Text." In *Mahāmudrā and Related Instructions: Core Teachings of the Kagyü Schools*, trans. Peter Alan Roberts, 379–400. Boston: Wisdom, 2011.

Shonin, Edo, William Van Gordon, Angelo Compare, Masood Zangeneh, and Mark D. Griffiths. "Buddhist-Derived Loving-Kindness and Compassion Meditation for the Treatment of Psychopathology: A Systematic Review." *Mindfulness* 6, no. 5 (October 1, 2015): 1161–1180. https://doi.org/10.1007/s12671-014-0368-1.

Shönu Gyalchok and Könchok Gyaltsen, eds. *Mind Training: The Great Collection.* Trans. Thupten Jinpa. Library of Tibetan Classics. Boston: Wisdom, 2006.

Shukla, N. S. *The Buddhist Hybrid Sanskrit Dharmapada*. Tibetan Sanskrit Works Series no. xix. Patna: K. P. Jayaswal Research Institute, 1979.

Silk, Jonathan A. *Materials Towards the Study of Vasubandhu's Viṃśikā (I)*. Harvard Oriental Series 81. Cambridge, MA: Department of South Asian Studies, Harvard University, 2016.

Smith, Gene E. "Mi pham and the Philosophical Controversies of the Nineteenth Century." In *Among Tibetan Texts: History and Literature of the Himalayan Plateau*, 227–234. Boston: Wisdom, 2001.

Smith, J. Mark. "Apostrophe, or the Lyric Art of Turning Away." *Texas Studies in Literature and Language* 49, no. 4 (Winter 2007): 411–437.

Sommers, S., and P. Ellsworth. "White Juror Bias: An Investigation of Prejudice Against Black Defendants in the American Courtroom." *Psychology, Public Policy, and Law* 7, no. 1 (2001): 201–229.

Sopa, Geshe Lhundub. *Steps on the Path: A Commentary on Tsongkhapa's Lamrim Chenmo*. 5 vols. Boston: Wisdom, 2004–17.

Stein, Edith. *On the Problem of Empathy*. Trans. Waltraut Stein. Washington, DC: ICP Press, 1989.

Stowers, Stanley. "Letters of Exhortation and Advice." In *Letter Writing in Greco-Roman Antiquity*. Philadelphia: Westminister Press, 1986.

Strawson, Galen. "Cognitive Phenomenology: Real Life." In *Cognitive Phenomenology*, ed. Tim Bayne and Michelle Montague, 285–325. Oxford; Oxford University Press, 2011.

——. "Religion is a Sin; Review of Mark Johnston.' *London Review of Books* 33, no. 11 (June 2011): 2.

Strong, John S., ed. *The Experience of Buddhism: Sources and Interpretations*. 3rd ed. Belmont, CA: Thomson Wadsworth, 2008.

Sweet, Michael. "*Bodhicaryāvatāra* 9.2 as a Focus for Tibetan Interpretations of the Two Truths in the Prāsaṅgika Mādhyamika." *Journal of Indian Philosophy* 2, no. 2 (1979): 79–89.

——. "Mental Purification (*Blo sbyong*): A Native Tibetan Genre of Religious Literature." In *Tibetan Literature: Studies in Genre*, ed. José I. Cabezón and Roger R. Jackson, 244–260. Ithaca, NY: Snow Lion, 1996.

Tatz, Mark, trans. *The Skill in Means (Upāyakauśalya) Sūtra*. Delhi: Motilal Banarsidass, 1994.

Teal, C., A. Gill, A. Green, and S. Crandall. "Helping Medical Learners Recognize and Manage Unconscious Bias Toward Certain Patient Groups." *Medical Education* 41, no. 1 (2012): 80–88.

Thanissaro Bhikkhu, trans. "*Samaññaphala Sutta: The Fruits of the Contemplative Life* (DN 2)." *Access to Insight (BCBS Edition)*, November 30, 2013. http://www.accesstoinsight.org/tipitaka/dn/dn.02.0.than.html.

Tharchin, Lobsang. *A Commentary on Guru Yoga and Offering of the Mandala*. Ithaca, NY: Snow Lion Publications, 1981.

Thokmé Sangpo (1295–1369). *Ocean of Excellent Utterances* (*Legs bshad rgya mtsho* in *rgyal sras kyi spyod pa la 'jug pa'i chos skor*), 9–188. Delhi: Institute of Tibetan Classics, 2006.

Thompson, E. *Mind in Life*. Cambridge, MA: Harvard University Press, 2007.

——. *Waking, Dreaming, Being*. New York: Columbia University Press, 2014.

Tomasello, Michael. *A Natural History of Human Thinking*. Cambridge, MA: Harvard University Press, 2014.

Tomasello, Michael, and Malinda Carpenter. "Shared Intentionality." *Developmental Science* 10, no. 1 (January 1, 2007): 121–125. https://doi.org/10.1111/j.1467-7687.2007.00573.x.

Tracy, David. *Plurality and Ambiguity: Hermeneutics, Religion, Hope*. Chicago: University of Chicago Press, 1985.

Tripathi, Sridhar, ed. *Bodhicāryāvatāra of Śāntideva with the Commentary Pañjikā of Prajñākaramati*. Darbhanga: Mithila Institute, 1988.

Tsering, Geshe Tashi. *The Awakening Mind*. The Foundations of Buddhist Thought, vol. 4. Boston: Wisdom, 2008.

Tsong kha pa. *sKyes bug sum gyi rnyams su blang ba'i rim pa thams cad tshang bar ston pa'i byang chub lam gyi rim pa/ Byang chub lam rim che ba*. Zi-ling (Xining): Tso Ngön (mTsho sngon) People's Press, 1985.

——. *The Great Treatise on the Stages of the Path to Enlightenment*. Trans. the Lamrim Chenmo Translation Committee. 3 vols. Ithaca, NY: Snow Lion, 2000–2002.

Tucker, Herbert F. "Dramatic Monologue and the Overhearing of Lyric." In *Lyric Poetry: Beyond New Criticism*, ed. Chaviva Hošek and Patricia Parker, 226–243. Ithaca, NY and London: Cornell University Press, 1985.

Vaidya, P. L., ed. *Bodhicaryāvatāra of Śāntideva with the Commentary Pañjikā of Prajñākaramati*. Buddhist Sanskrit Texts 12. Darbhanga: Mithila Institute, 1960.

Vairocanarakṣita (circa tenth century). *Bodhisattvacaryāvatārapañjikā* (*Byang chub sems pa'i spyod pa la 'jug pa'i dka' 'grel*). Tengyur, Comparative Edition, vol. 62, 248–399. China, 2000.

Vasubandu. *Abhidharmakośabhāṣya*. French trans. L. de La Vallée Poussin. English trans. L. M. Pruden. Berkeley, CA: Asian Humanities Press, 1990.

Viehbeck, Markus. "An Indian Classic in 19th-Century Tibet and Beyond: Rdza Dpal sprul and the Dissemination of the *Bodhi(sattva)caryāvatāra*." *Revue d'Etudes Tibétaines* 36 (2016): 5–44.

Vimuktisena and Haribhadra. *Abhisamayālaṃkāra with Vṛtti and Āloka. Volume One: First Abhisamaya*. Vṛtti by Ārya Vimuktisena. Āloka by Haribhadra. English trans. Gareth Sparham. Fremont, CA: Jain Publishing Company, 2006.

Wangchuk, Dorji. *The Resolve to Become a* Buddha*: A Study of the* Bodhicitta *Concept in Indo-Tibetan Buddhism*. Studia Philologica Buddhica Monograph Series XXIII. Tokyo: The International Institute for Buddhist Studies, 2007.

Wangyal, Geshe. *The Door of Liberation: Essential Teachings of the Tibetan Buddhist Tradition*. Boston: Wisdom, 1995.

Watkins, Calvert. *How to Kill A Dragon: Aspects of Indo-European Poetics*. Oxford: Oxford University Press, 1995.

Westerhoff, Jan. *Nāgārjuna's Madhyamaka: A Philosophical Introduction*. New York: Oxford University Press, 2009.

——. *Twelve Examples of Illusion*. New York: Oxford University Press, 2010.

Williams, Bernard. *The Sense of the Past: Essays in the History of Philosophy*. Princeton, NJ and Oxford: Princeton University Press, 2006.

Williams, Paul. "General Introduction." In Śāntideva, *The Bodhicaryāvatāra*, vii–xxvi. Trans. Kate Crosby and Andrew Skilton. Oxford World Classics. New York: Oxford University Press, 1995.

——. *Altruism and Reality: Studies in the Philosophy of the Bodhicaryāvatāra*. New York: Routledge, 1998.

——. *The Reflexive Nature of Awareness: A Tibetan Madhyamaka Defence*. Surrey: Curzon Press, 1998.

——. *Mahāyāna Buddhism: The Doctrinal Foundations*. Second Edition. New York: Routledge, 2008.

Williams, Rowan. "The Other as Myself: Empathy and Power." Tanner Lectures on "The Paradoxes of Empathy," 1 of 3. Delivered at Harvard University and sponsored by the Mahindra Humanities Center, April 8, 2014. https://www.youtube.com/watch?v=v79tL7uYTrA.

Wilson, Liz. *Charming Cadavers: Figurations of the Feminine in Indian Buddhist Hagiographic Literature*. Chicago: University of Chicago Press, 1996.

Wittgenstein, L. "Lecture on Ethics." *The Philosophical Review* 74, no. 1 (1965): 3–12.

Xiao, W., G. Fu, P. Qin, J. Tanaka, O. Pascalis, and K. Lee. "Individuation Training with Other-race Faces Reduces Preschoolers' Implicit Racial Bias: A Link Between Perceptual and Social Representation of Faces in Children." *Developmental Science* (2014): 1–9.

Yangsi Rinpoche. *Practicing the Path: A Commentary on the Lamrim Chenmo*. Boston: Wisdom, 2003.

Yao Zhihua. *The Buddhist Theory of Self-Cognition*. London: Routledge, 2005.

Yuasa Yasuo. *The Body: Toward an Eastern Mind-Body Theory*. Albany: State University of New York Press, 1987.

CONTRIBUTORS

Amber Carpenter is associate professor at Yale-NUS College. She publishes in ancient Greek philosophy, especially the ethics, epistemology, and metaphysics of Plato. Her book *Indian Buddhist Philosophy* appeared in 2014. She has taught at Oxford, Cornell, St. Andrews, and York; and held research fellowships and visiting appointments at the Einstein Forum (Potsdam), University of Melbourne, Yale University, and with the Templeton Religious Trust. She collaborates with Rachael Wiseman on the Integrity Project (integrityproject.org), which is currently producing a volume called *Portraits of Integrity.*

Douglas Duckworth (PhD 2005, University of Virginia) is associate professor at Temple University and the director of graduate studies in the Department of Religion. He is the author of *Mipam on Buddha-Nature: The Ground of the Nyingma Tradition* (SUNY Press 2008), and *Jamgön Mipam: His Life and Teachings* (Shambhala 2011). He is a coauthor of *Dignāga's Investigation of the Percept* (Oxford 2016) and introduced and translated *Distinguishing the Views and Philosophies: Illuminating Emptiness in a Twentieth-Century Tibetan Buddhist Classic* by Bötrül (SUNY 2011). His latest works include *Tibetan Buddhist Philosophy of Mind and Nature* (Oxford 2019) and a translation of an overview of the Wisdom Chapter of the *Guide to Bodhisattva Practice* by Künzang Sönam, entitled *The Profound Reality of Interdependence* (Oxford 2019).

John Dunne (PhD 1999, Harvard University) holds the Distinguished Chair in Contemplative Humanities, an endowed position created through the Center for Healthy Minds at the University of Wisconsin–Madison. He also holds a coappointment in the Department of Asian Languages and Cultures. His work focuses on Buddhist philosophy and contemplative practices, especially in dialogue with cognitive science and psychology. His publications appear in venues ranging across both the humanities and the sciences, and include empirical studies and theoretical works on Buddhist philosophy, contemplative practices, and their interpretation within scientific contexts.

Bronwyn Finnigan is a senior lecturer in the School of Philosophy, RSSS, at the Australian National University and an early career research fellow with the Australian Research Council. She works primarily in metaethics, moral psychology, and philosophy of mind in Western and Asian philosophical traditions and is currently working on two related research projects. The first investigates the nature of practical rationality involved in skilled action taken as a model of moral agency. The second examines Buddhist moral psychology and the meta-ethical grounds for rationally reconstructing Buddhist ethical thought. Bronwyn is a member of the Cowherds who authored *Moonshadows: Conventional Truth in Buddhist Philosophy* (Oxford), and has recently published articles on Buddhist arguments concerning animal welfare and vegetarianism (2017), idealism (2018), and the reflexive awareness of consciousness (2018).

Jay L. Garfield is Doris Silbert Professor in the Humanities and professor of philosophy, logic, and Buddhist studies; chair of the Philosophy Department; and director of the Logic Program at Smith College. He is also visiting professor of Buddhist philosophy at Harvard Divinity School, professor of philosophy at Melbourne University, and adjunct professor of philosophy at the Central University of Tibetan Studies. He has taught in Australia, Singapore, Japan, and Germany and is a regular lecturer at major universities, Buddhist studies centers, and research institutions around the world. Professor Garfield is author or editor of 27 books and over 150 articles and book reviews. His most recent books are *The Concealed Influence of Custom: Hume's* Treatise *from the Inside Out* (Oxford 2019), *Sellars and Buddhism: Freedom from Foundations* (Routledge 2019), and, with Emily McRae, a translation of Patrul Rinpoche's *Essential Jewel of Holy Practice* (Wisdom 2017).

Jonathan C. Gold (PhD 2003, University of Chicago) is associate professor in the Department of Religion and director of the program in South Asian studies at Princeton University. His research examines Indian and Tibetan Buddhist approaches to language and the ethics of personal cultivation, with an emphasis on how these are relevant to contemporary conversations in philosophy, politics, and social thought. He is the author of *The Dharma's Gatekeepers: Sakya Paṇḍita on Buddhist Scholarship in Tibet* (SUNY Press, 2007) and *Paving the Great Way: Vasubandhu's Unifying Buddhist Philosophy* (Columbia, 2015) as well as numerous book chapters and articles, including the online *Stanford Encyclopedia of Philosophy* entries on "Vasubandhu" and "Sakya Paṇḍita."

Charles Goodman is professor in the philosophy department and the Department of Asian and Asian-American Studies at Binghamton University. His first book was *Consequences of Compassion: An Interpretation and Defense of Buddhist Ethics* (2009). As a member of the Cowherds collaboration, he is also a coauthor of *Moonpaths: Ethics and Emptiness* (2016).His translation of the *Śikṣā-samuccaya* has recently been published as *The Training Anthology of Śāntideva* (2016). He holds a BA in physics from Harvard University and a Ph.D. in philosophy from the University of Michigan. He has published articles and book chapters on the works of Mahāyāna Buddhist philosophers, including Śāntideva, Bhāviveka, Nāgārjuna, Dharmakīrti, and Vasubandhu. His work emphasizes aspects of Buddhist thought that can offer valuable insights for the philosophy of today. He has also published on applied ethics and political philosophy in the Western tradition. His writings on Buddhist philosophy have explored a range of topics, including ethical theory, conceptions of well-being, free will, and personal identity.

Janet Gyatso is Hershey Professor of Buddhist Studies at Harvard University. Her writing has centered on Tibetan Buddhism and its cultural and intellectual history. Topics of her scholarship include traditional medicine and religion in Tibet; the reception of *Kāvyādarśa* and new kinds of poetics in Tibet; sex and gender in Buddhist monasticism; the current female ordination movement in Buddhism; visionary revelation in Buddhism; lineage, memory, and authorship; the philosophy of experience; and autobiographical writing in Tibet. She is the author of *Being Human in a Buddhist World: An Intellectual History of Medicine in Early Modern Tibet* and *Apparitions of the Self: The Secret Autobiographies of a Tibetan*

Visionary, as well as several edited volumes. She is currently also working in the field of animal studies and ethical phenomenology.

Paul Harrison holds the George Edwin Burnell Chair in Religious Studies at Stanford University, where he joined the permanent faculty in 2007. Prior to that he taught at the Universities of Auckland and Canterbury in his native New Zealand. He holds a PhD in South Asian and Buddhist studies from Australian National University. Harrison's published research deals primarily with Buddhist literature, in particular Mahāyāna sūtras, on the basis of Sanskrit, Chinese, and Tibetan sources. His interests also extend to the Mahāyāna *śāstra* tradition and the history of the Tibetan Buddhist canon. Current projects include editions, translations, and studies of the *Vajracchedikā*, the *Vimalakīrtinirdeśa*, the *Bhaiṣajyaguru-vaiḍūryaprabhārājasūtra*, the *Saṃghāṭasūtra*, and the *Śikṣāsamuccaya*. Harrison is also engaged in research on Buddhist manuscripts, and is a member of the editorial board of the series Buddhist Manuscripts in the Schøyen Collection.

Eric Huntington is a postdoctoral fellow in the Ho Center for Buddhist Studies at Stanford University. He is the author of *Creating the Universe: Depictions of the Cosmos in Himalayan Buddhism* (University of Washington, 2018), which exposes the complex cosmological thinking behind many different examples of Buddhist literature, ritual, art, and architecture. His current research investigates new approaches to Buddhist visual and material cultures. He has also published articles on the role of illustrations in ritual manuscripts and visual, spatial, and temporal understandings of tantric mandalas. Prior to joining Stanford, he served as a Cotsen Postdoctoral Fellow in the Society of Fellows at Princeton University and received his PhD from the University of Chicago.

Roger Jackson is John W. Nason Professor of Asian Studies and Religion, emeritus, at Carleton College, where for nearly three decades he taught the religions of South Asia and Tibet. He also has taught at the University of Michigan, Fairfield University, and McGill University. He has a BA from Wesleyan University and an MA and PhD from the University of Wisconsin, where he studied under Geshe Lhundub Sopa. He maintains a scholarly interest in Indian and Tibetan Buddhist systems of philosophy, meditation, and ritual; Buddhist and other types of religious poetry; the study of mysticism; and the contours of modern Buddhist thought. His books include *The Wheel of Time: Kalachakra in Context* (with

Geshe Sopa and John Newman, 1985), *Is Enlightenment Possible?* (1993), *Tibetan Literature* (with José Cabezón, 1996), *Buddhist Theology* (with John Makransky, 1999), *Tantric Treasures* (2004), *The Crystal Mirror of Philosophical Systems* (with Geshe Sopa et al., 2009), and *Mahāmudrā and the Bka' brgyud Tradition* (with Matthew Kapstein, 2011). He has written dozens of articles, book chapters, and reviews, and presented regularly at national and international scholarly conferences. He was editor-in-chief of *The Journal of the International Association of Buddhist Studies* from 1985 to 1993 and has served as coeditor of the *Indian International Journal of Buddhist Studies* since 2006. His study of Mahāmudrā in the Geluk tradition of Tibetan Buddhism, *Lamp So Bright*, will be issued by Wisdom in 2019.

Thupten Jinpa, PhD, holds a Geshe Lharam degree from the Shartse College of Ganden Monastic University, South India, as well as a BA Honors in philosophy and a PhD in religious studies from Cambridge University. Jinpa has been the principal English translator to H.H. the Dalai Lama since 1985 and has translated and edited numerous books by the Dalai Lama, including *The New York Times*' best-seller *Ethics for the New Millennium*. His own publications include numerous works in Tibetan and English, and translations of major Tibetan works. His latest book is *A Fearless Heart: How the Courage to be Compassionate Can Transform Our Lives*. He is the main author of CCT (Compassion Cultivation Training), an eight-week formal program developed at the Center for Compassion and Altruism Research and Education (CCARE), Stanford University. Jinpa is an adjunct professor at the Faculty of Religious Studies at McGill University, the founder and president of the Institute of Tibetan Classics, and the chairman of the board of the Mind & Life Institute.

Matthew T. Kapstein is professor emeritus at the École Pratique des Hautes Études, PSL Research University, in Paris, France, and Numata Visiting Professor of Buddhist Studies at the University of Chicago. He has published widely in the fields of Indian and Buddhist philosophy and Tibetan studies.

Sonam Kachru is an assistant professor in the Department of Religious Studies, University of Virginia. A student of the history of philosophy, with a particular focus on the history of Buddhist philosophy in South Asia, he is especially interested in the history of such concepts as minds, persons, and selves. He is currently working on a monograph on the Buddhist philosopher Vasubandhu, tentatively titled *More and Less Than Human: Life and Mind in Indian Buddhism*.

Reiko Ohnuma is professor and chair of the Department of Religion at Dartmouth College, where she is also affiliated with the Asian Societies, Cultures, and Languages Program and the Women's, Gender, and Sexuality Studies Program. Her research focuses on South Asian Buddhist narrative literature preserved in Sanskrit and Pali, and she is the author of *Head, Eyes, Flesh, and Blood: Giving Away the Body in Indian Buddhist Literature* (Columbia, 2007); *Ties That Bind: Maternal Imagery and Discourse in Indian Buddhism* (Oxford, 2012); and *Unfortunate Destiny: Animals in the Indian Buddhist Imagination* (Oxford, 2017).

INDEX

Abhidharma, 10, 23n31, 88, 92, 96n33, 186, 194, 218, 222–225
Abhidharmakośa, 96n21. *See also* Vasubandhu
act-consequentialism, 211–212
act-utilitarians, 210–212
adhyeṣaṇā (request [for the buddhas to teach]), 135
afflictive mental states (*kleśa*), 241, 243. *See also kleśa*
Ākāśagarbhasūtra, 30–31, 38–39, 139
Akṣayamati, 19, 24n35, 28
ālayavijñāna (store consciousness), 55
Amitābha, 137
Amitāyus, 141
Ānandavardhana, 79n14
anātman (no-self doctrine), 10, 54, 87, 124, 130n45, 154, 229–231; *Guide* on, 56, 105, 126; karma and, 56, 59n17
anger, 6, 9, 46, 56, 80n26, 104, 181; at *Guide* narrator, 103; as poison, 149; Tsongkhapa cites *Guide* on, 166, 170–171
anuttarapūjā (Supreme Worship, unexcelled worship), 35–36, 40, 43n19, 59n13, 122, 133, 135, 139; stages of, 135
Apabhraṃśa, 68
areteic ethics, 192, 195
Aristotle, 214, 215
Āryaśūra, 156, 164
Asaṅga, 138, 157, 169, 224
asceticism, 117, 78n4
aspiration to buddhahood (*bodhicitta*), 115. *See also bodhicitta*
Aśvaghoṣa, 22n2
Atiśa, 14, 146–147, 154, 158n2, 159n6, 164–165, 167, 176n9, 178n81; *lojong* sources of, 155, 160n25
ātman (self), 9, 77
ātmasneha (self-attachment), 245. *See also* attachment: to self or "I"
attachment, 103, 127, 155, 226, 238; anger, ignorance, and, 149; to body, 104, 116, 118, 127; desire and, 198; passion, lust, and, 116; to perspectives or views, 100, 102, 109; to self or "I," 100, 106, 112, 168, 245; to sensual pleasures, 118
attention (*manasikāra*), 224
Avalokiteśvara, 111
awakening (*bodhi*), 3, 66, 133–138; aspiration to, 35–36, 39, 134–136, 138, 142, 168, 174; body and, 116, 121, 128; descriptions of, 136–137; full, 163, 241, 244; of all beings, 84, 135; path toward, 137, 143, 156, 164, 169; ritual and, 137; for sake of all beings, 163, 168, 174; as universal principle, 84, 215. *See also bodhi*

Awakening (*bodhi*), 3, 128, 210. *See also* *bodhi*
awakening mind (*bodhicitta*), 138–139, 143, 155–156, 164, 166; arousal of, 135; aspirational, 152; development of, 134, 150, 166, 167; praised, 134, 135, 167; self–other exchange and, 150, 155; self–other equalization and, 150; Tsongkhapa on, 167; two kinds of, 134, 136, 148, 152–153. *See also bodhicitta*
Awakening Mind (*bodhicitta*), 3, 5, 22n5, 51, 123. *See also bodhicitta*

Barnett, Lionel D., 253–254
Batchelor, Stephen, 58n10, 255
beneficence (*maitrī*), 197. *See also maitrī*
Bhagavad Gīta, 17–18, 24n33
Bhartṛhari, 68
Bhattacharyya, 194
Bhavacakra (Wheel of Existence), 205–206n23
bhāvanā (meditation), 240. *See also* meditation
Bhāvanākrama (*Stages of Meditation*). *See* Kamalaśīla
bhoga (enjoyments, possessions), 33, 121
bias, implicit, 192, 194, 198–203, 205n9
blo sbyong. *See lojong*
bodhi (awakening, Awakening, enlightenment), 3, 66, 103, 178n82; of all beings, 84, 135; aspiration to, 35–36, 39, 134–136, 138, 142, 168, 174; body and, 116, 121, 128; descriptions of, 136–137; for sake of all beings, 146, 148, 163, 168, 174; full, 163, 241, 244; path toward, 59n12, 137, 143, 149, 150, 156, 164, 169; ritual and, 137; sudden, 58n8; as universal principle, 84, 215
Bodhicaryāvatāra. *See Guide to Bodhisattva Practice*
Bodhicaryāvatārapañjikā, 159n15, 160n27. *See also* Prajñākaramati
bodhicitta (aspiration to buddhahood, awakening mind, Awakening Mind, enlightened mind, mind of awakening, Mind of Awakening, spirit of enlightenment, thought of enlightenment), ix, 22, 102, 129, 135, 177n29, 177n32, 217, 231–233, 241; of advanced bodhisattvas, 3–4; aspirational, 3–5, 8–9, 11–12, 14, 115, 152, 168, 196–197, 204; Atiśa on, 147, 154, 158n2; conventional vs. ultimate, 148, 152; defined, 2–3; development of, 101, 104, 134, 150, 155–157, 159n12, 159n15, 164–169; engaged, 168, 196–198; fear and, 231–233; Gelukpa method of developing, 174–175; as *Guide*'s theme, 1–6, 101; metaphors for, 2, 101, 167, 169; mind training (*lojong*) and, 20, 146–150, 152, 155–156; praised, 5, 101, 123, 134, 135, 167, 216; self–other equalization and, 150, 155, 159n15; self–other exchange and, 104, 150, 155, 168, 174; sudden arrival of, 102, 108; translations of, ix, 22n5; Tsongkhapa on, 167–169, 171, 174; two kinds of, 3, 128, 134, 136, 148, 152–153, 148, 196–198; vegetarianism and, 14
Bodhipathapradīpa (*Lamp on the Path to Enlightenment*), 165
bodhisattva, 22n6, 30, 40, 42n17, 111–112, 172–173, 219n3; accomplished, 50; advanced, 3, 4, 9, 121, 122, 160n26; animal, 4; aspiring, beginner, or in training, 8, 16–17, 84, 22n4, 111, 122, 128; bodies of, 115, 117–124, 127–128, 211; compassion of, 101, 120, 123, 124, 227, 240–241, 244; dedication of merit by, 33, 135–136; fearlessness and, 221, 223; generosity of, 33, 35; harm done by, 214; human, 116, 122–123; Mahāyāna ideal, 134, 150; male, 22n4, 118–119; mind training of (*see lojong*); mindset or mental state of, 2, 11, 15, 50–52, 101, 111, 127, 159n12, 173 (*see also bodhicitta*); monastic, 121; perfections of, 136, 150, 163, 167, 241; refuge taken in, 221, 223, 226–230, 233; self-sacrifice of, 33, 121–122, 129n30, 130n33, 211, 216–217; *vinaya* (code of conduct) for, 37, 38; virtues of, 215–216, 231–232; worshiped, 122–123, 139–140
Bodhisattvabhūmi (*Bodhisattva Stages*), 138

Bodhisattvacaryāvatāra, 30, 95n7. *See also Guide to Bodhisattva Practice*: Dunhuang [*Guide*$_{1}$] version
bodhisattva path, 36, 85, 114, 121–124, 135, 142, 150, 153, 194, 210, 241; downfalls along, 138; early stages or start of, 196, 204, 243; late stages of, 121; preconditions for, 115; stages of, 2; *Training Anthology* on, 31, 33; Tsongkhapa on, 169, 172, 174
Bodhisattva's Jewel Garland, 147
Bodhisattva Stages (*Bodhisattvabhūmi*), 138
bodhisattva vows, 55, 124, 133, 168; in contemporary world, 192; in *Guide*, 5, 6, 137–139, 204; of Samantabhadra, 141–142. *See also* vows
bodies, 103, 105, 109, 112, 114–115; of bodhisattvas, 37, 115, 117–124, 127–128, 211; of buddhas or the Buddha, 117, 122–123, 128; Dharma, 29, 30; emptiness of, 126, 128; female, 119, 169; giving of (own), 45, 121–122, 130n33, 172, 211; human, 115–119, 123; loathsome or worthless, 70–74, 115–120; meditation on, 70–72, 116; self and, 124–128; worth of, 116–117, 119–120
Brentano, Franz, 90, 96n25, 223
bstan rim (stages of the doctrine), 164
Buddha, the (Śākyamuni): asceticism of, 117; as bodhisattva, 3–4, 55, 121; child of, 152, 167; images of, 39, 132–133, 138, 140; teachings or discourses of, 8, 10, 24n33, 87, 135, 139, 141, 175, 227–233, 241
Buddha-gem, 123, 129
Buddhaghosa, 58n9, 80n26, 164
buddhahood, 2–3, 22n6, 104, 115, 121, 123–124, 128, 155, 172, 177, 210, 241, 243–244; attained for sake of all beings, 11, 165, 167; for all beings, 5
Buddha mind, 190n21
buddhas, 141, 169; compassionate, 102; fully enlightened, 2–4, 122; illusory vs. truly existent, 189; images of, 14, 140, 142; recollection of, 55, 59n16; rejoicing in, 50; sons of, 29, 30, 222; supplication of, 135; teaching by, 135; thirty-five, 133, 142; virtues of, 215; visualizations of, 139, 142

caitasika (determining factors), 223–225
Candragomin, 139, 167
Candrakīrti, 86, 95n6, 96n23, 174
care (*karuṇā*), 197, 204. *See also karuṇā*
Carpaṭi, 80n29
Carpenter, Amber, 20, 21, 75
Caturdharmakasūtra, 39
cetanā (intention), 224
Chekawa Yeshe Dorje (Che ka wa ye shes rdo rje), 147–148, 152–155, 159n6, 178n81. *See also* "Seven-Point Mind Training"
cherishing (*gces 'dzin*), 154
chimpanzees, 235–237
China, 176n10. *See also* Dunhuang
Chinese (language), 6–7, 13, 40
Chinese (people), 15–16
Cīvaravastu, 78n8
Coan, Jim, 238
code of conduct (*vinaya*), 37. *See also vinaya*
compassion. *See karuṇā*
Compendium of the Perfections (*Pāramitāsamāsa*), 156, 164
Compendium of Training, 147. *See also Training Anthology*
Concise Presentation of the Perfections (*Pāramitāsamāsa*), 156, 164
confession, 5, 35–36, 43n21, 48; thirty-five buddhas visualized in, 142, 144n23; Three Heaps (*Triskandha*), 138, 142, 144n23. *See also pāpadeśanā*
confusion (*moha*), 241, 243–244
consciousness, 89–93, 96nn24–25, 97n35, 111, 112, 183, 217, 223; basic (*kun gzhi*), 187, 189; of self (*see* self-consciousness)
consequentialist ethics, 192, 195, 211–213
contact (*sparśa*), 224
conventional truth (*saṃvṛtisatya*), 88, 183–185, 188. *See also saṃvṛtisatya*
conventional usage (*saṃvṛtisatya*), 87–88. *See also saṃvṛtisatya*
cooperation, 235–238, 246
cosmology, 10, 164, 193
Crosby, Kate, 77n2, 254

Dalai Lama, H.H. the XIVth, 17, 18, 24n32, 41n4, 146, 157, 160n29; *Guide* studied by, 14; *Guide* verses quoted by, 11, 16
Dalai Lamas, 163
dāna (generosity, giving), 3, 35, 43n21, 84, 152, 196, 211, 215, 239; of body, 33, 130n33, 170; of body, enjoyment, and merit, 121; perfection of, 34, 36, 46, 150, 165, 169–170, 194, 196; Sanskrit word, 33, 169; of vegetables, 45, 172
death, 115, 116, 148, 221, 226; anxiety or fear of, 48–49, 200, 205n22, 206n23; inevitable, 17–18, 166; moment of, 23n31, 226, 227, 230
defilements, 54, 174
delusion, 10, 116, 125, 203, 204
deontological ethics, 192, 195, 211–214
dependent origination (*pratītyasamutpāda*), 124, 229, 231
Descartes, René, 79n20, 89
determining factors (*caitasika*), 223–225
dge lugs order. *See* Geluk School
Dharma, 28, 29, 34, 38, 103, 121, 130n33, 140, 165, 211, 229, 230
Dharmākara, 137–138
Dharmapada, 63, 78n7
Dharmarakṣita, 160n25
dharmas (fundamental phenomena), 10, 87, 88
dhyāna (meditation), 33, 169, 173. *See also* meditation
Dignāga, 96n26
diligence (*vīrya*), 58n6. *See also vīrya*
discernment (*saṃjñā*), 224
discipline (*śīla*), 46. *See also śīla*
Discourse on the Fruits of the Contemplative Life, 24n33
Dka' chen Ye shes rgyal mtshan, 174
downfalls (*āpatti*), 38, 138–139, 151, 216
dran pa (mindfulness), 204, 206n26. *See also* mindfulness
Drigung Kagyu School, 160n26
Dromtönpa, 146
Duckworth, Douglas, 20, 21, 85
Dunhuang, ix, 7, 21, 42n7, 176n10
Dunne, John, 21
Durgā, 17, 18
Dza Paltrül (Patrul Rinpoche), 14, 147

"Eight Verses on Mind Training," 146, 148, 155–156, 158n3
Emory's Cognitive-Based Compassion Training (CBCT), 158
empathy, 100, 105–106, 157, 247
emptiness. *See śūnyatā*
enlightened mind (*bodhicitta*), 101, 104, 108. *See also bodhicitta*
enlightenment. *See bodhi*
Entrance of the Bodhisattvas (*rgyal sras 'jug ngogs*), 160n22
epistemology, 9, 194
equanimity (*upekṣā*), 10, 167, 174, 210. *See also upekṣā*
ethical discipline (*śīla*), 170. *See also śīla*

faith, 3, 10, 29, 34, 37, 103, 116, 132–133, 139, 142, 160n27, 202
Faure, Bernard, 116
fear, 16, 52–53, 55, 68, 76, 107, 160n27, 166, 193, 195, 215, 217; Abhidharma view of, 222–226; of death, 48–50, 200, 205n22, 206n23, 226–227; of karmic consequences, 6, 227, 228, 230; as motivator, 200–202, 205n22, 221, 229, 232–233, 239; no-self view and, 230–232; refuges and, 222, 223, 227–229; Śāntideva's incitement of, 21, 221–222, 227, 229, 232–233
fearlessness, 21, 111, 221, 222, 223, 226, 229, 230, 232, 233
feeling (*vedanā*), 224
Finnigan, Bronwyn, 21
Finot, Louis, 254
Flower Array Sutra, 141
fortitude (*vīrya*), 33–34, 36, 43, 52. *See also vīrya*
Four Immeasurables (Divine Abidings), 10, 210, 219n1

Gadamer, Hans-Georg, 12–13, 18
Gaṇḍa-vyūha Sūtra, 141
Gāndhāri, 78n7
Garfield, Jay, 21
gces 'dzin (cherishing), 154

Geluk (*dge lugs*) School or order, 20, 23n30, 163–165, 174
generosity (*dāna*), 3, 33, 35, 84, 152, 196, 211, 215, 239; perfection of, 34, 46, 150, 165, 169–170, 194, 196. *See also dāna*
Gerow, Edwin, 78n14
giving (*dāna*), 33, 34, 35, 36, 43n21, 45, 121, 169, 171–172. *See also dāna*
giving and taking (*tonglen, gtong lan*), 146–148, 153–156, 160n26, 168, 174–175, 178n81
Gold, Jonathan C., 36, 95n7, 136, 162
Gómez, Luis O., 41n2, 60, 78n5, 253–254
Goodman, Charles, 21, 58n7
Great Treatise on the Stages of the Path to Awakening (*Great Treatise on the Stages of the Path to Enlightenment*; *Byang chub lam rim chen mo*), 163–170, 173–175, 175n3, 176n5; on *bodhicitta* or bodhisattva, 167–169; editions of, 175n3; on guru, 165; on perfections, 169–173
greed, 10, 103, 111
Greeks, 8, 20, 51, 52
gtong lan. See tonglen
Guide$_1$. *See Guide to Bodhisattva Practice*: Dunhuang [*Guide*$_1$] version
Guide$_2$. *See Guide to Bodhisattva Practice* (*Bodhicaryāvatāra*)
Guide to Bodhisattva Practice (*Bodhicaryāvatāra*): as "classic," 1, 11–13, 18–21, 162, 175, 254; audience of, 17, 38, 66, 102; author(s) of, 7–8, 18, 41n3 (*see also* Śāntideva); commentaries on, 6, 13, 22, 85, 94–95n5, 152–153, 176n4 (*see also* Kṛṣṇapa; Prajñākaramati; Tibetan: *Guide* commentaries in; Vibhūticandra); Dunhuang [*Guide*$_1$] version, ix, 30–32, 39, 42n7, 42n9, 43n22, 43n34, 95n7, 176n10; as guide, 2, 84, 162; as inspirational piece, 37; intertextuality of, 31, 38–40, 43n30; as literature or literary qualities of, 20, 21, 27, 60–62, 64–65, 77n2, 78n5; manuscripts of, 7–8, 18, 21; as merit-generating engine, 12; modern views of, 8, 12–13, 15, 18; monastic context of, 17; newness of (or not), 2, 8, 29–30, 102; in nineteenth century, 13–14, 20; phonetic figures in, 61–62, 64–65, 78n10, 80n31; political readings of, 13–15; prayer as or prayers in, 2, 5, 12, 111; pronouns in, 71, 75, 102, 108–109; reason in, 57; reception history of, 1, 8, 19, 85; as ritual manual, 162 (*see also under* ritual); ritual uses of (*see under* ritual); themes in, 1, 8; *Training Anthology* and (*see under Training Anthology*); translations of, ix, 6–7, 13, 157, 176n10, 253–255
Gyaltsap Jé, 154, 160n22
Gyatso, Janet, 20, 23n20, 63, 75, 150

Hadot, Pierre, 8, 94n1
Haribhadra, 9
Harrison, Paul, 5, 7, 19, 60, 134
hatred, 10, 15–16, 23n31, 103, 107
hells, 4, 5, 10, 15, 18, 103, 109, 166, 171, 187, 203; Avici, 195, 204n6; becomes delightful, 64; distinctive character of, 51–52; suffering or tortures of, 16, 55, 115, 222, 226
heroism (*vīrya*), 33. *See also vīrya*
heteronomy, 74–75
Hindus, 11, 17–18
Holy Teaching of Vimalakīrti, 154, 219n3
Hugh of St. Victor, 76
Hume, David, 200, 204n3
Huntington, Eric, 5, 20
Husserl, Edmund, 100

illusion (*māyā*), 89, 94
impartial benevolence, 209–210, 213, 215, 219n2
impartiality (*upekṣā*), 197, 203, 204. *See also upekṣā*
impermanence, 10, 116, 118, 148, 229
insight (*prajñā*), 33–36, 47, 84, 136, 142. *See also prajñā*
insight (*vipaśyanā*), 85, 173, 198
intention (*cetanā*), 224

Jackson, Roger, 20
Jatakas, 3
Jenkins, Stephen, 120, 243, 245
Jinpa, Thupten, 20, 23n20, 63, 178n81

Johnston, Mark, 73
Jones, Karen, 222, 227
joyous perseverance (*vīrya*), 170, 172. *See also vīrya*

Kachen Yeshé Gyaltsen, 174
Kachru, Sonam, 20, 21
Kadam (*bka' gdams*) School, 146–148, 155, 159n11, 164–165, 174–175
Kālāma Sutta, 10
Kamalaśīla, 58n8, 164, 167, 168
Kant, Immanuel, 89, 213
Kapstein, Matthew, 8, 20, 21, 75, 158n1
karma, 1–6, 11–12, 15, 23n31, 46, 158, 172, 214, 224; bad, 39, 56, 147, 150, 166, 169, 170, 171, 227–228, 230; good (*see* merit); Künzang Sönam on, 188; *lojong* practice and, 148, 153, 155; mental acts or state and, 4–5, 23n31; no-self doctrine and, 56, 59n17; *Training Anthology* emphasizes, 37
karuṇā (compassion), 157, 171; *bodhicitta* and, 2, 241; of bodhisattva, 227, 231; body and, 121, 124, 126–128, 130n33; confusion and, 243–244; defined, 210; emptiness and, 136, 184, 241; for enemies, 15, 16; immeasurable, 10; practices for cultivating, 150, 158, 167–168, 174, 235–236, 238–247; secular practices for cultivating vs., 158; self–other exchange and, 101–102, 106; suffering and, 57; universal, 6, 12, 14, 149
kāvya, 65, 77n2
Khunu Lama, 14
kleśa (afflictive mental states, psychopathology), 6, 194, 198, 202, 241, 243
Könchok Gyaltsen, 156
Krishna, 17–18
Kṛṣṇapa, 152, 159n12, 159n19
kṣānti (patience, patient acceptance), 6, 15, 56, 156, 177n54, 181, 196; perfection of, 33, 34, 36, 165, 170, 173, 194, 215; Tsongkhapa on, 170–173
Kunzang Pelden, 123, 130n33
Künzang Sönam, 20, 180–181, 183–189
Kyopa Jikten Gönpo, 160n26

lam rim (stages of the path), 155, 164, 174
Langri Thangpa, 147, 148, 155, 158n3. *See also* "Eight Verses on Mind Training"
Laṅkāvatārasūtra, 97n33
La Vallée Poussin, Louis de, 77n3, 253–254
Locke, John, 96n29
lojong (*blo sbyong*; mind training, Mind Training), 7, 14, 20, 23n20, 146–150, 152–158, 160, 164; *bodhicitta* and, 146–149, 152; Chekawa's text on (*see* "Seven-Point Mind Training"); basic structure of, 148; defined, 146, 156; Langri Thangpa's text on (*see* "Eight Verses on Mind Training"); teachers of, 146–147
loving-kindness (*maitrī*), 10, 210, 216. *See also maitrī*
lust, 116, 118–119
lyric poetry, 65–66, 68, 80n23, 80n29

Madhyamaka, 42n15, 47, 174; emptiness in, 9–10, 85–86, 88, 93, 218, 240, 243; illusion in, 20, 86; *Guide* as digest of, 2; *Guide* chapter on, 6–11; mental states in, 222; no-self view in, 230; reality or truth in, 47–48, 193, 242–244; Śāntideva and, 6, 59n12, 86, 173, 180–181, 218, 222, 230; subschools of, 86, 95n6 (*see also* Prāsaṅgika; Svātantrika); Yogācāra and, 10, 91, 93
Madhyamakāvatāra, 96n23, 97
magic, 89, 123, 181; powers, 18; trees, 64, 124
mahākaruṇā (great compassion), 231
mahāmudrā, 174
Maitreyanātha, 157
maitrī (beneficence, loving-kindness), 10, 197, 210, 216
Maitriyogi, 155, 160n25
manasikāra (attention), 224
Mañjughoṣa, 111, 174, 178n79, 204, 222
Mañjuśrī, 40, 137
māyā (apparition, illusion, magical appearance, etc.), 89, 94
McCrea, Lawrence, 78n14
McGinn, Bernard, 69
meat, 14

meditation, 1, 2, 14, 55, 66, 79n18, 102, 152, 158, 159n12; *bhāvanā*, 240; on body, 69–70, 112, 116–117, 126; breathing and, 148, 156, 174; *dhyāna*, 33, 169, 173; early sources on, 80n26, 164; eleven-point, 174–175, 178n79; ethics and, 198, 200, 219; fear ameliorated by, 200; *Guide*'s chapter on, 104–105, 147, 150, 169, 197–198, 200, 240, 245; *mahāmudrā*, 174; perfection of, 33, 34, 36, 150, 169, 173, 215; philosophy and, 8–11, 85; ritual and, 133–134; *samādhi*, 6, 8–10; *śamatha*, 84–85, 169, 173; textual practices and, 8, 76, 79n18; *vipaśyanā*, 85, 173. *See also lojong*; *tonglen*
memory, 91–93, 96n29, 97n34
merit (*puṇya, śubha*), 1, 3–4, 12, 33–36, 106, 116, 135–137, 197, 202; awakening and, 4, 136; of *bodhisattva*, 4, 121, 136, 172; dedication of, 6, 11, 35–36, 63, 121, 135, 137; destruction of, 15, 23n31; enhancing of (*vardhana*), 42n16; generosity and, 3, 170; importance of making, 102; of mental acts, 5, 136; rejoicing in (*puṇyānumodanā*), 135
metaphors, 41n6, 48, 54, 56, 57, 74, 96n17, 101, 119, 124
Milinda, King, 125, 130–131n45
Mill, John Stuart, 66, 212, 218
mind (*citta, manas*), 2, 6, 9, 58n6, 68, 69, 72–75, 223–224; Buddhist vs. Freudian view of, 53–54; as block of wood, 55, 56, 103, 201–202; as menagerie, 48, 53–56, 75; of others, 100; as wound, 56
mindfulness (*saṃprajanya/shes bzhin, smṛti/dran pa*), 6, 59n16, 156, 173, 195, 200–201, 216, 239; of body, 112; as restraint, 54–55; words for, 206n26
mind of awakening (*bodhicitta*), ix, 2, 3, 22n5. *See also bodhicitta*
Mind of Awakening (*bodhicitta*), ix. *See bodhicitta*
mind training (*lojong, blo sbyong*), 20, 146–150, 164. *See also lojong*
Mind Training (*lojong, blo sbyong*), 7, 14, 156. *See also lojong*
Mipam, 14, 22n11
moha (confusion), 241, 243
mokṣa (liberation), 2–3, 16, 17, 22n4, 165, 194, 215; of all beings, 11, 172; as *paramārtha*, 88
monasteries, 13–14, 17, 21, 64, 78n8, 106, 164, 219; libraries of, 38, 40; Narthang, 159n11; Royal Bhutanese (Bodh Gaya), 140; Samye, 58n8; Shankh (Mongolia), 140; Vikramaśīla, 85, 95n7. *See also* Nālandā
monastic code of conduct (*vinaya, prātimokṣa*), 37, 38, 43, 213
monastic schools, orders, or lineages, 13, 14, 86, 159n11, 163
monasticism, 13–14, 17, 18, 22, 23n25, 39, 112, 119, 163
Mongolia, 140
Mongolian, 13
moral behavior, 10
moral discipline (*śīla*), 150, 152, 166. *See also śīla*
morality (*śīla*), 33–36, 43n21, 58n5, 194, 215. *See also śīla*
morality, 10, 21, 46, 55, 67–68, 75, 80n32, 114, 195, 202; bodies and, 114–115, 121, 123, 127; cultivation of, 21, 115, 134, 192, 198; empathy and, 106; Greek views of, 52; karma and, 2, 4–5, 59n17; perspective shifts and, 99, 108; phenomenology and (*see* phenomenology: ethical or moral); psychology research on, 194; universal, 12–13. *See also śīla*
mouse, venomous, 20, 86, 90–92, 95n7, 95n9, 96nn27–28, 96n33
Mrozik, Susanne, 37, 43n24, 114, 130n39
muditā (rejoicing), 35, 36, 50, 197, 219n1
Mūlamadhyamakakārikās, 42n12

Nāgārjuna, 31, 59n12, 85, 88, 156, 168, 174; *Mūlamadhyamakakārikās* of, 42n12; *Ratnāvalī* of, 153
Nāgasena, 125, 130–131n45
Nālandā, 7, 18–19, 28, 32, 40, 41n4, 106, 112
Nance, Richard, 81n39
Nectar of Immortality, 14
Newari, 13

Ngok Loden Sherab (Rngog blo ldan shes rab), 176n10
Ngulchu Thokmé Sangpo, 147, 152, 154, 159nn17–18, 160n22
nirvana (*nirvāṇa*), 10, 18, 170, 194
Nōh, 101. *See also* Zeami Motokiyo
nonegocentricity (*upekṣā*), 197. *See also* *upekṣā*
no-self doctrine. *See anātman*

Ohnuma, Reiko, 20
Olivelle, Patrick, 78n4
overhearing, 20, 65–68, 70, 73, 77, 79n20

Pabongkha Dechen Nyingpo, 174
Padmakara Translation Group, 253–254
Pāli, 10, 24n33, 68, 78n7, 80n26, 130n45
Panchen Losang Chökyi Gyaltsen (Paṇ chen Blo bzang chos kyi rgyal mtshan), 174, 178n79
pāpadeśanā (confession), 132, 133, 135
paramārtha (ultimate significance, highest goal), 88
paramārthabodhicitta (ultimate *bodhicitta*), 148, 150
paramārthasatya (ultimate truth), 86–87, 183–184, 187
pāramitās (perfections), 19, 33–37, 85, 124, 134, 150, 163, 167, 169, 170, 215, 241; as mental attitude, 46; ten, 35. *See also dāna*; *dhyāna*; *kṣānti*; *prajñā*; *prajñāpāramitā*; *śīla*; *vīrya*
Pāramitāsamāsa (*Concise Presentation of the Perfections, Compendium of the Perfections*), 156, 164
parātmaparivartana (exchanging self and other), 63, 67, 75, 99–100, 104–112, 150, 155, 168, 174; *tonglen* and, 147
Parfit, Derek, 218
pariṇāmanā (dedication), 135. *See also* merit: dedication of
passion, 69–71, 80n27, 116, 118–119
Path of Purity (*Visuddhimagga*). *See* Buddhaghosa
patience (*kṣānti*), 6, 15, 56, 156, 165, 170–173, 177n54, 181, 194, 196, 215. *See also kṣānti*
patient acceptance (*kṣānti*), 33, 34, 36. *See also kṣānti*
Patrul Rinpoche (Dza Paltrül), 14, 147
perfection of wisdom (*prajñāpāramitā*), 58n6, 124, 135, 152, 167. *See also* *prajñāpāramitā*
Perfection of Wisdom (*prajñāpāramitā*), 9, 85. *See also prajñāpāramitā*
perfections (*pāramitās*), 46, 136, 150, 163. *See also pāramitās*
Pha bong kha Bde chen snying po, 174
phenomenology, 101, 104, 106, 112, 194, 202, 203, 226; ethical or moral, 21, 47, 80–81n32, 192–196, 200, 204; of sense of self, 230–231; of thought, 73
philosophy, 1, 16, 68, 73, 79n20, 85–87, 242–243; Greek or Roman, 8–9, 45, 94n1, 214, 215; *Guide* as digest of, 2, 6, 19; Indian, 85, 91, 92, 95n15; meditation and, 8–11, 85; moral, 75; Western, 89–91, 94n1, 96n29, 100, 192, 204n3, 209, 212, 214, 218, 227. *See also* Abhidharma; Madhyamaka; Prāsaṅgika; Svātantrika; Yogācāra
Piṇḍārtha (*Summary Meaning*), 6
Plato, 45–46, 57, 59n15
Potowa, 148
Prabhāśrī, 142
praise (*vandanā*), 135
prajñā (insight, wisdom, understanding), 6, 45, 84, 124, 130n43, 142, 240; emptiness and, 136, 173; perfection of, 9, 33–36, 47, 85, 105, 173; translation of, 85
Prajñākaramati, 13, 22n11, 42nn9–10, 85–90, 160n27, 219n11; authors cited by, 86, 95n6; background and date of, 85; editions of, 77n3, 94n5; on *Guide*'s contents, 241; on *paramārtha(satya)*, 88, 242; on *saṃvṛti*, 87; on self–other exchange or equality, 151, 159n15; on self-sacrifice, 121–122; Yogācāra and, 89–90
prajñāpāramitā (perfection of wisdom, Perfection of Wisdom), 9, 47, 58n6, 85, 124, 135, 152, 167
Prakrit, 68, 79
pramāṇa (epistemology), 9

praṇidhāna (vow, bodhisattva vow), 35, 133. *See also* bodhisattva vows
Prāsaṅgika, 20, 95n6, 174, 180; on conventional truth, 185–189; Künzang Sönam on, 183–189; *reductio ad absurdum* arguments of, 85; Śāntideva as (or not), 86, 173, 180–181, 183, 189
prātimokṣa (code of conduct for monastic practitioners), 213. *See also* monastic code of conduct
pratītyasamutpāda (dependent origination), 124, 229, 231
prayer, 1, 2, 64, 111, 155; merit from, 12; refuge, 5; *Guide*'s tenth chapter as, 150, 152
precepts (*saṃvara*), 55, 138
Precious Garland (*Ratnāvalī*), 153
Presentation of the Perfections (*Pāramitāsamāsa*). *See* Āryaśūra
protreptic, 20, 45–48, 53, 57
psychology, 4, 96n25, 157–158, 203, 230; Buddhist, 4, 21, 193–195; contemporary research on, 21, 236, 247, 248n3; Freudian, 53, 55; moral, 21, 114, 199, 221–223
Public Explication, 156
pūjā (worship, offering), 135
puṇya (merit, goodness), 33, 121, 136, 210. *See also* merit
puṇyānumodanā (rejoicing in merits), 135
purifying (*śuddhi*), 33, 34, 39, 42n16, 121

quiescence, meditative (*samādhī*), 6, 8–10

racism, 199, 202
Rand, David, 239
rationality, 9–10, 47, 50, 57, 177n32, 212, 217
Ratnāgni, 142
Ratnamegha, 35
Ratnāvalī, 153
refuge (*śaraṇa*). *See* ritual: refuges
rejoicing (*muditā*), 35, 36, 50, 197
rejoicing in merits (*puṇyānumodanā*), 135
request [for the buddhas to teach] (*adhyeṣaṇā*), 135
resoluteness (*vīrya*), 58n6. *See also vīrya*
restraint (*śīla*), 46. *See also śīla*
rgyal sras 'jug ngogs (*Entrance of the Bodhisattvas*), 160n22
right efforts (*samyak-vyāyāma, samyak-pradhāna*), 42n17
ritual, 5, 11, 19, 20, 39–40, 75, 116, 132–139, 143n13; confession, 132, 133, 138, 139, 142; dedication, 132, 133, 135, 139; to Durgā, 17; *Guide* context or structure of, 132–134, 142–143; *Guide* recited in, 6–7, 36; images and, 133, 142; of offering, 133, 142; reading and, 39; refuges, 35, 39; tantric, 137; vows, 168 (*see also* vows). *See also anuttarapūjā*; *pariṇāmanā*; *pūjā*
Rngog blo ldan shes rab (Ngok Loden Sherab), 176n10

Saitō, Akira, 21, 24n35, 30, 95n7
Sakya Paṇḍita, 160n26
samādhī (meditative quiescence), 6, 8–10
Samaññaphala Sutta, 24n33
Samantabhadra, 141–142, 222
śamatha (serenity, tranquility, tranquility meditation), 84–85, 173
saṃjñā (discernment), 224
Sāṃkhya, 40
saṃprajanya (mindfulness), 206n26. *See also* mindfulness
saṃvara (restraint, vow, precept, etc.), 30, 33, 37, 38, 41n6, 138. *See also* vows
saṃvṛtibodhicitta (conventional *bodhicitta*), 148, 150
saṃvṛtisatya (conventional usage, conventional truth, relative truth), 86–89, 183–184, 188, 242
saṅgha, 37–38. *See also* monasticism
Sangyé Gompa, 156
Śaṅkara, 24n34, 79n20
Sanskrit, 78n5, 78n7, 253–255; *Anthology* manuscript in, 41n1; *Guide* commentaries in, 13, 22n11, 77n3, 85, 94–95n5, 241; *Guide* editions in, 7, 22n1, 77n3, 94n5, 159n18, 176n6; literary criticism in, 61, 65, 77n2; phonetics or sounds of, 62, 64; poetry or lyric poetry in, 65, 68, 77n2, 80n29; translations from, 13, 85, 253–255; word *saṃvara* in, 30, 33; word *viveka* in, 62

Śāntarakṣita, 86, 95n6
Śāntideva: as Akṣayamati, 19, 24n35, 28; as author or poet, 7–8, 15, 19, 27, 36, 40, 41n3, 60, 63, 75–76, 163; biography of, 28–29, 32, 106; date or historical context of, 1, 11, 12, 19; phenomenological ethics of, 47; vanishes into sky, 28, 32; works by, 19. *See also Guide to Bodhisattva Practice*; *Training Anthology*
Saraha, 80n26
Śatakatraya, 68
Sattasaī, 68, 79n14, 80n26
satyadvaya (two truths, two realities), 86–89, 183–184, 242
Schmidt, Richard, 254
scholasticism, 7–9, 88, 106, 163–164, 172, 175n2
self (*ātman*), 9, 77, 124. *See also anātman*
self, heteronomous, 74–75
self-consciousness, 90–93, 97n35, 111
self–other distinction, 236, 238–239, 244, 246–247
self–other equalization or equality, 150–151, 155, 159n15, 245
self–other exchange (*parātmaparivartana*). *See parātmaparivartana*
self-overhearing. *See* overhearing
serenity (*śamatha*), 173. *See also śamatha*
Serlingpa, 147, 154–155, 158n2, 160n25
"Seven-Point Mind Training" (*Blo sbyong don bdun ma*), 147–149, 152, 155–156, 159nn5–6; points listed, 148
sexism, 18, 22n4, 199, 202
Shabkar Tsogdruk Rangdrol, 13–14
shes bzhin (mindfulness), 206n26. *See also* mindfulness
Śikṣāsamuccaya of Śāntideva. *See Training Anthology*
Śikṣāsamuccayakārikā (*Verses of the Training Anthology*), 32
śīla (discipline, ethical discipline, moral discipline, morality, restraint), 33–36, 43n21, 46, 58n5, 150, 152, 166, 170, 194, 215
six perfections (*pāramitās*), 19, 85, 134, 150, 163, 167, 170. *See also pāramitās*
Six Perfections (*pāramitās*), 35, 36, 37, 215; listed, 33. *See also pāramitās*
Skilton, Andrew, 77n2, 254
smṛti (mindfulness), 195, 202, 204, 206n26. *See also* mindfulness
sparśa (contact), 224
spirit of enlightenment (*bodhicitta*), 164. *See also bodhicitta*
Spyod 'jug gi rnam par bshad pa, 159n12
Śrāvakayāna, 27
Stages of Meditation (*Bhāvanākrama*). *See* Kamalaśīla
stages of the doctrine (*bstan rim*), 164
stages of the path (*lam rim*, *lamrim*), 155, 164, 174
Stanford's Compassion Cultivation Training (CCT), 158
Stein, Edith, 100, 104, 106, 113n5
Steinkellner, Ernst, 254
Strawson, Galen, 73
Subāhuparipṛcchā, 39
śubha. *See* merit
suffering, 16, 50, 63, 94, 104, 116, 127, 183, 218, 245; compassion for, 2, 57, 227, 236; fear of, 16, 50, 227, 232; future, 48–50; of hell or bad rebirth of, 16, 115, 122, 128, 166, 203, 214, 215, 226; karma and, 56; *kleśas* and, 243; *lojong* meditation and, 147–148, 150–158; of others, 3, 11, 50, 52–53, 57, 101, 104, 137, 147, 151–156, 168, 174, 204, 210, 227, 231, 236, 241, 245–246; Ownerless, 217; Stein on, 113n5; Tsongkhapa on, 170–172; view of self and, 151; wrong view and, 47
Sukhāvatī, 78n8
Sumatikīrti, 176n10
Summary Meaning (*Piṇḍārtha*), 6
śūnyatā (emptiness), 6, 9, 21, 93, 124, 126, 137, 154, 180, 196, 197, 243; of body, 126, 128; compassion and, 136, 149, 184, 240–241; Kṛṣṇapa on, 152; Künzang Sönam on, 184, 188–189; *lojong* and, 148–149, Nāgārjuna on, 85; Prajñākaramati on, 88; Tsongkhapa on, 173; as ultimate reality, 88, 148, 188, 242; universal, 10, 85, 86, 88
supplication (for the buddhas to remain) (*yācanā*), 135

Supreme Worship. *See anuttarapūjā*
Supuṣpacandra, 43n30
sūtras, Mahāyāna, 27, 30, 31, 33, 35, 39, 164
Sūtrasamuccaya (*Sūtra Anthology*), 31, 38
Suvarṇadvīpa, 6
Suvarṇaprabhāsa, 39
Svātantrika, 86, 95n6, 180, 185, 187
sympathetic joy, 10, 15–17, 104, 204

Tāḷapuṭa, 80n26
Tanjur (Tengyur), 32, 42n15, 159n12, 159n15
tantrism, 11, 12, 23n20, 137–138, 165
Tathāgataguhyasūtra, 159n14
Teachings of Vimalakīrti, 154, 219n3
Tengyur (Tanjur), 32, 42n15, 159n12, 159n15
Theragāthā (*Elders' Verses*), 78nn4–5, 80n26
Therīgāthā, 80n31
Thokmé Sangpo. *See* Ngulchu Thokmé Sangpo
thought of enlightenment (*bodhicitta*), ix, 22n5. *See also bodhicitta*
Three Heaps, 139
Tibet, 14–16, 58n8, 146
Tibetan: canon(s), 7, 13, 21, 144n23; *Bodhisattvacaryāvatāra* in, 42n9; *Guide* commentaries in, 13, 22, 85, 94n4, 123, 130n33, 149–150, 154, 159n11, 163–164, 180, 254; *Guide* passages quoted in, 163, 164; *Guide* translations into, 13, 30, 85, 94n5, 159n18, 176n10, 254; mind training texts in (*see lojong*); Sanskrit commentaries translated into, 95n5; *Three Heaps Sutra* in, 142, 144n23; traditions or debates about Śāntideva in, 41n3, 86, 95n7, 97n35. *See also lam rim*
Tibetan Buddhism, 13–14, 23n30, 146, 157, 163, 165, 174
Tibetans, 13–16; *Guide* recited by, 6, 150; *Guide* studied or taught by, 14, 20, 22, 147, 150, 152, 154–155, 157, 163–164, 175; treasure offering of, 141
tonglen (*gtong lan*; giving and taking), 146–148, 153–156, 160n26, 168, 174–175, 178n81
Tracy, David, 162
Training Anthology (*Śikṣāsamuccaya*, *Compendium of Training*), 7, 19, 27–33, 35, 37, 43n34, 43n37, 60, 114, 164, 215; audience of, 38, 39, 121; Four Divine Abidings/Immeasurables in, 210; *Guide* compared to, 27–30, 35, 37–40, 76; *Guide* refers to, 29, 31, 37, 38; as Kadam treasure, 147; later verses of, 37, 40, 43n23, 76–77, 215; literary qualities of, 27; opening verses of, 30, 75, 81n39, 216; perfections in, 33; quotations or reading recommendations in, 27, 38–40, 43nn27–28, 210, 211, 219n3; Root Verses of, 32–33, 37; self-sacrifice in, 121–122, 211; translations and manuscript of, 41n1; as *vinaya*, 37
tranquility (*śamatha*), 85. *See also śamatha*
tranquility meditation (*śamatha*), 84. *See also śamatha*
truth, 86, 242; final or ultimate, 47
Tsongkhapa Losang Drakpa (Tsong kha pa Blo bzang grags pa), 20, 147, 162–179; Ganden Ear-Whispered Tradition (*dga' ldan snyan brgyud*) of, 174; seven-point instructions of, 167–168, 174. *See also Great Treatise on the Stages of the Path to Awakening*
Twenty Verses on the Bodhisattva Vow, 139
two realities (*satyadvaya*), 242. *See also satyadvaya*
two truths (*satyadvaya*), 86. *See also satyadvaya*

ultimate truth (*paramārthasatya*), 86, 183–184. *See also paramārthasatya*
understanding (*prajñā*), 9, 45, 105, 130n43. *See also prajñā*
unexcelled worship (*anuttarapūjā*), 133, 135, 139. *See also anuttarapūjā*
Upadeśasahasrī, 79n20
Upālipariprcchā, 39
upāya (method), 241
Upāyakauśalyasūtra, 219n6

upekṣā (equanimity, impartiality, nonegocentricity), 10, 167, 174, 197, 203, 204, 210
utilitarianism, 209–213, 217–219

Vairocanarakṣita, 159n15
Vajradhvaja, 39
Vajrapāni, 111
Vajrayāna Buddhism, 35
valor (*vīrya*), 33. *See also vīrya*
vardhana (enhancing), 33, 34, 42n16, 121
Vasubandhu, 88, 90, 96n21, 224
vedanā (feeling), 224
Vibhūticandra, 95n5
vigor (*vīrya*), 6, 115. *See also vīrya*
Vikramaśīla, 85, 95n7
Vimalakīrti, Teachings or *Holy Teachings of*, 154, 219n3
vinaya (code of conduct, disciplinary regulations), 37, 38, 43n30
vipaśyanā (insight), 85, 173, 198
virtue ethics, 215–217
vīrya (diligence, fortitude, heroism, joyous perseverance, resoluteness, valor, vigor, zeal), 6, 33, 58n6, 115, 170, 172
Visuddhimagga (*Path of Purity*). *See* Buddhaghosa
vocation (*saṃvara*). *See* bodhisattva vows; *saṃvara*
vows (*saṃvara*, *praṇidhāna*), 30, 32–33, 55, 124, 133; in contemporary world, 192; in *Guide*, 5, 6, 137–139, 204; ritual, 168; of Samantabhadra, 141–142

Wallace, Vesna and B. Alan, 255
Watkins, Calvert, 78n10
Williams, Paul, 11, 12
Williams, Rowan, 100
Wilson, Liz, 119
wisdom (*prajñā*), 33, 47, 124; emptiness and, 173. *See also prajñā*
worship (*pūjā*, *pūjanā*), 135

Yogācāra, 10–11, 40, 55, 89–93, 96n23
yogis, 13, 87, 188
Yongzin Yeshé Gyaltsen, 147

zeal (*vīrya*), 58n6. *See also vīrya*
Zeami Motokiyo, 101, 109–110

GPSR Authorized Representative: Easy Access System Europe, Mustamäe tee 50, 10621 Tallinn, Estonia, gpsr.requests@easproject.com

www.ingramcontent.com/pod-product-compliance
Lightning Source LLC
Chambersburg PA
CBHW021935290426
44108CB00012B/846
* 9 7 8 0 2 3 1 1 9 2 6 7 5 *